P9-BYB-731

ANGEL OF DARKNESS

ANGEL OF DARKNESS

DENNIS McDOUGAL

WARNER BOOKS

A Time Warner Company

Copyright © 1991 by Dennis McDougal
All rights reserved.

Warner Books, Inc., 666 Fifth Avenue, New York, NY 10103

W A Time Warner Company

Printed in the United States of America
First Printing: May 1991
10 9 8 7 6 5 4 3 2 1

Library of Congress Cataloging-in-Publication Data

McDougal, Dennis.
    Angel of darkness / Dennis McDougal.
        p.   cm.
    ISBN 0-446-51538-8
    1. Serial murders—California—Case studies. 2. Kraft, Randy
Steven, 1945–   . 3. Murderers—California—Biography. 4. Trials
(Murder)—California—Orange County. I. Title.
HV6533.C2M24   1991
364.1′523′097949—dc20   90-50530
                                                                                        CIP

Book design: H. Roberts

For Sharon and Amy,
the two most important women in my life

AUTHOR'S NOTE

Though novelized to the extent that anecdotes and remembrances were incorporated into the text in chronological order, this story about the reign of terror, capture, and conviction of America's worst serial killer remains as faithful as possible to the public record. Some scenes are reconstructed and a few names have been changed to preserve confidentiality, but the people, places, and events chronicled here are real. In most instances, actual quotes and first person accounts are taken directly from court transcripts, police reports, and public documents. Letters, newspaper accounts, and trial exhibits—including a pair of family photo and souvenir albums prepared by the defense—that are a permanent part of the nineteen-volume court record of the trial of Randy Kraft became the backbone of *Angel of Darkness*. In addition, dozens of interviews with friends, acquaintances, victims, neighbors, police officers, journalists, and attorneys were conducted in the course of researching Randy Kraft's story. With the exception of a handful of letters exchanged with the author while Kraft was living on San Quentin's Death Row, Kraft has maintained a total public silence since his conviction in 1989 on sixteen counts of the sixty-seven murders he is believed to have committed over a twelve-year period.

ACKNOWLEDGMENTS

Kristi Heim is not only a fine researcher; she is a fine reporter who sat through months of trial, pored over mounds of documents, taped hours of interviews and testimony, and compiled hundreds of pages of notes in order to deliver the correct quote or the telling fact. Without her, there would be no book. Likewise, the photojournalist's eye of Leo Hetzel, in and out of the courtroom, captured ideas as well as images. He is an artist who simply uses a camera instead of easel, paint, and brushes. Patient and encouraging, Rich Horgan is that rare editor with vision who cares equally for the writer and the reader. Alice Martell says she is my agent. She is not. A yenta, a yuppie, a guru, and a friend, perhaps, but not an agent. Agent is much too businesslike a term for an expectant mother who wants to know when the next chapter of the book will be in the mail while her labor pains are ten minutes apart. Likewise, Sharon McDougal is not just my wife, she is my best friend and my first line editor who kicks out the awful stuff before anyone in a position to have me fired ever gets a chance to see it. She keeps me going when nobody else can or will. Carl and Lola McDougal, my parents, are my first and still my most venerable fans. Likewise my sister, Colleen, encouraged me through tough times, and my brothers, Pat and Neal, have always been one phone call away. Thanks also to my editors and peers at the *Los Angeles Times* who sustained me and tolerated my time away from the paper, especially Bob Epstein, Lee Margulies, John Lindsay, Barbara Saltzman, and SCIII. Special thanks to Irv Letofsky who will always be, quite simply, the best editor I have ever worked for in my life. The courthouse reporters in Orange County and Los Angeles work hard, get it right, and are rarely shown the appreciation they deserve for keeping the public informed. I thank them all: Jerry Hicks of the *Los Angeles Times*; Larry Welborn, Patrick Kiger, and Greg Zoroya of the *Orange County Register*; Helen Guthrie Smith, Molly Burrell, Bob Zeller, Mary Neiswender, and Kristi Heim of the *Long Beach Press-Telegram*; Dave Lopez of KCBS-TV. Special thanks to Deborah Caulfield, Lorraine Hillman, Lloyd Thomas, Katie Sauceda, Wayne Rosso, Ray Richmond, Mark Gladstone, Bill Knoedelseder, Brian Zoccola, Dorothy Korber, Pat Broeske, Diane Goldner, the men and women of the *Los Angeles Times* Editorial Library, and Bill Cook's unsung staff in the basement of the Orange County Courthouse who went the extra mile in helping me in my research. To all those in law enforcement and both the prosecution and defense who gave of their time and resources in Orange County, Los Angeles, and Oregon to help me reconstruct the story of the worst and most baffling serial killer of our times, my thanks and gratitude. Their contributions, as well as the anonymous help given by former friends and acquaintances of Randy Kraft, were invaluable. Finally, thanks to those among Kraft's scores of living victims—the parents, sweethearts, siblings, and friends who were forced to bury a loved one years before his time—who swallowed their pain long enough to cooperate in the creation of this book. Hopefully, their candor may help prevent other sons, brothers, or husbands from trusting to demons in their haste to thumb a ride to the end of the road.

INTRODUCTION

Looking down on southern California from above, the strands of freeway seem to pump from the heart of Los Angeles like contorted veins that twist and knot and stretch out to Santa Barbara in the north, San Bernardino in the east, and as far south as the Mexican border. Only to the west are the freeways missing, sutured off at the coastline so that automobiles don't spill into the brooding Pacific Ocean like so much lost blood.

At daybreak, the freeways brim with slow-moving vehicles, clotting into traffic jams from one end of the megalopolis to the other. At night, the strands glow red and white with the head- and taillights of a million cars oozing homeward.

The rest of the time the freeway system is an open road—an invitation to move unfettered through this dense, smoggy wonderland of subdivision after subdivision, as far as the eye can see.

Freeways define southern California and the premium that its residents place on mobility. For the price of an automobile and a driver's license, anybody can move from one neighborhood to the next in a matter of minutes. Those who can't afford a car or license can always stick out a thumb and hitchhike downtown, to the mall or the beach. If they don't mind who they're riding with.

Strange things happen on southern California freeways. Things that happen elsewhere while people are usually stationary. People make love while they're on the freeway. They cook, brush their teeth, do and re-do their mascara, dress and undress. Men shave. Women have babies at seventy miles per hour. Incantations and aerobics, fisticuffs and fellatio, midwifery and mayhem . . .

They've all happened in the fast lane at one time or another on the matrix of cement thoroughfares that crisscross Los Angeles and environs and, usually, nobody pays much attention, until it involves murder.

During the 1970s and early 1980s, more than a hundred young hitchhikers caught rides on the streets and freeways of southern California and didn't live to tell about it. Some of them became nameless bodies, forever to be known as John Doe 16 or 229. Some have names but no bodies, their human remains never having been found. Some became headless torsos or disembodied heads, or worse—the living cadavers of amateur sado-surgeons who used liquor as anesthesia, fishing knives as scalpels, and ice picks for probes. Sometimes their body parts were stuffed in black plastic trash bags and left in the desert to rot. Sometimes they were tossed in restaurant garbage bins. Most of the time they were simply pitched from a moving car or van like empty Coke cans or used hamburger wrappers.

Law enforcement has always known that there are predators who troll the freeway onramps and beach highways for hitchhikers. The hunters range in perversity from harmless to heinous. Occasionally they're just looking for money. Usually they are interested in quick, impersonal sex. And, sometimes, they want more.

The term *serial killer* came into vogue in the early 80s—used by police to describe the peculiarly modern type of American demon who selects his victims like ripe tomatoes in a grocery store. Ted Bundy, John Wayne Gacy, Juan Corona were all members of the fraternity. Unlike mass murderers who go into a frenzied killing spree and are spent, a serial murderer devours, savors, and digests each victim before reaching out to pluck up another.

The victims themselves are usually society's helpless or disenfranchised. Children, derelicts, and hookers are the easiest targets because they are vulnerable and can't fight back. Young hitchhikers who are rootless, often broke and alone, are hard to trace back to hearth and home. They too have little in the way of support from the larger society.

Only when serial murderers begin violating the sanctity of the home or the family—as in the case of Richard Ramirez, the so-called Night Stalker of Los Angeles who broke into suburban homes in the summer of 1985—are they tracked down and caught by an outraged society.

If they are careful and fortunate and pick their prey well, there is no outrage; no alarm set off by hysterical parents, a confounded constabulary, or an infuriated press. The killers can practice their craft with virtual impunity, learning from their mistakes and developing a style that only they and their victims can appreciate, like the inevitable hypnotic dance of death that unfolds between cat and mouse, shark and fish. . . .

But rarely between human and human.

"The first murder would be like a good meal," Stanford University psychology professor David Rosenhan once told me. "A truly memorable meal. The kind that you can shut your eyes and remember for years afterwards. All the other murders stem from that first one, like you or me trying to recapture that perfect dinner we experienced once in a little Parisian cafe or wherever. The taste, the smell, the moment. But we never quite recapture it."

But knowing how it happens doesn't explain why it happens.

Serial killers are not crazy in the commonly accepted sense of the term. Most of the time, they are perfectly sane—"abnormally normal," as prosecutor Bryan Brown once described a young computer consultant named Randy Kraft who was believed to have picked up hitchhikers along southern California's freeways and spirited them away, into the night, never to return.

After years of study and experimentation, behavioral scientists like Rosenhan can explain psychotic disorders such as manic depression, paranoia, or schizophrenia; but the sociopathic personalities that put on one face for family and friends and another for their victims remain a mystery. They are without conscience, and no psychiatrist, psychologist, or medical doctor quite knows why.

"Why do they do it? They do it because they like to do it," said Pierce Brooks, a homicide detective in Los Angeles for more than thirty years before he retired and moved to the little town of Vida, Oregon.

When he isn't fly fishing, the venerable cop writes and lectures to law enforcement personnel across the nation about his favorite subject: serial murder. He has had an abiding interest in such predators since the first time he arrested one, back in 1958. The killer was a small, commonplace clerical employee who was normal in every respect save one: he liked killing young women.

Beginning with the Manson family and northern California farmer Juan Corona, who killed at least twenty-five transient farmworkers in the late 1960s, serial murder has gone from being bizarre to ordinary.

No one can say exactly why there has been an epidemic rise in that uniquely sordid crime during the past three decades, though freeway travel and the easy, anonymous mobility of urban life, for victim and killer alike, probably has something to do with it.

Brooks has heard all of the reasons given by and for serial killers. Brain damage, child abuse, sexual dysfunction are frequent explanations. But none of them wash with him.

"It is a personality disorder," he said. "They're not mentally ill. They're not going to change. That's their life-style. That's the reason. There's nothing more to it than that. It's just something they do."

After making a second career of studying the sociopaths who put on one face for the world to see while living a secondary life of blood lust, Brooks has no solutions. That they exist and will continue to exist is as obvious as the morning newspaper or the evening newscast, with their endless footnote reports of missing children, murdered prostitutes, and unidentified bodies of young hitchhikers.

His only advice is vigilance: watch your children, pick your friends carefully, and don't ride with strangers.

Even those common-sense cautions aren't foolproof because serial killers have the advantage of stalking their prey in complete disguise.

Former Los Angeles County Sheriff's Sergeant Al Sett, another retired veteran of the southern California homicide wars, tracked down several serial killers and brought them before the bar of justice during the 1970s and '80s, including "trash bag" killer Patrick Kearney. When he questioned their close friends, co-workers, or family, none of them had an inkling. The wisdom Sett learned from a quarter century of chasing down murderers is that "nobody knows anybody else."

"They think they do," he said, "but they never do. Not really. I wish I had a dime for every neighbor or sweetheart or mother who's told me, 'He didn't do it. He couldn't do it. I *know* him!' If there's one thing I've learned it's just that. Nobody knows anybody. That's how they get away with it. That's what they depend on. That nobody will catch on, because people never take the time to really know anyone else."

ANGEL OF DARKNESS

1

On the last day of the year, Mark Hall, Bill Holly, and Phil Holmer went out on an all-night drunk. With each beer, remembered conversations grew murkier and time telescoped. It wasn't all that clear where the three musketeers of beer had been or where they were going, but by midnight it seemed as if the trio had been out party hopping all over southern California.

Only two of them lived to see in the new year.

"It was payday, but we didn't have no money for drinks," Holmer said years later, remembering how New Year's Eve of 1975 began.

Both he and Hall, a skinny pal with shoulder-length brown hair that parted in the middle of his head, worked swing shift at Emerson Electric Company in Santa Ana. That's where they had spent the previous evening: running through their routine sheet-metal work and breaking long enough to drink lunch from the tap at the Holiday Bar across Standard Avenue. Like Holmer and Holly, the twenty-two-year-old Hall spent a lot of his time drinking.

Hall was quiet and seemed a little dull-witted. People compared him in looks and manner to Ringo Starr, the "slow" Beatle. Shortly after Hall hired on at Emerson in 1974, he was able to run the sheet-metal shear, box brake, drill press, and other general shop equipment, but not without guidance from some of the more senior employees like Holmer. He wasn't even an actual machine-shop employee. His official title was "maintenance man." Mostly, Hall stayed to himself.

The first time he ran into Holmer outside of work was at the

Holiday Bar, where regular patrons from Emerson could get their checks cashed each payday. Soon, Holmer and Hall got to be drinking buddies. Holmer kept a half-dozen six-packs of Bud in his refrigerator at all times. Drinking beer was how they spent most evenings and weekends. That's how they planned to spend New Year's Eve.

For a long time, Holmer was convinced that Hall was on the run from some kind of trouble. He and Holly, his surfer-blond roommate, counted themselves among Hall's few friends. But even they didn't know much about him. Beyond that dull, dazed air about him was a lot of hurt that Mark didn't want to talk about much. It wasn't until years later Holmer found out that the restive long-hair with the pocked complexion and the taste for both Budweiser and Jimi Hendrix had come from Pocatello to become a rock star.

Before and after work, the talk in Holmer's and Holly's one-bedroom crash pad on North Parton Street was about booze and broads and the pluses of staying stoned most of the time. Sometimes somebody would come up with a little pot. The triple whammy of alcohol, hard rock, and cannabis turned the apartment into one kick-back state of stereo catatonia. Dialogue was expendable. They just never seemed to talk all that much about where they came from or where they were going.

"I didn't even know where he lived," Holmer said later. "I know he lived close to me, but he always used to ride his ten-speed over to our place, so I never went to his place."

Hall usually pedaled over from his own apartment on North Main Street in time for a few beers just before the beginning of the four P.M. swing shift at Emerson. It was easier to work if you were a little loaded. They would all hop in Holly's blue convertible, tool over to Emerson a couple miles to the east, and clock in. At the eight P.M. lunch break, Holmer usually drank a rum and Coke for dinner while Hall knocked back a Schlitz Stout Malt Liquor or two. That would see them through the rest of their shift. They clocked out at midnight, but stayed on tap at the Holiday Bar until last call at two A.M. Most nights, Hall wouldn't even go home. He'd just sleep it off on Holmer's old recliner in the front room of the apartment, just the way he did the day before New Year's Eve. Holmer didn't mind. When he did finally get him to talking about something beyond babes and the best brands of beer, he discovered that Hall was a poet of sorts with a sweet disposition and a passion for the blues.

Hall owned a Gibson acoustic guitar that he played badly. He brought it over on his bicycle once and never took it home. He usually turned it over to Holly to strum. He also owned a mouth harp that he blew like a tortured angel. Sometimes late at night, while Holly plucked tunes from the Gibson and Hall jumped in with his sweet, sad harmonica sounds, Holmer would just burrow down into the tired old sofa with a beer in one hand and wait for heaven to arrive.

Mark Hall had come to California for rock 'n' roll. He was the drummer in a band that he and three other guys had put together back in Pocatello, where he grew up. There, he and the rest of Heavenly Blue, as they called themselves, were heavy metal heroes. They played the high school and the enlisted men's clubs at various military bases in southern Idaho, neighboring Utah, and as far away east as North Dakota. They did convincing covers of Cream, the Doors, and even a few Beatles' standards. There was even some loose talk of their opening once for the Steve Miller Band when the pop group toured the Northwest.

Hall lived for hard rock. He was especially into drums, which he took up when he was still a junior in high school. He talked briefly about becoming a lawyer, but a career in music was what he really wanted. After he dropped out of Highland High in Pocatello in 1971, his drums and the three other members of Heavenly Blue became his life, much to his parents' chagrin.

Said his father, Darwin Hall, "Of course Lois and I, like parents every place, were hoping he would change his mind and apply himself and go to school, and we had the money to put him through school. He could have gone to medical school or anything."

Mark was Darwin and Lois Hall's only son, and admittedly they spoiled him. Darwin, a vehicle services manager for the Pocatello Post Office, was a country and western fan, but he tolerated the Beatles music that leaked out of his son's bedroom.

When he decided to break into pop music, Mark and the other guys in the band made demo tapes out in the garage. They played a few school dances and actually got paid a few bucks for it. That got the group to thinking seriously about their music. They found themselves a booking agent and started playing the enlisted men's clubs at Air Force bases in the Northwest.

"Mark was pretty wild when he got away from his family," said Heavenly Blue guitarist Keith Brasseure. "He'd do pretty crazy things."

In high school, he was loud and a little rude—something of a show-off. That worked all right on stage with the band, but not with teachers or other students. He alienated more people than he needed to, including the members of Heavenly Blue, according to Brasseure.

After he dropped out of high school, Hall dabbled briefly in graphic arts at a vocational continuation school. He took a job for a little while in a print shop. But his heart was with Heavenly Blue.

"The last time he played with us was a two-week Christmas stint we had up in Sun Valley in 1971 or '72," said Brasseure. "He was an interim drummer by then and he knew it. I think he resented it 'cause he knew what was coming."

They all smoked pot now and then, but only Mark let his habit get the best of him when it came to concerts, Brasseure remembered. He liked the groupies and he liked the adulation, but he didn't like the practicing. He showed up late or, sometimes, not at all. By the time Brasseure and lead guitarist Bruce Monk mustered the courage to ask Hall to leave, he was injecting Methedrine and even an occasional shot of heroin. He started carrying his show-off behavior to extremes.

"Near Twin Fall there's this giant canyon where there's a water-fall," Brasseure said. "The one Evel Knievel tried to jump. Shoshone Falls. Three hundred fifty feet, straight down. Sheer death. So it's fenced off, and we stopped there one night on the way back from Twin Falls, and it was dark. He was stoned. So he jumps the fence and goes way out there, right to the edge, and just sits. It was just typical of the things he used to do, just to show off."

It wasn't tempting death that cost him his drumsticks, though.

"He just couldn't remember. You'd go over a riff with him fifteen times and then he'd forget it," Brasseure continued. "I think it was really tough on him when we let him go."

The band broke up a short time after that. Keith Brasseure and Bruce Monk both left for Vietnam, while the band's vocalist worked his way to Europe, where he eked out a living playing for francs outside the Paris Metro.

But Mark had already immigrated to southern California, bitter and broken-hearted about being bounced from the band. He knocked around with a few fringe bands in L.A., but he finally had to face facts. There were no gigs around that paid a Pocatello boy enough to keep up the rent, let alone provide himself with an adequate reserve of marijuana and malt liquor.

That's when he applied for the trainee position at Emerson. Making metal boxes for computer components didn't pay much above minimum wage, but it was enough to keep him clothed, fed, and anesthetized.

It was enough for Holmer and Holly too. In 1975, the Vietnam War was finally over, and so was the draft. That was worth celebrating. None of the three musketeers of beer were particularly knocking the world dead, but they were alive, young, and employed. On the last day of the year, they were well-equipped to party 'til they puked.

The trio crawled out of bed late on New Year's Eve, hung over from the night before. When they drove down to Emerson around two P.M. to collect their paychecks, Holmer picked up a flyer advertising a New Year's Eve blowout in the beach town of San Juan Capistrano. He pocketed it for future reference as they got in Holly's car and drove down the street to the Holiday Bar.

It may have been an hour or two hours that they shot pool and drank draft beer, but the Holiday didn't seem such a great place to spend a holiday. For one thing, it only served beer and wine. So at sunset, they moved on to another bar on Main Street in the downtown district of Santa Ana, where a shot of bourbon or gin could be had for the same price as a beer.

It was dark outside when fellow Emerson employee Steve Sanchez came through the bar, inviting everybody he knew to come to his house in nearby Westminster for a New Year's bash. Holmer followed Sanchez to his home in Holly's convertible while Hall and Holly rode in the back seat, tossing down a few more on the way.

At Steve's party, they mingled and drank some more, each drifting off to talk to other people. There was no telling how long they were there or which one of them finally decided that they ought to move on. Drinking has diminishing returns, however, even for virile young men in their early twenties. What they were interested in was women, and there didn't seem to be enough to go around at Steve's place. The flyer that Holmer had picked up back at Emerson's payroll office promised that loads of them would be showing up at the San Juan Capistrano party.

"By the time we ended up heading down to the other party in Capistrano, it was close to midnight already," Holmer remembered. "It was very late and we were very drunk. I don't know how we got down there. We were professional partiers, but this was New Year's Eve and we were very, very drunk. God knows how we made it down there in one piece."

When they arrived, there were no women. The bash had been reduced to a poker party with a half-dozen guys sitting around a dining room table peering at their cards. Holmer and Holly sat in, but Hall begged off. He stumbled over a coffee table and couldn't get up without some help. Holmer limped his friend into the living room, where Hall curled up like a baby on the sofa to sleep off his binge.

"He was so drunk he fell down in the house," Holmer said. "He was way far gone. To get to that condition would take a lot of booze because this was when we used to party, party, party. We could drink all night long and it didn't faze us."

At midnight, Holmer went to the kitchen for some pots and pans to bang in the New Year with. He got another beer from the icebox. Then he went to the living room to wake up Hall.

But he wasn't there.

"We may have looked around for him in the front yard. I don't know. We were so far gone ourselves," Holmer said.

When he heard that Hall had vanished, Holly still had enough presence of mind to check his pants pockets for his payroll cash. He came up about $200 short, Holmer remembered. Holly groused about it to Holmer all night long while they continued playing cards. They both stayed until dawn, waiting for Hall to return.

But he never did.

Melanie Ann Lane graduated from Westminster High School in southern California in 1975. She remembered the family's annual New Year's Eve celebration that year very well because it happened at her mother's home and not at Aunt Kay's house or at Grandpa and Grandma Kraft's place in Midway City.

It was the year that Aunt Kay separated from Duane Eastburn, her husband of twenty-two years. Kay was living by herself making ends meet with her teaching job in Huntington Beach. It was a cinch she couldn't hold the annual Kraft New Year's gala at her place.

And the extended family with its in-laws and cousins and other shirttail relatives literally could not fit into the Krafts' Orange County homestead anymore. The tiny wood-frame structure on Beach Boulevard had been a World War II Women's Army Corps barracks when Grandpa Harold Kraft bought it from the U.S. government back in 1948. He refurbished it into a chicken ranch and raised his growing brood there, but they had all grown up and moved on years before.

Uncle Randy's apartment in Belmont Shore was out of the question.

It had only recently come to light that Randy Kraft was gay, and nobody was particularly comfortable with the fact yet. He and his roommate, Jeff Graves, seemed normal enough, but there was no need to open newly healing wounds. Harold Kraft still had difficulty accepting his only son's homosexuality, and his wife, Opal, a leader in the local Presbyterian church, simply tried to deny it altogether.

Melanie's favorite uncle was working as a computer operator at the time, running payroll programs for businesses in Long Beach and Orange County. He only made $4 an hour, but there was no shortage of overtime. In fact, he had to work on New Year's Eve that year, he told his sister. He would be a little late to the party.

Randy was making a real effort to get his life back together after several turbulent years following his 1969 discharge from the air force. After thirteen months as an enlisted aircraft painter, he had finally confessed to his superiors at Edwards Air Force Base in the California desert that he was homosexual. That's when he first began to come out of the closet.

Melanie Ann was almost too young to remember, but it had been a trauma for just about everyone. He went through a whole roster of second-rate jobs—bartender, truck driver, dispatcher. At one point, he was going to follow his sister Kay's example and go into elementary education. He was a teacher's aide one semester, working in the classroom with third-grade students. But ultimately that didn't satisfy him either. That the conservative school system administrators had a history of shunning and firing admittedly homosexual instructors was a fact not lost on him.

Finally, he started getting into computers. He was not only good at it, he loved it. He took night classes at Long Beach State University and easily mastered the basics. It wasn't unusual for him to stay up all night working out a computer problem. What's more, he took his jobs seriously and instilled instant trust in his employers. At Aztec Aircraft, one of the businesses where he ran computer payroll and handled the budget spreadsheets, he was given a key within a few weeks of his going to work. He was often the first to arrive and the last to leave.

So Melanie wasn't at all surprised that her uncle didn't arrive at her mother's house on Homer Street until nearly ten P.M. on New Year's Eve.

At thirty, Randy Kraft was the youngest of Harold and Opal Kraft's four children. Melanie's younger sister, Diana, described her uncle as "very neat and clean" and "yuppie casual." He had a tight but ready smile and a short walrus mustache. Since he had settled comfortably into his new life-style, there was a relaxed air about him much of the time. The time he spent at the beach had left him tan and healthy-looking. There was none of the sashaying or limp-wristed vamping in his manner that Melanie and her cousins associated with gay men. If anything, she preferred him to the other men in the family, who tended to cloister themselves in the living room for football and lots of male bonding whenever there was a family gathering.

Uncle Randy listened to his nieces and nephews.

When he did show up at the New Year's Eve party, Randy should have been exhausted, but he joined in the card games and the feasting and the conversation like everyone else in the burgeoning Kraft clan. His nephew Donald Lane had just enrolled in a computer science class and got his uncle talking about career opportunities.

As midnight approached, Doris Lane broke out the champagne. There were other members of the family who drank to excess, but brother Randy wasn't one of them. In fact, he rarely seemed to touch the stuff at all. So when he took up his glass along with everyone else for the New Year's toast, Doris marked the moment in her memory.

It was 12:30 A.M. when he left, as she said later. When Melanie Ann and her mother dropped by Grandpa and Grandma Kraft's home at about eight the following morning, Randy was asleep on the couch. He lived in the young, affluent neighborhood of Belmont Shore in Long Beach, some twenty miles to the north, but he still had his own key to the family home and let himself in and out whenever he was in the neighborhood. Doris noticed that he was still wearing the same clothes he had worn the night before. Her "neat and clean" little brother was just as neat and clean, curled up on the sofa, as he had been the night before at the Lanes' house. Doris and her daughter tiptoed by the sofa and turned on the TV low to watch the Tournament of Roses.

Randy didn't get up right away, but he was wide awake and ready to join in more gin rummy games by noon. He watched the Ohio State Buckeyes get trounced by UCLA in the Rose Bowl before he finally left. And, as usual, he treated the nieces and nephews with the kind of respect they never seemed to be able to get from their parents.

"I always had a good time with Randy," Melanie recalled some years later. "He didn't seem any different that day than he always was."

A quartet of off-duty cops riding dune buggies near a ranger station in the Cleveland National Forest first came across the body.

According to the records of the Orange County Sheriff's Office,

Detective's Report 458–339, on Saturday, January 3, 1976, at approximately four P.M., a nude male was found in heavy brush on the west side of Bedford Peak at the east end of Santiago Canyon in the Saddleback Mountains, about thirty miles south of San Juan Capistrano.

The killer or killers had carefully wrapped the body's legs around a sapling and slumped it up against the tree like a crumpled scarecrow in a fetal position. The man's hair was long and chestnut brown, tangled beneath his shoulders, and he wore a thin, unkempt mustache that drooped with his permanently frozen frown. When he had been alive, the young man stood about five foot ten and weighed 165 pounds, according to the coroner who arrived about an hour after the body was found and pried the decomposing corpse away from the tree.

He had died of alcohol and asphyxiation, the pathologist said. The body contained the equivalent alcohol of at least five six-packs coursing through its veins at the time of death, which the coroner fixed as sometime after midnight New Year's Eve. The young man had a blood alcohol level in his body of .67—nearly seven times the legal definition of drunk in California. The blood alcohol level in the young man's brain was only slightly less at .59. There were also traces of diazepam or Valium in his bloodstream.

But if alcohol alone hadn't killed him, the leaves and loam packed into his throat had finished him off. An autopsy later revealed that soil had been jammed down his bronchial tubes deep into the tissue of the lungs themselves. He had gagged to death on dirt.

Before he had died, however, his killers had played torturous games with his body—games that would have made a Dr. Mengele squirm with envy. First, the drunken young man had been trussed up like a hog, once he'd been stripped naked. Then, in the cool quiet of the forest, a half-dozen miles from the nearest hamlet, the screaming began.

A cigarette lighter from an automobile had left neat, red circles singed into the skin around the left nipple of his chest. There also were lighter burns branded into the scrotum, eyelids, cheeks, nose, and upper lip. Both eyes had probably been brown in life, but it was impossible to tell when pathologists began their preautopsy protocol. All they saw were the dark red and black circles burned into the eyeballs by the same automobile cigarette lighter.

Nicks and grooves had been carved into the young man's legs, with one particularly long incision sliced deep into the muscle, close to the bone.

After sodomizing the hapless victim, the murderer jammed a cocktail swizzle stick into the young man's penis, all the way into his bladder. Then the killer or killers hacked off both the penis and testicles and plunged them into the victim's anus. More leaves and some burned material were also stuffed into his rectum.

Based on the way the blood had dried and the wounds had reacted to the trauma, medical examiners concluded that the young man was still alive throughout much of the ordeal.

Later that week, there was a knock at the front door of Phillip Holmer's apartment. He and Holly were in the middle of a dispute about the disappearance of Hall and Holly's $200. Holmer was defending Hall. He was too dumb, too trusting, and, at the time, too drunk to pull anything as deceitful as lifting Holly's money.

Holmer answered the door. It was a pair of Orange County Sheriff's homicide investigators. They hadn't found Wayne Holly's $200. But they had found Mark Howard Hall.

The members of the band were stunned at the news of Hall's death, but not nearly so much as his parents. To the boys of Heavenly Blue, Mark Hall was a variation of the cliche "an accident looking for a place to happen": their former drummer was a victim looking for a place to destroy himself.

"When I heard what had happened, it was a shock that it had happened, but I wasn't surprised," said Keith Brasseure. "My impression was that he must have been in a bar being a big man, got in with some wrong people, made some promises he couldn't keep and when he realized that he was playing ball with some heavyweights, he freaked out and they took him out. I don't know if that's what happened or not, but knowing Mark, I'll bet something like that happened."

Darwin and Lois like to believe it was different somehow. They remember taking their only son to Disneyland when he was eight or nine, wide-eyed and running ahead of them to all the next rides. He never stopped talking about what a great place southern California was. No snow. Lots of beaches. Great women. And the very heart and soul of rock 'n' roll.

"He could hardly wait to get back there," said his father. "Mark was down there for about two years. We came down there and visited him in May of 1975, and we talked on the telephone a lot. Once in a while he'd send letters, but usually he'd just call us collect. Telephone's easier."

Darwin Hall chokes up over the memory of going fishing with his only son. When Mark was still a boy, the two of them hiked into the upper reaches of the Salmon and Snake together, pulling in the trout and chuckling to each other about the paradise on earth they'd found in the Idaho wilderness. But, ironically, the boy wouldn't accompany the old man on hunting trips. It was just all too violent for him.

"He didn't like to shoot stuff," Darwin remembered. Something about guns just turned Mark off. It was the era of the Vietnam war, too, which may have had something to do with Mark's feelings about firearms. He and his father quarreled frequently about the war.

"A lot of us didn't feel that the war was illegal or immoral at the beginning, but he did," Darwin said. "Mark always did. After a while, we all did. I was in the air force at the end of World War II, so I think as patriotic as I always tended to be, it really wore on Mark."

In high school, Mark took up smoking—a nasty habit to which Lois and Darwin Hall had never fallen prey. Darwin used to get on him a lot about that. It would ruin his health, he warned. He has revamped his feelings about the war and smoking and a lot of other things in the intervening years. In a very profound way, he has his son to thank for that.

"He was very trusting," Darwin said, with as much calm as he could muster. "Mark figured that everybody had a right to do what they want, long as they don't hurt no one else. He had long hair and I guess that was okay. You know, after a while I got to feeling the way he did too.

"Back in the '60s when they had all those demonstrations against the war, of course, I was against the demonstrations. But then everybody changes a little bit and has a different attitude. So I think we all changed. The whole nation changed.

"The kids weren't wrong that didn't want to go to war. Hell, after a while, I figured they were right too."

Brasseure sees what happened to Mark as a metaphor for the times in which he lived. He was at once too daring and too naive—and too desperate—to survive.

His death was inevitable.

"It wasn't so much our generation," he said, "as it was the time, the situation, the war, the drugs, the politics, everything, you know. The late '60s and the early '70s were like some witch's brew, churning up the magic. All the concoction was there. Everything that needed to be there was there and causing that magic. And, then, the magic turned sour."

Darwin Hall has gotten better at talking about what happened to his only son. He can usually get through a conversation without losing control the way he did that first week of January in 1976, when the homicide investigator called him from California.

"I would have been a good grandpa," he said, maintaining a strong control, with only the smallest hint of a tremble in his voice. "I know my wife would have been one of the world's best grandmothers. But then that's all done. I have two brothers. She has two brothers. We have good neighbors and friends here in Pocatello. We've thought about moving to a different area but I can't think of any place that I'd want to move to, really. We try to go on. Always have."

LAPD Sergeant John St. John stood near the top of Bedford Peak and scanned the rugged hillside below.

It was still winter but the steep sides of Santiago Canyon were already wavy green velvet. The wildflowers in this pocket of wilderness, which had thus far escaped the developers' bulldozers, would be breaking through in a few weeks, dotting the landscape with purples and yellows and blues. It was a picture-postcard portrait of how southern California used to be, before all the out-of-state émigrés started converging on Los Angeles.

Los Angeles before the coming of the freeways.

The remains from the kid that the Orange County homicide crew had found wrapped around a tree halfway down the hillside had been shipped back to his folks in Idaho weeks ago. They had buried him and that would probably be the end of it.

The kid was into dope. A long-hair. His brain had been pickled in ethyl alcohol when he bought the farm, according to the toxicological report that came back on him. So maybe he was asking for trouble, but there was no way the poor young bastard could have known how much trouble.

There didn't seem to be a clue, let alone an answer. There never was. This one—St. John glanced at the name—Mark Howard Hall, was number thirty or forty. Somewhere around there. It had gotten to the point where it didn't seem to make much sense trying to keep an exact count. It was tough enough for the dozens of police and sheriff agencies all over the south half of the state just to keep each other briefed on the latest bodies that popped up. That was why the various sheriffs and police chiefs from San Diego to Kern County had put together the interagency task force that St. John had been picked to head up in the first place: to try to keep up on the growing catalog of unsolved murders that were quietly plaguing southern California.

Some of them showed up in one of the coastal canyons like this one. A lot of them were dumped out in the desert, beyond Palm Springs. Occasionally one of them would pop up in the surf or get tangled up in a fisherman's net. The newspapers might give a paragraph or two to one of them when it was first discovered, but nobody had seemed to figure out that there was a frightening regularity to the body count yet.

The victims really didn't have all that much in common beyond being young and male. Some of them, like this Hall kid, were self-styled party animals with Veronica Lake hairdos. But there were Marines, too, and married guys and homosexuals and little kids still in junior high school.

Some of them were shot. Some of them were strangled. Some of them were beaten to death. There were plenty of them that wound up buggered, either before they died or, in a lot of cases, afterwards. But then there were those that didn't get sodomized either.

Some had been drugged. Some hadn't.

Some were mutilated. Some weren't.

Some of them had been hitchhiking. Some hadn't.

The whole thing gave St. John a headache.

He had driven to Bedford Peak over the same two-track Jeep trail that the crime lab crew had traversed three weeks earlier, accompanied by three other task force members: his partner, Kent McDonald from LAPD; George Troup from the Orange County DA's office; and Sergeant Gary Buzzard from Seal Beach, where at least a half dozen of the bodies had been dumped. A lot of the obvious evidence had already been tagged and shunted away into an evidence locker somewhere in the bowels of the Orange County Sheriff's headquarters, but St. John and his cohorts insisted on getting into a four-wheel drive and coming down to the rugged back-country canyon themselves to take their own look.

He studied the landscape they had combed for bits of anything that might provide a clue. A tiny bit of fabric or a hunk of paper or something. Maybe a matchbook cover, just like in the movies.

The sonofabitch had been playing cat and mouse with half the law enforcement agencies in southern California during the past half-dozen years. Perhaps he had a sense of humor. God knew he had a sense of the diabolic.

St. John understood the game all too well. By the time this assassin had started picking up his prey, using them for his pleasure, and dumping their mutilated carcasses by the side of the road at the beginning of the 1970s, St. John had already been working homicide for more than twenty years. The portly detective with the wispy gray hair and the watery growl had developed a reputation from Chinatown to San Pedro as the premier homicide detective in the Los Angeles Police Department. "Jigsaw" was his nickname. Jigsaw John.

The lab crew didn't find a lot. Some dried blood from the raw skin of the dead kid where he'd been dragged over the rough terrain to his final resting place. An empty package of Half & Half cigarettes. Not much else. Typical, though. The freeway assassin or assassins were a vexingly careful lot. The biggest revelation turned up during the first check of the area on January 3 was a shattered vodka bottle a couple of feet away from the body. The brand of vodka, ironically enough, was Winner's Vodka. There was a fingerprint on the bottle and it wasn't the dead kid's. The next day, another piece of broken glass found near the corpse revealed a second fingerprint.

They weren't terrific. One of the prints was only a partial and could only be brought up to where it was visible to the naked eye with a new process that used superglue to lift the imprint left by the whorls and ridges of the fingertips from a viscous surface like glass or pottery. When the lab people finally did manage to get the prints photographable, they were matched up with all the usual sources: FBI, California Department of Justice, local police departments.

And there was no match.

Still, it was something. Just like the hundreds of other fingerprints, fabric samples, pubic hairs, bloodstains, fibers, and other bits of evidence, the broken vodka bottle would get logged and filed in the crime lab property room for future reference.

Later, on June 28, 1976, St. John entered the prints in the task force logbook he maintained to keep track of the mounds of evidence that had built up around this so-called Freeway Killer. LP-0345 was the name for the photo blowups of the two fingerprints—LP for latent print.

Might mean nothing, like the dozens of latent prints that had been logged in before it, St. John mused.

But you never knew. In police work, you just never knew.

2

Westminster High welcomed a
new principal in 1961—a nascent environmentalist who demanded that
students and faculty observe Arbor Day by planting a tree. Each day
brought a new round of flyers and announcements and awards for the
most trees planted. Every morning, homeroom teachers instructed
their young charges to go out there and plant one for the chief.

Late one afternoon before a varsity baseball game with rival
Huntington Beach High, Randy Kraft and Billy Manson met at Randy's
house to dig up a small locust tree from the backyard.

The two boys dressed themselves in black, made their faces up
like minstrels to blend in with the night, and carrying shovels, sneaked
back to the athletic field at the Westminster campus. There, halfway
between home plate and the pitcher's mound, Billy dug a neat, round
hole while Randy stood watch to make certain nobody caught them.
With a solemn little ceremony, they planted the sapling. They unzipped
their flies long enough to christen it and then ran off the diamond by the
light of the moon, giggling like loons.

That was how students defied authority in those halcyon days,
Manson recalled. The Westminster he remembers advertised itself as
crime- and corruption-free through the '50s and '60s, when Billy and
Randy were growing up. No broken windows. No graffiti. Just an
occasional tree planted in the infield.

"I suspect there was a good bit of crime before then, but it didn't
matter because it was only the Mexicans cutting each other up," said

Manson, who graduated with Randy in 1963 and never returned to his hometown. "There was certainly a dark underside to the utopia."

The dark side of Westminster wasn't boys in blackface planting trees at midnight. It was more subtle, according to the people who lived there. The dark side came along with urban sprawl, spreading like pestilence until even the most pristine enclave was somewhat tainted.

Ex-rancher Roy Hefley marks the coming of the freeways as Westminster's waterloo. With the big eight-lane concrete ribbons lacing one end of the county to the other came the flood of middle-class, blue-collar humanity from L.A. trying to find a safe place to raise their kids. Unfortunately, they brought the criminal element right along with them.

Up until then, the town had had its share of burglary or vandalism, but murder or sex perversion were rare. A sixty-four-year-old chiropractor who adopted young orphan boys from Tijuana was charged with molesting in 1952 and sent to the state hospital at Atascadero for observation. That was about it for the decade. If unspeakable evil did happen in Westminster, obviously nobody ever spoke about it.

Back then life was bucolic, if a little bigoted. The Mexicans lived on unpaved alleys off Hoover Street, and the upwardly mobile, middle-class white kids lived in the beige stucco three-bedroom subdivisions on the west side of town, near Westminster High.

Billy Manson and Paul Whitson lived on the west side. They became fast friends with Randy in junior high: the three musketeers. They were all bright and oozing self-confidence. Each one knew exactly what he was going to be when he grew up. Whitson was going to be a scientist. Randy and Billy were both destined to become Republican U.S. senators.

"We were both someplace to the right of Attila the Hun," Manson remembered. "Nixon was a liberal. Barry Goldwater was okay. But our real hero was William F. Buckley, Jr."

Manson, Kraft, and Whitson became the three musketeers as much out of self-protection as mutual interest. None of them was an angel, but neither were they likely to cover the wall clock in Mr. Tinder's history class with spitballs or drop their books in Mr. Carney's science class just to irritate a substitute teacher.

"We were perceived by our classmates as being highly intelligent, and that wasn't always the best thing to be in those days," said Whitson.

They were all passionate young conservatives, heavily crusading on behalf of fellow Orange County-ite Richard M. Nixon during the 1960 presidential campaign. Despite their shared belief that Nixon represented the left wing of the Republican party, John F. Kennedy was worse.

Even as freshmen, they were devotees of the right-wing tracts of the day: Barry Goldwater's *The Conscience of a Conservative*, Buckley's *Up from Liberalism*, and W. Cleon Clausen's *The Naked Communist*. They went to meetings of the Christian Anti-Communist Crusade, regularly read the *National Review*, and became apologists for Senator Joseph McCarthy.

Kraft, who did an about-face and supported Robert Kennedy in college, wrote to a friend about his right-wing adolescence many years later: "I have to chuckle remembering about this. Kids do the darnedest things."

The musketeers were bright. From junior high through high school, Manson and Kraft and Whitson were all identified in state intelligence testing as "mentally gifted minors" and were accorded special accelerated college preparatory status.

They were "your basic nerds," said Manson, down to the neatly ironed white shirts and ties, close-cropped haircuts, and—at least in Manson and Whitson's nearsighted cases—black horn-rimmed glasses.

Whitson remembers a cool, rational Randy with a pale, freckled complexion that went pink only when he was frustrated—usually during a political argument. Both of them belonged to the Presbyterian church, and both considered themselves bona fide Westminster "natives" who had actually grown up there, unlike the sons and daughters of carpet-baggers who rushed south from Los Angeles in the late 1950s.

"I think the bond that Randy and I and [Manson] shared was that we were set aside from the rest of our classmates by virtue of our historical background in the county," Whitson said.

The musketeers grew up in a different era. Like the rest of the country, Westminster families liked Ike, subscribed to the *Saturday Evening Post*, and bought 78 rpm bakelite recordings by Perry Como or the Andrews Sisters. The '50s and early '60s in general were an age of innocence, as the three musketeers remembered it. And Westminster in particular was a good place and time to be a boy, growing up where the streets were safe, the neighborhoods friendly, and the people warm and trusting.

Randy Kraft entered the world in the front ranks of the Baby Boom. The obstetrician who delivered him on March 19, 1945, reported no congenital malformations, no birth injuries, no complications either in Mrs. Kraft's pregnancy or delivery. Randy was as healthy as his three older sisters: Kay, Doris, and Jeannette.

Randy's parents had immigrated to California at the outbreak of World War II. The couple met and married in Wyoming, where Harold was a cook at a Standard Oil field and Opal waited tables in the company cafeteria. She bore him three girls before he lit out for California in 1941. When he found work the following year—for himself and for Opal—he sent for her and the girls.

"Harold was a production man at Douglas Aircraft," said retired Douglas engineer John Kirkpatrick. "I came in contact with him once or twice a day and I always thought very highly of him. He put out good work, handled his crew well."

Harold was thirty-nine and Opal was thirty-three when Randy was born. His first home was a modest two-bedroom bungalow in the middle-class Bixby Knolls section of north Long Beach. Randy's three older sisters doted on him, acting like little mothers to hear them talk about it years later.

"I used to rock him in my arms and sing him to sleep as a baby," recalled his sister Doris, twelve years his senior. "He was a very calm baby."

But an active baby too, at times. Shortly after his first birthday, Randy fell off the couch in the living room and broke his collarbone.

A year later, when the family was planning on moving out of Long Beach, Randy was hurt even more seriously.

"Dad had taken us out to look at the house that he was thinking about buying on Beach Boulevard," Doris remembered. "And it had large concrete steps up to the porch. And Randy fell down and he hit his head and was unconscious and we had to take him to the medical clinic—the only one in the town."

The toddler was unconscious when the Krafts arrived at the Westminster Medical Clinic on 17th Street. After some desperate moments, Randy came to. He was treated and released to his parents, apparently with no further complications, according to his sisters.

If Randy had ever been abused, family members don't remember it, and medical records of his accidents were destroyed long ago. There is no dispute, however, that he had advantages that his sisters never did. As the only son, Randy was spoiled at the same time he was disciplined.

In 1948, when Randy was three, the family moved from Long

Beach to Westminster in rustic, agrarian Orange County, eight miles inland from the Pacific Ocean.

Their new home was a small wood-frame Women's Army Corps dormitory on Beach Boulevard in the then-rural community of Midway City, a single unincorporated square mile of county land located on the Westminster border.

Harold turned the old WACS barracks into a three-bedroom house for his family and vowed to raise chickens. It was the only home on the block.

The devoutly Presbyterian Kraft women immediately became active members of the Women's Fellowship Circles of the Westminster First Presbyterian Church. Doris sang in the choir and became part of a traveling foursome that called itself the Presbyterian Youth Quartet. Mrs. Kraft rose to the position of chairman of the deacons committee. Randy spent Sundays in church and Bible study classes, usually taught by his oldest sister, Kay.

Harold Kraft didn't go to church.

"Harold Kraft was never around," said Eva Boyd, wife of church pastor Kenneth Boyd. "I mean, a lot of the men didn't come to church, but they at least showed up for progressive dinners and the festivals. Whenever I saw Randy he was always with his sisters and his mom. Harold was always . . . distanced."

The Krafts' means were modest. Unlike the Peek family, who ran the mortuary, or the Moores, who owned a ranch, Harold Kraft could barely pay the bills for his growing family with his assembly-line salary at Douglas Aircraft. To supplement her husband's meager paycheck, Opal Kraft worked as a sewing machine operator for a time at a Westminster garment factory and, later on, took a job cooking and cleaning and, eventually, supervising in the cafeteria at the 17th Street school.

But she still found time for Randy. She was a PTA officer at Midway City Elementary and baked cookies for Cub Scout meetings. Randy remained the darling of his mother and older sisters throughout those lean times.

By sixth grade, the kid with the flat-top haircut and the band of freckles across his nose and both cheeks tested out to be clever enough to go to accelerated classes at the 17th Street junior high.

In the eyes of the boys, Randy was a likable egghead: always good to crib homework assignments from, but not a first-round draft choice for the flag football team.

In the eyes of the girls, Randy was the perfect gentleman: always well-dressed, well-liked, studious, quiet. The only time he ever seemed to get animated was over politics.

"I knew absolutely nothing about politics," said Kay Frazel, who had a junior high crush on Randy. "Once, I was just shooting my mouth, repeating what my parents said about Republicans, not knowing what I was talking about. Randy was very much the Republican and my parents weren't. So he and I got into this heated discussion and he made me cry. That's about the only time I can remember anything loud, noisy, or troublesome coming out of Randy."

Beach Boulevard, the two-lane blacktop where Harold Kraft bought and remodeled his WACS barracks, grew to four lanes in 1954. The house where Randy grew up became almost invisible—a tired 1,100-square-foot shack recessed fifty feet from the highway, surrounded by new businesses. A blacksmith's shop opened to the north and the Red Garter cocktail lounge opened to the south of the Krafts' home, much to Mrs. Kraft's horror. What Randy learned about Presbyterian probity in Reverend Boyd's Sunday sermons he unlearned next door.

"Randy used to say he'd come home from church and have to shovel the condoms out of the backyard every Sunday morning," Manson recalled.

Generally, however, Westminster's civic image remained clean-cut and respectable: a stronghold of traditional conservative values.

When the three musketeers became Westminister High freshmen, they urged one of their history teachers to help them found a Westminster World Affairs Club and immediately passed resolutions condemning the United Nations and supporting the John Birch Society.

Miss Nova Kimzey, the no-nonsense head of the English Department, made her college prep classes write a three hundred–word essay every two weeks. Randy's were usually impassioned political tracts, but good enough to be entered in contests staged by the Rotary or Kiwanis clubs. He won his share of awards, she remembered.

"Randy sat right at the middle of my class," said Miss Kimzey. "He was sort of a square-faced kid and outgoing, very pleasant, always in class. He did all his assignments. I gave him an A."

He may have been a right-wing nut case, but he was bright. Most of his teachers did give Kraft good grades. One who didn't was chemistry teacher Leigh Manley.

"As a general rule, almost any teacher who had him would

generally concede that he was a good student. But I failed him," he recalled. "He was one of those people who felt that the rules didn't apply to him. He was never short of ability but he sort of made his own rules. What struck me at the time was that he wouldn't do the work in chemistry, and it wasn't because he wasn't able to. It's just that he decided he was going to graduate and nobody was going to stop him from graduating."

Kraft wasn't totally cerebral. He played saxophone for the school band for a while and took up tennis, despite the beginnings of a lifelong battle with flat feet. He wound up as one of the top four seeds on the Westminster High varsity team.

But academics were where the three musketeers—Randy, Billy, and Paul—shined. By the time they were in high school, they stopped being embarrassed about being smart. They even became trend-setters. Billy was the first to notice that the jocks and "soshes" started wearing shirts and ties to school occasionally, just like them.

Westminster was a reel straight out of *American Graffiti* in those days. Those lucky or rich enough to afford cars cruised Beach or Garden Grove boulevards on Friday nights after the weekly sock hops and hung out at Me 'n' Ed's Pizza, The Right Place, or Oscar's Drive-in. But despite owning a car, Randy was not a member of the sociable or "sosh" clique.

"He wasn't involved in any of the cheerleader stuff or anything like that," said Clancy Haynes, who was elected student body president the year Kraft graduated in 1963. "I was not aware of him having any kind of real social life outside of school, after school or anything like that."

Randy did in fact have a social life, but it was as a member of the "brainy" crowd, according to Manson. He bought a '53 Mercury when he was a sophomore and spent his off hours with the other high school intellectuals at Carolina's Pizza, several blocks away from sosh hang-outs.

"They made better pizza," explained Manson.

While others resorted to crude pranks, such as mooning teachers or cops on Golden West Boulevard, Kraft's crowd was more sophisti-cated. Theirs were the practical jokes, like the locust tree in the infield.

"I can remember Randy laughing, but it always seemed like he had probably a different, more wry sense of humor, and I would attribute that to his maybe being a little brighter than some of the rest of us," said Haynes. "I think that people who are bright don't have a silly sense of humor. What I remember of Randy was, he seemed to laugh at the more ironic stuff."

None of the musketeers were great lovers, but each did his share of escort duty at the Spring Flings, the Peppermint Balls, and the Junior/Senior Proms. Their dates tended to be interchangeable.

"There were a batch of girls that a batch of boys ended up spending a lot of time with, in rotation almost," remembered Manson. When summer rolled around, the three would pile into Randy's Mercury, rub on some suntan oil, and tool down to Newport or Balboa to ogle women. Randy leered and learned to wolf whistle as well as his pals, panting appreciatively at the latest European import on the Huntington Beach strand: the two-piece bikini.

By the time Randy was in high school, all three of his sisters had left home, married, and started families of their own. Randy had his own room, his own car, and his own wants, supplemented by money he earned during summer vacation as a fry cook at Dwight's, a hamburger stand near the Huntington Beach pier. He was as normal as normal could be, remembered Bill Manson.

Randy's brother-in-law, Duane Eastburn, a swim coach at Westminster High, had persuaded Harold to let him build a half-Olympic-sized swimming pool on the vacant land behind his father-in-law's home so that he could open his own swimming school. Eastburn's own four children, as well as their cousins, learned to be competitive swimmers there. Though Randy's game was tennis, he helped out at Eastburn's Blue Dolphin Swim School during school vacations and when he wasn't making burgers at Dwight's during the summer.

"When we were kids, we'd be playing in the pool out in the backyard over at Grandma's house," remembered his niece, Diane Lane. "Randy would always be down there playing with us, whereas all the dads would be in playing cards or watching football games and it would be like an act of God to get their attention. But Randy would always be out in the yard playing What's Up? with us."

Many years later, Randy maintained that he knew as far back as his high school days that he was gay. He didn't know how to show it or explain it, but he sensed even then that dressing up in a tux, black bow tie, and white dinner jacket to ferry Sybil Wiles to Camelot, the senior prom, was a farce. The bashful blonde was fooled, and it wasn't just because she was a year behind him in school.

"Promise to keep in contact with me after you're (sob!) gone," she wrote in his yearbook. "I need encouragement in my last year. You know me: muddle-head the first . . . Love, Sybil."

He couldn't put his finger on why he felt that way. But if Randy instinctively knew he was different, his friends, family, teachers—and certainly the other musketeers—never did.

"In those days nobody would ever let it be known that they were horny, let alone gay," said Clancy Haynes. "We probably had all kinds of desires to do all kinds of things, but nobody ever did. And whenever somebody *did* do something, everybody in the world knew about it. If somebody got a piece of ass, everybody knew. The next day they knew! So, you know, I can't *imagine* that somebody who was a homosexual in those days would ever have done anything to let it be known."

In 1963, when Kraft graduated, the hallucinogenic youth revolt that caused legions of homosexuals to emerge from the closet was still several years away. Then and now, there are no gay bars, bath houses, or social clubs where gay men or women gather in Westminster. Then and now, gayness is viewed as a mental and moral sickness that can be cured.

"We kind of had a feeling that he had a propensity for boys even back then," said former Westminster science teacher Al Stone, who gave Randy the nickname "Crafty Randy." The "we," he explained, were teachers who gossiped about such matters in the faculty lounge, outside the earshot of the students. "We had several boys like that, but most of them straightened out later on."

When the three musketeers took their diplomas from Westminster High on June 13, 1963, Randy graduated tenth out of a class of 390.

Kraft wrote an entire page in Whitson's yearbook, extolling Whitson's "natural wit and humor" and waxing philosophical: "Now we're just on the threshold of our lives and many problems and uncertainties face us. I naturally wish you the best of luck. We can all use it. I'm sure that your faith in God will be an asset as you feel your way through life."

The summer after Randy's graduation from high school, Mrs. Kraft contributed the institutional cooking skills she had learned as the 17th Street school cafeteria supervisor to the Boy Scouts. She cooked for several hundred youngsters at a summer camp in the San Jacinto Mountains south of Westminster, and she brought Randy along for a few days, even though he was too old for scouting.

"I didn't trust him and I didn't like him," said Steve Manley, a scout four years Randy's junior who went to camp with the Kraft's that summer. "I'm not puritanical, but I have a certain moral feeling about things, and Randy didn't fit well. He was the kind of person who'd say one thing to the parents and then do almost the opposite. An Eddie Haskell type."

Because Randy was three or four years older and bound for prestigious Claremont Men's College, where he'd won a scholarship, his version of events was the one the grown-ups always seemed to believe.

"I got the feeling that he did enough to be surface unblemished," Manley continued. "I didn't ever feel comfortable around him and I never understood why. I was still aghast when I heard about his arrest, but it may not have surprised me as much as it surprised a lot of other people."

3

The God that holds you over the pit of hell, much as one holds a spider or some loathsome insect over the fire, abhors you and is dreadfully provoked," hissed the sophomore with the nickname of Moley, his voice rising with the flames.

He turned the page.

Dennis Mann, a long, tall international relations major with a pointy chin and a klutzy manner, threw some more wood on the fire. The autumn sky, which had been a smoggy gray orange just a few hours earlier, was now a black shroud hanging over the eastern border of Los Angeles County. The flames leaped higher, casting shadows against the granite walls of the quarry pit. Mann, who stood six foot nine in his stocking feet, looked like Frankenstein's monster lumbering around the edges of the bonfire. Moley raised one hand high, letting his finger shadows play against the rock wall like the tentacles of a huge, angry fist.

"His wrath towards you burns like fires," Moley said a little louder. "He looks upon you as worthy of nothing else but to be cast into the fire. . . . You are ten thousand times as abominable in His eyes as the most hateful and venomous serpent is in ours!"

Moley, so named for the nearsighted mole in *The Wind in the Willows*, adjusted his glasses and waited for his audience to shudder. Randy Kraft swaggered to the keg, pulling another tankard from the spigot. He drained half of it in one thirsty draught. The more imaginative of the dozen or so Claremont College students and their dates could hear a coyote or two baying at the moon as it rose over Mount Baldy. Moley focused on his book of sermons and read in an even louder, more malicious intonation. He tried to appear menacing, but all he did was look ridiculous standing by the fire in his bathrobe. He aimed his words at a huddle of freshmen, pointing an accusing finger into their midst.

"You have offended Him infinitely more than ever a stubborn rebel did his prince!" he shouted, his shadow hand undulating over the shadow head of one of the newly indoctrinated. Moley's hand dropped and so did its shadow, seeming to immolate itself in the flames that licked the very edges of the twenty-foot pit. His raging words dissolved into a hideous cackle and, finally, a helpless giggle. His flock giggled right back at him. If the freshmen were frightened, their faces didn't show it.

Soon, everyone was rolling around in the dust, snickering and snorting and sucking down beer.

Devotees of the regular Friday night Green Hall revival and beer bust had a special place in their hearts for hellfire and brimstone. The faithful offered cheers and applause while preachers like Moley quaffed their pints and stood next to the fire, spouting sarcastic sacrilege between handfuls of popcorn.

"After you'd had a couple pitchers of beer, you'd just sort of make it up," remembered one of the regulars. "And everyone'd cheer. Maybe Randy or someone else would sermonize. There was nothing degenerate about it. Nothing illegal, except underage drinking and building a bonfire without a permit."

The TGIF revivals were as rowdy as it got at Claremont College in the '60s. In the foothills behind campus, in the shadow of Mount Baldy, the residents of Green Hall would gather every week or two for a solemn reading from Cotton Mather or Jonathan Edwards while they polished off a keg. Sometimes they'd drive up higher on the mountain to Glendora Ridge Road, where they could drink and watch the sun set in the Pacific Ocean at the same time. But mostly they studied and wrote and read at a pace unheard of at most California colleges during the 1960s.

There were no fraternities or drinking clubs per se. Claremont was as deadly serious an all-male bastion of academics as any British boys' school. The dorms, like Green Hall, substituted for fraternities, but they were poor excuses for an "Animal House."

There was the time that the seniors built themselves an illegal brewery up on the third floor, but the dean found out about it and made them destroy it. To show how civilized he was, he shared a bottle with the boys before he made them get rid of it.

The fifty-acre campus of the Claremont colleges was like a cloistered anachronism from another century. Tucked away in the northeast corner of Los Angeles County, just off the San Bernardino Freeway, it was "like entering the Twilight Zone," said one of Randy Kraft's '60s contemporaries.

It hasn't changed much since then. Other than a perpetual layer of thick smog that hangs over much of the San Gabriel Valley, signs of urban decay still haven't penetrated Claremont. At the base of Mount Baldy, a mile off the freeway, stands a corridor of eucalyptus trees, thick and primeval, on either side of College Avenue. They lead onto a pastoral campus, undisturbed by the commuter hustle that defines much of southern California.

When Randy was a freshman, high tea was served each afternoon. Young women in tights practiced ballet exercises on manicured lawns. In the early evening, chamber music often seeped from the interior of Bridges Auditorium, blending with the twittering of songbirds in nearby sycamore groves. Students studied and teachers taught. There was no such thing as political demonstrations, women's rights, or gay students.

"If you believe what people say, that 10 percent of the population is gay, then it's probably true that there were some on campus back when Randy was attending classes," said former Claremont Men's College dean of students Clifton McLeod. "There was a movement to get the administration to recognize gays in the mid-'60s. But it was our position at CMC not to recognize any group based on sexual orientation. If there was a gay club, why shouldn't there be one for heterosexuals too?"

Randy wasn't ready to declare his own homosexuality in the fall of 1963, when he enrolled as an economics major at Claremont, even though he told friends in later years that he knew even then that he preferred men over women. And though he spent the next four years at an all-male school, few if any of his friends knew he was gay.

"First of all, in the '60s homosexuality was not accepted," said Randy's classmate Russell Chung. "Everyone was still in the closet. In the '60s you had an image of a homosexual as someone who was effeminate and had strange mannerisms. And you didn't suspect someone who appeared to be straight and had a hidden, secret life. That was completely something that you wouldn't imagine at that time."

An eventual move toward open homosexuality was not the only radical change that Randy Kraft underwent during his college career. As a freshman in 1963, he enrolled in Claremont's Reserve Officers Training Corps program along with Chung and Mann and Moley and all the rest of his circle of friends.

But two years later, he rejected ROTC, along with the Vietnam War. In the mid-'60s, when campuses all over the United States were erupting in protest, Claremont was one of the few places in the nation where students carried placards demonstrating *for* the presence of U.S. troops in Southeast Asia. Most faculty and students—including Randy—initially supported the nation's inevitable march toward war.

By the time the first Claremont graduate died in Vietnam two years later, the pro-war demonstrations had become antiwar. Randy was among the first to do an about-face. He didn't advise Doug Grimwood, his dorm roommate, to drop out of ROTC, but he did quit the program himself.

"That was one of the things I appreciated about Randy," Grimwood said of his roommate's tolerance. "You took a ration of garbage from a lot of people about being in ROTC, but Randy wasn't one of them."

Three months into Randy's first semester, John F. Kennedy was assassinated.

"I had been in college ROTC and that morning we had our only experience with firearms: an hour or so session at the National Guard Armory Rifle range in Montclair," Randy wrote in a letter to an acquaintance nearly a quarter century later. "In the weeks and months that followed, it became significant to me that when Kennedy was shot I was probably firing a gun."

But it wasn't until two years after the assassination that Randy would reverse his rightward drift. Up to that point he remained—in rhetoric, at least—a staunch conservative.

"I remember as a freshman getting into an argument with him over politics on the steps of the library," said classmate Fred Merkin. "It stands out in my mind because I remember he was *so* conservative and I was *so* liberal."

That kind of argument occurred often at Claremont. There wasn't much else in the way of entertainment. Students who weren't sucking down pots of coffee at nearby Story House while studying for exams were gathered around a TV set in the rec room at Green Hall, watching Huntley and Brinkley, old Japanese horror movies, or Mort Sahl.

Unlike the major West Coast universities at Berkeley, Stanford, and UCLA, which accommodate thousands of new students each year, enrollment remains small and select at Claremont. Students, particularly those who live in the same dormitory for four years, get to know each other well. Less than three hundred entering freshmen are admitted annually. CMC's total number of alumni since it first opened its doors in 1948 adds up to less than ten thousand.

When Kraft was a freshman, there was strict sexual segregation among the cluster of five colleges that included Claremont. At monastic Green Hall on the Claremont campus, where Kraft lived with sixty other male students, women were both rare and revered.

"Sundays were the only time you were allowed to have female guests in your room," recalled Chung, one of the "Gang Green" residents of Green Hall. "You had to keep the door ajar and there was always someone checking up on you. It got to be a big deal to have a woman in your room."

Men outnumbered women nearly two to one, and it was a given that upperclassmen had the pick of the freshmen women at nearby Scripps, Pitzer, or Pomona. Claremont Men's College further handicapped its freshmen by discouraging them from owning cars. They were not normally allowed to park on campus until they were upperclassmen. Kraft was one of the few entering students who stubbornly ignored the administration's roadblocks and drove his '53 Mercury to the school every day.

Otherwise, he was the quintessential Claremont freshman, circa 1963.

"My impression of him, I guess, was that he was kind of a stereotyped Orange County conservative Republican John Bircher," said Chung.

Kraft later maintained that he was just mimicking his parents' views. They were not his own. At eighteen, he was still the dutiful son. He joined the Barry Goldwater Victory Squad on campus because Harold and Opal Kraft were for Goldwater.

"His mother was pretty classically a mother," recalled one of Randy's closest Claremont friends, who used to accompany Kraft on the thirty-mile trip back to Midway City during weekends and holidays. "She was nice. Baked cookies. But his father definitely was not one of Randy's favorite friends. And his father and mother didn't get along real well. That was real obvious to visitors, and it *shouldn't* have been obvious to a visitor, I didn't think. I mean, you're only going to be there for half an hour. You would think that people could get along, and it was very clear that they didn't."

Publicly, however, the image of the Kraft family remained spotlessly all-American in the "Leave It to Beaver" mold. His sisters gathered at their mother's house to drink coffee and bicker about their own growing families. Harold Kraft, fast approaching retirement age, receded further and further from family functions. He got his son a job at Douglas Aircraft one summer, where Randy joined him in the machine shop, operating a routing machine.

The Krafts seemed no different from other ordinary working middle-class families. But the passionate Presbyterian values that inspired Randy to scribble "May God bless & keep you" on the back of his high school senior photos before passing them out to his friends had begun to come into question.

"By the time we'd hit college, I think he'd become agnostic or atheist, I'm not sure which," said his old friend Bill Manson, who stayed in touch by letter from his own college in Illinois. "He was a rationalist in one sense or another anyway."

Manson also remembers Randy parlaying his high school fry cook's job at Dwight's hamburger stand into a similar fast-food position at Disneyland the summer between high school and college. With his clean-cut, square-jawed good looks, Manson said, Randy conformed perfectly to the Disneyland image.

But the image transformed along with his politics and his sexuality the following summer. The demise of Goldwater conservatism and the beginnings of a gay life-style turned Randy's world upside down.

"I was a poll watcher at a precinct in Pomona, even though I wasn't old enough to vote," Randy said, remembering the summer and fall of 1964, before the voting age was reduced from twenty-one to eighteen. "It was probably the last gasp of the conservative ideology in me. I wasn't that upset about the loss. My heart wasn't in it.

"Of course, the summer before that election I had had an affair with a black guy, and that had thrown much of my 'beliefs' into chaos. Ah, Mike . . . I really loved him and cared for him . . . took him home to meet Mom and Dad. What an awkward meeting. . . ."

Randy took on a part-time job far removed from the Disneyland image, tending bar at the Mug, a Garden Grove cocktail lounge with a gay clientele. Meanwhile, his parents and sisters still had no suspicion that his sexual preference was male, not female. While he was tentatively emerging from the closet, bringing male friends home to meet his folks, he continued to live his double life at Claremont.

By the time he was a junior, Randy had traded his Mercury in for a classic white Jaguar XK convertible. He sported longer hair, a mustache and, briefly, a beard. Occasionally, some students heard rumors that Kraft and at least one other CMC student might be involved in sadomasochistic "bondage and discipline" parties.

"The evening I met him has been embedded in my subconscious all these years, I guess," said Gregory Fall. "I was a freshman and Randy would have been a junior or a senior. He and another guy—one of the people he ran with—invited me to a party off-campus."

Fall remembered a Randy who wore a badly kept goatee and an inscrutable smile—almost a leer. He was friendly enough, but friendly in the manner of one who has ulterior motives and understands that freshmen are fish out of water, hungry to find any means of fitting in.

"Some of the older people in the dorm warned me not to go to the party," Fall said. "They were very subtle about it. I mean, they didn't say, 'He screws boys,' or anything like that. But I got the message, and the message was that Randy Kraft was a very dangerous person."

If there were such suspicions about Randy, however, they died in the minds of most of his classmates as soon as they were born. Even his closest Claremont friends didn't give much thought to Randy's odd habits until years later.

"The most bizarre thing about Randy as a person was that he would disappear with regularity," said Mac, his roommate that year. "Maybe two, three times a week. At odd hours of the night. Like you'd be going to bed and he'd be going out. He'd been up all day. And then he'd go out and about and whatever.

"He was very . . . well, he let you know that what he did wasn't really something he wanted you to know about. He let you know in just a subtle way. You'd ask him, you know: 'I went to bed last night and you went out and I heard you come back in at five o'clock in the morning. What the hell did you do all night?'

"And he would generally give you some vaguish answer if he bothered to answer much at all. But the signal always was: 'Don't worry about me, I'm fine and I'll go out and do what I want.'"

Randy also began to suffer from headaches and chronic stomach trouble. The stress of coming out, even tentatively, may have contributed to his psychosomatic ills, but it wasn't the only factor. His friends and family blamed school work and a general sense of floating futility that often accompanies the realization that graduation is not far off.

"He had a lot of physical problems with his stomach and a lot of migraines. This was over a long period of time. He had them in college. He had them after college," remembered one of Randy's closest friends. "I don't know that they were all that serious, but they were the kinds of things that I associate with stress."

The same Westminster health clinic to which Randy's parents had taken him when he fell and was knocked unconscious as a toddler was now the grown Randy Kraft's source for prescription pain relievers and muscle relaxants. Over the years, Dr. Wilson C. McArthur, the general practitioner who acted as family physician to the Krafts, prescribed hundreds of pills for Randy's headaches, dyspepsia, and nerves.

Remembered another friend, "He took Valium or something like that. He took those kinds of things to calm you down. And a lot of times he'd talk to me about it. He couldn't understand why he was having all these problems with his stomach and his head and headaches and stuff like that."

One of the reasons could be traced to a brush with the law the summer following his junior year, when the carefully hidden life-style he began developing shortly after he graduated from high school was briefly exposed to public view.

When Mac, Randy's Green Hall roommate who was a year ahead of him, offered to get an apartment with Randy at Huntington Beach the summer following Mac's graduation, Randy jumped at the chance.

"That was '66," Mac recalls, "when Vietnam was really starting to happen. I had two Peace Corps assignments that I'd turned down. There was all kind of things going on in my mind at that point. So that was my present to me: getting the Huntington Beach apartment and going down to Laguna to lie around on the beach. And Randy lived down there with me when we did that. He was living as a gay then, but I didn't know that until quite a while later on."

By 1966, Randy was well aware that there was a different, secret life that existed in southern California, even if Mac wasn't. Randy had heard it alluded to back at Westminster High and was already scouting the gay bar scene by the time he'd joined Gang Green at Claremont. In Orange County during the '60s, gay life was centered in Laguna Beach, where homosexuality flourished with limited interference from the local police. Randy drove his Jaguar down to Laguna often during the

summer, but it was at the Huntington Beach pier that he had his first
run-in with the law.

Stretching along the oceanfront, all the way from Seal Beach to
Costa Mesa, is a series of lifeguard shacks and restroom facilities.
During hot summer days, the sand is packed wall-to-wall with tanning
bodies and squealing children. In the evening, beach party bonfires dot
the horizon, and small bands of teenagers hunt grunion when the moon
is full.

But after midnight, around the yellow stucco men's rooms that are
spaced at intervals of a few hundred yards up and down the beach, gay
hustlers and their tricks emerge from the shadows. It is usually the
older men who are the buyers. The sellers tend to be young and jaded
beyond their years.

When Claremont College junior Randy Kraft offered to have sex
with a man near the Huntington Beach pier during the summer of 1966,
he didn't know he was about to be busted by a vice officer for lewd
conduct.

All that remains of the records of that first run-in with the law is an
entry in the Huntington Beach Police Department incident log. Randy
wasn't cited and was apparently told what most first-time offenders
were told when caught soliciting tricks around the beach restrooms:
Don't get caught doing it again.

Residents of Claremont's Green Hall dormitory, more boisterous
than most, were dubbed the Green Weenies, and during his senior year,
Randy became the head Green Weenie: he was elected dorm president.
Randy the academic had become Randy the socialite. He organized
late-night poker games, beer busts, and the dances with all-girl Scripps
and Pitzer.

Perhaps it was pretense, or perhaps it was continuing confusion
over his sexual identity, but Randy dated, just as he had in high school.
Doug Grimwood remembers him sneaking girls up to the room and
cooking for them on contraband frying pans and hot plates. He
conducted himself as if he were just as exaggeratedly macho as the next
student. When the guys lumbered down to Willie and Ethel's Midway
Bar on Foothill Boulevard to toss off a few beers, Randy was right there
with them. Wednesday night was seventy-five-cents-a-pitcher night,
and the Gang Green usually dropped in for several pitchers around
midnight.

As a senior at Claremont, Randy was beset by the same complacency that had earned him an F in Leigh Manley's chemistry class during his final semester at Westminster High.

"I have an image of Randy in our senior year holding a beer bottle, walking around the dorm with a smirk on his face, wearing some strange hat—like a hat that your dad would wear but you wouldn't," said Mike Donovan, another Green Weenie nicknamed "Grumpy" by his roommates. "It was a black hat with some sort of a flat rim. He seemed to wear black a lot. I think he had a black vest he used to wear too."

When Donovan staged an all-night bridge game following the last football game of the season, Randy was among the revelers who moved the game outdoors and played by candlelight in the quad outside of Green Hall. Russ Chung was only half joking when he said that Randy changed his major from economics to bridge during his senior year. Randy didn't like to lose at cards and seldom did.

When he did crack the books, it was usually to cram. Randy was one of the worst of the senior goof-offs, but he wasn't the only one to pull all-nighters. Sometimes he needed a little help. A *Claremont Collegian* ad, circa 1967, pushed caffeine capsules: "When you must keep alert, take Verv—continuous action capsules, safe and non–habit forming."

But everybody used at least caffeine to buzz them through finals, said Donovan. Randy may have been listless about his studies, but he did seem to have boundless energy.

"I remember Randy had a beard," he said. "It wasn't real full. Just a little tuft at the bottom of his chin. I wouldn't use the word 'mephistophelean' ordinarily, but it sounds like a good description. I won't say that he looked evil, but in retrospect I think that he did, only because—I know this sounds corny, but—he seemed to have an evil glint in his eye, you know? And his sense of humor was strange. He would make snide little comments that were jokes or something, but they seemed funny only to him. Not funny ha-ha but strange funny. Odd funny."

Randy did not graduate with his classmates in June of 1967. His senior lethargy caught up with him and he had to repeat four units of D in econometrics over the summer. He finally earned his bachelor of arts degree in economics the following February.

The war caught up with Claremont that summer. The placards students had carried to the ROTC parade grounds two years before asking WHAT CAN WE WIN BY LOSING? and proclaiming VICTORY IS ESSENTIAL

TODAY gave way to block-long protest banners chastising the ROTC enrollees.

Randy finally abandoned his Midway City politics and registered as a Democrat, campaigning as avidly for Robert Kennedy as he once had for Goldwater. He became a grassroots Democratic party organizer in the very heart and soul of California conservatism. In a personal letter, the senator from New York wrote his encouragement and thanks for Randy's efforts:

"The campaign is a great challenge. It is my hope that you will choose to join with our Orange County Committee in this effort. They have set a number of local events which I will attend. In addition, we have arranged for your participation, Mr. Kraft, in the Gala scheduled for the Los Angeles Sports Arena. . . .

"Looking forward to meeting you in Orange County, I am respectfully yours, Robert F. Kennedy."

Bill Manson got married that summer to a girl he'd met at college in Illinois. Randy hitchhiked back to the wedding in upstate New York, surprising his old friend and fellow Westminster High reactionary. They'd both changed, but Manson didn't know how much. He didn't learn until some years later that his boyhood chum had taken his first tentative steps out of the closet, living near the beach and cruising the growing gay bar scene.

Randy had, by then, come to grips with the worst of his misgivings about his politics and his future, and was beginning to deal more openly with his sexuality. Most of the time, he appeared well-adjusted and at peace with himself.

But there were moments when all did not seem so well, and intimate friends glimpsed a facet of Randy Steven Kraft they didn't want to see.

"We used to have these big soul-search things," recalled Mac, who'd lived with Randy at Huntington Beach. "There was a time when I was a senior and he was a junior and he looked at me one night . . . We were out somewhere and he said, 'You know, there's a part of me that you will never know.'"

Twenty-five years later, Mac still shudders as he recites Randy's words, a chill attached to each syllable. He shakes his head in a futile effort to shake away the memory.

"The way that he said it was real scary, and that was a hell of a long time ago so . . ."

His voice trails off again as he shuts his eyes tight.

"You know, you have these little things you remember about people over time? That was a point in time in my relationship with Randy when I remember his expression, and I remember the depth that he used to express that thought.

"And he was right: there was a part of him that I never knew."

In June of 1968, his college defer-
ment having evaporated, Randy joined the air force. Abandoning
Reserve Officer Training Corps as a sophomore left him without much
of a bargaining position when he went to his recruiter. Despite his
bachelor's degree, he entered as an enlisted man. But he did well for
himself anyway. Recruiting records show that he scored in the mid-
nineties in just about every category of the Air Force aptitude tests.
The Defense Department also put him through a background check and
granted him a "secret" security clearance.

Following boot camp and technical school in Texas, Kraft was
stationed at Edwards Air Force Base in southern California. He posed
for his boot camp graduation photo wearing a scarf, leather flight jacket,
and airman's patent leather visor hat, looking as dashing as a still from
a Spencer Tracy movie.

The reality was not nearly so romantic. For the next year, he
worked at the Air Force Flight Test Center as a protective-coating
specialist—translation: he painted test planes. Worse, he pulled duty as
a house painter on base when he and his crew ran out of planes. He rose
to the rank of airman first class and supervisor–manager at Edwards,
but spraying planes and broad-brushing buildings was never his idea of
what a Claremont economics graduate ought to be doing with his life.

The enlisted barracks where Randy lived on base were the same
dorm-style buildings as Green Hall back at Claremont. There was little
to do outside of driving thirty miles to Rosamond, the nearest town, and

getting drunk each night. Nobody likes living at Edwards for very long, especially if they have a less-than-glamorous job.

Randy didn't.

Though he quickly lost touch with most of the members of his old Gang Green, Randy remained close to Mac. By then, he trusted Mac enough to tell him the truth about his sexuality.

"He used to write, not often but maybe every other month or so," Mac remembered. One letter in particular, mailed from Edwards shortly after Randy got out of basic training, stuck in Mac's memory.

"At the top, like a letterhead, he had drawn a boat with SS KRAFT written on the bow and the boat was sinking," he said. "Then he wrote this letter mainly about the fact that he was going to have to get out of the service because he couldn't stand the pressure of worrying about being discovered in his life-style."

He wrote of his parents' reactions when he admitted that he was homosexual. His father went into a rage, howling that no son of his could possibly turn out queer. His mother was more understanding, if disapproving. She held out hopes that he was just going through a phase and would get over it.

Randy was close to his family until 1969 when he "decided to become a homosexual," said his oldest sister, family matriarch Kay Plunkett. "He never made a grand announcement."

"Kay was in absolute shock when they found out that her brother was a homosexual," said Eva Boyd, the minister's wife. "And that would have been after he graduated from college and joined the air force.

"She said it was really hard on her parents, and we tried to guide her as to how to treat him and not to ban him from the community and the family."

Kay blamed Randy's gayness on his attending an all-male college. She said that the family tried to understand. Nobody attempted to "excommunicate" her little brother. He still came to all the family gatherings and stayed in contact by phone. But he did begin to distance himself, she said.

There is probably "a whole side" of Randy about which she knows nothing, Kay said much later.

But there was a lot more than just the pressure of being gay on Randy's mind while he was in the air force. He wrote Mac about the humiliation of working for and with people he considered to be beneath him at Edwards. He complained about the isolation of the base, an hour's drive from the nearest outpost of civilian civilization. He complained about the grinding routine of military life: up at dawn, lousy food, manual labor, hurry-up-and-wait . . .

The letter was "just real negative," said Mac. "I got the sinking-ship letter and that was sort of a waterloo. We lost contact with each other for maybe a year. It was the year he was at Edwards."

On weekends, Randy drove the 150 miles back to Midway City in Orange County to trade in the desert dirt for beach sand. He visited with his parents and his sisters occasionally, but most of the time away from the base Randy was cruising, lying on the beach at Laguna, learning more about the gay life-style. He heard about the quick, impersonal liaisons in the subway and restroom stalls at Cherry Park near downtown Long Beach, the back-room action at Wellington bathhouse in Wilmington and the gymnasiums in downtown L.A., the all-male singles cocktail lounges along Hollywood Boulevard, the tricks in the bushes at MacArthur Park and Pershing Square after dark . . .

But most of all, he heard about the beach.

While he was doing his house painting time in the air force, something was happening at the beach. Gays were coming out of the closet in droves. Each time he returned to his old haunts in Laguna and Long Beach, Randy met more and more gay couples who were living together, openly, in an increasingly liberal atmosphere. Churches that catered primarily to a gay congregation were forming. Gay community centers were opening their doors for the first time. A gay newspaper, the *Advocate,* began publishing in 1967 in Los Angeles.

Randy decided to declare himself too. When he did, the SS *Kraft* finally did sink, just as he wrote Mac that it would. On July 26, 1969, a year and a month after he enlisted, the air force discharged Randy Kraft for "medical" reasons.

"I think he got principled about being gay and not being allowed to be gay. So he just told them," said one friend.

For a time, Kraft tried to fight it. Because he was discharged for homosexuality, the discharge itself was classified "general," not "honorable." Though not as stinging a rebuke as a dishonorable discharge, a general discharge is often viewed in a pejorative light by employers. It tends to raise questions—something Randy knew would be a big problem for him in the future. He immediately saw an attorney about contesting the general discharge and filed a formal protest, but the air force would not renege.

With this new curse on him, he knew he wasn't likely to find himself elected a Republican senator—or any other kind of senator—the way he and Bill Manson once dreamed. He wasn't likely to get elected dog catcher—or even to land much in the way of a job.

That summer, Randy kicked back. He moved back into his old room at his folks' house. Sometimes he slept there and sometimes he didn't. He took an apartment on Fir Drive in Huntington Beach, a few miles south of his parents' house, and spent a lot of time at the beach. Moley ran into him in Newport once. He was on leave from the service and assumed Randy was too. No, Randy told him. He was out.

How'd he pull it off? Moley was ready to take notes.

Simple. He went to his commanding officer and announced that he was homosexual.

"That was a real shocker to me," said Moley. "I mean, he never showed anything like that in school.

"He'd lost a lot of weight too, so I asked him how he got so skinny. 'A diet of speed and beer,' he told me."

It wasn't long after that Randy had to have his appendix removed. Randy started writing to Mac again.

There was a fatalistic tone that Mac didn't remember seeing in his letters before. At one point, Mac remembers Randy almost sounding suicidal though, at the time, he dismissed it as histrionics.

Randy became a bartender for a while after he was discharged.

Along a commercial strip of Pacific Coast Highway between Seal Beach and Huntington Beach, just south of the exclusive shoreline colony called Surfside, is Sunset Beach, where a modest offshoot of the Laguna life-style developed in the late '60s.

It centered around three bars: Broom Hilda's, Stables, and the Buoys Shed.

"None of them are still around," said Ben Paniagua, a student at nearby Long Beach State College who was just beginning to come out of the closet himself around 1970. "I think the Buoys Shed where Randy worked is an animal hospital now. They were essentially beer bars, though I think Broom Hilda's might have served mixed drinks. They had pool tables and like that, but no entertainment or films or anything. Just social gathering places."

Ben met one of his first steady male companions at the Buoys Shed. When he wasn't pouring another beer, Randy was in the market for mates too. One of the fringe benefits of working in a bar, he discovered when he had worked at the Mug in Garden Grove a few summers before, is finding someone to go home with at closing time. In those days, Randy's preference leaned toward older and more experienced men, according to people who knew him at the time. During his off hours, Randy hit Broom Hilda's and Stables too, striking up conversations about the war, the Beatles, politics. About being homosexual in a heterosexual world.

"The thing about the gay life-style is that it's just that: gay," said one of the Sunset Beach regulars of the late '60s. "I mean, it was like: have a good time. I didn't think of sex as any big mysterious thing, and I suppose there was a lot more promiscuity among us, if that's what you want to call it. But it was just never any big thing if you went home with somebody or you got quick sex at a bathhouse or whatever. Men are different than women in that way—both gay and straight. They can have sex and just walk away. Women can't."

Randy had quick, impersonal sex and walked away regularly the year or so while he was tending bar. Even after he quit and moved on to other jobs, he came back: the Surfside bars were a regular pit stop on the weekend run back to Los Angeles from Laguna. Every Sunday afternoon, people who had spent the weekend sunning in Laguna stopped at Stables or Broom Hilda's for one last beer before returning home to start the work week.

When old friend Paul Whitson and his new bride returned to southern California for a visit in 1970, he took her to meet Randy. His hair bleached to a surfer blond and sporting Joe Cocker muttonchops as well as bell-bottom denims, Randy was a liberal fop—not the dead-serious white-shirt-and-tie Goldwater youth crusader Whitson remembered from Westminster High. Randy surprised his old friend with far more than just his rhetoric about the immorality of Vietnam, the military/industrial complex, and Kent State, however. He entertained the Whitsons by taking them to the Buoys Shed for a drink.

It didn't dawn on Whitson right away that the Buoys Shed was any different from any other bar. It was dark, with the requisite red Naugahyde booths, and there was a waiter in jeans, T-shirt, and apron who took orders but wasn't particularly interested one way or the other in whether or not he sold them burgers or beer. But after Randy proudly proclaimed to Whitson that he had come out of the closet and that he worked there as a bartender, Whitson made the connection. He rescanned the room and noticed that only men seemed to be sitting with other men. Whitson and his wife stood out like sore thumbs.

He finished his drink in numbed shock.

*   *   *

The two-lane Ortega Highway snakes from San Juan Capistrano over the Santa Ana Mountains into Riverside County, through Viejo Canyon and some of the most remote backwoods areas in southern California. Motorists have had heart attacks on that stretch of road and not been found until a day or two later, stiff and lifeless, the surprise still etched in their chalky faces.

On October 5, 1971, the body of a man was found at the bottom of a ravine off Ortega Highway. The corpse was bloated and rank, but deputies could tell even from a relatively redolent downwind position several yards up the hillside that it was naked.

The coroner was able to fix the day the man died at around September 20, but two weeks of putrefaction made an exact cause of death impossible to determine. If there were any marks on the body or other telltale signs of foul play, the sun and wind and morning dew had erased them.

"Other conditions" listed on the autopsy report, however, put his blood alcohol level at the time he died at .36. For death certificate purposes, the medical examiner settled on acute alcohol poisoning as a cause of death.

Right away, police knew they had a body dump on their hands. The easiest way to turn a person into a John Doe is to remove all his personal effects, including his clothes, and toss him out the car door a long way from home. Despite his nakedness, however, it didn't take long to identify the Ortega Highway body.

Wayne Joseph Dukette, thirty, hadn't been to his Long Beach apartment for more than two weeks. Though nobody had reported him missing, police discovered his car still parked next door to a beach area bar where he had last been seen. Dukette worked there nights to supplement his day job at Harvey Aluminum. He was the bartender at the Stables, located next door to Broom Hilda's and just down Pacific Coast Highway from the Buoys Shed.

The police reasoned that naked men don't leave their cars behind and fall off mountain highways, no matter how drunk they might be, so an investigation began. But there were no leads—no trace of foul play or witnesses to a pickup or an argument. It was apparent after detectives asked just a few questions of friends and bar patrons that Dukette had been gay. They determined that his car might have been on the blink the night he disappeared, accounting for his abandoning it in the parking lot. Or he may just have gotten so resoundingly drunk that he needed a ride home. His Newport Avenue apartment was five miles away in Belmont Shore.

But the trail was two weeks cold before the body was even discovered, so the odds of discovering the good samaritan who helped remove the drunken bartender's clothes and get him to the Ortega Highway were slim or none.

On October 8, Wayne Dukette was buried without ceremony in Pacific View Memorial Park in Newport Beach.

5

Joey Fancher was a tough kid.

He didn't like school and he didn't like it at home. His eyes were set wide apart and his nose was slightly flat, giving him a perpetually dazed, angry look. That might have accounted for the hassles he was always running into at school, from smartass punks who thought they were smarter than him or coaches who were always running his ass all over the playing fields to "get him in shape" or teachers who just wanted to give him a bad time.

Life sucked. His salvation was his bike. Joey would get on it and ride, away from the bickering mother and stepfather who finally got divorced, away from the beatings he underwent for misbehavior, and away from the doldrums of junior high in the Orange County suburb of Westminster.

When you're thirteen, in eighth grade, the escapes are limited and you grab them when you can.

Joey grabbed his chance one March day in 1970. He'd run away from home before and he would run away again. But this particular day would stick out vividly in his memory nearly twenty years later.

"I wasn't going nowhere in particular," he says. "I went down to what they used to call the boardwalk."

The boardwalk was an extension of the Huntington Beach pier—a great place to ride a bike. He'd been there before. You just got on Edwards Street and pedaled like mad for about two miles due west, past the new subdivisions and shopping centers, over the wide-open coastal steppe to the Pacific.

The boardwalk was terrific for claustrophobia. The sea wind would whip through a kid's hair as the slats of the wooden walkway rippled beneath the bicycle tires. Fancher raced his bike back and forth several times before he noticed the stranger staring at him. To a thirteen-year-old, the man appeared to be tall and hip: a sandy-haired guy with a mustache and a mild, urbane manner about him.

Joey was smug, self-assured. He wore a new pair of shoes, owned a fast bike, didn't have to answer to anybody now that he'd run away from home. He felt good.

"I asked him for a cigarette," Fancher remembers.

The stranger obliged. As the boy took his first draw, the conversation turned to Fancher's being a runaway. Fancher railed a bit about school and his unhappy home life.

The stranger asked him if he needed a place to stay and the boy quickly answered yes. Then the stranger asked him if he'd ever slept with a woman before.

"I said I never had no sex with no woman," Fancher recalls.

It looked like his lucky day, because the stranger not only had an apartment, he also knew a willing lady. He asked Fancher if he wanted to lose his virginity, and there was no hesitation. The boy walked his bike across Pacific Coast Highway, the four-lane strip of blacktop that separated the beach front from an oil field, and hid his bicycle between a pair of petroleum storage tanks. The stranger, who had a dark green Honda motorcycle, piloted over to the tanks and invited Fancher to hop on.

As they roared north up Pacific Coast Highway, Fancher held on tight around the stranger's middle, smiling secretly to himself, his adolescent fantasies racing as fast as the motorcycle's 450 cc engines. It was a short ride from Huntington Beach to the trendy beach enclave of Belmont Shore in Long Beach. Affluent, ambitious young college grads occupied the dozens of studio apartments that fronted on or near the beach. Even in March, when the surf is cold and the skies are often overcast, saucy, nubile females in bikinis can often be observed wandering the palm-lined Second Street shopping district.

Fancher couldn't believe his good fortune.

The stranger pulled up at a corner apartment building on the fashionable Belmont peninsula behind a blue customized van. Fancher remembers admiring the mag wheels. According to the stranger, it belonged to him. He opened the door and showed the boy the plush, carpeted interior and the stereo. Growing more impressed by the minute, Fancher followed his venerable new acquaintance upstairs to his second-story apartment, overlooking Ocean Boulevard with a view of the Pacific beyond.

"He asked me if I liked music," Fancher says.

He also asked him if he'd ever smoked dope before. Sure, answered the boy nervously. Who hadn't? The stranger lit up a stick of marijuana, and Fancher settled onto the couch.

The boy took a few drags off the joint the way he'd learned to draw on a Marlboro, inhaling deeply. All at once, he felt fatigued, famished, and a little nauseated. He told his host he wasn't feeling too well and the stranger perked up. He had just the thing to make the boy feel better. He disappeared from Fancher's woozy range of vision for a moment.

While he was out of the room, the boy phoned home. When his sister answered, he boasted that he had run away from home. He hung up as the stranger returned.

He offered him four red capsules and Fancher obediently plucked them up. He dropped all four pills on his tongue and chased them with Spañada.

No reaction.

"I told him I felt the same," Fancher remembers.

The stranger waited a few minutes, then gave him four more capsules. The reaction this time was swift and profound.

"I started feeling drowsy. I started blacking out, like I'd know what was going on but I couldn't answer or anything."

Then the same hands that gave him the wine and pills set a sheaf of black and white photos in front of him: eight-by-ten enlargements of men engaged in various sexual activities. Fancher blinked, recognizing one of the men in the photos as the stranger.

With herculean effort, the now-apprehensive thirteen-year-old pushed himself up and off the couch, mumbling something about playing some more music. As soon as he took a step, he fell forward, flat on his face.

As Joey crawled back to the couch, the stranger wanted to know if Fancher had ever had "sex with a dude before." The boy tried to say no, but his tongue wouldn't obey him. The room seemed to wobble and spin and he was powerless to do much about it.

"It was like somebody'd slapped me real hard in the face and I couldn't respond."

The stranger unzipped his trousers and began touching himself. At the same time, Fancher heard the man's voice ordering him to disrobe. Fancher couldn't move.

The stranger's T-shirt came off and he wavered over him obscenely. Fancher could not recall if the stranger said anything or not, but the next horrible moment, he found his helpless mouth being used as a receptacle for the man's sperm.

"He put his hands on both sides of my head and forced me," Fancher remembers. "I couldn't do nothin'. Period. It was like I was a rag doll."

The boy retched. The stranger disappeared into the bathroom, tossing a warning over his shoulder before he left: if the boy moved, he would kill him.

He hadn't paid much attention to the Hollywood bed that folded out of the wall when he and the stranger first came upstairs, but now it became as big a part of the boy's expanding nightmare as the wine, the pills, and the lewd photographs. Somehow, he dragged himself to the mattress and lay down.

"It seemed like eternity but it—you—it was . . ." Fancher recalled in a halting voice, his words trailing off in painful memory. "I would pass out, come back in. I didn't want to follow his instructions. I wanted to go home. He threatened me. He said, 'Take your clothes off or I'll take them off for you.'"

All Fancher remembered about the sodomy was pain, intense and awful, as he lay on his stomach across the bed. There was a brief intermission when the pain stopped and the stranger was back in the bathroom again. The eight pills the boy had downed were now in full force and "it was like I was in space," he remembered.

Then the stranger was back, angry this time.

"He didn't slap me around the first time, but the second time he did. It was like a distant pain. It was like sticking novocaine in your finger, then smashing it in a door and then two hours later it would start to throb."

Again, he was lying face forward on the bed. Again, there was shooting pain as the stranger used him for his pleasure.

The stranger returned to the bathroom while Fancher lay on the bed, weeping and vomiting. When he emerged, he told the boy he was going to work.

The front door slammed and, for a time, the apartment was silent. Eventually, the boy heard a knocking. He pulled his pants up and stumbled off the bed, opening the door. Two boys not much younger than himself wanted to know where Randy was. Fancher mumbled that he didn't know and shut the door.

Painfully, he pulled on the rest of his clothes, save his shoes. He stepped to the door in stocking feet and cracked the front door cautiously, scanning for the stranger. "I half walked and half fell down the stairs."

Out in the sunshine again, he sobbed until someone came to his aid. He remembers being helped across Ocean Boulevard and almost getting hit by a car. He walked to a neighborhood bar where someone called for an ambulance while he waited on a bus bench out in front.

At the hospital, his stomach was pumped.

"I remember two hoses going up my nose," he recalled. "I remember a lot of puking."

When he said how many pills he'd taken, the doctor told him two more would have killed him.

When his parents showed up, one of the first things they noticed was that Joey's brand new shoes were missing. Joey was still in a daze, only mildly aware of the two police officers seated in the examination room with him and his folks. They wanted to know where he'd left his shoes too.

Once his stepfather signed him out of the hospital, they all drove over to the apartment where Joey had left his shoes, his lunch, and his innocence.

The shoes were by the fold-out bed, right where the stranger had left them after pulling them off Joey's helpless feet. While Officers Sprague and Booth from the Long Beach Police Department cased the apartment, Joey slowly put the shoes back on, aware the entire time of his parents' angry eyes.

Sprague found a treasure trove in the kitchen: a Skippy's peanut butter jar filled with Benzedrine tablets and another jar of Seconal. In another cupboard was a baggie of marijuana and a cigarette-rolling machine.

There were also several vials of prescription sedatives and antidepressants, made out by a Dr. Wilson McArthur from the Westminster Medical Clinic. The patient was a Mrs. Doris Lane.

The rest of the apartment didn't look much like a woman's place, though. On an end table was a framed color photo of a foppish-looking man in his twenties flanked by two older women. Joey stopped dawdling with his shoes when he saw it, picking it off the table and pointing out the man as his assailant—the stranger that the two kids at the door had called "Randy."

One of the cops took a statement from him while the other continued to roam around the apartment. He found some greenish blue capsules in the bathroom called "Pep Aid" and further evidence that the apartment was definitely not the home of an older woman.

A handbill for a gay bar lay on the coffee table, near the wineglass Joey had used when he washed down his dose of reds just a few hours before. There was also a stack of snapshots, depicting men and women in various stages of undress and orgasm. Some featured men and women. Some were taken of men only. The man called Randy was a featured player in most of these pictures.

Officer Booth flipped through the stack. He counted out seventy-six photographs in all. By the time they left, the police knew they'd stumbled into a gay crash pad, but they weren't sure they had a crime—at least, a crime they could prove. The kid had apparently taken the pills voluntarily from the story he told and nothing happened except he passed out and got his stomach pumped. Besides, he was truant and had been in trouble before and would undoubtedly get in trouble again. It would be hard to get the D.A. to file charges and harder still to get any kind of conviction. To complicate things, they had done their inspection of the place without benefit of a warrant.

When they got back to the station, Sprague and Booth filed their formal report. It went into a file folder and remained there for the next thirteen years. It was a runaway's story, not all that different from dozens of such accounts, often embellished, that law enforcement hears every year. The report detailed Fancher's drug overdose and gave the name and apartment number of the stranger who gave him the pills. The report said nothing about sex because Joey Fancher didn't mention any of that.

Joey got a licking when he got home. He said his stepfather beat him with a board that had a nail in it, though his mother swore that she and her husband never used anything more formidable than a rubber beach thong to punish him. The licking was for cutting school more than anything else—that and embarrassing the hell out of his parents by getting himself picked up by a fruitcake and taking drugs. His stepfather was also stuck with a hospital bill. Worst of all, Joey had gone off and nearly lost his brand new shoes. He had no respect for property, no respect for school, no respect for his elders.

Joey took his beating in stride. It didn't hurt anywhere near as much as his torn and bleeding rectum, which took weeks to heal. The other wounds the stranger had inflicted, to his psyche and self-respect, never did heal.

"How you s'posed to tell your mom that something you didn't understand happened to you?" he says years later. "She never listened anyway. Who was I gonna tell? The cops never came back. I was only thirteen. Nobody listened. So I never told nobody."

After his parents drove him back to Westminster, nothing more was ever said about the incident.

6

Pouring beer was no way to make a career or much in the way of money—despite the after-hours fringes. Randy finally moved on from the Buoys Shed, but not on a career path leading to the executive suite. Still dogged by the stigma surrounding his military discharge, in 1971 he took a day job running a forklift for Arrowhead Water in Huntington Beach. Results of a standard intelligence test he took for the job showed that he had an I.Q. of 129.

It wasn't an overly demanding job, but it suited his needs. It was his "surfer" period, when Randy was getting into grass and Led Zeppelin and nightly rounds of Miller draft at the pickup bars along Pacific Coast Highway between Huntington and Long Beach.

Randy's hair was long by Orange County standards, though it hardly qualified as shaggy compared to the generally accepted shoulder-length locks of the time. He peroxided it, affecting a Troy Donahue look, accentuated by loafers and Levi's. His Jaguar had burned its last case of thirty-weight oil years before. Randy now cruised the beach in a van and, later on, a Mustang. It turned more than a few heads and kept him broke much of the time.

At night, when he wasn't cruising, he went to Long Beach State University, following his oldest sister's lead, and taking courses in education so he could get teaching credentials. That's where he met Jeff Graves, a Minnesota boy four years Randy's junior who was also enrolled in teaching classes. Though he was younger, Jeff knew a thing or two about the gay life-style that even Randy hadn't dabbled in, like threesomes and the double high of sex combined with drugs.

"I know he couldn't have been too much younger than Randy because Randy was only like twenty-four or twenty-five then, but Jeff seemed much, much younger physically and mentally and emotionally," recalled Mac, Randy's ex-Claremont roomie.

Graves, a slightly thinner and darker version of Randy, had a tiny studio apartment on the beach at Seal Beach and offered to share it with Randy. By 1971, they were a sometime couple, hitting the Sunset Beach bars as well as a few more that they had discovered in the burgeoning gay community in Long Beach: Ripples near the pier at Belmont Shore, and the Prospector, kitty corner from the 7th Street entrance to Long Beach State.

"He and Jeff used to go there a lot," said Mac. "It wasn't exclusively gay by any means, but a lot of gay couples went there too. It was a college bar where you'd go after class or on Friday nights."

It was also a great place to pick up third parties for a menage à trois—an occasional diversion for the pair now that Randy had gradu-ated from older men to younger men and had learned the full and indulgent meaning of the term "recreational sex." Theirs was always an "open" relationship at the mercy of the ebb and flow of their respective hormones. It was understood that Randy's late night driving habits and Jeff's own predilection for cruising the rougher bars along Broadway and downtown Long Beach were not cause for jealous outbursts—at least, not at first. They were just giving full rein to their own natural impulses.

"The first time I had any impression at all that Randy was into kinky stuff was when he was with Jeff," said Mac. "Jeff was into leather and he had a bunch of biker friends. That really shocked me because I had this naive notion that they were all dopers, and Jeff never came off that way at all. I recall vividly coming across all this leather stuff in their closet once—leather suspenders, pants, jackets. I asked about it and he just shrugged it off and told me that was Jeff's."

Randy and Jeff moved out of Jeff's cramped quarters on the Seal Beach boardwalk, but—wanting to remain just a few steps away from the warm, sandy existence that remains the universal image of the California life-style—they found a slightly larger, more expensive apartment within walking distance of Ripples and the shoreline along Ocean Boulevard at Belmont Shore. By then, the high-rent waterfront apartment buildings and specialty shops along Second Street had already made Belmont Shore the swinging singles beachfront headquarters of Long Beach.

During his infrequent visits to Midway City for Sunday dinner with his family, Randy endured his father's barely disguised intolerance and his mother's concern. There was still a room for him at home, and he used it from time to time when he and Jeff were on the outs. Most of his time, however, he tried to spend in the bracing environment of Long Beach's gay renaissance.

Long Beach has been a quiet haven for gay men and women as far back as World War II, when the city boomed as a home port for much of the Pacific Fleet. Sailors interested in sex stalked the seedy dives along Ocean Boulevard and Pine Avenue, looking for someone, anyone—male or female—to spend the night with. More often than not, they found them. After the war, according to local lore, many of those same gay sailors blended into this five-hundred-thousand-population bedroom community. They created their own subculture in a city on the outskirts of Los Angeles.

On the surface, Long Beach reflected middle-class, midwestern values, far removed from its larger, more cynical and sophisticated sister city to the northeast. The white, heterosexual majority of Long Beach characterized itself as "Iowa by the Sea," a reference to the turn-of-the-century Iowa farmers who emigrated from their cornfields almost two thousand miles to the west to help found the city. For decades, Iowans from throughout California converged on Long Beach each summer for an old-fashioned Fourth of July picnic, parade, and concert in the park. In the '50s and even into the '60s, long after the founding fathers were outnumbered by thousands of returning veterans of all classes, colors, and political persuasions, the civic identification and the conservatism that went along with it remained.

With a burgeoning gay population, a municipal schizophrenia developed. As late as 1981, the Long Beach Police Department officially stated, as a matter of policy, that the city had no gay community at all—a policy that has since been radically revised. The best educated guess is that roughly 12 percent of Long Beach's population is gay. Unlike San Francisco or West Hollywood or Greenwich Village, however, Long Beach's gay population remained discreetly anonymous until the early '80s when the combination of intensified police harassment, AIDS, and the gay community's newly discovered political clout in municipal elections forced homosexuals out of the closet.

Until then, gays remained invisible to mainstream heterosexual residents, unless they were familiar with the overt signs: bars with names like Impact, Forced Heat, and the Mine Shaft, the private clubs and male-only bath houses, the homosexual sections of adult bookstores and moviehouses.

Despite its official position, the seven-hundred-man police force did recognize the influx of gays by stepping up loitering, pandering, and lewd conduct arrests along Broadway and around the restrooms in several city parks and in the "hot" beach areas along a four-mile stretch from Cherry Avenue on the north to Granada Avenue on the south, where gays tended to congregate after dark. Vice cops delighted in taking heterosexual "civilians," male and female, on ride-alongs to the most notorious pickup areas in the late-night world of gay Long Beach to point out men looking for other men as well as what they regarded as other gay oddities: the transvestite bar and the leather bar, the biker bar and the lesbian bar.

But easily the most popular gay bar of all in Long Beach during the '70s was Ripples.

"Going to Ripples was sort of like being a freshmen in high school: the bright lights and dancing," remembered Richard Tenney, who knew Kraft as a regular. "The line to get in stretched around the block. On Sundays, we'd play volleyball across the street, and then there was always a tea dance at Ripples in the afternoon where you'd just dance until you dropped."

Ripples and the Granada Avenue beach area nearby were both wholesome meeting places by gay standards.

"Our life-style isn't that much different from the straight life-style in that respect," said Tenney. "You go to a bar in hopes you'll snag something in one of two ways: either a one-night stand or a relationship that'll last awhile.

"Once you set up housekeeping, you don't need the bar scene so much. Then you start entertaining. You have a couple over and they have you back. The only difference is we don't have kids. We have dogs. Lots of dogs."

Randy and Jeff were Ripples regulars. They openly lived the gay life in Long Beach, strolling Second Street on Saturday afternoons hand in hand and cruising bars together on Saturday nights.

Randy occasionally put up beefcake posters featuring shirtless studs and dour-looking men on the apartment walls. Randy's general discharge from the air force, once his mark of Cain, was on open display in the apartment—a kind of fierce defiance of accepted social mores.

Jeff's collection of biker magazines and gay pornography was scattered throughout the apartment. Randy bought heterosexual pornography as well as the male-only variety. For more personal pornography, they had a Polaroid camera.

They had other couples over for dinner and spent weekends together sunning in Vegas, drinking beer at Busch Gardens, or watching the swallows return to Mission San Juan Capistrano. Randy and Jeff vacationed in Europe in '71 and Mexico the following year. Increasingly they were identified among their peers as a permanent item: Randy-and-Jeff.

"Unfortunately, couples don't last too long in the gay life-style," said Tenney. "We tend to play musical chairs together a lot."

Jeff was into drugs. A hit of speed or a rush of amyl nitrite, especially just before sex, doubled the sensation. With all capillaries open, blood rushing to every tingling nerve end, orgasm was no longer a simple, clinical release of sperm. It was ecstasy. Pure sensory pleasure, by Jeff's measure, was what sex and, maybe, life was really all about.

Randy was also experimenting more with pharmacological sensations, but he tended to be more judicious about getting loaded than his roommate. He liked grass and trifled with Benzedrine and "reds," but his drug of choice continued to be beer.

The anxiety and brooding fits of periodic depression he developed while he was at Claremont persisted, and he regularly renewed his Valium prescriptions with Dr. McArthur, but he was disciplined enough to know not to abuse the tranquilizer. He preferred to be alert, especially with one-night stands, and learned early on that he couldn't do that if he drank too much or dropped too many capsules.

Once, not long after they began living together, Jeff came home from work one day and found the police there. They had received a complaint from the parents of a thirteen-year-old Westminster boy that a man named Randy had given their son drugs and beaten him up. The youngster had to have his stomach pumped, they said.

Nervously, Jeff let them look around, but he denied that his roommate would have done such a thing. Neighborhood kids came by the apartment all the time, and there had never been a problem. In their report, the officers noted that there were homosexual literature, posters, and pornography throughout the apartment, as well as drugs, but they made no arrest.

Randy and Jeff were still close then. Randy assumed the stronger, older, wiser role, while Jeff was impulsive and adolescent, but still deferential and attentive. For months at a time, they seemed to get along, only to explode in door-slamming, expletive-shouting scenes that led to one of them leaving in anger. Psychologists might have characterized them as co-dependent, boosting each other's egos only to tear them down and start all over again in an endless cycle of nurturing and destroying.

After a few years in the fast lane of the gay life, they began to follow separate paths, even though they remained roommates.

They both paid for their promiscuity with venereal disease and hemorrhoids, but Jeff ultimately paid the dearest. Several years after they separated, he developed AIDS.

"We had different friends and we were just kind of going our own way and I wasn't paying much attention to him," Graves said in an interview years later. "I was busy working. I was teaching or I was starting to teach, and I was gone a lot."

He was out with other men too. By 1972, the open relationship was beginning to take its toll on both of them. Jeff hit Ripples and the other gay nightspots, looking for sex highs and calling it love. Randy was out trolling too, but not in the bars.

When he and Jeff had a fight, Randy got in his car and drove: up north through Torrance and San Pedro, weaving through the night along the San Diego or Hollywood freeways. Or south, through his old high school haunts, in and around Huntington Beach and Costa Mesa, along the Santa Ana and Garden Grove freeways. Or farther west, along the San Bernardino and Pomona freeways, near Claremont.

He got into his car and drove until the flush of his anger and frustration went away. Sometimes, it took all night long.

In the beginning, the corpses didn't even have names. The cops didn't know who they were or where they came from. If the manner of their deaths hadn't been so bizarre, it could easily have been concluded that they simply came from another planet. Nobody ever claimed the bodies. The only connection that seemed to make much sense was the hitchhiking angle: drifters from God knows where, bumming a ride with the devil.

At 11:30 A.M. on February 6, 1973, the nude body of an unidentified male was found next to the Terminal Island Freeway in the Wilmington area of Los Angeles, a couple of miles north of the Long Beach Naval Station. He was thin, average height, and bearded, lying face up in a ditch like a medieval Christ figure, with sad, unblinking brown eyes staring permanently at the sun.

His only clothing was a brown sock, jammed into his rectum, and the only mark on his body was a maroon ligature ring on the skin around his neck. Investigators put it down as garroting, probably with piano wire. He was about eighteen and had been dead for a day or two before the Long Beach Police found him. Sketches of his face were printed up, distributed around the gay bars, and even reprinted in the local newspaper. Nobody came up with a name, although a few homosexuals said they remembered seeing the dead man soliciting tricks along the Belmont Shore bluffs that overlook the beach near Cherry Avenue.

Fingerprints and missing persons reports came up negative, so he was given a name: John Doe 16. He never got another.

Two months later, on Easter Sunday, at approximately 1:30 A.M., a passing motorist reported another body lying in the roadway on Ellis between Gothard and Goldenwest, according to the records of the Huntington Beach Police Department. In the 1950s, students at nearby Westminster High School called the spot Airplane Hill because there was a sudden dip in the roadway and cars driven fast enough—say, forty or fifty miles per hour—simply flew across the pavement and landed on the other side.

Unlike John Doe 16, the corpse they found on Airplane Hill was dressed and wearing socks but no shoes. He was also about eighteen with long brown hair that touched his shoulders. He wore a tattoo of a cross on his arm, but any medieval Messiah comparisons ended there. He also had tattoos of a swastika, spider, and the number 13 stenciled in black on his shoulders and arms.

Judging from the abrasions, he had been tossed from a moving car, and cord marks around his wrists indicated that he had been bound for the last hour or so of his life. When police arrived, the first thing they noticed was the dark red stain on the seat of his blue trousers. The autopsy later revealed that his penis and scrotum had been sliced off about fifteen minutes before he died and that he had also been sodomized. The medical examiner couldn't be certain of the cause of death. His lips were a puffy purple, indicating suffocation, but the loss of a quart or more of blood could also have killed him.

He carried no wallet, no key chain, no identification. His clothes looked like those of a gas station attendant, and a flyer that went out to the gay community in the Long Beach area a few weeks later got some response: yes, several people had seen the young man in the rundown

Long Beach amusement park area known as "the Pike" where hustlers, carnies, and petty thieves were known to hang out. But nobody knew who he was.

Like the bearded body in the Terminal Island ditch, police had to give him a name: John Doe Huntington Beach.

John Doe 52 wasn't as lucky as the others. He, too, may have met his fate on Easter Sunday, but those who found his remains could not be sure. A head in a brown paper sack behind a Long Beach Alpha Beta supermarket; arms, torso, and right leg in plastic trash bags left by the roadside in San Pedro; a left leg dropped behind a beer bar in Sunset Beach—a place called the Buoys Shed.

John Doe 52's body had been carved and carted all over southern California. By the time most of it was reassembled on a stainless steel morgue table in the Los Angeles County Coroner's office two weeks after the discovery of John Doe Huntington Beach, the bloodless body parts were so decomposed that it was impossible to tell whether he had been drinking or taking drugs before he died, let alone where he spent his final hours.

The medical examiner was able to say with some certainty that he had been trussed up like the other John Does: a ligature mark remained visible about four inches above the heel on both of the severed legs. He had also been emasculated and his eyelids removed—apparently so that he could not shut them while his torturers performed their experiments upon his body.

The body parts also showed signs of having been stored in a refrigerator for a while before finding their way to the alleys and frontage roads of southern California.

The hands were never found.

"I went out a lot, with other guys," Jeff Graves said.

What began as a fairly permanent if tempestuous relationship strained at the edges as the years passed. The arguments and temporary splits became more frequent, and Jeff answered Randy's rage by doing more of what angered Randy in the first place: finding one-night stands. When he didn't come home at night, or for an entire weekend, Randy went out driving, making wider and wider circles. Jeff wasn't the only one who could still turn a trick. Randy used to boast in the bars of picking up marines. Sometimes they came home with him for the weekend, he said.

Despite his troubles with Jeff, the other facets of Randy's multifaceted life seemed to be going well. He actively campaigned for George McGovern for president in 1972 and shocked his former Westminster High classmates at the ten-year reunion the following year, not so much by his rumored sexual preference, as by his politics. The one-time junior John Bircher showed up in turtleneck and bell bottoms, calling for legalization of marijuana and spouting the liberal party line.

Randy quit his forklift job with Arrowhead Water in 1973 when his sister Kay encouraged him to land a teacher's aide position in the Long Beach schools. For a while, he and Jeff had something more than cruising, drugs, and sex in common: they were both going to become teachers. But at about the same time, Randy began to dabble in computer science.

He got a part-time job as a dispatcher at Aztec Aircraft near Long Beach Airport and worked there two years, soon switching from the phones to the office computer, where he taught himself to handle the payroll, scheduling, and other data-processing tasks.

In the quiet, antiseptic hum of the big IBM mainframes and the new, revolutionary smaller desktop versions—the so-called "personal" computers—Randy found what he was looking for. Computers had just begun to come into their own as he was leaving Claremont, and later he often regretted not majoring as an undergrad in the fledgling science of ROMs and RAMs and bytes and bits, instead of dreary economics.

But it wasn't too late.

His postmilitary identity crisis seemed to be over. He finally seemed to his family and friends to have found his path in life. He had the beginnings of a real career in data processing. He had what appeared to be a steady relationship with an apparently intelligent, if flighty, younger man. He was a fixture in the growing Long Beach gay community. The trauma of emerging from the closet seemed behind him at last.

7

Charles Wendell Vines, Jr. had been in the army once. The frail-featured Southerner with the doe eyes and high Randolph Scott cheekbones was commissioned a second lieutenant the day after he graduated from the University of Arkansas.

He liked the military well enough, spitting and polishing and putting the new recruits through their paces. There was something exciting about shouting out orders early in the morning and seeing young men stand at attention, salute, and punctuate their every sentence with "sir."

Vines might have been a career soldier if things had gone differently. He might have been a surgeon or a poet too. But some things in life seem to happen that are beyond one person's control. Things that change the course of events subtly, irretrievably, sometimes fatally.

Charles Vines knew he didn't fit in as far back as high school. It was a problem he traced back to the secret thrill he got masturbating in the woods when he was a youngster in Buckner, Arkansas. Self-abuse, as the ministers called it, was a rite of passage for most of the kids in his Boy Scout troop. Everybody did it at least once. But everybody else seemed to outgrow it.

"I was just a kid, and probably a lot of people have done that and it has never affected their lives," he remembered. "They have done it and it has been washed out of their lives and they have forgotten about it."

But Charles Vines couldn't forget about it. He remembered each detail of himself and the other boys, sneaking off into the underbrush for a round of guilty pleasure. The thought stayed with him, the way the recollection of a first kiss or a delightful Christmas morning might stay with someone else. It stayed with him through adolescence, college, and the army.

"Those years went by and then I had an experience with a civilian," he recalled, "a man. And I don't even know who he was."

Vines didn't advance beyond second lieutenant in the army. It didn't look like he ever would. He related differently to his fellow soldiers than they did to him. It became clear that the army was not the career he thought it might be.

When he was discharged in '62, Vines entered graduate school. For the next several years, he studied English at Harvard and Ohio State and Trinity College in Hartford, lumbering after a muse who would not respond. If he couldn't write, he could teach, he reasoned. He took a job teaching and coaching at a military academy in Saint Louis. It wasn't the army, but it was close. The ceremony, the uniforms, the discipline . . .

After an hour of Twain or Shakespeare in the classroom, it was exhilarating to move out to the parade grounds and put the boys through their paces, instructing them in the bearing of arms, returning their snappy young salutes. That's how he got his nickname. The boys gave it to him.

The Major.

At a massage parlor in Saint Louis, Vines continued to explore the pleasures of his boyhood memories. He learned that there were other ways to exercise his indulgence than simple masturbation. But it was always with men. He preferred their company to that of women. He liked to believe that he was always the aggressor. In matters of intimacy, the Major concluded that it was always better to give than to receive.

By the time he took over as second-in-command at San Diego Military Academy in 1971, he had a reputation as a tough, no-nonsense educator. He had a full-flowing mustache by then, filling out his thin features and adding strength to a weak chin. His hair was thinning a little, marking the approach of middle age, but he kept his weight down and tried to be an example for his cadets. All in all, it was a good life, if not the one he had envisioned for himself so many years before.

At thirty-six, he counted himself a modest success. He drove a new brown '72 Gremlin and lived in a trailer near the beach.

Still, it was lonely at times, especially around the holidays, when all the boys packed up their civvies and went home. The parade ground was empty and the barracks silent. The Major grew restless during those periods. He would drive up Pacific Coast Highway to Oceanside, just outside the main gate at Camp Pendleton. Chances were usually good he'd meet someone at the bars or restaurants on the Strand or run into an off-duty marine at the USO. They'd pal around, shoot some pool, watch football on TV from a barstool, maybe catch a movie.

He met Eddie Moore that way one morning during one of those lonely periods. It was the long Labor Day weekend of 1972.

"I was walking down Hill Street in Oceanside," he said. "Third Street, I believe, is the cross street that goes in front of the USO/YMCA down by the beach, and right at the corner of the street is a little bar called Minnie's Tavern.

"I started to walk across that street, and I had not seen Eddie before. I did not know who he was. As he walked across the street, I was standing on a street corner waiting for a car to go by and he came up and looked at me and said, 'Do you know what day it is?'"

Major Vines knew exactly what day it was and talked to him for several minutes about the absurdity of asking such a question. They were both laughing by the time Eddie told Vines that he was broke and hungry. He didn't have enough money to get a place to sleep at night, he told the Major. Even though Labor Day marked the end of summer, it was still warm at night, so Eddie had slept out on the beach the night before.

He told Vines he was a marine, provoking another laugh from the Major. Even in his rumpled civilian clothes, it was obvious from the close-cropped haircut and the broad black shoes that Moore was a brash young jarhead. The blond, blue-eyed kid told him later on that he was with the First Engineers, First Marine Division at Camp Pendleton.

Probably AWOL, Vines thought, though he didn't say it out loud. Moore had just turned twenty, wore a shy smile that didn't seem to go with his panhandling impudence, and spoke with a Southern drawl to match the Major's. He had the vague beginnings of a mustache, but it was so fine and flaxen that you had to be a few feet away to even notice it.

They walked through the vacant Sunday morning streets of Oceanside to the Major's Gremlin, parked a couple blocks away near the Greyhound bus station. Vines sized him up as a hustler, but not a bad one. He didn't see much chance of getting rolled if he bought him breakfast. They drove to Sambo's Restaurant and the Major sipped at his coffee while he watched Eddie eat his eggs and bacon.

Between bites, Eddie wondered out loud what the Major was doing the rest of the day.

"I told him that I didn't have to go to work that day, and then he asked me where I worked and I told him that I worked at the academy," said the Major. "I explained to him that I wasn't working that day because the students weren't actually back in school at that time. So we went to my trailer."

It wasn't the first time Major Vines had brought a marine back to his trailer. They were usually tough-talking, hard-drinking knuckleheads who showed their machismo by liberally peppering their speech with "fuckin's": "fuckin' mess hall had fuckin' roaches all over the fuckin' deck fer fuckin' chrissakes." Some showed off their tattoos—death's heads and roses and MOTHER scrawled across a shoulder or an arm. Some chain-smoked filterless cigarettes. They all drank beer and hated both the military and fairies with equal fury.

But Eddie Moore was different. There was uncertainty behind the hustler facade. He squinted and smiled a lot and came on more like a cocker spaniel than a mastiff.

"There's something with his eyes," Vines remembered. "He had a way of squinting at people. When he would look at you, it was as if he were straining to try to see out of his eyes. In fact he told me that he had had some kind of surgery to help open up his eyes and help his vision. And he explained to me that was why he didn't have a driver's license."

They talked for about an hour in the Major's trailer. A lot of the grunts Vines picked up near the Camp Pendleton main gate, or Mainside as it's called in Oceanside, were about as eloquent as a water buffalo. If they spoke at all, it usually wasn't to do much more than complain about being stuck in the Marine Corps.

Eddie wasn't happy about being in the service either. He had been AWOL from Parris Island, his last duty station, and had done his share of disciplinary duty as a result. But he didn't harp on it. Eddie opened up to the Major. He poured his heart out, almost without having to be asked. And it touched Charles Vines.

"Eddie told me his mother died when he was young. Somewhere around when he was ten or eleven. He told me that he had a brother. He did not tell me his name."

His parents were both alcoholics, and both Eddie and his brother were taken away from them when Moore was twelve. His mother died of a stroke shortly thereafter. For a time, he lived with his older married sister, Patricia. Later, he moved to Chicago to live with another sister and eventually landed in a Methodist boys' foster home in Frankfort, Kentucky. At the foster home, he said later, both he and his brother were molested. And there, too, Eddie told the Major, he and his brother furthered their sexual explorations with each other.

It seemed natural enough to the Major to make the offer and Eddie didn't object. He went down on Eddie first, and then Eddie satisfied the Major. By late afternoon, Charles Vines and Eddie Moore were lovers.

"We left the trailer and drove around a little more," Vines remembers. "I got out of the car and he got behind the wheel and drove for a little while. I could tell he had not driven a car because he was very awkward about it. But having never had a license to drive, and then the problem he'd had with his eyes, it made sense. It just seemed very unusual to me that he would be on active duty as a marine."

At nightfall, they drove to a drive-in movie on Mission Avenue and huddled close to each other.

Then they drove back to Vines's trailer and slept together.

"Sometime early the next morning, around three-thirty or four, I drove Eddie back," Vines said. "I honestly cannot remember whether I drove him to Oceanside or whether I took him to an area called Mainside at Camp Pendleton."

As he got out of the car, Eddie asked the Major if he would mind picking him up in front of the base bowling alley the following Friday afternoon after he got off duty. Vines gave him a smile and a nod.

When the Major dropped tricks off, he usually despaired of ever seeing them again. Normally, there was shame and fear connected with the seduction even if Vines was the only one doing the fellating or masturbating. But Eddie was different. As the eastern sky over Pendleton lightened and Eddie turned to wave a good-bye to him, the Major was sure he'd see him again.

"Randy used to go away for a few days, come back and lock himself in his room for a couple more days," recalled one of his roommates at the time. "He'd go down by the Marine base. He wouldn't talk about it much—just mumble something about going down and looking for marines."

Randy remained aloof, even among his new circle of fellow gay friends in the early '70s. When he and Jeff had their inevitable quarrels,

Randy would either move back home to Midway City for a while or impose temporarily on friends until he and Jeff made up. Randy seemed especially restless and distracted during those times.

"He never would tell us where he was going or what he was doing," remembered one acquaintance from that era. "He was a very anal-retentive kind of guy: very uptight and very strict with himself. Everything had to be correctly done. Precise.

"Jeff Graves was the complete opposite of Randy. He was very jovial and fun. They'd come over, have dinner. Jeff was pretty nice to be around. I thought it was good that Randy had him in his life. He evened him out."

Outwardly, Randy's hedonism seemed to peak in 1972. Everything was subordinate to getting high, getting tan, and getting off. Preferably with a marine.

A vintage TV recruiting ad for the U.S. Marine Corps at the time features a montage of green-helmeted, rifle-toting men hitting the beach, followed by shots of marines working in various occupations—communications, chemistry, computers. The final seconds of the commercial displayed a young man in full dress uniform, saluting with a confident smile on his face and an announcer's voice-over growl of the familiar recruiter's exit line, "We're looking for a few good men."

The irony did not escape Randy Kraft or Jeff Graves, or nearly anyone in the gay community of the early '70s. They finally had something in common with the U.S. government: they were both looking for the same thing.

Beginning shortly after he moved in with Jeff, Randy's nocturnal driving habits took him to Tustin and El Toro and Oceanside—all cities that grew up around and flourished next to Marine enclaves. There were thirteen-thousand stationed at the Marine Corps Air Station in El Toro and five times as many at Camp Pendleton, the two-hundred-square-mile Marine Corps training reservation located on the coastline about an hour's drive south of Long Beach. Each weekend, most of them get to leave the base Friday night and don't have to report back until seven A.M. Monday. There are always a handful who don't make it back in time.

Randy and Jeff specialized in picking up marines who didn't mind getting loaded and laid without paying much heed to returning to the main gate before weekend liberty hours expired.

"If they do not show up one day, we call them UA, for Unauthorized Absence," said Captain Tony Rothfork. "After thirty days, if they are still missing, we classify them as deserters."

When they are reclassified as deserters, missing marines become truly "missing." The corps turns the "deserter" information over to law enforcement and makes no further attempt to find them. Only when they show up, either voluntarily or under the arrest of civilian authorities, does the Judge Advocate General's Office take over. Deserters, as well as UA's, generally wind up in the brig.

Occasionally they wind up in the morgue.

"On that Friday afternoon after I finished my work at the school, which would run up around five or five-thirty P.M., I drove to the bowling alley," Vines said.

There were another couple of marines with Eddie when they piled into Vines's Gremlin, but they were just looking for a ride into Oceanside. After they dropped them off, Vines and Eddie went drinking at the Playgirl bar and, later, at the Teen Club. They spent the night together again in Vines's trailer.

Saturday morning, Eddie joined Vines in a tour of the academy. Down on the football field, the Major introduced Marine Private Edward Daniel Moore to the assembled cadets who were up early for drill and told them that Moore would be helping him teach them the Manual of Arms. Together they put the cadets through their paces, ordering them to stand taller, speak louder, heft their rifles in unison, and, always, to address them as "sir." For the next several hours, it was like a page out of Hemingway, with the young, capable military man and the wise older soldier showing boys the path to manhood.

In the afternoon, they drove the twenty miles back north to Oceanside. They walked up and down the pier together and then strolled for miles on the beach until the sun began to drop into the Pacific.

Eddie played the harmonica, he told Vines. He had lost the one that he owned, along with most of his uniforms. While he had been gone on unauthorized absence from Parris Island, somebody had broken into his locker and taken everything, including his harmonica.

"We were walking around the beach and we went over and sat down on the benches and then Eddie saw this girl Alice. He said, 'I'm going to go over here and talk to this girl,'" Vines said.

While Moore joined several other marines who were flirting with Alice, Vines sat nearby cooling his heels impatiently. Then he spotted

Frankie, the homeless girl from Rhode Island who lived on the beach. He'd talked to her a few times before. When she crossed the street, he waved to her.

The minute they began to chat, Eddie came back. He glanced over his shoulder just in time to see Alice wander off down the beach flanked by the other marines.

"So that just left Frankie and Eddie and I," said the Major. "It was just the three of us. We got in my car and rode around for quite a while."

She had a daughter, but she was young and not ready to be tied down as a mother, so she left the baby with her own parents in Providence and hitched a ride to California.

Eddie and Frankie hit it off. Soon the three-way conversation became two-sided and the Major just drove. Frankie knew about an abandoned beach house five hundred yards or so from the Oceanside pier. Nobody ever checked there. She had been sleeping there for several nights and nobody ever bothered her. If Eddie had no place to spend the night, he might want to stay there.

The Major let them out of his car reluctantly. Eddie had his arm around the girl as he waved good-bye. The Major returned the wave like a stoic salute. Then he drove back to his trailer and spent the night alone.

The next time he saw Eddie, he was playing the harmonica. It was an afternoon near the end of November. The girl wasn't with him. He was standing with another marine next to the Amtrak rails that run through the center of Oceanside.

"How you been?" he called out to Vines.

"Been busy," he said, rummaging up a stoic smile.

The Major inquired after Frankie, and Eddie shrugged off the question. He hadn't seen her that day. It was nearly winter by then and getting too cold to sleep out on the beach. She was probably nearby, looking for some cash to buy blankets or hooch, he told Vines. Eddie sometimes sold a pint of blood to the blood bank to make a few extra bucks. Frankie did too. Maybe that's where she'd gotten off to.

Vines didn't have much money on him. He did have some change. He offered it to Eddie so that he and his friend, a guy named Tex, could buy some lunch. Tex had an old Plymouth Roadrunner. The two of them clambered in and shot off down the street without so much as a good-bye to the Major.

"Every time I saw Eddie, he seemed to need money," Vines said with a sigh. And every time he saw him, Eddie seemed to get it from him. With his shy grin and his ingratiating overgrown-kid mannerisms, Eddie Moore was a hustler to be sure, but not the sort who would hurt anybody.

Or anybody would want to hurt.

"He had a really strange temper," remembered Danny Carranza, one of Randy's younger acquaintances in the early '70s. "He would really wig out every so often. I knew he could get very upset very easily. He was seething underneath, but he would never express it. I thought, 'This guy keeps his anger in so much.'"

During one of his breakups with Jeff Graves, Randy needed a place to stay. He came to Carranza and his roommate because they had an extra room in their Neito Avenue home in Belmont Shore, and he asked if he could stay. He moved in for several weeks, until the Great Kitchen Massacre. It started after Randy had come home and cleaned up the kitchen following one of his all-night drives down to one of the marine bases. After tidying up the kitchen, he went to bed.

"The previous night, he was trying to sleep and we didn't realize he was home," Carranza remembered. "We came home with some friends and we were drinking."

Danny and his roommate and a girlfriend who also lived with them whipped up a batch of tacos and continued drinking well into the night, whooping and hollering and having a good time. Randy never made his presence known.

"The reason he held back, I think, was that he was our house guest," said Carranza. "We went out to the beach the next day and while we were gone, he just picked up a bucket of trash, coffee grounds and everything, and threw everything all over the house. He just did that and split."

Randy took every container in the kitchen and dumped it out on the floor—sugar, flour, coffee, salt. Anything that had any kind of foodstuff in it he poured all over the stove and the sink and the floors. Then he left a short note taped to the refrigerator apologizing for losing his temper.

Danny's roommate, Jon, remembers coming home from work that day and finding that Randy had "absolutely destroyed the kitchen. He'd dumped trash and shit all over the floors and I don't know what all. It was just a mess. He didn't physically break anything but, I mean, it was unbelievably trashed.

"I didn't have any interest in that and I told him so. I remember that we had an absolute 120-decibel yellathon at each other on my front porch. Then he left."

It was one of the few times that either Carranza or Jon could remember seeing normally cool, calm Randy Kraft lose his temper. When he did, it left a lasting impression.

"My father used to get really, really angry," said Carranza. "He could have a real mean temper too. When he got angry his face would completely distort.

"Randy was that way. He'd get very red in the face. His facial features would get very exaggerated. You'd say to yourself, 'This guy is pissed. I would not like to be around this guy when he's pissed.' It was so infrequent. But when it happened, it was frightening."

"Well, as I told you last night this is George Troup and my name's Bill Tynes," said the first of the two men who had stood in the doorway of Charles Vines's trailer the previous afternoon. "We're both from the Orange County District Attorney's Office and what we want to do with your permission is go over a few of the things that we discussed last night about Edward Moore pertaining to yourself and . . . I think that was what we agreed on last night, wasn't it?"

"Yes sir," answered Vines.

"And, I mean, you did come back here voluntarily and all that?" asked the man named Tynes.

The Major looked around the small interrogation room apprehensively.

"Yes sir," he said.

"To assist us in the homicide investigation," Tynes continued.

The Major winced. "Yes sir," he answered.

The two homicide investigators wanted to see his driver's license again, apparently to verify that he was, indeed, Charles Wendell Vines, Jr., from Buckner, Arkansas. That out of the way, the pair reprised the unbelievable details surrounding Eddie Moore's death. Vines blanched, as shocked by it as the first time he heard about it. That was about a week after New Year's when he ran into Dale Zielinski, one of the guys who used to accompany Eddie when the Major picked them up outside the main gate.

Zielinski spotted the Major sitting with a lance corporal in a booth at J.B.'s Restaurant in Oceanside.

"I thought he was joking," the Major told the two investigators.

Vines and the corporal got up, paid their bill, and drove down to La Jolla to watch the Major's cadets compete in a basketball game.

But Zielinski wasn't joking. The Major understood just how serious the marine had been when the two detectives from the District Attorney's Office showed up at the front door of his trailer.

He knew he was under suspicion. They wouldn't have asked him to come to the Orange County courthouse for a formal, taped interview unless he was. But he also knew he was innocent, and the only way to demonstrate that was to be openly, painfully honest about who he was and his relationship to Eddie Moore.

Tynes and Troup began with a bloodless, monotonic recounting of the details in the Seal Beach police report of December 26, 1972. On the westbound offramp of the 405 and 605 freeways, near the 7th Street intersection, the crumpled body of twenty-year-old U.S. Marine Edward Daniel Moore was spotted by a passing motorist at approximately 1:45 A.M. He wore no belt or shoes and had on only one sock. The other sock was jammed into his rectum. He wore a jacket with a USMC patch and a Confederate flag sewn on it. ED MOORE was stenciled on the waistband of his jockey shorts and the collar of his T-shirt. There was a rabbit's foot tied to one of his belt loops.

He had been dumped from a car. It probably slowed down, but it didn't stop. The last time anyone remembered seeing him alive was in the barracks at Camp Pendleton about six P.M. on Christmas Eve.

His face had been beaten with a blunt instrument, possibly a pipe. The autopsy showed that the face injuries had occurred minutes before death. What had killed him, though, was the garrotting, according to the coroner. Red ligature marks ringed his neck. Faint red rings encircled his wrists and ankles too, leading investigators to conclude that he had been tied up during his ritual killing. There were also fingernail scratches on his testicles and a bite mark on his penis.

He had a blood alcohol level of .01, but even the medical examiner conceded that could have been just a false positive result in his toxicological report, caused by body putrefaction. He had no drugs in his system when he died either.

"Here's a photograph that shows Edward Moore and his male sex organ," said Tynes, sliding a photograph across the table to Major Vines. "As you can tell, someone has done a job on his testicles, either with their hands or fingernails or a knee or something. . . . Have you ever seen this man in Oceanside or do you know him?" Tynes asked, pushing another photograph across the table.

"No sir."

Tynes explained that it was a mug shot of a black hustler who sometimes worked the bars along the Strand in Oceanside. Vines couldn't recall ever seeing Eddie with him.

Tynes leaned across the table, poking a finger at the picture of poor, dead, strangled Eddie Moore.

"Do you yourself have any idea why Eddie Moore would end up like that?" he demanded.

"No sir, I do not," the Major said, finding himself wanting to elaborate. "Eddie, uh, Eddie was a . . . my impression of Eddie was that he is a lonely kind of person and kind of lost. And the kind of person that, uh . . ."

"Whether he's lonely or lost, the fact remains that somebody did a job on him," Tynes interrupted, a hard edge suddenly in his voice. "There was violence involved and from everybody we've talked to, including yourself, people indicate to us that Moore was not a violent type person."

"No sir," the Major said. "He wasn't."

"This has to have a relationship to something," Tynes persisted. "His particular death. His stocking. His male organs. The fact that he'd been beaten about the head. This has to have a relationship to something.

"Now what in your estimation could this be related to if he wasn't a violent person? Why would that have occurred? From all the people we've talked to who knew Eddie Moore, you're probably the person who knows him better than anybody, including the guys in his outfit. So we're asking you for your help. We're asking you why. You know, why did this happen?"

The Major swallowed and looked to the blank wall for help. He knew how a POW must feel during the first round of interrogation, when the enemy is trying with thinly disguised disgust to ferret information out of a subject who might know some crucial bit of counter-intelligence—or might know nothing at all.

"The only . . ." he began, then shook his head slowly and stared down at the mug shot of the black suspect side by side with the lewd eight-by-ten closeup of Eddie Moore's scratched and torn genitals. "I can't explain why it happened. I can talk, if I may just talk about Eddie. Just, my, what I saw, what my . . ."

Tynes pulled the photographs back and waved his approval.

"Sure. Go ahead," he said.

Vines sat up in his chair, more sure of himself now that he had the floor. He spoke from the heart, hoping that the two hard-boiled cops sitting across from him would sense that and listen.

"Eddie is the kind of person, or was the kind of person, that would befriend or try to become friends with anybody who would talk to him for very long," the Major said softly. "If somebody in a restaurant or on the beach or anyplace would stop and talk to Eddie for four or five minutes, Eddie would want to become that person's friend.

"Eddie had this thing . . ." Vines continued, growing more animated. "I'm not a psychologist and I don't pretend to be, but Eddie had some kind of compulsion, some kind of desire to have friends, to want people to like him."

Tynes was not persuaded. He pulled another photo from his folder, showing Moore's body as it had been originally found on the freeway offramp, with fresh skid marks on the forehead, hip, and knee where it had bounced like a lost piece of furniture that had fallen off a moving van.

"Is this the result of a friendship?" Tynes challenged.

"No sir," Vines said, retreating into his chair. Weakly, he began again. "I think that Eddie may have been hitchhiking or maybe he left Camp Pendleton or got on the bus or something. Eddie told me that he did hitchhike. He told me that he had, a lot of times in his life, since his mother had died, that he had gotten away that way. He said that the way he traveled was that he would just go stand on a road and put his thumb up and that he would hitchhike and people would come by and pick him up."

Eddie was lonely and Eddie was likable. He had his problems and the Major tolerated them. The begging, the irresponsibility, the flitting from relationship to relationship like a butterfly. They were irritating flaws. But there was nothing in his personality that should have cost him his life.

"I think . . . I mean, my interpretation of this is that Eddie tried to befriend somebody," Vines said softly. "The wrong person."

8

Du:ring the past two years there have been eleven separate homicides in the general area of Long Beach, Seal Beach, Los Angeles Harbor District, city of Irvine, Salton Sea area in Imperial County, and the city of San Bernardino," began George Troup's January 21, 1975, process report on efforts to solve southern California's baffling string of grotesque killings.

The media hadn't caught on to it yet, which was good. Troup and the other investigators from a half-dozen different police departments weren't ready to deal with reporters, tossing scare headlines out onto the streets just to sell newspapers while the killer or killers calculated their next move in the cat and mouse game they were playing with law enforcement.

But the task force wasn't making much headway either. That was the bad news.

Another meeting was scheduled the following week and Troup's boss, Orange County chief deputy district attorney James Enright, wanted an update. The FBI was showing up this time, along with a couple of forensic psychologists who might be able to nail down a suspect based on his behavior patterns.

The progress report, detailing the eleven murders that had been laid to a single killer or killers over the previous two years because of their similarities, was supposed to show Enright that the task force was making progress. But that, of course, was an exaggeration at best.

Typing it up was anything but a labor of love for Troup, a terse, husky law enforcement veteran who fancied himself more a man of action than a wordsmith. Each sentence was an exercise in frustration. He stared at the blank sheet of paper and it stared back, challenging him to write down a solution and justify the homicide task force he had helped create to track down the maniac driving the southern California highways.

The killings dated back to the very first one that Troup had ever gotten involved in: Edward Daniel Moore.

That had been late 1972, and since then Troup had followed dozens of leads in a vain attempt to crack the case. He and Bill Tynes thought they were pretty close a couple of times, especially with the gay "Major" who worked as a vice principal at a military school and turned out to be Moore's on-again off-again boyfriend. When the Seal Beach police first found the kid's body on the Seventh Street offramp of the 605 Freeway, right at the Long Beach city limits, "jealous homosexual lover" seemed to be the obvious suspect to hunt down. Troup had been a cop in Orange County for five years by the time he wound up on the Moore case, and he recognized the signs immediately: gay killings were always the worst.

Husbands and wives, boyfriends and girlfriends—they beat up on each other, shot each other, stabbed and strangled and slapped each other. But they rarely went in for torture and dismemberment and all of the other imaginative mutilation that seemed to delight a small and perverse—but all too active—segment of the gay community in southern California, particularly around Long Beach.

They had their dungeons and their whips and chains, all for fun. Just make believe, they said. Heterosexuals did it too, of course: tying each other up and going through crazy rituals of submission and punishment. One enterprising escort service near the Disneyland Hotel specialized in catering to conventioneers who liked dominant women in spike heels with raven hair, red lips, and mascara slits for eyes.

But when it came to body dumps of nude young males, raped and maimed at the hands of another, it could generally be traced back to a lover whose anger or ecstasy—or both—got out of hand. The results were almost always ghastly. Witness Eddie Moore, with the stocking stuffed up his ass and the bite marks around his penis and testicles.

But if it was a lover, the homicide investigators who had worked the Moore case couldn't find him. And it wasn't long after Moore's body showed up on the freeway shoulder that a regular roadside corpse parade began. Bodies popped up regularly all over the place, from

Surfside to the Salton Sea. Three unidentifieds alone in Wilmington, Huntington Beach, and Long Beach within six months of Moore's murder.

Then there was Ronnie Wiebe, the first one who broke the jealous-gay-lover mold and seemed to obliterate what remained of Troup's original theory: that maybe Moore and the three John Does simply had a one-night stand with a boyfriend and things got out of hand.

Wiebe, a twenty-year-old from Fullerton, was another Seal Beach case. The body drop was in almost the exact same location where they had found Eddie Moore six months earlier.

Troup read over the bare-bones, just-the-facts-ma'am Seal Beach detective's report, looking for something to put into his own progress report to Enright.

"On July 30, 1983, at approximately 6:20 A.M., officers were dispatched to the eastbound 405 onramp at 7th street regarding a body lying in the ice plant. The victim was fully dressed except for shoes and one sock, which was later found stuffed into his anus.

"His pants were unfastened though zipped, and his penis was partially exposed. Ligature marks around his neck and facial trauma were apparent. There were no valuables or identification. When found the victim had been dead for two days. He had been dumped from a moving vehicle."

Of course, the police report didn't go in for the wretched details, like the teeth marks on the stomach and penis where the killer did some leisurely gnawing while a hog-tied Wiebe probably shrieked in agony. The settling of the blood and the stretch marks left by ropes on his wrists and ankles also seemed to show that the pathetic wretch had been suspended somewhere from the rafters, his head and chest hanging down.

It also didn't mention that this killing, more than any of the previous ones, looked like the work of more than one murderer: how the body almost had to have been carried from a car to the patch of ice plant next to the curb where it was dropped like a sack of fertilizer.

Of course, it was possible it could have been pushed out the door of a moving vehicle and landed, without disturbing the ice plant, by the roadside. And it was equally possible that one man could have slung a five-and-a-half-foot, 135-pound corpse over his shoulder and carried it there from an idling car.

But not likely. Nothing is as heavy or as cumbersome as a dead body. Troup concluded at least two people carried Wiebe: one lugging the feet and the other grasping the body beneath the arms.

But perhaps more troubling than anything else, Wiebe was married. Separated, yes. Living with his father after leaving his wife, yes. Seeing another woman on the side, yes. But definitely not a homosexual.

That took the entire investigation out of the realm of gays killing gays and put it into a more general arena: anybody who happened to be young, male, and naïve enough to get sucked into whatever scam these killers were laying on their prey was susceptible. That meant kids hitchhiking to the beach, young husbands with a flat tire and no ride home, sailors and soldiers off on weekend liberty—anybody.

The last time anyone saw Wiebe was closing time on Saturday, July 28, at the Sportsman Bar on Katella Avenue in nearby Los Alamitos. It was a quarter to two and Wiebe wandered out the door, waving good-bye to everyone. He owned a car, but it had a flat tire. When his sister got worried and went looking for Wiebe the next day, she found the car still parked next door to the bar.

The following morning, Wiebe turned up dead in the freeway ice plant with abrasions all over his body and a sock jammed in his anus. His scratched and bruised face wore an amazed, wide-eyed look.

The police report continued in cold, dry investigatorese: "The autopsy revealed that some of the injuries to the victim's face occurred before death. He died of ligature strangulation. However he had also received two or three blows to the top of the head with a blunt instrument heavy enough to pierce the skin and fracture the skull. The victim's blood alcohol level was .02, however that may have been an incorrect reading due to putrification. No drugs were found in his system."

Nothing about his dad or his family or his estranged wife, Glenda, or his girlfriend, Julie, who entered a couple of dance contests with him at the Honeymooner Club in Long Beach, or the people he'd worked for the past four years at Eurton Electric Company in San Pedro.

Nothing to make him sound any more human than day-old round steak at the local Safeway.

After Wiebe, the list just kept on growing:

• **December 29, 1973**. Hikers find twenty-three-year-old Vincent Cruz Mestas, a Long Beach State University art student, at the bottom of a ravine in the San Bernardino Mountains. Except for shoes and one sock found forced inside his rectum, Mestas is fully clothed. Someone has shaved his face and head, probably after he was dead, and cut off both his hands, wrapping plastic sandwich bags around the bloody stubs. The hands were never found. A stick or toothpick or, maybe, a pencil has been jammed into his penis before he died.

Mestas was bisexual, had a male roomie, and had been caught a few times trying to hustle sex at the Belmont Shore bluff area, a few blocks from his Temple Avenue apartment. A couple of days before his body turned up, he had told his roommate he was going to the mountains to do some drawing. He took a sketchpad, some drawing pencils, and left.

• **June 2, 1974**. The nude body of Malcolm Eugene Little, who had just turned twenty, is found propped up against a mesquite tree along Highway 86, just west of the Salton Sea. His legs are spread wide and his genitals are missing. A mesquite branch has been forced six inches up his rectum.

Little was an out-of-work truck driver from Selma, Alabama, who had just arrived by Greyhound the previous week for a visit with his brother, Bill Little, who lived in Long Beach. But no sooner did Malcolm arrive than his girlfriend called from back home, reading him the riot act for leaving her behind. Malcolm complained that all he had was ten dollars to his name and no return bus ticket. She was unappeased. The next morning Malcolm had his brother drop him off at the junction of the Garden Grove and Santa Ana freeways so that he could hitch a ride back to Alabama. He had on purple pants and shirt, Western boots, and a new army field jacket when Bill Little left him by the side of the road. The last time he saw his kid brother, he had his right thumb aimed east and a green suitcase at his side, waving good-bye forever.

• **June 22, 1974**. The nude body of eighteen-year-old U.S. Marine Roger E. Dickerson is found off a dead-end street in Laguna Beach above a golf course. His killer has chewed his penis and left nipple, sodomized him, and then strangled him to death.

The night before, Dickerson had been drinking beer at Bud's Cove Bar in San Clemente with several buddies from Camp Pendleton when he told them he'd found someone who'd drive him to Los Angeles for the weekend. He left without telling anyone who that someone was.

The autopsy shows a modest amount of alcohol in his system, but it also shows something else: diazepam, the generic name for Valium.

• **August 3, 1974**. Morning shift employees in a Long Beach harbor oilfield find the fully clothed body of Thomas Paxton Lee, a twenty-five-year-old waiter at the Princess Louise restaurant. He is lying halfway down a steep, nine-foot embankment. His blood alcohol shows he drank more than a six-pack of beer the night before, but that's not what killed him. He died from manual strangulation.

A regular at gay bars like L'il Lucy's in Long Beach and the Diamond Horseshoe in Wilmington, Lee was a well-known "troller" or solicitor who worked the Granada Beach and Belmont Shore bluff area for one-night stands. The last time his roommate had seen him alive was near closing time at the Diamond Horseshoe on Friday, August 2.

The next day, he's dead.

• **August 12, 1974.** The shoeless, sockless body of Gary Wayne Cordova, twenty-three, is found down an embankment near Cabot Road and Oso Parkway in southern Orange County.

Cordova had just moved out of his house in Pasadena and told friends he was hitchhiking to Oceanside.

Cause of death is acute intoxication due to ingestion of alcohol and diazepam.

• **November 29, 1974.** Shortly after four P.M., Irvine police receive a report of a partially clothed body near the San Diego Freeway. Except for a white, blood-soaked T-shirt, nineteen-year-old James Dale Reeves is naked, face down between two trees, about twenty feet off the southern edge of Barranca Road. His white denim Levi's, a bloodred stain at the crotch, lie in a heap at the base of one of the trees. His legs are spread a yard apart, forming a human Y, and a four-foot-long tree branch, three inches in diameter, is jammed into his rectum.

A gay who still lived with his parents in the Long Beach suburb of Cypress, Reeves took the family car for a spin on November 27, Thanksgiving Day, and drove to a newly formed gay community church in Costa Mesa, where he shared Thanksgiving dinner. He eventually wound up at Ripples in Belmont Shore, where the family car was later found abandoned.

Troup stared at his report.

All the names and bodies and times and places were blurring together. There had to be a common thread somewhere: an overlooked clue that would unmask this guy. Something that would even the odds. They never seemed to be short of longshot suspects. That was one ironic beauty of the task force system. Get enough self-described cynics from enough homicide divisions into a single room and they'd fall all over themselves coming up with possible perpetrators. They had mug books and profiles and make sheets on a couple dozen potentials, but nothing—absolutely nothing—solid enough to even make a case against any one of them to the point where they could drop everything, declare the guy under suspicion of murder, and make an arrest.

Yet the list of victims kept growing. The best evidence ought to be just lying there at each body dump, waiting for some forensic specialist to pick it up like one of Hansel and Gretel's bread crumbs and trace it back to the source of the evil.

But it wasn't. At the end of each thumbnail sketch on the facts of each case, Troup was forced to write a single, aggravating sentence, over and over and over: "At this time there are no known suspects under investigation in this crime."

The most recent victims were so fresh they hadn't even made the distinguished task force list yet. A little over two weeks before Troup sat down at the typewriter to update Enright on the investigation, a seventeen-year-old high school kid from Long Beach was found with a wooden surveyor's stake up his rectum, floating in the surf off Sunset Beach. John Leras had had a few drinks, been tied up and strangled to death. His body was dragged through the sand and dumped in the ocean. Two sets of footprints in the sand indicated that two people did the dragging.

Leras was last seen alive boarding a bus for a Long Beach skating rink with the set of roller skates he had just received as a Christmas present. So far, he was the youngest victim.

Just a ten-minute car ride away from where Leras was found, another body turned up two weeks later.

Just after noon on January 17, 1975, construction workers found Craig Victor Jonaites in a vacant lot near the Golden Sails Hotel on Pacific Coast Highway in Long Beach. Except for missing shoes and socks, the twenty-one-year-old victim was fully clothed. In fact, he was wearing two pair of pants, not just one. The red ring around his neck and the blackened tongue protruding from his mouth told how he died: a string pulled tight around his trachea, cutting off the air supply long enough to strangle him to death.

Troup did a quick mental statistical survey of the facts and dashed off his conclusion:

It is to be noted that all victims have been male, Caucasian, between the ages of seventeen and twenty-five, and all have had the same physical characteristics. It is believed that all except three of the victims were homosexuals. With the exception of the victim found in San Bernardino, all of the bodies were placed in a location where they could have easily been found by the police or passing motorists. Four of the victims had stockings inserted into their anus, and on two of these victims there was also found white tissue which appeared to have been used to plug the nose. Investigation revealed that this is a procedure used by the military forces on bodies of servicemen usually after they have been killed as a result of military action to keep the body from purging. Investigators feel that the stocking technique was used on all four victims to keep the bodies from purging while being kept in a room or while being transported in the vehicle prior to being dumped. Investigators also feel that there are two or more subjects committing the crimes as it would be difficult for one suspect to accomplish dumping the bodies.

And that was about it.

The joint meetings with other investigators, the hundreds of witness interviews, the interrogation of possible suspects, the polygraph tests, and the careful cataloging of thousands of pieces of evidence all turned up nothing. Young men had been slaughtered and scattered over four counties for two years and investigators were no nearer an explanation than they had been in the beginning.

Troup sat back in his chair and reread the sixteen-page memo he had cranked out. Not bad for a cop who didn't like to talk much.

At nine A.M. on January 24, 1975, homicide investigators from the sheriff's departments in San Bernardino, Orange, and Imperial counties as well as the police departments of Los Angeles, Long Beach, Seal Beach, Irvine, and Huntington Beach met in a large conference room at the Orange County Sheriff's headquarters in Santa Ana.

A special investigator from the California Attorney General's Criminal Investigation Index in Sacramento and FBI special agent Howard Teton from the Bureau's Multiple Murder Investigative Unit at FBI Academy headquarters in Quantico, Virginia, were also on hand.

Agent Teton, who took the floor to keynote the session, described a different kind of killer at work in the country—one whose like had been seen only rarely in the past.

Just five years earlier, the notorious Tate-LaBianca murders had been carried out by the Manson family, steeling the public to the danger of LSD-crazed hippie killers. The headlines devoted to those murders further widened the generation gap that had been opened in the 1960s by drugs, political disenchantment, and Vietnam.

But there was a different kind of killer plaguing the Southland since the arrest of the Manson gang, and he was far more deadly than any hallucinogenic hippie. This murderer wasn't drug-crazed or otherwise obvious the way Manson was. He didn't surround himself with adoring women who carved Xs in their foreheads. He didn't try to hide by escaping to Death Valley in a pre-Armageddon dune buggy battalion.

This killer, or killers, was far more clever, clear-headed, and insidious. The kind of monster who was out on the freeways stalking young men was so new and unusual that the term "serial killer" had not even come into common usage in the language yet. Even police called him a "mass killer," though he was clearly not in the same class as a Manson or a Richard Speck or a Charles Starkweather, all of whom killed in a frenzy once or twice and then were caught.

This was a new brand of killer with few precedents in times gone by: Bluebeard, Jack the Ripper, the Boston Strangler.

He killed, waited, then killed again.

And again.

At the Behavioral Sciences Unit of the FBI Academy in Quantico, there was a general alarm being sounded about this new kind of human shark. At one point, the FBI estimated that the U.S. had as many as thirty-five such murderers at large in various regions of the nation. In Quantico, such a killer was known as a "lust killer" because his periodic murders were usually committed to satisfy a sexual urge.

Quoting from a general FBI profile of such a killer, Agent Teton pointed out that he "exhibits complete indifference to the interests and welfare of society and displays an irresponsible and self-centered attitude. While disliking people in general, he does not avoid them. Instead, he is capable of displaying an amiable facade for as long as it takes to manipulate people toward his own personal goal. He is a methodical and cunning individual, as demonstrated in the perpetration of his crime. He is fully cognizant of the criminality of his act and its impact on society and it is for this reason that he commits the crime. He generally lives some distance from the crime scene and will cruise seeking a victim."

Investigators finished their coffee, then started their discussion. A handful of psychologists and physicians who regularly attended inmates at the Orange County jail were also invited, among them Dr. E. Mansell Pattison, an associate professor and vice chairman of the Department of

Psychiatry and Human Behavior at the California College of Medicine, University of California at Irvine.

At the end of the day, there were still no likely suspects.

Dr. Pattison was not jaded by it all. What he saw revealed in the discussion was a homosexual maniac who, in a bizarre paradox, was no homosexual at all.

Another week passed before he decided to write Teton his own analysis of the "remarkable similarity" in the string of unsolved homicides and the kind of pseudo-gay person capable of committing them. This person was angry, insecure, brilliant, and completely baffled as to his sexual preference.

"He desires to be masculine and virile, but does not feel masculine. He vicariously identifies with the beautiful masculine image of the victim. Sodomizing the victim affirms . . . that he is a potent, aggressive, virile, heterosexual male. Biting of the nipples and genitals or the excision of them symbolically makes the victim a female, thus reinforcing the killer's self-image of masculinity."

The way he mutilated the corpses was a road map to what made him tick: Better that *they're* castrated than *him*. Stripping the bodies of clothing and removing all identification is a further kind of degradation, all designed to turn the victims into repugnant objects, not people. That's also why he stuffs a sock or a stick into the victim's anus, Pattison theorized. Anything rammed in the rectum is not only a "typical homosexual sadistic symbol," he wrote, it's also a "symbolic penis," which shows that the victim, not the killer, has been the one castrated.

As Dr. Pattison pictured him, the killer actually hated committing homosexual acts and projected that self-loathing onto his victims. In his subconscious, the equation went like this: destroy the victim and you also destroy your own lust. Temporarily, at least, the killer doesn't hate himself as much, and he doesn't set out to kill again until he builds up another head of steam.

For up to several months after a murder, the urge is reduced. But when pornography or sadomasochistic fantasizing builds up tension again, another attack is inevitable, said Dr. Pattison. And, he added ominously, there is little likelihood that the killer feels any guilt.

He played the game so often and so flagrantly that he appeared to know southern California like the back of his hand. He might be a truck driver or a traveling salesman or someone else who drove the back roads as well as the eight-lane interstates professionally. Or perhaps he just liked exploring likely places for body drops late at night and had learned all the best ones over a period of years.

It seemed fairly certain that he was no Johnny-come-lately. He knew precisely how to dispose of the remains of his prey by plunking them down in plain sight. He was like a cat who drops a fresh bird in the middle of the front porch once he has feasted on its entrails, then perches in a nearby tree to watch what happens when the humans find the carcass.

Maybe the freeway killer was just a particularly quick study from another state who had come to California and learned how to get around fast. But to detectives who would soon inherit the case from George Troup, like Orange County Sheriff's sergeant Jim Sidebotham and Los Angeles County Sheriff's sergeant Al Sett, it seemed far more likely that he was a native son.

In the predawn hours of Saturday, March 29, 1975, nineteen-year-old Keith Daven Crotwell caught a ride from Long Beach to nowhere in particular. He rode all the way down the San Diego Freeway to the Laguna Hills in southern Orange County, forty miles away. He and the guys he hung out with from Wilson High School had bummed rides plenty of times before. But this ride turned out to be Keith Crotwell's last.

He wore glasses when he was in high school, but what scholarly appearance they might have given the slim six-foot-one dropout was misleading. He looked older than he was, partly because of his height and build. Crotwell played baseball and basketball, so blithely and so well that some of his friends still believe he might have made it to the pros if he'd been given half a chance at home.

His parents were divorced and the entrance to the Crotwell home was "a revolving door," according to his friends. Like his two brothers, Keith could be gone for several days without raising much concern among his family. Sometimes his mother invited him to leave. Sometimes he just left.

When he dropped out of Wilson High in the middle of his senior year, things got worse at home for Crotwell. His friends Frank and Terry Ditmar asked their parents if it was all right for Keith to move in for a while. The Ditmars agreed to unofficially adopt Crotwell as a third son until he could get a job and get on his feet, "figure out what he was gonna do with his life," Frank Ditmar remembered. At nineteen, long-term goals like career and family tend to be postponed, if they come up at all. For Keith Crotwell, a timorous and unambitious student when he was in school, the future didn't extend much beyond the next six-pack.

"He was an advanced motorcycle rider and a decent mechanic," remembered Kent May, one of the guys who hung out with Frank and Terry Ditmar. They all lived in the same East Long Beach apartment complex—perhaps as many as a dozen boys, all in their teens. It was a loose-knit fraternity: they played softball together, went out partying together, tinkered with motorcycles together, hitchhiked to the beach together. Crotwell was a swimmer as well as a ball player. He spent summers body surfing at places like Huntington Beach, Newport, or Seal Beach. The rest of the guys he ran with spent their summers browning at the beach too, studying bikini mammography while drinking a Bud.

"He could really hold his liquor," said Frank Ditmar. "He was one of those guys who could drink and drink and drink and never act drunk and then just fall asleep."

On weekends he and his pals went to the desert to run their cycles through the sand or hit pickup places like Big John's pool hall near the municipal swimming pool in Belmont Shore. For those who weren't scouting for women or didn't like billiards, there was always prevideo arcade games to play like air hockey and foosball. For those who liked neither, there was Schlitz in the trunk of one of the guys' cars out in the long beachfront parking lot, bordered on the north by Granada Avenue and on the south by the city pool.

That's where Crotwell and fifteen-year-old Kent May sat, commiserating on a Saturday night in the spring of 1975 following a fight Kent had had with his new girlfriend. She had just waltzed off with another guy. Kent was seething. He spent his last $20 on her. Life, like his girlfriend, he told Crotwell, was a bitch.

Nah, Keith told his callow young friend. Women were just that way. You couldn't let them get to you. You had to roll with the punches. The stupid broad was just trying to make him jealous. Kent couldn't play into her hands by showing her that she had succeeded.

It was about then that they noticed the doofus in the Levi's jacket and sailor's cap laughing at them from across the parking lot.

They both stiffened a little when he walked up. It was after midnight and the lot near the municipal swimming pool was pretty much deserted. The guy was older, had a mustache, and seemed far too eager to join in the conversation. Both boys edged off. He was friendly enough, with his quick smile and brown eyes that crinkled at the corners when he laughed.

But he had cruised from the direction of Ripples, a bar at the Granada end of the lot, notorious for its long-standing reputation as a hangout for homosexuals. Gays often cruised the beach area, and even high school sophomores like Kent May knew what they were cruising to find. On the beach itself, just a few steps from Big John's, was a row of restrooms where almost every night gays met for whatever the hell it was they did to each other. By 1975 the practice was so blatant that even the Long Beach vice cops only made token lewd-conduct busts. There was no real intent to stop the hustling.

Crotwell asked the man in the sailor's cap what he thought about queers. When he answered that he hated them, the two boys began to relax.

The stranger drove a classic black and white 1974 Mustang that he had parked nearby. He had something in it, he told them, something that a broke, frustrated fifteen-year-old and his bored buddy might find very tempting.

"Wanna beer?" he asked the pair.

Within moments, Crotwell was in the front seat of the Mustang. May was close behind. He hopped in the back and held out his hand like a tot at Christmastime. The stranger handed a bottle back to him and opened another couple of beers for himself and Crotwell. Then he started to drive.

"I had been in that situation before where gay people or people who I suspected of being gay picked me up when I was hitchhiking up and down Pacific Coast Highway on the way to or from Seal Beach," May recalled. "I had many times been offered drugs or money or alcohol."

It was a given that gay cruisers would pick up young hitchhikers, so May was careful about accepting booze or pills or anything else from a driver when he thumbed his way to the beach.

This particular night was different. To begin with, he was miserable.

When the stranger pulled up to a stoplight and turned around in the seat to hand something to him, Kent held his hand out obediently. The dude poured a mound of yellow tablets from a plastic prescription vial into Kent's outstretched palm. Then he offered some to Crotwell. As the Mustang pulled away from the light, Kent held one of them up to the streetlight and examined it closely. Each pill was inscribed with the numeral 10.

He deferred to Crotwell's judgment. Keith thought it was all right. He was three years older and seemed to know about women. So why wouldn't he know about pills?

Crotwell spoke to the fifteen-year-old like a Dutch uncle, warning him to go easy on the pills. He recognized Valium when he saw it and told May that taking too many at once would result in a blackout, not a high. Crotwell took about ten of the tablets. May followed Crotwell's wise counsel and counted out only seven tablets for himself. They swallowed them with the remaining beer and waited for the buzz to set in.

That's when May recalls things getting peculiar. Within fifteen minutes, the buzz came and went, giving way quickly to a helplessness bordering on catatonia. One of the last things May recalled was that the stranger seemed perfectly sober. It was only then that he realized that he hadn't seen him drink any beer or take any pills. All the stranger seemed to do was drive and drive with a passion, like a man on a mission.

He steered his Mustang with deadly precision through the streets of Belmont Shore, prowling the avenues and purring to an impatient idle at stoplights. Dimly, May remembers him getting on a freeway and riding, riding, riding into the night. Maybe they stopped once. Some place in Seal Beach, perhaps. Another pool hall parking lot or some other kind of parking lot. Maybe next to another cocktail lounge. May wasn't sure because he passed out in the back seat at some point, his mind as well as his body numbed into unconsciousness by the combined wallop of Valium and beer. There was some movement, a dim sense of falling, like a paratrooper without his chute. But that subsided and Kent remembered nothing more.

The next thing he did know for certain was that he had a terrible headache and that the sunshine was streaming in his bedroom window. It was Sunday afternoon and he had visitors. The Ditmars and Randy Cooper and Cooper's sister, Vicki, wanted to know what had happened to Keith the night before. Kent was at a loss. How he had even gotten home to his bed was a genuine mystery to him. The preceding twelve hours were a blank.

Not to Frank and Terry Ditmar, though. Frank got tired of the partying at Big John's early on Saturday night and headed home before the stranger and his Mustang ever showed up. But Terry had walked out into the night air some time after midnight, just as the Mustang reentered the parking lot. He and Cooper and some of the other guys tried to catch up with the car. Terry got a good look at the driver—a confident, sober face accented with dark bushy brows, blond hair, and cold, blank shark's eyes.

Before Ditmar could reach the car, the rear door swung open and the driver pushed May out on the pavement.

Terry found a phone and called his older brother for help. Frank rolled out of bed and, by two A.M., he showed up in the beachfront parking lot. They all helped get Kent May home.

But they couldn't help Crotwell. The last Terry saw of their friend, he appeared to be unconscious, leaning against the stranger's shoulder in the front seat of the car as it slid into the darkness, up Third Street, and into the night.

When Crotwell failed to show up in the next several days, Vicki Cooper coaxed the Ditmars to get their parents to file a missing person report. The following week, Keith's older sister, Sharon, showed up at the apartment complex in east Long Beach where the Ditmars, the Coopers, and the families of most of the other teens who formed Keith Crotwell's crowd all lived. Sharon berated them for not looking after her brother and accused them of knowing what had happened to him. The Ditmars responded by lashing out at the Crotwells for failing to offer even minimal care for their son.

But all of the accusations and counter-accusations ended on May 8, a little over a month after Crotwell's disappearance.

On a Thursday afternoon, three teenagers from nearby Bell Gardens clambered over the rocks that form one of the jetties that create the channel leading into the Long Beach Marina. They went exploring in search of starfish and, near the end of the jetty about three hundred yards offshore, one of them spotted something wedged in the rocks. Weeks of decomposition in the sun and salt water had reduced the object to something less than human, but it was still intact enough upon closer inspection to be recognizable as a grinning skull with rotting strips of creamy white flesh still attached to the brows and cheeks and temples. Though police scoured the surrounding rocks, they could find no body to go with the head.

Two days later, William Lystrup, a dental X-ray technician with the Orange County Coroner's office, matched X rays taken of Keith Crotwell's teeth when he was ten years old to the teeth in the skull the teenagers found floating off 72nd Place in Belmont Shore.

The Ditmars and the Coopers and all the rest of Keith's friends wasted no time waiting for police. Right away, they suspected that their friend died at the hands of one of the regular patrons at Ripples bar. While Long Beach homicide detectives Mike Woodward and Robert Bell opened their investigation, Terry Ditmar and Randy Cooper began a block-by-block search of the densely populated Belmont Shore area for the black and white Mustang. Five days later, they found it, parked in front of an apartment at First Street and Gaviota Avenue, less than a mile from the parking lot where Keith Crotwell was last seen alive.

The following week Woodward ran a Department of Motor Vehicles make on the registered owner and came up with the name of Randy Steven Kraft. The Mustang registration gave an Orange County address from which Kraft had moved several months before, so Woodward quizzed several mail carriers in the Belmont Shore area about the name. One recognized it and directed Woodward to 1727½ Ocean Boulevard.

Woodward, a tall, black veteran cop born and raised in Long Beach, confronted an average Joe in Randy Kraft. Aside from a slightly prominent chin and a mildly ruddy Teutonic complexion, Kraft was indistinguishable from dozens of young professionals of the Baby Boom generation who had flocked to the beach areas of southern California to live following the tumultuous '60s. He sported a mustache and bleached the forelock of his brown hair in an affected attempt to advertise that he lived near the beach, but Kraft was not otherwise unusual.

When Woodward knocked at the door of the apartment, Kraft invited him in. The detective immediately began to suspect that the thirty-year-old computer consultant was gay. Kraft's roommate was male, a poster of an apparently gay male was hanging on the living room wall, and a copy of a gay magazine rested on the coffee table.

"He spoke with a very mild, timid type voice, and he appeared to me to have some gay tendencies," Woodward said.

Kraft was indeed gay, but so were half the residents of Belmont Shore in 1975. He worked as a dispatcher and part-time computer operator, running payroll and accounts receivable programs at Aztec Aircraft, a charter flight company at the Long Beach Airport.

"He was a little bit affected," said Aztec president Clifford Smith. "He held his fingers kind of like he was gay and talked effeminate a little, but he was a good employee. Very dependable."

He also had a reputation among his friends for loyalty, caring, and an even-tempered nature. He was a regular patron of Ripples bar, just as Crotwell's friends had suggested, but Woodward could find no arrest record on him.

When Woodward asked him about the evening of March 29, Kraft nervously denied ever meeting Crotwell or May at first. Woodward didn't believe he was telling him the whole truth, but he was also not ready to suspect murder. The area around Ripples was a well-known gay cruising spot and, though there was no evidence Crotwell was gay, a likely scenario began to hatch in Woodward's mind: The teenager drinks too much, finds himself propositioned by an older man, and opts for a quick liaison out on the marina jetty. In the dark, the drunken boy falls into the water, loses his bearings, and drowns. The older man panics, fears that his homosexuality will be discovered if he reports the accident, and simply walks away.

Woodward felt only slightly comfortable with his theory, so he asked Kraft to come down to the station for an interview anyway. Kraft said he'd been ill and really didn't feel up to it, but Woodward insisted. Back in the patrol car, Woodward radioed back to headquarters to put Kraft under surveillance, just in case.

Later that afternoon, Kraft told his roommate he was going to the Long Beach Police Station.

"Randy was on his way out of the house [when he] mentioned he was upset," recalled a friend at the time. "He said he had to get help—that he'd met someone on the beach and had a physical relationship and the next day, he turned up dead."

On May 19, 1975, at five P.M. in Room 346 of the five-story police building, Kraft sat down with Woodward and his partner. After he introduced Detective Bell, Woodward began taking notes. One of the first things he jotted down was that Kraft seemed far less rattled than he had that morning.

He also had changed his story.

Woodward: Now, Mr. Kraft, on or about March the 29th, the Saturday prior to Easter day, do you recall picking up or seeing a subject in the area of the Granada parking lot?

Kraft: As I say, I'm not certain about the time. It's somewhere in the past . . . two or three months.

Woodward: Okay, when you picked this subject up, uh, did you later take him for a ride somewhere?

Kraft: First of all, I didn't pick the person up. As I told you before.

Woodward: Okay.

Kraft: I'd been to the bar, to Ripples, drinking that night. Just, you know, talking to some friends. And I went and got in my car, which was at the Granada end of the parking lot.

Bell: Now that's directly across the street from Ripples. Is that correct?

Kraft: Right. And I started to drive home and, uh, as I got toward the other end I noticed on the other side of the parking lot that there was a person I knew.

Bell: Do you know this person's name?

Kraft: No, I don't. Just somebody I've, you know, seen.

Bell: You don't even know his first name?

Kraft: In the gay world, lots of people you know by sight. Perhaps you don't know their name or occupation or whatever. I chatted with this fellow for a while. Then I saw a guy and a girl having an argument right in the first aisle of the parking lot.

Bell: Was this on the Granada end or was this down at the other end by the pool?

Kraft: It was down at the other end, by the Olympic pool.

Bell: And they were having some sort of personal disagreement?

Kraft: I don't know what it was, but they were very vocal about it. A lot of arm waving and stuff like that. And I sat in my car and I was sort of, you know, watching the show take place. And finally the girl had evidently had it, and I believe she got in a car and left with some people. And the guy comes over and was talking to me, right there at my car. I believe I was sitting on the hood. I don't know. And, uh, I had some beer in the car and I asked him if he wanted to have some beer. He said yes, so we had a beer. Only one or two. Could be Budweiser. Could've been Busch. Like I said, I don't drink Coors. Doubt that it was that.

And so then this other guy came over to the car, I guess he got out of, like, a Datsun truck. Either he came over or the other guy went over and got him. He said to him, "Come on over." You know, partake with us.

So the guy that I first met who was arguing with the girl got in the back seat and this other guy got in the front seat 'cause only two can sit in bucket seats and, uh, you know, he proceeded to have another beer. It was just the new guy's first beer and, uh, we were probably on our second beer.

But there were three of us in the car and I don't like to draw attention to myself out in the parking lot. Like I said, I like to drink and drive. So we went driving around a little bit. And we went, uh, just around Belmont Heights, I think. Not for very long, you know. Just wandering around.

Bell: About twenty minutes?

Kraft: Maybe twenty minutes.

Woodward: Did you ever leave Belmont Heights? Did you head toward Huntington Beach or Seal Beach or anywhere down in that area?

Kraft: Not that I remember. I don't recall ever going in that direction.

Woodward: Did anyone suggest anyplace to drive, or did you just drive wherever you felt an urge to go?

Kraft: I think I just drove wherever it popped into my head to go.

I don't recall any directions. So, then we went back to the parking lot. I think the one guy mentioned something about a party or something. You know, lots of girls and the usual thing. Maybe. I don't know. That just popped into my head.

Anyway, if that were the reason, then that's why we went back to the parking lot. Perhaps we just got tired of running around and went back. We got back, pulled up, and parked just about where we left from. And like I said, there were some other people. They drove up and they were already there or I don't remember the situation. But the guy in the back seat wanted to get out. He said he was tired of riding around and drinking beer. He was tired of it. So he got out and asked his buddy if he wanted to leave. The other guy said, no he didn't. He just stayed. So he and I took off and went driving around some more.

This time I really got into one of my driving fits. Drove on down on the San Diego Freeway down south. I don't know. We might have stopped for gas. We might not have. We did stop one time just on an offramp. I don't remember which one. This guy wanted to drive the car and I said he could. We kept going on down south and having some more beers. Got off somewhere around the El Toro offramp.

And this guy went off on, like, a side road. I don't know where it was. It was dark. And he high-centered the car on an embankment. We couldn't go anywhere. We got out and tried to get it unstuck, trying to dig it out.

Bell: How did you try to dig it out?

Kraft: Well, I looked all around to see if I could find anything I could use for a tool. We tried jacking it up, but the dirt was really soft and wouldn't hold. So then I found, like, a long stick and we tried to use it 'cause the dirt was loose. I thought maybe I could shovel it out from underneath. It was right up into the oil pan. The whole thing was just sitting there in the dirt. There was no way I was going to go anywhere. And I tried to dig it out from under the tires and put stuff underneath them. I don't remember what I found for traction. I had something, maybe, you know, a large board or a plank or something. And he was helping me do that but it didn't work. We tried jacking it to get the wheels up on some traction and we tried to get the dirt out from under the front of it. It didn't work. So, like I said, I had to go to work the next morning, so, uh, I wanted to get some help and I asked the dude if he . . .

Woodward: Excuse me.

Kraft: Yeah?

Woodward: You had to go to work the next morning?

Kraft: Yeah.

Woodward: Well, the next morning was Easter Sunday. You had to work on Easter Sunday?

Kraft: Yeah.

Woodward: You did?

Kraft: Yeah.

Woodward: Where? At the aircraft place?

Kraft: It's open seven days a week, fifty-two weeks a year.

Woodward: Okay. Go ahead. Excuse me.

Kraft: Sure. So I went to see if I could get some help like a tow truck or anything to get the car unstuck. I walked about a mile, two miles. I don't know how far I actually walked to this Bob's Big Boy. There was some gas station around there, but I don't believe it was open. It must not have been because I couldn't get any help. I didn't have any money anyway so I couldn't have paid for a tow truck. But, you know, possibly I could have got somebody with a chain or something to yank it loose. I couldn't find any help so I called my roommate, Jeff, to see if he could help.

Bell: What's Jeff's last name?

Kraft: Graves.

Bell: Jeff Grace?

Kraft: Graves.

Bell: Graves.

Kraft: I called him, got him out of a sound sleep, and, uh, he said yeah, he'd come down and pick me up or help me out. I didn't tell him there was anybody with me. Jeff's not just a roommate. He's my, uh . . .

Bell: Yeah.

Kraft: He's my other half. So I sat down and had some coffee at this restaurant where I called him from. It was probably about, say, three-thirty or four A.M.. Something like that.

Bell: When you'd left to go get help?

Kraft: Yeah. Now the thing was, as I was having some coffee, I was thinking: Well, wow, you know, I'm dragging Jeff all the way down there and he's just got a Volkswagen. He's probably not going to be able to help me anyway.

So I was looking around to see if anybody could help me out. And that's how I got the car unstuck. This guy and his wife had a pickup and they drove me back. When I went back, it was getting light. They helped me get it unstuck. The guy was gone—the guy who had driven down there with me.

We tried to push forward, but we couldn't do that. So once again I started looking for stuff that this man could tow it with. There was this building, kind of across the street. When I first got there, it was so dark I didn't know what was around. I couldn't see. But it was getting light now. I could see this building, so I went over and I found a rope. We yanked the car out of the dirt with his truck. After I got the car unstuck, I went around looking and the guy I'd driven down with wasn't there.

I walked around, you know, looking for him. I didn't see him anywhere. We were pretty drunk, so you know, it crossed my mind that he might have passed out. I didn't see him anywhere. I had the car going so I drove back to the restaurant because Jeff was going to show up to help me out. I got some breakfast or just some more coffee—I don't remember which. Jeff showed up and I told him that I already had the car unstuck, that some people had helped me get it off the dirt. So he sat down and had some coffee and then, you know, drove back.

Woodward: So your roommate was there shortly after you called him?

Kraft: No, I'd say about forty-five minutes to an hour after that. See, I got him out of a sound sleep and he had to get up and put his clothes on. It takes a while to drive down there.

Bell: Are you sure it was the El Toro Road offramp of the San Diego Freeway?

Kraft: Yeah, that's where the restaurant was.

Bell: And you were approximately a mile from there?

Kraft: I'd say so. Yeah.

Bell: Which direction?

Kraft: South.

Bell: Do you think you'd be able to recognize this area again if you saw it?

Kraft: Yeah, I think so. It was dark when I first got there and as it lightened up you could see more of what it looked like. As it turned out, just right next to where I was stuck was another onramp to the freeway. I don't know what the name of that one is because it was down past El Toro Road.

Woodward: Were there any lights or anything down there or was it kind of out of the way?

Kraft: It was pretty black. It lightened up in the morning. There were some street lights, I think. There were lights on the hills and that kind of thing.

Bell: Remember the name of the guy who disappeared at all?

Kraft: No I don't.

Bell: Was he white?

Kraft: Yeah.

Bell: About how old do you think he was?

Kraft: I'd say about twenty-four.

Bell: About how big?

Kraft: Smaller than me but I couldn't be sure about that.

Bell: How tall are you?

Kraft: I'm five-ten and a half. I think he was five-nine or five-ten.

Bell: How about weightwise? Was he skinny, fat, medium-build?

Kraft: Average.

Bell: How about hair?

Kraft: Uh, hadn't thought about that. I guess it was longish. Longer than mine.

Bell: Yours is just a little bit down over your collar so his would have been a little bit longer than that?

Kraft: I think so. Yeah.

Bell: What color do you think? Dark, light, red, black?

Kraft: At night it's hard to tell. You know, brown is all that sticks out.

Bell: Was there anything distinguishing about him? Like a scar? Broken nose? Missing tooth? Amputated finger?

Kraft: No.

Bell: Do you know what he was wearing?

Kraft: No, not off hand.

Woodward: Did you recall whether he was wearing glasses?

Kraft: It doesn't stick out in my mind. Maybe, maybe not.

Bell: Did he leave anything in the car?

Kraft: No.

Bell: You don't recall what his name was during your two rides with you? Did he ever take any pills or narcotics or anything like that you know of?

Kraft: Not that I know of.

Bell: Was there any talk about dope while you guys were riding around?

Kraft: There may have been. Just ordinary chitchat, you know. It's a popular subject to talk about.

Bell: But nothing that you recall specifically? When you left him by the car what condition was he in?

Kraft: About the same as me.

Bell: Well, what was that?

Kraft: Well, we were kind of drunk but we maintained.

Bell: Able to maintain.

Kraft: Yeah. Both having all our faculties.

Bell: Did he say he'd wait for you?

Kraft: Uh huh.

Bell: Did you kill him?

Kraft: No.

Bell: Did you, in any way, help dispose of his body?

Kraft: No.

Bell: Do you know how he died?

Kraft: No.

At 5:27 P.M., the interrogation was over.

There were still a lot of questions, but the mild-mannered subject with the unblinking brown eyes and the confident manner had offered a plausible enough explanation to the two investigators, at least for the moment. They told him he was still under suspicion and took photos of him before he left the station. Woodward asked if it would be all right for the detectives to take pictures of his car and Kraft balked at first but did agree to take them out in the front of the station where his Mustang was parked.

While Bell snapped photographs, Woodward snooped inside the car. Sitting on the seat was a half-smoked package of Half & Half cigarettes, but what caught Woodward's eye was a bottle of Coricidin and a plastic prescription vial lying on the floor. When asked about them,

Kraft answered that he'd been sick and that both the over-the-counter decongestant and the prescription medicine had been for the flu.

After Kraft had left, the investigators decided to check out the stuck car story. They drove the forty miles to El Toro, a then thinly populated valley in southern Orange County, and began following Kraft's general description of where he and Crotwell had stalled the Mustang. Just about a mile from the freeway was a dirt road with ruts deep enough and soil soft enough to satisfy both Woodward and Bell that Kraft's car might, indeed, have bogged down on the night that Keith Crotwell disappeared.

They already spoke with Jeff Graves, his roommate, who corroborated his story.

Bell and Woodward still weren't mollified. How did the teenager get from southern Orange County to the Long Beach Marina in the middle of the night, especially if he were as drunk and drugged as Kent May said he was? And why his head—only his head—surfacing in the ocean waters? Where was the rest of Keith Crotwell?

Perhaps nibbled away by fish or lying somewhere in the silt in San Pedro Bay. The conclusion they were asked to buy was that Keith Crotwell, a powerful swimmer, stumbled and fell or dove into the rocks, rendering him unconscious, and drowned. What became of his body was anybody's guess.

Still, there seemed to be enough to charge Kraft with suspicion of killing the kid. His innocent act over the pill business didn't jibe with May's account.

When the two investigators tried to file homicide charges against Randy Steven Kraft the following week, however, they were told to forget it. No body, no evidence. No evidence, no murder. The Los Angeles District Attorney's Long Beach office reviewed the case and sent it back to the third floor of the cop shop.

Historically, the dozen or so prosecutors in the Long Beach office had a reputation for refusing to pursue all but the most airtight cases. Bell maintained that enough circumstantial evidence existed to at least charge Kraft and build the case from there, but nobody listened.

Bell raged about the decision but was powerless to do anything except half-heartedly keep the investigation open. Woodward stayed in contact with Crotwell's friends and family for several weeks, hoping for a break that didn't come.

When the final coroner's report was returned, the medical examiner concluded in his autopsy on Keith Crotwell's scant remains that the young man had died of accidental drowning. The body had floated around in the surf, decomposing until the nibbling of sea creatures simply separated the head from the body. If anybody wanted to go deep-sea diving, they might eventually find the rest of Keith Crotwell.

Bell and Woodward weren't satisfied. But, in time, other murder cases with better evidence or eyewitness accounts came along, occupying the two detectives' time and energy. The file on the Crotwell case found itself buried deeper and deeper in the back of a file drawer.

10

June of 1975 was a bad month for Randy.

The Long Beach cops called Jeff in for a lie detector test to see whether his story held up about the disappearance of the Crotwell kid. He passed, but that didn't make Randy feel any more secure. The two detectives who had interviewed him and Jeff didn't strike Randy as being satisfied with the version of events they gave, and Randy simply had no idea how relentless they wanted to be. His headaches came back. The indigestion and insomnia that had plagued him as far back as college began acting up again. He eventually took a battery of tests to get to the root of the trouble and discovered he suffered from hypoglycemia.

To make matters worse, while Randy was walking on eggshells over the prospect of being a murder suspect, he got caught in a vice sweep at the restrooms in Cherry Park near the Belmont Store bluffs: "lewd conduct," they called it, just like the misdemeanor charge he'd beaten in the restroom bust ten years earlier in Huntington Beach. That was the price you paid for taking a leak in a "known" hangout for gays and "looking" gay, whatever the hell that was.

And the same month, Randy's boss laid him off of the first job he'd had since college that he could genuinely say that he looked forward to every day. Tinkering with computers was his calling—he knew it the first time he ever ran a program, watching the screen take his punched-up numbers, whirl them around, and spit out flawless spreadsheet figures. There was something about the clean, structured operation of computers that had an esoteric appeal to him, over and above the obvious intellectual prestige of being in on the ground floor of a technical profession that, Randy sensed, would shape the rest of the century.

But in June, Aztec Aircraft owner Clifford Smith was having troubles and had to sell his company. He had to let Randy go at the same time.

A few months before calling it quits, Smith had installed an early model IBM business computer in Aztec's business offices and given Randy the job of punching in the payroll. Randy was a quick study. When Smith laid him off, Kraft had enough experience to switch over with little trouble to Pacific Computing Systems, the fledgling consulting company that Smith had hired when he originally set up his system. Pacific Systems paid Randy $4 an hour to run similar programs for its other customers. But it wasn't steady work.

"He certainly was no gifted programmer," said Pacific president Tim Jensen. "We've had a lot better."

But he was good enough to work off and on for the next two years as Jensen needed him. On his resume, Randy later boasted that he was a "data entry manager" for Aztec . . .

"He was a keypunch operator," said Jensen.

. . . and a "senior programmer" for Pacific Computing.

"He did some real basic work for us," said Jensen. "When he didn't work for me anymore, he became an independent computer consultant. That's what someone calls themselves when they're generally out of work."

At the same time he was losing his job at Aztec, Randy wound up paying a $125 fine for the lewd conduct misdemeanor. The charge, he told friends, was a bum rap. There was plenty of times Randy had dawdled around one of the midnight stalls in the men's room at Granada or Cherry Avenue beach, scoping out some strange stuff for a quick trick. But this was not one of those nights. A couple of vice cops had a quota to fill, so they approached him, set him up, and arrested him even though he did not proposition either of them, he said. Randy felt as indignant about the citation as a speeder who gets a ticket the one day of the year he's driving under the limit. It was just one more example of his run of bad luck.

Things were not going well with Graves either. He had grown cool, drifting off with his own leather-and-party crowd more and more, especially since he began teaching.

As he approached thirty, Randy Kraft had grown more conservative, at least in his social life. He wanted more homegrown hedonism and less bar-hopping; more dinner parties and group vacations to gay havens like Palm Springs and Key West and less cruising. In other words, he wanted to settle down into a monogamous relationship and Graves didn't.

The Crotwell business seemed to have iced it. Randy confessed to one of his closest friends that he had, indeed, picked the kid up for a few hours of sex and that they had, in fact, gotten each other off. But then he let him off at the side of the freeway and that was that. It was partially out of frustration with Graves that he did it in the first place. The murder charge was both outrageous and absurd. And the fact that the cops had tried to link him to it did little to help his failing relationship with Graves, who was none too happy about Randy's infidelity anyway.

For most of the final year they were together, Kraft and Graves were roommates and little else. Jeff was talking to Randy about moving out for good—talk that became reality by the end of 1975.

Randy hated going back home during that year, even to visit. After his father retired from Douglas Aircraft, he and Randy's mother seemed to quarrel endlessly about the most petty things. When he did go home, he found himself mediating the latest battle rather than sitting around the kitchen having a cup of coffee and shooting the bull, the way he used to when he was in school. At the same time, his oldest and most favored sister, Kay, was breaking up with her husband, Duane, after more than twenty years of marriage. The only family members he really got along with were the younger nieces and nephews who seemed to just accept him for who he was without judging him or discreetly trying to "cure" him of his homosexuality.

The summer of '75 looked like it was destined to be a sorry rerun episode in the "Sinking of the SS *Kraft*" soap opera. Then he got invited to a party and met Jeff Seelig, a chubby apprentice baker from a well-to-do Jewish family from Long Beach. Randy was twenty-nine. Jeff was nineteen.

In a letter he wrote to Seelig's parents years later, Randy described their courtship: When he met Jeff, it had been over a year since he'd broken up with Graves. Randy was self-sufficient and in no hurry to settle down again. If he did, he told himself, it would be with someone his own age.

Jeff told him he was twenty-six. He looked it and seemed even older than that. "He can be a real showman when he wants to be," Randy wrote. He came after Randy very intensely, taking over his kitchen, redecorating his apartment, and even cleaning up Randy's appearance.

"Well, I relented and told myself that the three-year age difference was more than compensated by his being so mature," Kraft wrote. Six months later, when Jeff and Randy were living together, Jeff found himself surrounded by several gushy, very young teenage girls at a party he and Randy attended. The girls kept talking about when all of them, Jeff included, had graduated from high school the previous June.

The next day Randy found out Jeff was only nineteen and they had their first major crisis, according to Randy.

But not their last. They fought and made up, over and over, for the next eight years. By the beginning of 1976, Seelig and Kraft had moved in together into an apartment in Laguna Hills.

A husky, dark-haired young man with brown eyes, thick eyebrows, and a baby face, Seelig nevertheless looked far older than his years. He hired on in the kitchen of Grandma's Gazebo, a Long Beach restaurant located near the Castro Street South concentration of gay businesses near Broadway in Belmont Shore. When he wasn't cooking at work, he cooked for Randy, preened him, behaved in some respects like a traditional working wife.

"Jeff was a Jewish princess," said Michael Wiles, a longtime friend of both Kraft and Seelig. "Here's a young kid with a mouth that wouldn't stop. You couldn't shut him up. And there was a big age difference. He was a teenager and all the rest of us who knew Randy were in our thirties. Jeff was very immature in many things."

His feelings were easily hurt and his naïveté about almost everything—culture, sex, politics, music—was genuine. While Kraft played the strong, quiet, wise role in the relationship, Seelig fussed and fumed and flitted. He was Lucy Ricardo with a mustache while Randy was Ricky without an accent, according to one friend.

"You have played a very special part in my life and I know you see it," Seelig wrote to Randy early in their relationship. He praised his older, wiser lover for helping him grow and develop.

Among other things, Randy introduced Jeff to theater and travel, but he also taught his young charge how to troll the freeways for a threesome fantasy according to court records. The best places were Camp Pendleton and nearby El Toro Marine Base, where svelte young marines decked out in their liberty civvies had their thumbs out for a ride as soon as the sun went down each Friday night. Most of them could be coaxed for the price of a six-pack or two, and the sex was as anonymous and unfettered as any pick-up bar because "real men" marines don't go running off to the cops with tales of fellatio and fornication.

Randy was also Seelig's basic mentor in the gay world. He introduced him to the Broadway bar scene, to Ripples, and to the baths. Seelig said it was not Randy who introduced him to S&M. He got into that scene by himself later, wearing leather vests, uniforms, chains, and hats fancied by the gay subculture who prefer master-slave fantasies.

Randy was far too serious to play "dress up." He analyzed everything, often brooding for days over a faux pas Seelig might have made at a party before trying to talk about it. After several years together, Kraft summarized for Seelig what was right and wrong with their relationship, down to the way Seelig got along with Randy's dog:

"I like our relationship with Max and am extremely glad that you two have come to accept one another. There was a time that I was being forced to choose either one or another of you and fortunately that is past us."

Despite the age difference, Seelig remained with Kraft through several years, a home purchase, and a couple of tempestuous breakups. "Jeff and Randy were kind of on and off," said Phil Crabtree, another close friend. "It wasn't Randy who talked so much as Jeff. Jeff can't shut up. He has to talk about everything. So if they had a disagreement or something, everybody kind of wound up finding out about it."

For some reason, there seemed to have been a lull in the body drops through the spring and summer of 1975. But by the end of the year, they started to pick up again, beginning with a twenty-one-year-old from Inglewood. Larry Gene Walters died on Halloween. It was a Los Angeles County case. There always seemed to be more murders in Los Angeles, until the last few years.

Mark Howard Hall, another twenty-one-year-old, from Pocatello, Idaho, was murdered on New Year's Eve. The Orange County cops rang in 1976 by prying Hall's hacked-up corpse off a tree near the Ortega Highway, south of San Juan Capistrano—a favorite byway to get rid of bodies. The nation's Bicentennial started off in southern California as a banner year for murder. There were two more dumps along Ortega Highway alone before the year was out: Mark Andrew Orach, twenty, of Ottawa, Canada, shot and dumped alongside Ortega Highway on October 6, 1976; and a John Doe, whose body was found August 22, 1976, along the same stretch of highway.

Jim Sidebotham, a tall Texan who wore a relaxed scowl and had a permanent droop in his eyes that some felons mistook for good ol' boy denseness, was part of the permanent Orange County Sheriff's robbery-homicide team investigating the string of freeway killings. It had been three years since George Troup's first task force meeting on the subject, held in the Seal Beach City Council chambers in April of 1973, and there were still no solid suspects.

Up in his office at Santa Ana headquarters for the Sheriff's Office, Sidebotham regularly went over the growing catalog of names and evidence, looking for the pattern or the clue that would narrow the field of several dozen possible suspects down to the one or two killers. But the only thing that had changed in 1976 was that the victims were getting younger and the killer was starting to use bullets instead of steel wire.

Oliver Peter Molitor, thirteen, Manhattan Beach—March 21.
Kenneth Eugene Buchanan, seventeen, Inglewood—April 7.
Larry Armendariz, fourteen, Los Angeles—April 19.
Michael Craig McGhee, thirteen, Redondo Beach—June 11.
And so on.

The bodies were still usually dumped by the side of the road, though the killers were now getting a little more tidy about it. Instead of simply tossing a corpse out the car door, they were stuffed into a plastic trash bag and deposited in a dumpster or left in the desert. A nineteen-year-old Merced youth turned up in a sack a few miles south of Borrego Hot Springs in September, and Randall Lawrence Moore, sixteen, of Phoenix, was bagged and dropped on Highway 80 east of El Cajon a month later. A couple more were dumped right on the Mexican border, near Calexico.

Sometimes the bodies weren't discovered until a trash tractor at a garbage dump accidentally ripped open a sack and an arm flopped out. There was no telling how many solutions to cases involving runaway children were buried each year at the bottom of a landfill.

For a time, it looked like the killers just killed gays. But not any more. They were growing bolder, picking up servicemen and straights and young kids now. None of them so far had been young enough or affluent enough or well enough known to catch the imagination of the press, but it was just a matter of time. There were already a few reporters sniffing around, wanting to know how many unsolved homicides southern California had the previous year or two and how those figures compared to the rest of the country.

Sidebotham looked over the list. It seemed to go on forever.

Wilford Lawrence Faherty, twenty, Redondo Beach. Body found August 28 next to Otay Lakes Road in southeast San Diego County. Shot to death.

David Allen, twenty-seven, a Camp Pendleton marine. Body found October 9 on a remote road in the Fallbrook area about two miles west of Interstate 15. Shot to death.

It looked like 1976 would be a bumper crop year for unsolved murder in southern California. Maybe in 1977 the good guys would finally get lucky.

Paul Fuchs sat down to Sunday dinner with his family on December 10, 1976, but finished early and ran out the front door of his Redondo Avenue home to catch a ride with some friends. He left so quickly he forgot his wallet.

His parents, Hungarian refugees Paul and Elizabeth Fuchs, never saw their son again.

He was nineteen, parked cars for pocket change, and planned to become an artist, his parents told police when they reported him missing the following week. And he was attached to the family, especially Elizabeth, who doted on him. She had three older boys, but Paul was her baby. He would never simply disappear without leaving word, she told the desk sergeant. When he left even for a few minutes, he always left a note saying where he was going and when he was coming back.

The desk sergeant was sympathetic, but firm. Fuchs would be listed as a routine runaway unless something came up that showed foul play or made his departure out of the ordinary. He was nineteen, after all. Maybe he joined the navy.

The Fuchses did check ships' crew lists for his name in later years. By then Elizabeth wept a little each day for her son. Her husband would try to console her, but usually gave up and left the room after a while. Stopping her tears was as impossible as stopping the memories of a boy who simply left one day and never came back—not even in a casket.

Paul liked to drink. A few weeks before he disappeared, the boy had been to a beer bust in San Pedro and was cited for misdemeanor drunkenness. Elizabeth dutifully went to court in hopes that he would show up for his scheduled appearance. He didn't.

The couple went through every name in his address book. None of his friends knew who Paul had been with the day he vanished—whose car had stopped outside the redwood gate to the Fuchses' home to pick their son up. They checked with the bank. There had been no withdrawals from Paul's account.

The police found out quickly what Paul's parents probably knew but found hard to accept—that their son was probably homosexual and that the last place anyone remembered seeing him was Ripples, the best-known gay bar in Belmont Shore. There, his nickname was obvious: When detectives from the Long Beach missing persons detail showed up to ask questions, there were universal shrugs all over the room. No one knew what had become of Fuchs.

On the first day of July 1977, an unlikely pair of murder suspects walked into the Riverside County Sheriff's Office fifty miles east of Los Angeles, pointed to a wanted poster, and said, "That's us."

In black hornrim glasses, black slacks, white short-sleeved shirt and tie, thirty-seven-year-old Patrick Kearney looked more like a life insurance salesman who made house calls than a $20,000-a-year engineer for Hughes Aircraft. His close-cropped black hair and receding hairline, together with exaggerated ears that stuck out Clark Gable–style from the side of his head, gave him a boyish appearance. Ten years earlier, he might have been compared to Jerry Lewis; ten years later, to Pee Wee Herman.

His thirty-four-year-old roommate, David Hill, was a tall, slightly built high school dropout from Lubbock, Texas, who'd been married briefly and done a short stint in the army before meeting Kearney and moving to California in 1962. Hill went through a rocky divorce before finally moving in with Kearney in 1967. At six foot two, he towered over his spindly roommate and lover, yet Hill was outwardly the more docile of the pair. He couldn't hold a job, so he kept house while Kearney went off to work each day.

But it was far from a storybook match. As time went on, they would scream at each other like couples on the verge of divorce. Hill would stomp out and remain away for days at a time, staying with friends or picking up a one-night stand at a gay bar, as much out of spite as lust. Sometimes he'd hit the road and return to Texas. Once he got arrested for vagrancy in Louisiana. But he would always return. Unless he was in one of his tempestuous tirades, Hill tended to follow Kearney's lead on most things, including the decision to turn themselves in.

They had been on the lam for close to two months following the March 13 disappearance of a seventeen-year-old El Segundo youth. For weeks, they had been hounded by police snoops, so they finally just left town the first week of May.

Now, Kearney told the desk sergeant, he was ready to talk about it—"he" meaning Kearney; "it" meaning murder.

Hill, he explained, had nothing to do with any of the things they probably wanted to know about. They might have been living together for ten years, but Hill never knew what Kearney did with the victims. In fact, Hill didn't even know there were victims.

Yes, "victims," Kearney said. Plural.

The first one whose name he could remember was "George." He didn't know his last name. He was buried beneath the driveway at the home he and Hill once shared together on Van Buren Avenue in Culver City.

His secret life as a gay pickup artist began with the glittery-eyed boys with the big Mexican smiles who Kearney picked up in the back streets of Tijuana or down near the border around San Diego. Kearney had a keen interest in Latino culture and was proud of his fluency in Spanish. He also had pen pals with whom he corresponded in Russian and Japanese.

And there were the barflies. And the bus stop blueboys looking for a quickie in the bushes at Pershing Square or MacArthur Park in downtown L.A. And the hitchhikers. And the druggies and the hippies and the wayward, aging flower children, fresh off the bus from San Francisco . . .

The very first victims were transients. The earliest killing he remembered was a young man he picked up at the Pike, a sleazy Coney Island–type midway area in downtown Long Beach where sailors and winos and carnies and minor-league criminals hung around. That would have been about 1964 or '65. There were also two or three out-of-state hitchhikers Kearney killed before he got around to George.

This wasn't about bragging or boasting or anything like that, he explained. This was about something just snapping, was all. Something just giving way inside of him that made it necessary for Kearney to take control—ultimate control—of someone else's body. It wasn't personal. In fact, he barely spoke to most of them.

Yes, "them." There were a lot of them.

The kid from El Segundo—John Otis LaMay was his name—was only the latest of many, Kearney was about to explain.

On March 13, John LaMay had told a next-door neighbor, Michael Trainor, that he was off to Redondo Beach to see a guy he'd met at a gym in downtown Los Angeles. The guy's name was Dave, Trainor remembered when Los Angeles County Sheriff's sergeant Al Sett questioned him about it some time later. It had been about 5:30 P.M. on a Sunday, Trainor recalled. It was the last time anyone remembered seeing LaMay alive.

When her son didn't come home that night or the next day, Mrs. LaMay contacted the El Segundo police. She was bordering on hysterical, claiming that Johnny didn't just go off for days at a time without letting her know where he was. The police chalked it up as a typical teen-runaway case, calmed her down, and sent her home to wait. It wasn't until five days later, when John LaMay did turn up, that law enforcement began to take his mother seriously.

On March 18, neatly carved parts of John LaMay's body were discovered among the greasewood and manzanita near Temescal Canyon in Corona, just east of Orange County. They were packed into five transparent trash bags, three of which the killer had crammed into an empty eighty-gallon oil drum. The remaining two sacks lay in the dust nearby like so much toxic waste. The bags were identified as Mipro 6160, an industrial brand of trash sack. They had been carefully sealed with heavy one-inch-wide nylon filament tape. The Riverside County Coroner's medical examiner guessed from the decomposition that the dismembered body had been there for about four days.

The head was missing, but a horseshoe-shaped birthmark on one of the arms matched a birthmark visible in snapshots that LaMay's mother had given to police when she first reported her son missing.

Breathing through their mouths to keep from gagging, the investigators waded through the brush and picked over the rotting flesh. Using tweezers and baggies, they found some other unusual artifacts: several pubic hairs that, as it turned out, did not belong to LaMay.

Back in the lab, the nylon tape wrapped around the opening of the trash bags also yielded evidence: fine, green nylon fibers that appeared to have come from a carpet.

LaMay's wasn't the first body that had turned up in a canyon or a trash bin or a lonely stretch of desert highway, sliced up like a frying chicken and neatly packaged in a heavy plastic sack. Sometimes there wasn't even any blood to speak of. The sliced and packaged bodies had been desanguinated, the way undertakers drain them before pumping embalming fluid into the veins. They had been turning up regularly around southern California for months, but rarely with the kinds of fiber and hair evidence recovered in LaMay's case.

Sergeant Sett and his partner, Roger Wilson, began retracing John LaMay's last day of life. The gym that LaMay told Trainor he had visited before setting off for the mysterious Dave's house in Redondo was the Midtowne Spa, one of the oldest discreetly gay bathhouses in downtown L.A.

"We knew the kid was probably gay," Sett remembered. "That helped. What straights do when they're looking for sex is go where they're known. What gays do is go where they are strangers."

A pair of lanterns flank the entrance to the white stucco building, marked only by a bronze plaque next to the door that reads MIDTOWNE SPA. Inside, a sign warned those who might be offended that the Midtowne was a GAY-ORIENTED BUSINESS.

There was no pretense about the primary raison d'être of the Midtowne. Men dressed only in towels walked hand in hand through the halls, and women simply never appeared. Newcomers were quizzed about their sexual preferences, but from that point on, first or false names were perfectly acceptable.

Once a patron signed in, he was free to go upstairs to the weight rooms, exercise equipment, steam baths, or one of the smaller private rooms where strangers could get to know one another better. Bankers, lawyers, and businessmen mingled with bodybuilders, actors, and young men fresh from the Greyhound bus station a half dozen blocks to the west on Sixth Street.

Times and clientele have changed somewhat, but in the pre-AIDS atmosphere of the 1970s, the Midtowne was one of L.A.'s premier gay meat markets, according to investigators. When homicide detectives asked the owners for a list of patrons, they got dozens of names. Hill and Kearney were among them.

Another infrequent visitor was a twenty-four-year-old gay hustler from Oxnard: Arturo Ramos Marquez. Marquez was on his way to a Mexican restaurant to meet a Beverly Hills lawyer three weeks before

John LaMay disappeared. Marquez's friends claim he and the lawyer were sleeping together, though the attorney denied it.

On March 3, just fifteen days before John LaMay's carved remains were found, a couple of linemen for Southern California Edison were working on a dirt road about a mile north of the I-10 freeway near Palm Springs. They saw buzzards circling and landing near a ditch and drove over to inspect, fully expecting to find a wayward calf that had been attacked by a coyote.

Despite the desert heat, they rolled the windows up on their truck as they drove near. A fly-blown bloated brown body was baking in the harsh, high desert sun. Marquez had been dead for about five days, according to toxicological tests. His killer had fired a single .22 slug at point blank range into the side of his head.

Except for an Oxnard High School class ring with the initials A.R.M. engraved inside, the body was naked. It had not been dismembered nor stuffed in a trash bag, though it had been stabbed once midabdomen. Not even a hair or a fiber could be recovered.

But Marquez, nonetheless, was to lead the way to LaMay and, ultimately, to the nondescript Hughes Aircraft engineer and his hand-wringing, ne'er-do-well roommate.

A couple days after Marquez disappeared, a manila envelope showed up in his apartment mailbox in Oxnard. It contained several keys on a key ring and a short message typed in Spanish, explaining that these were the keys to Marquez's car. Marquez's roommates, who had already reported his disappearance, took the keys and envelope to the Oxnard police who, by then, had heard from the homicide detectives in Banning, near Palm Springs, assigned to investigate the Marquez murder.

At first, the Beverly Hills lawyer whom Marquez had told his roommates he was going to visit became the prime suspect. The attorney handled immigration cases and lived in a remote, if affluent, canyon area in the Hollywood Hills—a fine site for torture and murder.

The attorney flatly denied that he was gay or carrying on an affair with Marquez when questioned by police. He also denied meeting with Marquez the day he disappeared, even though an autopsy analysis of Marquez's stomach contents showed that salsa and tortillas like that served at the restaurant where Marquez's friends said Marquez was to meet the lawyer were, in fact, his last meal.

But the Marquez investigation also led to an examination of the Midtowne Spa's sign-in sheets to see which regular patrons might have been sitting around the sauna at the same time that Marquez was there. While suspicion continued to hover over the hapless attorney, the discovery of John LaMay's dismembered body focused new attention on a pair of names that came up repeatedly on the Midtowne list: David Hill and Patrick Kearney of 1906 Robinson Avenue, Redondo Beach.

Michael Trainor's last memory of John LaMay began to resonate in investigators' minds: "I'm going to Dave's house in Redondo Beach."

Riverside County Sheriff's deputies Larry Miller and Dan Wilson didn't expect much cooperation when they knocked on Hill's door more than a month after LaMay's body had been discovered. They got no confessions, but Hill and his roommate didn't turn them away either. They were invited in and asked to wait for a bit while Hill and Kearney made themselves presentable. As the two deputies shuffled around the living room waiting to speak with the pair, Miller pulled a few fibers from the green carpet and put them in his pocket.

Kearney and Hill entered and invited the detectives to sit. They listened to the news of LaMay's death with keen interest. Kearney offered up the fact that he and Hill were, in fact, gay and that they were as much in fear of being murdered as anyone else. There had been a rash of gay murders in recent years, he pointed out, with ghastly details reported in the press about victims being impaled on wooden stakes and raped and tossed like naked voodoo dolls down mountainsides or from freeway offramps. It was a dangerous world in which to be homosexual, he exhorted.

But Kearney himself had been at work the evening that LaMay had disappeared. And Hill had been visiting a friend. Neither man could offer a clue as to what might have happened to the boy.

Wilson and Miller thanked them for their time and left.

Back in the police lab the next day, the deputies got their first hint that they might not be hearing the whole truth.

The carpet fibers Miller had pocketed matched perfectly with the minute green threads that homicide investigators had found stuck to the nylon tape that had been used to seal shut the trash sacks in which LaMay's body had been found.

Next, the deputies visited Hughes Aircraft to check out Kearney's alibi and found a bonus: unused Mipro-brand trash bags just down the hall from Kearney's office. A quick inventory of Hughes's office supplies also showed that the company bought the same kind of nylon tape used to seal shut John LaMay's death bags.

The deputies knew they had their killers, but now they had to prove it, and Miller's pocketful of fibers was not enough to do it. To begin with, he had pulled them from the floor without permission— something that could blow the whole case for them if and when it got into court. A handful of pilfered fibers wasn't even strong enough evidence to seek a search warrant, the prosecutor in the case told Miller. They would have to go back and *ask* for some carpet samples.

On May 3, Miller and Wilson mustered the nerve to return to the quiet suburban street where Kearney and Hill lived and make their appeal for carpet fibers. They fully expected a demand for a warrant, followed by a door slammed in their faces. But to their pleasant surprise, Hill and Kearney invited them in one more time. While Wilson clipped the carpet fibers, Miller went one step further: he asked both of them for a sample of their pubic hair. Again, they both obliged.

Within a few days, Miller and Wilson knew they had found LaMay's murderer. Again, the carpet fibers matched under the microscope. But this time, they also had a match on the hairs found on LaMay's body. Under the microscope, cross sections of Patrick Kearney's pubic hair were identical with those found in the trash bag.

While Miller and Wilson prepared their search warrant, however, Kearney and Hill were making other plans. Three days after the two detectives visited, Kearney called in sick at Hughes and never reported for work again.

When the deputies showed up two weeks later at Kearney's front door with their warrant, the two fugitives were already in El Paso, Texas.

Kearney had written his grandmother in the California desert town of Barstow, asking her to put the house up for sale. A resignation letter was also on its way to Hughes Aircraft, where Kearney's plodding consistency and facility with foreign languages had been about to land him a plum position as an overseas engineer in Saudi Arabia for the defense contractor. The government had granted him a secret security clearance, and he was earmarked for special company-sponsored classes in Arabic.

In the meantime, the search warrant turned up dozens of items, from film and magazine pornography to toy handcuffs and rubber gloves. One of Kearney's well-thumbed volumes was titled *Bluebeard,* the story of Giles de Rais, a fifteenth-century French nobleman who was burned at the state for raping, killing, and drinking the blood of an estimated two hundred teenage boys. There were also several yellowing newspaper accounts about a string of Houston homosexual murders in the early '70s.

A forensics specialist the deputies brought along with them sprayed the bathtub, shower, walls, and floor of the bathroom with a green compound that glows in minimal light everywhere except where there are traces of human blood. When the lights went out, there were dark spots all over the room.

"I washed a lot of the bodies because, with dried blood, you can leave fingerprints," Kearney said later. "I was worried about leaving bloody prints around. And they begin to smell if they're not clean."

But by far the most damning evidence turned out to be a hacksaw. It had a new, unused blade in it, but a microscopic inspection turned up bits of human flesh and blood embedded in the two points at which the blade is fitted into the saw.

The blood type was O positive—the same blood type as John LaMay.

On June 1, the Riverside County District Attorney's Office issued murder warrants for the arrest of Hill and Kearney.

"As many as 43 slayings may be connected with two murder suspects who are cooperating with authorities in pinpointing the locations where the bodies may be found, law enforcement officials said Saturday," reported the *Los Angeles Times* in an article published on the front page on July 3, 1977.

Patrick Kearney, thirty-seven, and David Hill, thirty-four, of Redondo Beach were booked on two murder charges and put under investigation for six others following their surrender in Riverside County, reported the newspaper.

"However," the article continued, "Los Angeles County deputies said 'there may be as many as 30 to 35 more bodies' of victims who were killed during the last decade and the remains scattered throughout Southern California. The possibility of additional victims was based on statements made by the suspects, a deputy said."

The deputy, homicide sergeant Al Sett, went on to tell the newspaper reporter in lurid, off-the-record detail how the eight victims that he and partner Roger Wilson had traced to Hill and Kearney so far had been shot in the head with a .22 derringer, usually while they were sitting in the passenger seat of a car.

All of the victims were young men between sixteen and twenty-eight whose naked bodies had been discarded near freeways. Some had been known to patronize bars and bathhouses and parks in downtown Los Angeles frequented by homosexuals. Four of the eight victims had been cut up, loaded into trash bags, and dumped.

"The papers were already calling it 'the trash bag murders,' but homicide was calling it 'the fag-in-the-bag case,'" Sett said in an interview about the investigation several years later.

Like his counterparts in the Riverside, San Bernardino, San Diego, and Orange County Sheriff's departments, Sergeant Sett half-hoped and half-believed that they had finally closed in upon the killers who had been plaguing southern California freeways for the better part of a decade.

When they grilled Kearney about picking up marines and, perhaps, feeding pills and lager to his victims, they got a blank look from him at first.

Then a flash of recognition came over him as they persisted, wanting to know if he had ever put anything but his penis into his victims' rectums.

He used towels to keep bodies from leaking offal all over his bathroom before he dissected them, Kearney answered, with a shrug.

His interrogators persisted: How about torture? Did he ram anything into an anus for the sheer pleasure of . . .

Kearney shook his head, interrupting them. He evenly pro-nounced, "I am *not* the Wooden Stake."

He knew exactly what the detectives were getting at, but he himself didn't go in for impaling his victims or garrotting them or torturing them.

"Did you have any association with someone else who had been killing people?" they wanted to know.

"Inadvertently," Kearney answered cryptically. "I lived in Long Beach and I did a lot of corresponding with people who put ads in the *Free Press.*"

But that was as far as he would go.

There was someone else out on the freeways—an anonymous competitor Kearney knew through gay bar gossip and news items that appeared in the papers whenever another of the killer's victims showed up near a freeway offramp, mutilated and raped with tree branches, poles, or sticks. He knew about the other killer, but he didn't know him. In fact, he was somewhat offended that Sett and the others considered him a suspect.

The spindly middle-aged engineer had pride of craftsmanship when it came to murder. He never confronted his victims with his intentions before killing them. He always used a gun, aiming with his right hand just above the ear at the temple. Usually he carefully steered his Volkswagen bug along the interstate with his left hand, observing the speed limit, while committing murder with his right. It was all so quick that the dead man's facial expression was rarely even surprised.

The deed done, Kearney would continue driving down the freeway with the corpse slumped upright in the bucket seat next to his until he got to an isolated locale. Then he went about his necrophilia uninterrupted before disposing of the body.

He killed his last victim, John LaMay, that way.

The boy came to visit one Sunday in March when Hill wasn't home, so Kearney invited him to watch television until his roommate returned. As the boy got up from the sofa to change a channel, Kearney reached for his derringer on an impulse, walked up behind him, lifted the gun to the base of LaMay's skull, and fired.

It was far more clean and simple than stabbing or strangling, he explained.

As for his roomie, he was innocent of all of it. According to Kearney, Hill was usually out on a week-long bender or threatening to move out all together when Kearney went into one of his black moods and felt the itch to pick up a victim. The Riverside District Attorney's Office believed Kearney after a week of questioning and turned Hill loose. He returned to Lubbock and never came back to California.

"When I was eight years old, I had a feeling I was going to do these things," Kearney told investigators the day he turned himself in.

Temperatures were in the nineties and the air conditioning was broken as interrogators from four counties converged on the Riverside County Jail that July 4th weekend. While they listened, Kearney recounted murder after murder, beginning with George in 1968. Kearney met him in San Diego and took him home to Culver City. What happened next was the beginning of a ritual that Kearney repeated off and on for the next eight years.

As soon as George walked through the front door, Kearney shot him in the head, dragged him to the bathroom, chopped him to pieces, and skinned him with an Exacto knife. He drew a map for his interrogators, showing where they could dig up George's bones, behind the garage of the triplex house on a residential street behind the Culver City movie studios, where he and Hill had lived from 1968 to 1970.

Later on, he got rid of many of the bodies by just driving to the

desert and finding a remote area where animals, insects, and the
weather would turn flesh into food or dust.

"I used to live in Arizona, and I noticed that things disappeared
very rapidly in the desert," he told investigators. "You can put a small
animal on an anthill and it disappears right in front of your eyes."

When he recounted the killing of George for Sergeant Sett and the
others that sweaty summer weekend in 1977, Kearney was a little fuzzy
on how it happened.

"He didn't remember exactly when it was, but he guessed it was
around Christmas time in 1968," said Sett. "This was about the time
that Hill got busted in Louisiana. He went back there for some damn
reason and got arrested for vagrancy. Hill was a real winner. He wasn't
home for the holidays and Pat got lonely. So he picked up George. We
never did find out what his last name was. He was just plain George."

One detail Kearney did remember of the first murder, and
repeated with the dozens of killings that came afterwards, was post-
mortem sodomy. His pattern was fairly clear on that point: a bullet to
the brain, anal penetration, orgasm, and disposal of the body.

He read about a homosexual killing ring in Houston during the early
'70s in which three men participated in torture, rape, and murder. Led
by one Dean Corll, the trio did in nearly two dozen runaway boys before
they were caught. One of the things they did to their victims was yank
out their pubic hair. That inspired Kearney to do the same with many of
his victims, he told investigators.

He also hit his victims once they were dead, usually pummeling
their faces and torsos with a rage that had built up since childhood.

Kearney didn't start experimenting with dismembering and disem-
boweling his victims until several years after George. One of his
trademarks involved slicing the dead man's stomach open.

"It was curiosity," he told investigators. "The gore of it, you know.
What it would be like. Cutting somebody open does tend to sound a little
bit exciting when they're dead. But it didn't give me any thrill when I did
it. I did it for curiosity to see if it would, but it didn't."

He didn't kill again for more than a year after George's death, out
of his own ghastly dread over what he had done. After a while, though,
no one came knocking at his door inquiring after George, and Kearney
began to understand that he had literally gotten away with murder.

The grim ritual of dissecting victims in his bathtub, loading their
parts in Mipro trash bags, and dumping them by the roadside didn't
happen until several years later.

He had his close calls.

Once, he told investigators, he had a flat tire during one of his desert drops. When he discovered that the spare was flat too, he had to call a tow truck to get his VW hauled to a service station. The station attendant fixed the flats and sent Kearney on his way. He never asked about the two bags in the back seat of the car, which contained arms, legs, a rib cage, and intestines.

On another desert visit, he parked at the side of a road to inspect possible dump sites, and managed to lock his keys and freshly loaded trash bags inside the car. It took him the better part of an afternoon to jimmy the lock with a coat hanger while he nervously looked over his shoulder to make sure no good samaritan stopped to help him.

After he was rid of the bodies, he felt a tremendous sense of relief, accomplishment, and power, he said.

Kearney traced his first feelings of impotence and anger to grammar school, when he was the target of bullies. He was the oldest of three sons in a stable middle-class family, but he was small, thin, and sick much of the time. So when another boy hit him or a teacher dressed him down, he rarely retaliated.

"He states that as a kid he was often beat up by others since he was small and called queer by his peers, though he was interested in girls," court-appointed psychologist John McMullin said in his report on the case.

Kearney would go home and complain to his parents, who told him to stand on his own two feet and learn how to fight his own battles.

He did learn how to cope with his frustrations, but not in public. In the safety of his bedroom late at night, Kearney first began fantasizing about killing his enemies. He shut his eyes tight and rehearsed how he would do it, over and over again, skinning them like animals once he'd finished with them.

Kearney had other fantasies too. He dreamed of having sex, any kind of sex, with someone over whom he had complete control. When he was thirteen, he experimented with intercourse with the Kearney family dog, he told psychologist Seawright Anderson. Bestiality was a secret sexual exercise that he continued long after adolescence.

"I went through a period of frustration through my late teens and I was slow to grow," he told Anderson. "I wanted to get even with people who were taking advantage of me."

Many years later, Kearney recanted his dog-molesting confession in a letter to the author:

There are some things that I don't want to talk about; things that are personal, embarrassing or none of anybody's business. When people insisted, I either misled them or they misled themselves.

For example, when Dr. Anderson asked what I did with that dog, I refused to answer. The truth would have been embarrassing and humiliating . . . more so because the doctor had another guy in the room listening. Dr. Anderson was determined to have an answer. He said, "Did you do such-and-such?" And I said, "Yes," just to get away from the subject.

If you think about it, the act that Dr. Anderson described with the dog sounds highly improbable. I've never tried it, but I'd be willing to bet that most dogs, especially a large strange male, would bite you before you got started. It might not even be physically possible.

You might consult a vet or other dog expert about that, or you might approach a large, strange male dog with a banana and see what he does. Ha, ha! I think you see my point. In fact, your own pet might bite you, even if you only used a pencil.

He also denied his guilt in many of the killings he once admitted to having committed, suggesting to the author that "you might find evidence that other people were involved in my case.

"You could look at confiscated photographs and films that the police have," he wrote. "They should have obtained quite a few while investigating other cases similar to mine. You might find photos of some of the alleged victims of my case. You should especially look for movies showing live torture or evisceration."

In December, six months after his surrender, Kearney pled guilty to three murders in Riverside Superior court. Two months later, on February 21, 1978, Kearney pled guilty to another eighteen murders in Los Angeles Superior Court. In exchange for his cooperation with investigators, he was given twenty-one life sentences instead of the death penalty. There were at least seven more investigators believed he killed, but for lack of evidence—sometimes even a body—he was never formally charged.

"If he hadn't gotten sloppy, consciously or unconsciously, he'd probably still be doing it today," said Sergeant Sett.

There was a momentary relaxing among southern California homicide divisions after the arrest and conviction of Patrick Kearney. When he was escorted from the Los Angeles County Jail to the maximum security state prison at San Quentin the first week of March

1978, some of those assigned to the freeway killer task force that LAPD sergeant John St. John had helped put together three years earlier thought their job was done.

Sergeant Sett and Orange County Sheriff's sergeant Jim Sidebotham were not among them.

According to the records of the Anaheim Police Department, on April 16, 1978, at approximately seven A.M. the body of a male was found on the eastbound onramp of the 91 Freeway at Euclid Avenue by an employee of Martin Luther Hospital in Orange who was on his way home from work.

The victim, later identified as eighteen-year-old Scott Michael Hughes, was fully dressed, though the laces were missing from his running shoes. Yellow nylon fibers that clung to his shirt and pants were tweezered off the body, dropped into plastic bags, and deposited in the Anaheim Police property room, along with the rest of his clothes. There was blood on the crotch of his pants and ligature marks around his neck. The coroner fixed the time of death at about three A.M.

The autopsy revealed that Hughes hadn't been drinking, but did take a therapeutic dose of Valium before he died. The cause of death was strangulation, but his killer didn't stop there. He slit his genitals open, from the base of the penis to the scrotum, and removed Hughes's left testicle.

Hughes was a U.S. Marine stationed at Camp Pendleton who drank, smoked marijuana, and dropped LSD from time to time. Friends described him as "boisterous." He had girlfriends and occasionally visited prostitutes.

The last time anyone saw him alive was at the base barracks about two P.M. the previous Friday. At the time of his death, Patrick Kearney had just ended his seventh week in San Quentin.

12

Randy didn't show it, but he hated to lose at cards.

"He didn't express much," said Phil Crabtree. "I mean, I'm a Virgo and I tend to keep things inside, but it needs to come out enough to where I don't explode. Randy seemed to be pretty much the same way. I never saw him angry."

By the time Randy and Jeff joined the Friday Night Poker Club in 1977, the very first foursome was ancient history. No one remembered where the first game was played or who played it. It was an institution, with a dozen or more couples, rules and rituals. They met in a different member's living room once a week and played for precisely three and one half hours with drinks and dinner in between. It had been going on for years. Randy and Jeff were just the latest additions.

"We'd have cocktails from seven to eight P.M., then play cards from eight to nine-thirty. Dinner was from nine-thirty to ten, then we'd play cards again from ten to midnight," said Bob Day, another of the regulars and the unofficial recording secretary for the club. He took attendance; sent out invitations for special events, like New Year's Eve or surprise birthday dinners; and handed out certificates of recognition to those couples who managed to host six months' worth of poker games, punctuated by a blowout dinner party.

The prospect of big money wasn't the enticement. Stakes were limited to a nickel a chip, three raises and call, and the hours of play were also rigid. No extensions beyond midnight for showdown hands or bigger pots. Even big losers only left five or ten dollars lighter in the wallet. People like Randy, who almost always came out on the plus side, didn't win enough to buy a pizza. The rules were one of the reasons the club was able to last for twenty years without major squabbles or hard feelings. Jealousy and pride and greed were all kept to a minimum.

Randy was there nearly every week with Jeff at his side.

"It was just the kind of thing that his brain enjoyed, you know, the challenge of cards like that," said Crabtree, who was also a data-processing consultant.

Where he excelled wasn't in poker, though. Soon after he and Jeff became regulars, Randy split off from the main group and began a side table where bridge was the game. While three or four rounds of five-card draw kept most of the club members busy in the living room, Randy rounded up the quasi-intellectuals, like Crabtree, and a couple of the three or four professors from Long Beach State University who were regulars, and started a bridge game in the dining room.

Bridge, with its chesslike precision and demand for near total recall, became Randy's passion.

"You could tell he was really challenged the same way I am," said Crabtree. "I could be addicted if I had the opportunity, but I never let myself. It takes a lot of time. You could see his brain clicking along and he was very average-good at it. For somebody who didn't play a whole bunch, I thought he was very good."

After Randy and Jeff moved from their Laguna Hills apartment to a condominium on Molino Avenue in Long Beach in August of 1977, they hosted the Friday night ritual a few times themselves.

"They went all out," remembered Day. "They used to have shrimp. Nobody else would have shrimp. Two or three inches long. Jeff was a cook, so they had just the very best of everything. They had bouillabaisse one time."

The ritual was as sociological as it was social. From the moment the front door opened, there was a schism in the ranks, not unlike the split between the men and women at holiday get-togethers that Randy remembered as a youngster, growing up in Midway City.

There, the men floated off to play cards or drink beer or watch sports on TV while the women gathered in the kitchen, kibitzed, and made supper. At the poker parties, the role-playing was just as pronounced, with the strong, silent partners like Randy sharing cigars and cocktail conversation in the living room while the effusive, emotional, and usually more effeminate partners like Jeff carried out hors d'oeuvres, emptied the ashtrays, and made last-minute dinner preparations in the kitchen.

"There are care-givers and care-takers in this life-style," said one of Kraft's poker buddies. "Care-givers, like Jeff, tend to always want to rescue someone. The Randys demand a lot of attention, even though they look like they're stronger. I don't think they always are."

When the cards were dealt, Jeff was still serving his latest culinary delight with scant attention to whether he had a pair or a royal flush lying on the table. Randy was almost always at the bridge table, chain-smoking and playing hardball. But not drinking as much as the others. Drink too much, he used to say, and you lost your competitive edge. Better to let others do the heavy drinking.

"He was pretty competitive and dragged his tail a little bit when he lost, but not to the point that it seemed to screw up his emotions or anything," said Crabtree.

Randy kept his composure and sense of humor about him, though he never seemed to forget the few times he'd been trounced and made subtle references to those minor moments of humiliation when he was having a good night at the table. He also remembered every trump and never let his opponents forget them when he was down on his luck.

All things considered, however, Randy was just one of the guys: no green eyeshade, no trick decks, no marked cards.

"It was pretty routine stuff," said Harry Eylar, a Long Beach State professor and one of the club regulars. In fact, he and others pointed out, the most unusual thing about the Friday Night Poker Club was that they seemed to play bridge as often as they did poker, and that the games were played on Thursday or Saturday as often as Friday.

Still, when Friday Night Poker Club came around to Randy's house, there were the occasional oddities. Like the drunken hitchhikers in the bedroom.

"I was invited over with about six others on a Saturday night and we were sitting there having dinner and so forth and in conversation it came up that Randy had picked up some sailor," remembered Michael Wiles. "I'm just thinking that's what it was, but it might have been a marine.

"Anyway, Randy said the guy was hitchhiking and he picked him up and they went out drinking in the afternoon and the guy was so bombed out of his mind that he passed out in the bedroom. The bedroom was across the hall from the bathroom and you could go by and hear the guy snoring."

Randy laughed it off and the rest of the guests seemed to accept it as nothing special, but in later years the incident haunted Wiles as one of the most peculiar during his fifteen-year friendship with Randy Kraft.

"I thought that was rather strange, especially when you're planning to have people over to your house for dinner," he said. "If you're going to entertain in the evening, why would you go out in the late afternoon drinking with a stranger you picked up hitchhiking and get him so drunk that you have to bring him back and let him pass out in your house? That was weird."

On January 3, 1978, the freeway killer task force held one of its irregular sessions at Parker Center in downtown Los Angeles. John Breault, the deputy district attorney from Los Angeles who prosecuted the "trash bag" case and was about to put Patrick Kearney away for several life terms, was toasted all around. Al Sett and Roger Wilson of the L.A. Sheriff's Homicide Division, who put the case together, got their share of kudos too.

But the dozen or so law enforcement specialists from Orange County, Los Angeles, and San Diego weren't fooling themselves either. Though there was a general hope they were wrong, every cop in the room knew Kearney had not been the only killer on the southern California highways.

For starters, Kearney used bullets, not rope. If by some bizarre point system, a serial murderer could be rated on how humanely he did in his victims, Kearney was probably near the top of the list. They were dead within seconds of the .22 slug entering their brains and didn't feel any of the emotional or physical humiliation that followed.

Kearney was a necrophiliac and would never consider sodomizing or dismembering or torturing a victim who was still alive. He made sure his prey was dead before he began performing his indignities upon them.

The bags of body parts and entrails he left around southern California were deposited in out-of-the-way places, where they stood a chance of never being discovered. Indeed, Kearney literally had to lead his captors to several of the bodies he'd dumped out in the Mojave or they might never have been found. Patrick Kearney might be a cold-blooded killer and a sexual psychopath, but he was not a showoff.

The killer who was still out there, on the other hand, was as morbid an exhibitionist as Caligula. At first, he was discreet enough to throw corpses in a remote canyon or off a mountain road. But increasingly he seemed to get a little extra kick out of tossing his victims on busy freeway offramps or city streets, where grandmothers or school children or hospital orderlies or unsuspecting young women out walking their dogs could stumble across them.

What is more, they were not eviscerated, dissected, bled, and scrubbed up in the bathtub before being neatly packaged and dumped. This guy's victims were billboard advertisements for the rankest kind of front-seat sadism. They had cigarette-lighter burns all over them, incisions up and down the legs and torsos where the killer played tic-tac-toe with a knife blade, and deep red welts around the wrists where the cord bit into the skin as they strained to get away. He cut their balls off. He cut their cocks off. And he did it all while they were still alive.

He—whoever "he" was—sent a shudder through even the most hard-bitten task force members when they thought about it.

They knew how he did it. Thirsty young hitchhikers, naïve enough to mix beer with a few pills in order to get high, apparently never heard of or understood the term "Mickey Finn." Young men, whether felons or marines, always test their limits to see how much they can drink, how far they can go, how fast they can travel without getting caught.

In the bars where task force members like Al Sett and John St. John had done some of their first police work as street patrolmen many years before, the hotshots who drank too much were also the ones who always got into the most trouble. When brawls had to be broken up and bungled robberies had to be investigated, the swingers who had had one too many beers were usually at the core of it all. Some wound up alcoholic and some wound up in jail. Most of them lived long enough to know their limits.

But occasionally, one of them would play poker with the devil, try to outbluff him, try to outdrink him, and wind up with a dead man's hand.

Roland Young woke up in the D block of the Orange County Jail on June 10, 1978, with a screaming headache, the shakes, and a cotton mouth. It was a real struggle just to gather up his personal belongings from the property deputy and sign himself out of jail. Once he got out into the early evening air, he had no place to go and no one to turn to. He'd exhausted just about any goodwill he had left among his handful of acquaintances, and his parents were absolutely disgusted with him.

At twenty-three, Roland Young was already halfway to the cemetery with a liver that went through more vodka in a week than most people digest in a year. He was trained as a machinist, but the longest he could hold a job was five or six weeks. Besides losing interest and coming in hung over, he always seemed to get in fights.

Officer Gil Bowman, a cop for the city of Maywood where Young lived, made a habit of picking him up, busting him, and sending him home the next day. He'd gotten him on both marijuana possession and cocaine use and helped send him off to the sheriff's honor ranch for a sobering-up sentence. It didn't do any good. The rumor around the department was that Young was into a lot heavier stuff and that he might be dealing drugs as well as using them. No one had ever proven it, though. Young was just a petty thief, a druggie, and a drunk on the official police rolls.

But it wasn't Officer Bowman who'd sent him to jail this time. Young managed to do that without the aid of the Maywood Police Department by partying his way down into Orange County forty miles away with one of his drink-and-drive buddies in search of TGIF action. Young got loud and belligerent at the Clubhouse bar, making enough of a spectacle of himself to have the Santa Ana police called in. The cops did him a favor and booked him.

He'd spent the previous weekend in the Los Angeles County Jail for the same thing, so it was no big deal to Young. The biggest problem was getting bailed out. His girlfriend drove to downtown L.A. and got him out that time. They spent the next few days the way young lovers do: shooting up heroin with a couple of their friends in Young's mother's garage. The rest of the time, they were out cruising crash pads to see about acquiring more drugs. Maywood was at the very edge of the East L.A. ghetto, long a headquarters for gangs and gang warfare; and anything that could be shot up, snorted, or ingested whole was available to the highest bidder or the lowest thief.

"In the neighborhood, in Maywood, if there were drugs and alcohol sitting around, it was a given that they were yours," Young's girlfriend recalled. "That's just the way it was."

They lived high for a week and then she lost touch with "Rol" when he and David and Robert took off drinking Friday night in Santa Ana. He didn't call her the next day when he finally got out of jail either. The booking slip that the Irvine police found later in his jacket pocket said he'd walked out a free man at 8:19 P.M.

Danny Van Pool, a bail bondsman who claimed that one of his relatives once bought drugs from Young, said he got a call from him some time after midnight and his voice was panicky. Young told him over the phone that he was at a party where he'd run into some drug dealers he'd stiffed a few weeks before and that they were now looking for their money. Could Van Pool make him a loan?

Van Pool hung up and went back to sleep.

At 3:30 A.M., an off-duty Santa Ana fireman was heading east on Irvine Center Drive when he caught something in his high beams that was too big to be a dead dog.

Even by flashlight, it was apparent he'd been dumped head first from a fast-moving car. There were scrapes and cuts all over him. His shoes read LACO—a clear sign that Roland Young had been a ripoff artist clear to the very end. The Irvine police recognized them as jail-issue high-tops lifted from the Los Angeles County Jail. A single shoelace was missing from the left shoe.

The crotch of his jeans was soaked with blood, he wore no jewelry or belt, and his right wrist bore an all-too-familiar red ligature ring. He had been stabbed four times in the chest. One stab pierced his heart.

Someone had given him Valium with his beer, according to the blood tests, but he was still awake enough to feel the edge of the knife when it cut into his scrotum. His torturer had carefully removed both testicles and the end of his penis. A woman who lived nearby heard the screams and told police about it two days later when she read about the body in the newspaper. She concluded that he must still have been alive, a passenger in a van or a car driven by the killer past her house.

Mrs. Eleanor Young held a wake for Roland the following week.

The same day Mrs. Young buried her son, Lance Corporal Richard Keith hitched a ride from Camp Pendleton to the Los Angeles suburb of Carson to visit his girlfriend, Wanda Lynn Shepherd.

"He looked high. You know, his eyes were glassy," she remembered.

It was late Sunday evening when her Indiana farm boy from Company Third Battalion, First Marine Division, showed up on her doorstep, full of grins and hormones. He didn't smell like he'd been drinking, which was normally what she ran into when he was all hands and mouth, trying to pin her to the edge of the sofa in her parents' living room. He was amorous, though, and she wasn't.

"He wanted to touch me and I didn't want him to," she said. "I was mad at him for hitchhiking out to see me."

He was a smooth talker, though, and could wax on for hours at a time about the terrific life they were going to have together once he finished up the remaining year on his hitch in the marines. He talked for hours, it seemed, though it couldn't have been more than a couple. Wanda softened.

By the time the clock in the kitchen read eleven P.M., she relented enough to let him kiss her good night. Then he laughed and told her he was hitchhiking back to the base. She told him he'd better not, and he left her fuming on the front porch with her hands on her hips. Wanda walked back in and slammed the door. She didn't even peek out the window to see if he'd caught a ride.

Jim Sidebotham visited Corporal Keith seven hours later on a two-lane road off Moulton Parkway, near the entrance to a water district building in southern Orange County. As in the Young case the previous week, a fireman was the first to find the body. This time, he was an off-duty captain from the L.A. Fire Department on his way to work a little before sunrise. His call was relayed directly to Sidebotham's bedside and the detective was out the door before he finished his coffee.

If he was perturbed, the Orange County homicide detective didn't show it. Sidebotham's slicked-back hair and egret eyes rarely displayed his feelings. He cultivated his good ol' boy image, wading around like a stork through the weeds, carefully taking it all in. If his profile weren't so distinctive, with its long, sad cheeks giving him more the appearance of an undertaker than a cop, he could have been described as poker-faced. Nobody—not even his partners—knew exactly what Jim Sidebotham was thinking at any given moment.

Ironically, it was an undertaker who gave Sidebotham and his crew the only real lead they had on the twenty-year-old marine. Robert McCormack, a funeral director who convincingly pled that he knew a newly dead body when he saw one, told police he had seen a camper parked directly ahead of where the body lay when he drove by shortly after five A.M. Unfortunately, that was the only description he could provide and nobody else remembered any camper.

The ninety-foot arc of blood and skin left on the pavement where Keith's body bounced and rolled to rest in the middle of the road argued persuasively for more than one killer. The body had to have been pushed out of a car moving up to fifty miles per hour to have left such a long trail of gore. How could one man handle the steering wheel at the same time he pushed someone out the car door?

The investigators might have liked to believe the camper story. A body bouncing out the back door of a Winnebago made more sense. Everything else about the Keith murder was achingly familiar and excruciatingly empty of clues. Naked body, no I.D.; dumped from a moving vehicle; ligature marks on wrists and neck; Valium and alcohol in the blood. The lab also came back with a couple of new twists. He had overdosed on flurazepam along with the Valium. Flurazepam was a prescription drug used to treat insomnia. The froth in his strangled throat yielded another piece to the puzzle. An analysis indicated that Keith might have been slowly drowned in salt water before—or at the same time—that he was garroted.

Keith Klingbeil limped out his father's front door in Everett, Washington, and kissed his girlfriend good-bye for the last time before setting out to hitchhike to southern California.

A records search some weeks later showed that he made it safely as far south as Sacramento. A California highway patrolman wrote Klingbeil out a ticket for thumbing rides on the Interstate out of the state capital, but that didn't deter him. As soon as the cop was gone, he shouldered his backpack, stuck his thumb out again, and caught a ride south to the end of the road. It wasn't the first time he'd defied the law.

Klingbeil was a hard case—a Navy brat whose family moved back and forth across the nation while he was growing up, settling in base housing wherever the old man happened to be home-ported that particular year. He never actually stayed in one place for more than six months at a time until after his parents were divorced and he went to San Diego to live with his mother.

He started out smart enough, she said. A real athletic over-achiever: Little League, football, scouts. But he was hit during a motorcycle ride when he was seventeen, and his life changed forever. The handlebar went through his spleen, broke his collarbone, and butchered his leg. He had to have the bone fastened with a metal pin just to be able to walk again, and for the next year of his life, Klingbeil was confined to a hospital bed where he learned first-hand the pleasant pain-killing effects of Demerol.

He got a $50,000 insurance settlement from the accident and spent it all before he was twenty on sex, drugs, and rock 'n' roll. When the money ran out, he joined the marines until his crippled leg caught up with him. He was discharged before he got out of boot camp and wound up in a Veterans' Administration Hospital, back on Demerol, until surgeons removed the pin in his leg.

Then he hit the road.

Keith was a wanderer. Never a bum in the workless, wageless sense of the word, but definitely a wanderer. He was a day worker on construction jobs in Florida for a while and tinkered with motorcycles for a few bucks here and there.

The last summer before his twenty-third birthday, he worked in a traveling carnival around Washington state. He started collecting tattoos—a green snake wrapped around a dagger on his upper left arm; a rose on his forearm; KEITH written on his other arm; a skull and crossbones above his left nipple—always smoking a joint or two to ease the sting of the needle. In a spaghetti-strap T-shirt with a cigarette dangling from his lip, Klingbeil was a natural carny who alternately soothed and snarled at youngsters spending their quarters at the midway game booths. A six-foot-tall tough guy with beery breath, bad teeth, and a bitter smile.

With his thumb stuck defiantly back out toward the passing semis south of Sacramento, Keith Klingbeil seemed more raggedy, restless, and innocent than tough and bitter. Two days before Independence Day, that's how he looked in the receding reflection of a rearview mirror as the CHP squad car left him there on the side of Interstate 5.

Two days after Independence Day, he was lying in one of the northbound lanes of Interstate 5, six hundred miles to the south near the Orange County city of Mission Viejo. He was dying of a massive overdose of Tylenol, washed down with beer. It was 3:30 A.M. when the paramedics arrived, but there were enough life signs to warrant an ambulance to Mission Community Hospital.

By the time Sheriff's deputies arrived, he was dead. Detective Thomas Wallstrom, subbing for Sidebotham, found a matchbook from a Long Beach business in one of the pockets in his Levi's and a ligature mark around his neck. One lace was missing from his left hiking boot.

And just beneath the black skull and crossbones Keith had etched across his left breast with a black and red ring, encircling his left nipple—the seared mark of an auto cigarette lighter.

Nearly twice as many showed up for the year-end freeway killer task force meeting as the one at the beginning of the year. San Bernardino, Huntington Beach, and Anaheim were represented along with the regulars from L.A., Orange County, Seal Beach, Imperial County, and Irvine. Christmas was still twelve days away, and 1978 had already set a record for unsolved body dumps in southern California.

The worst of the year was probably Michael Inderbeiten, a twenty-one-year-old Long Beach truck driver dumped in morning rush-hour traffic at the Seventh Street offramp, intersection of the San Diego and 605 freeways.

His eyelids and hand had been branded with a cigarette lighter and he had been emasculated. The body was dumped not twenty feet from the spot where Seal Beach police had found one of the very first victims back in '72: the marine, Eddie Moore.

One of the task force members got up and spoke about procedure and escalating tactics on the part of the killer. Troup emphasized the need to share information as much as possible: leads, suspects, questionable homicides that might be traced back to another jurisdiction. He had composed a notebook of possible suspects—more than a dozen of them, with mugs and criminal histories. There would be more in the coming months.

But at the end of the last meeting of the year, they were no closer to a solution than they were at the first.

The final 1978 session of the Friday Night Poker Club wasn't for poker at all. It was, as Phil Crabtree put it, "an opportunity for us to don our gay apparel":

> Our Great Auntie Respighi's first annual tree-trimming party is to be held at the Pines in Idyllwild December 18, 3:30 P.M. . . . food, booze, local tricks . . . rooms will be reserved at a local motel upon request or take your chances with local tricks. Bring a country tree ornament for Auntie's tree and a humorous gift. High camp, low porno: let your imagination run but not your purse. $5 limit on the gift. Please advise Auntie of your intention to attend so that she may know how many fruitcake, lube, drugs, etc. . . . to have on hand. Your hosts are Great Auntie Respighi's favorite nephews, those boys Jay Boulton and Phil Crabtree.

The invitation sounded far more racy than the actual event, Crabtree said afterward. Some guys came in drag, several got ripped on wallbangers and gin, and there was even a little card playing among a few of the older members—poker, but no bridge. Randy didn't play that night. He liked a game with a challenge and, less and less, poker met that description.

Randy liked a challenge, but he also liked to win.

"The game of bridge seems to me to relate to the type of work that Randy and I both did," Crabtree said. "We were both challenged to find out what was wrong with a computer program and solve the problem. Bridge is the same way: when you solve a hand, you win."

Occasionally Randy lost at bridge and the game of finding the bug in a computer program. But there was one game that he never lost.

"I think the first death was probably accidental somehow," said Crabtree. "Maybe it was intentional, but whether it was or not, it must have clicked something that made it a challenge to him: if you can get away with one, then it was almost like playing bridge. Because it didn't matter. Once you've done one, it really didn't matter if there were more. From then on, it was strictly the challenge of how clever and cunning and skillful you could be. Bridge is the same way: once you've started, you just go and go as long as you possibly can until you lose.

"In the murder game, if you've never experienced losing, if you didn't know what losing was and it was *always* winning, that would be satisfying.

"Now, there are many things in life that you don't have absolute control over. A relationship, for instance. It's too humanized, too emotional for one person to control. But a bridge game or a computer program or a murder, one person really can control it. Randy had things under his control, and he could control what was happening and what was going on.

"They're all games—bridge, computer programming, and murder. And there's winning and there's losing in all of them. But the odds are that, sooner or later, you'll lose at all three."

13

Psychic Joan Julian, AKA Reverend Joan, couldn't get the helicopter pilot to go in the direction she wanted him to go.

One hundred feet below the copter was Silverado Canyon where, in Reverend Joan's vision, the killing had taken place. It was primeval California: steep draws and brown chaparral, dotted here and there with tiny oases of green live oak. The dry southern California summer weather hadn't hit yet, so there were still wildflower patches of purple and pink among the dusty yellow weeds that carpeted the hillsides. An occasional squirrel or jackrabbit could be seen from the cockpit, high-tailing it from one oak oasis to another in the wake of the copter's wind-whipping blades.

And somewhere down below, Joan was certain, Donnie Crisel had lost his life.

"It was so strange because the helicopter man—the policeman who was driving—would not go the way I wanted him to go," she remembered. "This was the strangest thing. I would say go *this* way, that sucker would go *that* way. He would *not* go in the direction that I wanted."

She had been up the same canyon a few days earlier with police in a four-wheel drive, trying to pin down the spot where her mind's eye pictured the twenty-year-old marine taking his final, bloody breaths. The boulders and rock faces along the dirt road twisting up the canyon were embellished with names and signs and years that students graduated, courtesy of reckless high school kids set loose in the wilderness with cans of spray paint.

CLASS OF '80 inscribed in black on an outcropping. CLASS OF '79 done in Day-Glo red on the side of a cliff. Donnie Crisel, class of '77 would never see the rest of '79, let alone '80.

Gang logos appeared here and there, like the territorial markings of animals that instinctively want others to know they have been there and are claiming the area as their own. But it wasn't gangs who had done in Crisel. Other markings were there too: pentagrams in circles, crosses in boxes, and symbols that might have been lifted, wholesale, off a deck of tarot cards.

The canyon floor was littered with the refuse of a disposable society: beer and soda cans, pop tops, used Pampers, Styrofoam cups, doughnut sacks. Use once, then throw them away. There was no reason for the Reverend Joan or the police to believe Silverado might not be a handy dump for discarded bodies too.

It looked different from the sky—tranquil and untouched by urban madness. Odd how deceptive something can be until you look up close with unblinking eyes, thought Joan.

"I can only go by sense and feeling," she said. "You know, I don't know streets, I don't know anything. I just get a sense."

That's what she was getting, hovering over Silverado Canyon one afternoon in the summer of 1979. A sense of murder and madness, of at least three people who'd hauled a drugged and trussed-up marine into the canyon and sacrificed him to some erotic demon on a flat rock beneath the light of the June moon.

On June 16, 1979, a slowly moving vehicle dumped a body on the northbound onramp of the 405 Freeway at Irvine Center Drive, a thirty-minute car ride away from Silverado Canyon. The body was still warm and clad only in boxer shorts when the Irvine police arrived. It was ten o'clock at night and there were plenty of spectators around, but nobody could describe the vehicle that had dumped the body. Best guess was that it was a van.

The young man hadn't been dead long. He was still sanguine. The cold gray of death hadn't even begun to settle over his face. Blood dripped from his nostrils, and his nose was as red as a cherry. He had two loose teeth and scrapes on his arms and sides where he had hit the pavement. There were red rope marks around his neck and one of his wrists. His left nipple was still scarlet from an automobile cigarette lighter burn. He had died from drugs and alcohol, mixed to a lethal level, according to the pathologists who found alcohol equal to a couple of beers in his system. But it was the alcohol combined with toxic doses of Tylenol, antihistamine, decongestant, stimulant, and appetite suppressant that had killed him, they said.

There were tire marks on his shorts and his back, as though someone had backed over him after tossing him out the car door. Stenciled on the waistband of the shorts was D. H. CRISEL.

Nine days earlier, Arkansas-born Donald Harold Crisel celebrated his twentieth birthday. He'd been transferred to the Marine helicopter base in Tustin after more than a year with the Marine Corps in Okinawa. Friends at the base knew him as a hell-raiser—the kind who smoked marijuana, drank like a fish, and propositioned Japanese barmaids with his last dollar. But Donnie Crisel was no homosexual or bi-guy.

A couple of buddies from the base, Mark Panunzio and Gerald Smith, saw him weaving toward Taylor's Restaurant across the street from the main gate around two A.M., ostensibly to get some coffee and sober up long enough to limp back to the barracks and sleep it off. Panunzio shouted at him that they were going to Barstow the next day and that Crisel was welcome to come along. Crisel waved and disappeared inside, and Panunzio never saw him again.

Twenty hours later, Crisel lay crumpled with a beatless heart on the pavement near the juncture of the Santa Ana and San Diego freeways.

When the Seal Beach police called Joan a month later, it was a last resort. She was a major flake by traditional law enforcement standards. Joan Julian had her name legally changed to just Joan in 1977, after she discovered she had a talent to deal with an unseen spiritual dimension. Everybody has the ability to some degree, she preaches, but few people know it and even fewer nurture it. In her yellow stucco Bellflower tract home, she founded a Universe of Metaphysics Center where she conducted guidance sessions for followers who wanted to learn about the psychic world. And she took the title of reverend, though her frizzy strawberry blond hair and streetwise manner made her look more like someone's fun-loving grandmother—which she was.

Nevertheless, Detective Gary Buzzard came to the sixty-year-old psychic about the Crisel case on the recommendation of the South Gate police after they had successfully used Joan on their own murder case the previous year.

After exhausting all of their leads, the South Gate police heard about Joan from a hypnotist they sometimes used to help witnesses remember details of crimes. He suggested they seek Joan's help in the case of Carl Carter, a missing seven-year-old. She listened to the details, meditated, and gave a description to a police artist, who showed his completed sketch to the boy's parents. They recognized a family acquaintance, who turned out to be a triple murderer. Before he kidnapped and killed the Carters' son, thirty-three-year-old Harold Ray "Butch" Memro confessed to police that he had similarly molested and slit the throats of two other youngsters.

"I knew the boy was dead and I got a flash of the person who'd killed him," Joan recalled. "I kept seeing two people. One man occasionally wore a mustache or beard. When they arrested him, it solved that case as well as two others of boys killed two years previously in Bell Gardens. That's what started this thing with me and the police and solving these things."

She had a built-in rooting section at the South Gate Police Station after Memro was convicted, but that meant very little to other law enforcement agencies. About the only time somebody comes to a psychic is when they exhaust their suspect list and they're desperate. Joan didn't condemn them for it. In fact, when Buzzard came to her about Crisel, she told him upfront she wasn't sure she could help him.

"People a lot of times think that police arrest indiscriminately," she said. "They can't afford to do that. They've got to prove it. They've actually got to prove information that I give them down to the minute. So the stuff I give is just information and if it works, it works. If it doesn't, it doesn't."

Joan forewarned Buzzard that her visions didn't play like a feature film. Conditions had to be right, she needed absolute cooperation, and the cops had to understand that playing footsie with the spirit world demanded a lot of patience. In her own experience, law enforcement types had little patience and seldom went in for esoteric talk about time and motion and otherworldliness.

"Time is elusive," she told them. "It's kind of here and it isn't. Human beings are the ones who put the twenty-four-hour day in."

She recalled, "When Crisel showed up dead, the Seal Beach police came to me and I gave them some sketches and information and described one particular man—what he did, what his actions were."

What she was seeing in the Crisel case was a mishmash of visions, she told police. One involved a gay party animal who lived in an Irvine trailer court. Another involved three human sacrifice cultists in a van: a fifty-year-old man, a short thirtyish Hispanic woman with a big bust, and a balding former marine combat pilot in his late thirties with a penchant for knives, a tattoo on his right arm, and an earring. And there were bikers and satanists, all mucking up her visions.

"Then the Irvine police came into it and I saw an area where people were being killed, in the canyon. That's when they put me in the helicopter."

What she was looking for was a large, flat stone with blood on it. On a map, she drew a circle around the area where she thought the rock would be found, and police joined her in looking for it. By then, the serial killer task force was involved.

"We had a meeting with about ten different police departments," she said. "I kept seeing a lot of motorcycles and one particular night, when people kept going into a canyon. This was separate and away from the other stuff I was talking about. I was seeing so many different things involved in this that it was confusing. And eventually they said it was a waste of money and time because they didn't know what the heck I was dealing with. But you don't know when you work with a psychic. That's what I told them from the very beginning."

The exploration of Silverado Canyon turned up nothing, but Joan said she wasn't surprised. The rock where she saw human sacrifice performed, she said, was farther up the canyon, in terrain so rugged even high school kids with spray cans couldn't find their way in. What is more, everyone who saw the rock thought the dried blood was from animals. It was not, she said. It was from the wanton torture of drugged and dying young men. She also began to sense that her "flashes" of the human sacrifice gang represented only one of three or four groups picking up children or hitchhikers and killing them in the southern California outback.

"I knew there was like a satanic group that was involved," said Joan. "There are many people into satanism who do not believe in human sacrifice and would never do it, but with every organization—a religion or whatever—you've got those groups that spin off that are really bizarre.

"There was some other group too, which I don't think has ever been uncovered. I saw one dark-haired man in particular. He acted alone usually. I think he got involved in some kind of a group and that occasionally he worked with them, but he preferred to work alone. It was like a bunch of lions who chase their prey and have to share it, as opposed to wanting it all to yourself."

Murder, as Joan has said in conversations with police detectives over the years, is the most natural unnatural thing in the world. Cain did it to Abel. People have been doing it to other people ever since and then standing back in horror once it's done.

"There's not one person in the world who hasn't thought about killing somebody. There's not a person alive who hasn't contemplated someone's death," she said. "You see people driving on the freeways and someone cuts in front of them, and it's almost like this machine has now become a power tool to destroy. People chase people down the freeway. What're they going to do when they get them? Their intention is to hurt them.

"The only reason they don't do it is they don't know what the hell to do with the body. That's the only reason. Their consciences said, 'I've got to do something with that body.' So they found another way out. People who kill other people either find ways to do something with the body or just don't give a shit about the body and kill 'em anyway. That's the very thin difference between civilized man and freeway killers."

Donnie Crisel had the misfortune of meeting someone who knew what to do with the body and didn't give a shit either, Joan said, with a sigh that was one-third sad, one-third sorry, and one-third matter-of-fact.

Nineteen seventy-nine was a banner year for cadavers found on or near southern California freeways. The lifeless bodies of more than a dozen young men, ranging in age from thirteen to twenty-four, were tossed from passing cars to the ground like so much rubbish.

Thomas Lundgren was picked up just before eleven A.M. May 28 in Reseda and let off two and a half hours later a hundred feet off Mulholland Drive in Agoura, about fifteen miles away. He'd been stabbed and strangled, his throat was cut, and the back of his head had been caved in. He had on a T-shirt, shoes and socks, but his cutoffs and underwear were lying in the weeds nearby, along with his severed genitals. He was thirteen.

Marcus Grabs hitched a ride at ten P.M. August 5 from Pacific Coast Highway in Newport Beach. The car that picked him up took him to Las Virgenes Road, a couple miles south of the Ventura Freeway near the Los Angeles County line. He had been strangled, stabbed, and sodomized when a rancher found his body at 6:30 A.M. the next day. His clothes were strewn in an open field. He was seventeen.

Donald Hayden was walking down Santa Monica Boulevard in Hollywood at one A.M. August 27. Ten hours later, construction workers at a housing project in Liberty Canyon, just off the Ventura Freeway, found Hayden in a trash bin, strangled and sodomized. His wrists had welts on them, as if he'd been handcuffed, and both his neck and testicles bore knife wounds. He was fifteen.

David Murillo caught a ride south on Highway 101 just after noon on September 9. Three days later, his naked body was found in the ivy on the highway shoulder, the back of his cranium crushed to rubble and his neck ligatured shut. He had handcuff marks on his wrists, rope marks on his ankles, and sodomy marks on his rectum. He was seventeen.

Newspapers and television began to sound the antihitchhiking alarm as frequently as high school principals, Sunday school teachers, and youth group counselors. Before the year was out, the menace had a name—the Freeway Killer—and headlines in southern California newspapers issued summertime warnings to blasé teens: "Hitchhiking Dwindles, Parents' Outrage Grows in Unsolved Freeway Killer Case" . . . "Freeways Stalked—Agencies Seek Cause of 41 Deaths" . . . 'Freeway Killer' Cruises for Murder" . . .

In the gay bars of Hollywood and Long Beach and as far away as Palm Springs and Laguna, police distributed Special Bulletin posters with pictures of dead John Does so frequently that the bartenders had the format down by heart and joked about it: "Information wanted . . . unidentified murder victim . . . John Doe #—— . . . victim dumped . . . autopsy revealed the subject was a victim of a homicide . . . LAST CALL! Careful who you go home with . . ."

If they were bothered by the rash of killings, Randy Kraft and Jeff Seelig didn't show it. There was safety in numbers and it seemed as if they rarely went out alone at night. If they didn't go on a pub crawl together, they were in the company of some other couple, usually from the poker group.

Besides, they were way beyond their hitchhiking days. Seelig was now a partner in Grandma's Sugar Plums in Belmont Shore, which was doing a box-office business in specialty candies and pastries among the young and affluent beach dwellers. Kraft went to four months of Erhard Seminars Training sessions and became an "est" convert, asserting himself and creating his own space. Once, according to friends, he asserted a bit too much with Jeff and wound up with a black eye, but his newfound self-confidence seemed to hold him in good stead in the business world.

"He has an even disposition; knows systems and programming; is always available, thorough, neat, quick; has worked off and on since 1976; is clean cut, ethical. I couldn't say anything bad about him," wrote Gertrude Baron, Randy Kraft's supervisor at Jay-El Products, where he helped set up computer programs for several months on a freelance basis.

Randy S. Kraft was a data-processing consultant proficient in IBM System/3, System/32, and System/34, according to his business card. By then, he was competent enough to find regular work setting up small business systems on his own and earn a good living at it.

Good enough, in fact, to buy a house. On July 30, 1979, Randy and Jeff moved into a white stucco bungalow with a red tile roof on Roswell Avenue in Long Beach, a few miles from the beach and their great old Second Street neighborhood in Belmont Shore, but not so far that he and Seelig couldn't drive down to Ripples whenever they wanted.

The Roswell house was a fixer-upper, but built solid, the way the sturdy mission-style houses had all once been built back in the '20s and '30s. Two avocado trees grew in the front porch patio.

The front room had a white ceiling, natural wood around the windows, dark full-length drapes, hardwood floors, and a picture window with a small yellow and black Neighborhood Watch decal in the lower right-hand corner. They put in a bar in the front room and stocked it with scotch, Bloody Mary mix, and Galliano for Harvey Wallbangers. Jeff loaded the built-in hutch in the corner of the living room with lots of potted plants: ficus, fern, azalea. There were soon so many they spilled over onto the white adobe fireplace.

A chandelier hung over the dining room table, and the kitchen reflected the fact that a professional cook lived here: oak cabinets, espresso machine, white lace curtains, a large refrigerator stocked with melon, grapes, bananas, apples, jams, and jellies.

Randy and Jeff found themselves thoroughly anchored in the gay community, though they were just as comfortable in straight Long Beach. They visited couples like Miriam and Russell Phillips and shared problems common to many young couples, including scraping up enough money to buy and remodel a house.

The Friday night poker party institution became their social circle. Marjorie Rubenstein, another straight friend from Sacramento, hosted Randy and a half dozen of his poker pals on a week-long trip to Lake Tahoe in May. The same group spent the previous August in Puerto

Vallarta and Acapulco, where Randy took up parasailing. He was keenly competitive and liked to take calculated risks.

"He remembered things, specific little things that nobody else would ever care about or remember," recalled Rubenstein. "I'd forgotten all about it, but apparently I skunked Randy at Scrabble once. He never forgot it."

Years later, he brought the Scrabble loss up in a conversation. Rubenstein said she was sure he remembered the precise word she'd beaten him with, though she had forgotten long ago.

Randy and Jeff were an item at the close of the '70s. They went to the movies, to plays like *Annie* at the Shubert Theater, to discos and dances, pot lucks and seders. At year's end, they celebrated their newfound affluence with an extended vacation to the East Coast where they visited the top of the Empire State Building in New York, the Capitol in Washington, D.C., and every swinging gay cocktail lounge Key West had to offer.

When they weren't on the town or feuding, theirs was a splendid marriage in the ironic modern sense, because they rarely saw each other.

"They had bizarre hours," remembered Michael Wiles. "Jeff was an apprentice baker with his own business, so he was gone from two in the morning on because they'd cook all night long. And Randy being a computer person had his own bizarre hours. Computer people can sit in front of a machine for days without getting up."

Then, said Wiles, they can simply disappear for an equal number of days and never say where they're going or where they've been.

"I think that some people can be invisible," said Reverend Joan. "They create an environment around them where you just don't see them. They just cover themselves somehow. You see them, but you don't see them. I know that sounds weird, but they just learn this. I think a lot of government agents learn it."

The man responsible for most of the murders of young marines and other hitchhikers during the 1970s was such a person, she said. Sitting in her Bellflower home years later, musing on the subject of her own dead-end search in Silverado Canyon for a killer, Joan Julian remembered the suspect the authorities believed had murdered Donnie Crisel. He was a blood addict, like so many serial murderers before him. As far back as Jack the Ripper, there have been men and women whose blood lust keeps them coming back for more, according to the Reverend Joan.

142 • DENNIS MCDOUGAL

"The first murder is probably a tremendous high and they're always trying to get that high again," she said. "Sometimes they get a lot of frustration because they never achieve that. It never comes back.

"When people become serial killers, they become addicted: they need it. That becomes their form and force of energy. Something happens and the addiction becomes so great that it increases and increases and increases.

"In the past, people in the so-called uncivilized nations used to feel that when they killed an animal or a person and they drank the blood, they took on that person's strength and energy. And sometimes I think on the psychic level, when we kill a person, we assume that energy somehow or we attempt to or we think we do. It's very savage, it's very bizarre, and it's very brutal, but that was something that people did for centuries."

There are murderous cults at work in southern California, she insists, and they have haunted her meditations on unsolved murder more than once, including the killing of Donnie Crisel. But the lone killer Joan saw ranging through her dreams during much of the '70s, looking for an evil eucharist in the form of real human blood, genuine human suffering, and eternal orgasm, began as a kind and gentle soul.

"He's a brilliant man," she said, her eyes narrowed with cynical wonder. "I think at one time he was an extraordinarily spiritual young man with a tremendous belief in God and the goodness of everything. I think that with him something happened really traumatic, that other people thought meant nothing but which meant a lot to him.

"I think it probably happened when he was between about thirteen and fifteen, and I think that it made such an impact and he lived with that pain and couldn't express that pain for so long, it just bore down deeper and deeper and deeper, like a cancer, to where it took over and he lost touch with who he was. I don't feel he was a brutal child. I don't feel he was a brutal young adult. I think something happened to him and it made such an impact that it just twisted him.

"It could've been something to do with his homosexuality. But whatever it was, it was not a nice thing."

When the serial killer task force gave up on her visions of Donnie Crisel's killers and returned to more traditional means of sleuthing, the Reverend Joan returned to other forms of connecting with the spirit world. But she never gave up on her sense that a troubled killer was stalking the southern California night, seeking one more thrill kill as good as the first one.

Three years after the Crisel episode, a woman whose son was missing came to ask Joan for help. The boy had gone to visit a friend and his mother never saw him again. When he was found by a CalTrans crew beneath the Hollywood Freeway several weeks later, sixteen-year-old Robert Avila was a decomposing corpse.

"She came to me. Her name was Theresa. I didn't even know her last name. I described the man who had killed her son. Well, this Mexican lady was going to go out and do harm to someone. I said you can't do that. Because part of what I've described here could fit a lot of people. What're you gonna do? Go shoot a man who looks a little fey with kind of sparse, light brown hair and walks with a stoop? I mean, you know, this is not good enough.

"She took the tape to the police who were working the case and I told her to let them work. They know what they're doing. How she could be effective, I told her, was to get her family together and every day for a few minutes imagine a big searchlight shining down on the person who'd killed her son. Do *that*. Don't take the law in your own hands. Just imagine a huge searchlight. And within months they will arrest the man who killed your son."

It was nearly a year after the July 29, 1982, discovery of Robert Avila's body that police arrested the man who killed Theresa Avila's son.

The Reverend Joan credited the Avila family with patiently running through their daily ritual, as if they were saying a rosary for Robert: shutting their eyes and focusing their mental spotlights on the highways, visualizing the freeway killer as he droned through the night looking for unsuspecting victims. Their concentration helped chase him to earth, she insisted. Their own silent nonviolent vengeance helped end the reign of terror of the tortured, vicious, but seemingly normal freeway murderer.

But his arrest didn't happen right away. Before he was caught, police had arrested and the courts had convicted another man venerated with the dubious distinction of having molested and killed more young hitchhikers than any other person in southern California history. He was called the Freeway Killer.

14

When the squealing from inside the light green Chevy camper van grew loud enough, the plainclothes officers scrambled, aiming a half-dozen guns at the side and rear doors. As the doors swung wide, a thirty-three-year-old pale, pudgy truck driver from Downey took his hands off the naked bottom of a teenage hitchhiker and raised them high above his head. He knew the drill. He'd been arrested plenty of times before.

The seventeen-year-old boy he'd picked up an hour earlier lay facedown on the floor, his hands cuffed behind his back, still moaning from being sodomized when the cops helped him out onto the pavement behind the Shell Service Station near the Hollywood Freeway.

The boy told police the sex was purely voluntary, the handcuffs were just part of the fantasy, and that the truck driver was not entirely responsible. What he didn't know was that he was fortunate he was still alive.

A couple dozen other teens who'd gotten into William Bonin's van and let him perform his magic handcuff trick on them weren't so lucky. The magic didn't end once the dark, heavyset former cab driver and bartender shoved his manacled prey to the metal floor of the van and forced himself on them. The real squealing began when he pulled their T-shirts off and knotted them around their necks while they squirmed on their bellies, gagging for air. He then calmly reached for a tire iron that he slipped through a sleeve of the T-shirt and used as a tourniquet, slowly shutting off the oxygen to his victims' lungs as well as the blood to their brains.

And he chuckled about it as they each gurgled their last breaths, musing out loud about finding even more victims before he'd gotten rid of the bodies of the last ones.

Bonin's arrest June 11, 1980, shortly before midnight, ended the deranged Vietnam veteran's two-year killing spree in southern California at a time when media hysteria surrounding the Freeway Killer had hit unprecedented highs.

Both Lieutenant Wyatt Hart, spokesman for the Orange County Sheriff's Department, and Lieutenant Dan Cooke, veteran spokesman for the LAPD, issued statement after statement during the twelve months prior to Bonin's arrest, calling the Freeway Killer a creation of the media's exaggeration, not law enforcement's.

Yes, someone was out there picking up young men, raping them, killing them, and leaving their lifeless bodies at the side of the road. And, yes, when Bill Bonin was finally arrested, he became an immediate prime suspect. But to call him *the* Freeway Killer was, well, irresponsible. Patterns and signs and evidence showed that he was probably responsible for many murders, but it was equally likely that he was not the only—or the most prolific—of southern California's highway assassins.

For months, the press had been keeping a box score. Each time a young hitchhiker turned up dead near a freeway, the Associated Press or at least one of the local newspapers picked up the story and added all the others that came before it so that the headlines came out: "Teen-ager May Be the 34th Victim of 'Freeway Strangler'" or "Freeway Killer May Have Claimed 41st Victim." Sound-bite teasers for the eleven-o'clock news on Los Angeles TV delivered the same numbers: Victim 36 discovered in a dumpster, victim 38 found by the roadside. . . .

To investigators who had been tracking the case from victim 1, U.S. Marine Edward Daniel Moore back in 1972, it was deadly clear within hours of his arrest that William George Bonin was *a* freeway killer, but probably not *the* Freeway Killer.

The swarthy, dark-haired psychotic with the deep, piercing shark eyes and smarmy Tom Selleck mustache had been in and out of institutions, jails, and mental hospitals most of his life. His father was an abusive alcoholic who'd beaten him, his mother, and his two brothers. His mother was an overbearing, overly protective co-dependent who'd refused to acknowledge her middle son's constantly escalating antisocial behavior.

Robert Bonin, who'd gambled away the family's home, died an early death from cirrhosis. The other boys had been boxed around by the old man as much as Bill when he was growing up, but neither his younger brother, Paul, nor his older brother, Robert Jr., ever had the trouble Bill had.

Bonin was born in Connecticut but grew up in a white stucco tract home on Angell Street in the Los Angeles suburb of Downey, just a few blocks from the home of singing stars Karen and Richard Carpenter. He was first arrested when he was only ten years old, sent to a detention center, and molested by an older man in charge of youthful offenders. His unstinting, often schizophrenic, interest in pedophilia developed as a teenager according to psychologists who examined him years later. His mother pushed him into an early marriage and coaxed him to do his patriotic duty in Vietnam by joining the army, but he failed miserably at both.

By the time he was twenty-one, Bonin was once again single, a veteran, and a bona fide sexual psychopath. Torrance police arrested him in 1969 with a sixteen-year-old boy in his car, handcuffed and ready for Bonin's favorite pastime. It didn't take long for the district attorney to make a case. Complaints from four other young hitchhikers about a long-haired, easygoing young driver who raped them once he had them in cuffs also turned up in law enforcement files. Bonin was indicted on five counts of kidnapping, four counts of sodomy, and one each of oral copulation and child molesting.

He spent his twenty-second birthday in the Atascadero State Hospital, going through a battery of psychiatric tests. Bonin had a higher than average I.Q. score of 121 and a personality profile that showed he had a dangerous internalized tug-of-war over his mother. Alice Bonin kept him emotionally tied to her apron strings while at the same time she maintained that he was pretty much worthless as a human being. She shrugged off his overriding sexual interest in boys as a curable, transitive aberration.

Bonin spent the next five years in the mentally disordered sex offenders ward at Atascadero. His doctors set him free May 20, 1974, writing on the release order that he was "no longer a danger to the health and safety of others."

It took Bill Bonin just sixteen months to prove them wrong. In September 1975, fourteen-year-old David McVicker hitched a ride from

Westminster to his home in nearby Garden Grove, but the man who picked him up took a detour to an open field. McVicker turned in the seat to ask him where they were going and looked down the barrel of a revolver. The man parked, undressed, ordered McVicker to disrobe, and proceeded to rape him.

Then he took him to McVicker's home and let him off as if nothing much had happened.

His parents both worked, so McVicker sat and rocked and cried inside his empty house for several hours before he called a child abuse hotline. When he contacted his mother at work, she picked him up immediately and went to the Garden Grove police.

"The look in his eye when he raped me scared the hell out of me," he recalled in an Associated Press interview five years later.

McVicker's testimony put Bonin back in prison at the California Men's Facility at San Luis Obispo for three more years, but on October 11, 1978, he was again set free. The parole board put him on eighteen months' probation and admonished him to start his life fresh. On the surface, Bonin appeared to take the board's advice. He got a job driving a truck for $5 an hour at Dependable Drive-Away Company in Montebello, got an apartment in the Kingswood Village complex about a mile away from his parents' house, and found a girlfriend who, he told friends, he took roller skating each Sunday.

But he also made the party circuit with a curious circle of friends and often spent Saturday nights a long way away from either girlfriends or skating rinks.

Everett "Scott" Fraser was twelve years older than Bonin. He was an ex-bank officer who lived in the same apartment complex as Bonin. He liked sports and having a good time with lots of people, whether he knew them all or not, and threw parties almost every night of the week during the first several months after Bonin was released from prison. Bikers, druggies, and ex-cons mixed freely with rootless young men and curious high school coeds who drifted in and out of Fraser's front room. It was inevitable that Bonin would wind up there sooner or later too.

Fraser also shared Bill Bonin's preferential lust for young men and made no secret of it with his young friend. They traded descriptions of lithe young bodies and the sensual pleasure they each took from sharing intimate moments with males, not females.

But Fraser's hedonism was more fantasy than reality, whereas Bonin's was unrelenting and insatiable.

One day in August 1979, ten months after he was released from prison, Bonin called Fraser from the Orange County Jail. Sheriff's deputies had caught him molesting a seventeen-year-old boy in the coastal community of Dana Point. It ought to have been a parole violation, but a records error at the jail put Bonin back out on the street.

As Fraser drove him home, Bonin told him that he had finally learned from his mistakes, but the exact words that he used to express what Fraser interpreted as remorse came back in later years to haunt Bonin's party pal.

"No one's going to testify again," he told Fraser as they drove the short distance north on the Santa Ana Freeway from the jail to Bonin's home in Downey. "This is never going to happen to me again."

Fraser didn't connect what his young friend was saying with anything as radical as murder at the time. That didn't come until much later.

Fortunately, Bonin hadn't learned enough from his past run-ins with the law to silence all of his potential or actual victims with a T-shirt and a tire iron, or to remain modestly silent about his sexual exploits. For Bonin, murder was group sport: it wasn't nearly as much fun if you did it alone all of the time. He wanted company.

It was another seventeen-year-old who tipped off the Freeway Killer task force nine months later to an incident that put Bonin under surveillance and, in less than two weeks, led to his arrest.

Billy Pugh accepted a ride home from a party with Bonin late one Friday night in March of 1980 and almost immediately the heavyset truck driver asked the boy if he wanted to have sex. The teenager panicked, stammered, and at a stoplight, he later told police, tried jumping out of the van. But Bonin angrily caught him by the neck and pulled him back in. The boy sat back in the seat in cold fear. As Bonin drove over the city streets, he seemed to get over his momentary irritation and began chatting pointedly about picking up young hitchhikers on Friday and Saturday nights, getting his rocks off with them, and using their own shirts to strangle them to death. Bonin's delivery was so matter-of-fact it left the boy speechless.

"If you want to kill somebody, you should make a plan and find a place to dump the body before you pick a victim," he explained to the boy.

Perhaps because he knew he had been seen by others leaving a party with the younger man and perhaps because he believed that he had successfully recruited the teenager as a co-conspirator in his murder game, Bonin let him off at a house that the boy said was his. It was not Pugh's home, however, he told police. He had no intention of letting Bonin know where he lived. He waited in the driveway until the van had left and then ran home like a kangaroo rat who has just escaped a rattler.

It wasn't until two months later, when Pugh was being held at a juvenile detention center for car theft, that he told a counselor about the incident. The counselor informed police, who passed on the tip to LAPD homicide sergeant John St. John. After questioning Pugh, St. John knew he had something more substantial than another one of the hundreds of media-driven Freeway Killer sightings or "death van" rumors that came into one or another of southern California's dozens of police agencies every week.

He assigned surveillance of Bonin, beginning June 2, 1980. The team didn't begin tailing him early enough in the day, however, to save eighteen-year-old Steve Wells.

At about dusk on Monday, June 2, Bonin's last victim was waiting at a bus stop near El Segundo Boulevard and Main Street in south central Los Angeles. The tall, slightly built eighteen-year-old had just finished his shift at the print shop where he worked. Five hours later, two brothers from Long Beach stopped at a Mobil service station in Huntington Beach to fix a flat tire, walked out back behind the garage, and found a naked, six-foot corpse with light brown hair and blue eyes, wedged between a truck and a chain-link fence.

In chilling testimony delivered at Bonin's trial eighteen months later, Steve Wells's last moments were spelled out in grim detail by James Munro, one of four accomplices who helped Bonin in one or more of the twenty-one killings he was eventually accused of committing.

Munro, who agreed to tell his story in exchange for being allowed to plead to second-degree murder, explained how he and Bonin picked Wells up at the bus stop and brought him to Bonin's parents' home. Munro helped hold him down while Bonin tied Wells up with clothesline, took his wallet, sodomized him, and then used Wells's own T-shirt to strangle him. Together, they loaded the body back into the van around nine P.M. and drove to the nearby home of another of Bonin's friends, Vernon Butts.

A self-styled magician whose apartment resembled a Halloween costume shop, Butts came to the door in a Darth Vader cape carrying an iridescent white sword. His coffee table was an inverted coffin and strobe lights flashed on an eerie, cavelike living room with artificial spiders hanging from the ceiling and heavy metal playing from the stereo. Bonin invited Butts to "come look what we did" in the van.

After he showed off the body, Bonin asked Butts's advice: dump the body "in the canyons where the other bodies are" or someplace nearby?

Butts told him it was too late, the canyons were too far away, and that they might get caught roaming around with a dead body in the back of the van at daybreak, which could be very dangerous, given the mass hysteria whipped up by the media and the stepped-up vigilance of the cops.

Munro remembered Butts's answer: "'Try a gas station like'—or 'where,' I don't know which—'we dumped the last one.'"

Back in the confined space of the van, Wells's body had begun to throw off the fetid odor of death, so Bonin and Munro rolled down the windows and hung their noses outside as they set out looking for a suitable dump site. They stopped at McDonald's for hamburgers and paid for them with $10 from Wells's wallet. After they unloaded the body, they drove back to Bonin's parents' house and switched on the TV. They munched burgers while flipping around the dial in search of bulletins about the Freeway Killer's latest victim turning up behind a Huntington Beach gas station.

Bonin bit into his Big Mac, looked at the ceiling, and said, "Thanks, Steve," according to Munro. Then he looked at the floor and added, "Thanks, Steve, wherever you are."

"He started laughing and I started laughing too," Munro said in his courtroom testimony.

In the summer of 1980, Randy Kraft had arrived.

After years of uncertainty and experimenting, he was a full-fledged, up-and-coming young urban professional—or, as magazines would form the acronym a few years later, a yuppie. He and Jeff were homeowners in a modest but upscale section of Long Beach. Jeff was doing very well in his own right with his Belmont Shore goldmine, Grandma's Sugar Plums specialty chocolate shop. And Randy was a suit-and-tie troubleshooter for Lear Siegler Industries. Not a computer consultant, but an on-the-payroll data-processing expert complete with his own expense account, subordinates, and travel allowance. Randy began to make plans to enroll in the University of Southern California's M.B.A. program the following year so he could climb even higher up the ladder of success.

He traded in the old Mustang for a brand new sporty Toyota Celica that he proudly parked out front in the driveway for the neighbors to drool over. He began to become active in gay politics, using his new Erhard Seminar Training assertiveness skills to overcome his residual inhibitions about his homosexuality and get the message out to friends and neighbors to vote against the anti-gay Proposition 6 proposal to keep homosexuals out of government jobs in California.

On the home front, Randy's father had developed high blood pressure and heart trouble and his mother was studying astrology. Randy stayed away as much as possible, though he played the dutiful son and did go home for birthdays and some of the holidays. Increasingly, however, he spent holiday seasons with Jeff's family whose acceptance of their son's life-style seemed unconditional. Randy was a part of the family, just as much as Jeff's older sister's husband.

Randy did continue to visit his oldest sister at every opportunity. Kay was still teaching while her new husband, Don Plunkett, worked as an accountant. They honeymooned in Hawaii and couldn't stop talking about it years afterward. Randy made a mental note to take Jeff there someday, though their own immediate sights were set for Europe.

Randy's new job satisfied his passion for travel. He traveled to the Bay area for Lear Siegler, carrying out programming chores in Silicon Valley and, in the summer of 1980, he got his first out-of-state assignment in Oregon, working out a computer system for Lear Siegler subsidiary Peerless Trailers in Tualitin, just outside of Portland.

It was while he was there that news broke of the capture of the Freeway Killer. Jeff and a number of the Friday Night Poker group were pretty excited about it, relaying the information as it unfolded to Randy. At one point shortly after William Bonin was arrested, a well-respected gay activist organization offered $50,000 for information leading to the arrest of the Freeway Killer. A supermarket chain had already pledged $30,000 to the reward fund. But southern California's growing gay community was feeling the pinch from negative publicity surrounding the gay life in general as a result of the Bonin incident, so the donation contributed by the gay-oriented Great Outdoors carried with it this admonition from its president, Greg Carmack: "There's quite a bit of concern that, as we get into the summer, hysteria in the community from the murders is creating a backlash against the gay community. People are misdirecting their rightful upsettedness against the wrong people and we as an important part of California society feel a responsibility to make our resources available."

But Randy's concern and interest in the set of events unfolding near his home was muted at best. He was a thousand miles away from the Freeway Killer frenzy that had hit southern California, after all. The comparatively benign mood of northern Oregon with its unhurried pace and friendly people was a natural tranquilizer to Kraft—a man who had grown up with the fearful daily froth whipped up by the *Los Angeles Times* and the Eyewitness News Team. Someday, it might be nice to retire to the Oregon woods.

In the summer of 1980, though, his only real concern was to get the computer system up and running for Peerless, so that his blossoming reputation as a "can do" computer technician at Lear Siegler would grow even stronger in the years ahead.

The capture of the Freeway Killer was the last thing Randy Kraft had to worry about.

Michael O'Fallon mailed his last word home to Golden, Colorado, from British Columbia. He addressed the postcard, featuring a color picture of Mount Robson, the tallest mountain in the Canadian Rockies, to Mary Jo Halfin, his mother, as well as to his brother and sister. It arrived the last week in July, several days after the Oregon state police called to tell Mary Jo about Michael's death.

"Just entered British Columbia after spending a couple of days in Jasper and Banff national parks," he wrote to his mother, his kid brother Kevin, and his little sister Jeannie. "The people there were great, and the mountains and glaciers were gorgeous. Now we're on Highway 5 heading toward Kamloops—destiny unknown. Money decreasing rapidly. Still riding with Steve from Fort Collins. Stopped for shower. Bye, love, Mike."

A man hauling beans to a cannery found the body on the northbound Talbot onramp of the Interstate 5 highway, about ten miles south of Salem, at approximately 4:15 A.M. on July 17, 1980. He stopped because he thought he saw a stuffed animal in the middle of the road.

But it was the naked body of a boy whose hands had been bound behind his back with shoelaces. His ankles were also tied, pulled up behind his thighs and secured to the same laces that secured his hands. A separate cord was tied around his scrotum and secured to the ties which bound his hands and feet.

At seventeen, Michael Sean O'Fallon became Marion County murder case 772007. He had been strangled to death.

"He graduated from high school and wanted to see some of the country before he went to college in the fall," his mother told the Oregon homicide investigators who came to visit after she buried her son in Mount Olivet Cemetery. "He took a backpack and a sleeping bag and a tent. He didn't want to take a car, so he hitchhiked. His intention was to go to Canada."

He did make it as far as Canada and was on his way down the Pacific Coast, heading toward California, when he picked the wrong person to ride with. Somewhere in northern Oregon, he met a driver who gave him a drink or two along with a near-toxic dose of Valium and Tylenol, according to the autopsy lab report.

Everything he had with him when he first thumbed his way out of Colorado disappeared: his hiking boots, his backpack, his identification, the camera that his mother had bought during a trip to Mazatlán the previous year.

All Mary Jo had left to help remember her first-born son's final days was a picture postcard from the Canadian Rockies that arrived in the mailbox one ironic week too late to match the breathless exuberance of his words. For several years after, the only phrases that kept echoing all too true as she read the lines over and over again were "destiny unknown" and "Bye, love, Mike."

It was more than the mother of John Doe Oregon had to remember her son by, though.

Marion County murder case 772008 was opened just two hours after Michael O'Fallon was found on the Interstate, when a truck driver on his way to work spotted a man in his thirties lying on the gravel shoulder of I-15 about a mile south of Woodburn, Oregon.

He was fully dressed and still warm to the touch when police arrived, but he wore no belt and had no laces in his high-top shoes. He'd been drinking and had a near toxic level of Valium and Tylenol in his system, but he died of ligature strangulation.

Pictures were taken, clothing cataloged, and red carpet fibers plucked off his trousers and tagged away as possible evidence before any effort was made to find out who he was. Like Michael O'Fallon, he'd been seen hitchhiking on the freeway a few hours earlier, but nobody was ever able to give him a name.

Throughout the year before and after the arrest of Bill Bonin, dozens of stories appeared in the southern California media, document-ing every imaginable aspect of his murder spree. Friends, family, co-workers, psychologists, prosecutors, investigators, civil libertarians, gay activists, Christian fundamentalists all held forth in print or over the airwaves, speculating on the elements that went in to creating a Freeway Killer.

Ironically, the stories themselves were one element.

Bonin collected news clippings about his latest victims and kept them in the glove compartment of his car. He would show up at his job the morning after a body had been discovered with a grin on his face and a deep sigh for his fellow employees.

"He did it again," he would say. "They found another one, a strangler victim."

Munro was just as obsessed with the secondhand reports of the Freeway Killer's handiwork. His own preoccupation with the latest body drop radio reports almost sounded as if he were vicariously rooting for the murderer. The Freeway Killer would never be caught because "he's too smart," he told his co-workers.

The day after Bonin's arrest, Munro quit his job and moved back to his native Michigan until LAPD homicide detectives went back to get him a month later. It didn't take long for investigators to unravel the loose-knit gang of hedonistic drifters who helped Bill Bonin become the Freeway Killer.

Scott Fraser didn't contact police after Bonin was caught. They contacted him first, after discovering from kids around the neighborhood that Fraser had a well-stocked refrigerator, a laissez-faire attitude about what went on in his apartment, and a close friendship with Bill Bonin.

At first, Fraser didn't believe a word of it. Bonin liked boys and cruised known pickup spots to find the thin, pale, long-haired types that appealed to him the most, but he never struck Fraser as a killer. When the coincidences and probabilities the cops suggested to him became too obvious, too logical, and too certain to merit Fraser's doubt, he told them to start taking notes. He spun a tale of casual partytime depravity that became one more ingredient in the murderous recipe that was William George Bonin.

Fraser supplied enough detail to lay claim to the reward money that had been put up for information leading to the capture of the Freeway Killer. He told of how Bonin had a hypnotic, Pied Piper effect on young wanderers like Munro and impressionable weirdos like Vernon Butts. They, too, blamed Bonin's Rasputin-like spell for their fall from grace.

Gregory Miley was another one of Bonin's worshipful young hangers-on who came by Fraser's apartment for a time. He was a little more easy to explain than the others. The nineteen-year-old odd jobber from Texas had an I.Q. of fifty-six and followed Bonin around like a puppy. Before he ran out of money and returned to Houston in the spring of 1980 to live with his stepfather, Miley happily helped Bonin with a couple of nocturnal projects.

On Saturday night, February 2, 1980, Bonin and Miley picked up fourteen-year-old Charles Miranda hitchhiking down Santa Monica Boulevard toward Hollywood. At 9:15 Sunday morning, Miranda's strangled, naked body was found lying next to a trash bin in an industrial area on east Second Street in downtown L.A.

With the focused glint of unrequited blood lust in his eyes, Bonin turned the "death van" south and found twelve-year-old James McCabe standing on a street corner in Huntington Beach that same Sunday afternoon. His ninety-seven-pound body was found three days later in a new home construction site in the city of Walnut fifty miles away, strangled, beaten, and naked from the waist down.

Fraser's recollections also raised questions about Billy Pugh, the first witness to tie Bonin to the Freeway Killer murder spree. Pugh knew Bonin better than he initially let on, according to Fraser. Pugh did not simply ride home from a party listening to Bonin's fearful tales of murder and get out of the van never to see Bonin again.

On March 25, after Miley was on his way back to Houston, Billy Pugh accompanied Bill Bonin on one of his chicken hawk expeditions. Harry Turner, a fifteen-year-old runaway from the desert community of Lancaster, turned up naked and dead at the rear delivery door to a west Los Angeles business the next morning. There was blood around his testicles and bite marks were on his chest. Someone had whacked his head eight times with a blunt instrument, but he died of strangulation.

Pugh had simply gone along for the ride, but the ride cost him six years' imprisonment for voluntary manslaughter.

Miley, who testified against Bonin, got twenty-five years to life for helping Bonin kill Charles Miranda.

Munro, the first of Bonin's accomplices to testify against his former hero, was sentenced to fifteen years to life for his role in the murder of Steve Wells.

But Vernon Butts, the tall, wan magician with the sad green eyes and the faintly Draculian obsession with death, paid the highest price for his role as Bonin's alter ego. At six-foot-three and 130 pounds, the twenty-three-year-old porcelain-factory worker with the long stringy blond hair went along on six of the murders.

An eerie figure even when he wasn't in costume, Butts fancied himself an undiscovered entertainer with a penchant for black magic. His business cards read: "Vern Butts, Magician for All Occasions. Stage Shows. Parties."

Until he was fired for his sloppy appearance and increasingly strange behavior, Butts had been a sales clerk in the Knott's Berry Farm magic store. For over a year before he met Bonin, he hired his talents out to private parties at $30 a show. He was a dungeonmaster in the complex teen fantasy game Dungeons and Dragons and used a coffin as a telephone booth in his apartment, as well as for a coffee table.

Once, he boasted to friends, he turned the coffee table over and made love to his girlfriend, a self-proclaimed witch, inside the coffin.

Butts was as fascinated and terrified by Bill Bonin as he was by death itself. When he teamed up with Bonin, he admitted in court testimony that he was "hypnotized" by the silky-smooth evil tone in Bonin's voice. But at first Butts thought it might be just a lot of talk. He didn't really believe Bonin would carry through with his boasts. He learned differently the first time he drove the van while Bonin selected his hitchhiker *du jour*.

He liked them slender, long-haired, and young. Once he had them inside, Butts helped Bonin tie them up and sodomize them. He admitted running a coat hanger up one victim's rectum, but swore that his participation in the torture didn't go beyond that. Most of the time, Butts remained at the wheel, cruising through the urban night and watching Bonin perform live sadomasochistic pornography in the rear-view mirror.

"He really loved those sounds of screams," Butt said. "He loved to hear 'em scream. . . . He loved every minute of it."

They picked up nineteen-year-old Darin Kendrick from a street corner near Knott's Berry Farm late one April night in 1980 and brought him back to Butts's apartment. Bonin and Butts wrestled Kendrick to the floor, tied him up, forced themselves on him, and made him drink chloral hydrate, the active ingredient in knockout drops. While Kendrick was fading out, Bonin finished him by gleefully wringing his neck. Then he rammed an ice pick in his right ear, Butts recalled.

They dumped his body behind a warehouse in Carson.

Another time they picked up a seventeen-year-old West German hitchhiker, trussed him up in orange nylon cord and ignition wire, and drove him home. After he strangled him, Bonin stabbed the body more than seventy times. An investigator who later discovered the body in the Santa Monica mountains likened the bloody results to "a rabid dog who has gone mad and does not know when to stop biting."

When he first confessed his part in Bonin's two-year odyssey of freeway terror, Butts told Los Angeles Sheriff's deputies that it had been "a good little nightmare."

But Bill Bonin's nightmare magic turned as bitter for Vernon Butts as any other deal with the devil. At year's end, his confession was released to the public and the lurid details of his part as Satan's chauffeur, listening to the muffled screams behind the driver's seat in the death van, made front page news.

On January 11, 1981, a jail deputy making his routine bed check at the Los Angeles County Central Jail found Butts lying on the floor of his cell with one end of a towel twisted into a noose around his neck and the other end tied to a towel rack three and a half feet off the ground.

The coroner ruled his death a suicide.

Exactly fourteen months later, Los Angeles Superior Court judge William Keene sentenced Bonin to die in the gas chamber for the murder of ten young men and boys.

"He had a total disregard for the sanctity of human life and the dignity of a civilized society," Keene said when pronouncing sentence. "Sadistic, unbelievably cruel, senseless, and deliberately premeditated," he said. "Guilty beyond any possible or imaginary doubt," he said.

Bonin propped one elbow on the defense table and rested his chin in his hand as he listened, but offered not a word in his own defense. He had already spoken, both in court and jailhouse interviews with the press, and it had only gotten him in deeper trouble, if that was possible. Reporters had deluged him with interview requests and he had obliged a handful of them, only to discover that their idea of a Freeway Killer was some all-encompassing predator who was now off the streets of Los Angeles and safely tucked away in his jail cell.

Bonin just laughed.

He might be guilty of some of the killings, and even bragged a bit about it on tape with KCBS-TV news reporter Dave Lopez. But the suggestions in some of the clippings he kept in his glove compartment that, somehow, he was responsible for all of the forty-two unsolved murders dating back to 1972 amused and, at the same time, griped him. He had been in prison or the sex felons' ward at Atascadero nine out of the previous twelve years. Besides, Bonin was openly offended by the degrading intemperance shown by the killer or killers who he knew to be his silent competition on the southern California highways.

"I don't cut the dicks off little boys," he huffily told one interviewer.

No one believed a word he said by the time his case went to trial. Bill Bonin was a monster with no more credibility than Charles Manson or Mephistopheles.

But Bill Bonin knew the truth: he might be a killer, but the title of Freeway Killer was one he must ultimately share.

Over lunch on Thursday afternoon, the twenty-first of August 1980, at San Diego's London Opera House, Assistant Controller Ben Wroblewski picked at his salad while he gave Randy Kraft a rundown of the computer needs of Accurate Elastimer Products.

The well-kempt young man sitting across the table from him had just returned a few weeks before from another subsidiary of the Lear Siegler Industries family up near Salem, Oregon. Dan Shobe from corporate headquarters in Santa Monica had nothing but glowing reports about this Randy Kraft, who had been doing consulting work off and on for LSI for several months before Shobe decided to take a chance and put him permanently on payroll.

It was one of the smartest moves he'd made. Randy got on well with everybody above and below him in the corporate hierarchy. He wrote crisp, to-the-point memos, and could carry on a decent conversation, whether it be about data processing or office gossip.

Before Kraft had even been with the company for six months, Shobe felt confident enough to praise his analytical approach and his "excellent problem-solving skills."

"A self-starter, Randy works well with little supervision and accepts any assignment cheerfully," Shobe wrote in an appraisal of his newest find.

The tanned, bright-eyed programmer sitting across from Wroblewski was definitely one to watch. As he launched into the problems he was having with the LSI computer accounting setup at Accurate Elastimer, the LSI Rubber Products Division, Wroblewski could tell Randy Kraft was as articulate and up to speed on MAPICS and the IBM System/34 as Shobe had promised.

Randy listened intently, injecting his comments from time to time, but his mind wasn't solely on Wroblewski's spreadsheet problems. He was also thinking about the drive back to Long Beach and a moonlighting job he had to do.

Ambition and money powered Randy at the time, and he wasn't so entrenched in the LSI corporate family that he wanted to turn down $25 an hour to handle some weekend programming. Dan Neuhar, who owned a small greeting card and novelty items company in Los Angeles, hired him to set up a software system for his business before Shobe ever offered Randy the LSI job.

Wroblewski might get Saturday off, but Randy had to work. He finished his coffee and drove back north from San Diego that Thursday afternoon with Neuhar's computerized inventory job on his mind. He would have to get right on it as soon as he finished up another pair of appointments he had the next day at two more LSI subsidiary companies: Anchorlok in Torrance in the morning and Energy Products in Santa Ana in the afternoon.

Randy put the rental car in gear and zipped through the light midweek traffic, out to the long, clean strip of highway that hugged the ocean for fifty miles, all the way to southern Orange County.

It had been over a year since he and Jeff bought their Roswell Avenue home. The mortgage payments were steep and the hours they spent together far too few. But it seemed all worth it when they found a few moments to work out in the garden together, sit around the fireplace in the front room watching cable TV, or take in an outdoor summer concert. Jeff still wore his souvenir T-shirt from the Village People's one-night stand at the Greek Theater. THE VILLAGE PEOPLE GO GREEK! it read. Jeff was a scamp.

Randy's guess about computer programming back in 1975 turned out to be right on the money—with an emphasis on the word *money*. He and Jeff could afford to go to the Hollywood Bowl or the Shubert or the Greek with some regularity. Shobe put Randy on the LSI payroll at $30,000 a year. Add in his freelance programming income and Jeff's profits from the burgeoning Belmont Shore candy business and you were talking about something in excess of $50,000 a year—twice what most middle class families earned in 1980.

The warm summer air and sandy beaches along the wide open Pacific Coast Highway between San Diego and southern Orange County reflected Randy's own warm, wide-open attitude about life in the '80s. Hard work and perseverance—the Protestant ethic that his sister Kay had taught him so many years before in Presbyterian Sunday school—turned out to be the keys to success and happiness after all.

Off to the left, the sun dipped low on the horizon. It would soon sink into the cloudless Pacific. Off to the right, Randy would soon be passing Camp Pendleton, where off-duty marines lucky enough to swing a three-day pass would just be leaving the main gate, looking for some way to spend money and excess energy on a long summer's liberty weekend.

Yes, life was good for Randy Kraft. He was a busy man, a driven man—some might even say an overachiever or a workaholic. But he was a satisfied man too. Most of the time.

The Orange County robbery-homicide detail wasn't particularly stunned with the news.

Everyone had sort of halfway hoped that Lieutenant Hart was wrong and that William Bonin and his band of loonies were, in fact, the whole Freeway Killer gang. After all, since they had been rounded up and tossed in the slammer in June, there hadn't been any more reported murders. Jim Sidebotham, George Troup, and all the rest of the rank and file who had worked the case for eight years crossed their fingers that 1980 would be the first summer in several years where bodies weren't popping up on freeway offramps or discovered collecting flies in some gully off of the Ortega Highway.

Summer vacation unofficially ended on Labor Day, so technically they got their wish.

Two days later, though, some children were playing one morning at the end of Paseo Sombra in a new housing tract near the El Toro Marine Air Base. They found a dark green trash bag dumped in the gutter with something so foul inside that they had to breathe through their mouths just to get near it. If they had been old enough to know what carrion was, they might not have gone any nearer.

When they peeked, what they saw was far worse than what they'd smelled. There was real terror in their shrieks as they raced home to tell their mothers of the kneeling remnants of a man, encased in plastic and all folded up together in a ball, like a newborn baby.

Pathologists got to see even more horror: flesh and bones and a cracked purple face, all bloated up like a mask with a gaping O for a mouth and the faintest hint of a horror-movie smile.

The coroner guessed that Robert Wyatt Loggins, Jr., known to his friends as Wyatt, had been hogtied and bunched up like a large, aborted fetus in the plastic trash sack for at least three or four days before the children found him. It was all but impossible to determine just what it was that had killed him. The skin that wasn't as dry as beef jerky had grown far too rancid even to fix how long he'd been dead. Maybe a few days—perhaps as long as a week.

The last people who saw him alive remembered how badly Loggins wanted to get out and party. Until Friday, August 22, the nineteen-year-old U.S. Marine had spent the best part of the southern California summer restricted to Barracks 134, Marine Corps Air Station, Santa Ana. He got violent when he was drinking and he liked to drink often, according to fellow marines. That's how he got restricted in the first place: a drunken brawl at the Miramar Naval Station down in San Diego at the beginning of summer.

After several thirsty weeks, Loggins gathered up buddies Jim Maddux and Pete Rachels, bought a bottle of Southern Comfort, and drove out to Laguna Canyon Road to do some serious celebrating that Friday night. They cruised around for a while before they ended up at a liquor store across the street from the Huntington Beach pier. They fancied themselves studs on the prowl and there was always the chance that they might come across some wahines in heat on that warm summer's eve.

But their primary mission—or at least Loggins's primary mission—was a good, heavy drunk to make up for the dry weeks on the base. The other marines couldn't keep up with him, though, and had to be back at the base for duty the following day. By midnight, when they were ready to leave, Loggins was riproaring.

When they got ready to go, Loggins didn't. Both Maddux and Rachels knew what an exercise in futility it was to order Loggins to do anything, even when he was sober. He swore and swung his arms, raving his displeasure at the world in general. This night, however, he wasn't angry.

"He was determined to spend the night on the beach," Rachels said.

He and Maddux left Loggins weaving south, down Pacific Coast Highway, looking for a place to sleep it off. They never knew whether he found it or not.

On the stainless steel morgue table a week and a half later, the medical examiner unfolded the body as best he could, discovering a sock next to the rectum and a cord around the neck. Loggins's blood alcohol level was .25, but even blood sheltered deep inside a body that has been baking like an apple in the sun for days can register a higher alcohol level than the victim actually drank. It was far more likely that what Loggins had drunk, mixed with therapeutic doses of two different kinds of antihistamine he had swallowed, had done him in. On the death certificate, the medical examiner wrote out a cause of death due to acute intoxication from the ingestion of ethanol, chlorphenaramine, and diphenhydramine.

As the examination of Loggins's body continued, one patch of skin appeared to be intact. A tiny red devil was permanently etched onto his right shoulder—a tattoo he'd had done during one of the great drinking bouts Robert Wyatt Loggins Jr. experienced during his short, angry life. In a scroll right below the red imp was a motto that seemed to sum up Loggins: DAZED AND CONFUSED.

The coroner's office officially labeled his death accidental. It wasn't refiled as a homicide until nearly three years later.

15

Dan Shobe knew a fast-tracker when he saw one, and he saw one in Randy Kraft.

In less than six months, the modest freelancer Lear Siegler had lured on board on a hunch had become a dynamo. He was a natural-born teacher in addition to being a crack programmer and troubleshooter. Put him in charge of a handful of operators who didn't know System/34 from a fire hydrant, who thought MAPICS had something to do with the motion picture industry—and, voilà! Kraft had them humming through program applications like pros in a day or less.

A supervisor would start to suggest that he try a different, more efficient approach to a problem only to find that Randy had already thought of it and gone right ahead and put it to work.

And he smiled that enigmatic, Mona-Lisa-with-a-mustache smile every time anyone asked him to handle something. No back talk. No grousing. Just a refreshing can-do attitude.

He commuted often from his Long Beach home, spending a great deal of time at the Peerless Trailer Division near Portland during the early '80s. What he managed to do among the computer illiterate there was nothing short of a miracle.

"We were floundering. We needed an expert programmer," said Jean Geddis, a young data-entry employee who developed a crush on Kraft. "Randy was attractive in that this old Oregon girl sees the California boy, so dapper, always looking sharp. He was someone you cared to be with."

163

Like many of the other younger employees, they went out for popcorn and beer after work once in a while and sarcastically discussed upper management. Randy might have been sent in by corporate-level executives to get the Peerless computer work force on track, but he came off to the people he was supervising like just one of the gang. Jean even did her best to get asked out, dropping little hints and enunciating her very best body language. She didn't know, and Randy never let on, that he was gay.

"My memory of Randy was that he was sort of passive," said Dana Lee, who worked with Kraft at the Lear Siegler subsidiary outside of Portland, as Randy spent more and more time troubleshooting for the company in Oregon.

"He was very much given to mediation and working problems out," said Lee.

After work, he socialized with Randy too. They were both young, single males and Dana didn't mind sharing a beer with him. Kraft had to spend long spans of time away from home and Lee sympathized with him. Once, he invited Randy to a tennis tournament at the Portland Coliseum, where Lee did a little moonlighting as a match umpire. Dana brought his financée along. Randy came alone.

"More than anything, I guess I saw him as a friend," said Lee. "I felt like Randy was someone that was not far from what I saw in myself."

Lee remembered one particularly hard case at Peerless—an older woman who had been with the industrial truck and tractor manufacturer for several years and consistently turned out mediocre work. Peerless's top management had given Kraft carte blanche to crack down on incompetence, but Randy chose a more diplomatic approach. He sat down with her and, step by step, walked through the program with her, showering her with praise each time she did anything correctly.

He was a very smooth manager of people. Kraft appeared just as deferential in the daily staff meetings.

"Randy probably appeared to be passive in the meetings, but he was giving everyone time to state their own problems," Jean Geddis remembered. "He allowed the other people to create the problem and he solved it."

Shobe had no problem at all recommending his prize programmer when Randy came asking for a raise. He'd spent weeks and weeks away from home, living out of Portland motels and driving rented cars, with very few complaints. The employees loved him and so did the Peerless management team, which didn't have much positive to say about its operation in 1981, when the Oregon recession had finally hit home, forcing layoffs and a general fear that the entire subsidiary might have to be closed.

Besides, Randy showed the same initiative in asking for more money that he demonstrated when he was working: a quiet, friendly determination—assertive, but never angry.

"It is my opinion that Randy is an exceptional employee and, as such, deserves exceptional treatment," Shobe wrote in a memo dated February 23, 1981. "I request your consideration for a merit salary increase in the immediate future and trust that such an increase would not impact his annual review in June. Thank you for your attention in this matter. Sincerely, Dan Shobe."

Duane Cluck had been a machinist for Jorgenson Steel for nearly twenty years and he didn't even earn $20 an hour. What made his smart aleck seventeen-year-old son think he could pull down that kind of change as an unskilled oilfield roughneck? In the spring of 1981, that's what Mike Cluck told his old man—not once, but over and over. There was more than one shouting match over the subject in the front room of the Clucks' home in the Seattle suburb of Kent, Washington.

"You couldn't tell him nothing," Duane said sadly. "He was seventeen."

Duane and Rosalie Cluck got married and got a house on Black Diamond Road eleven miles outside of Seattle nearly three years before their first child, Michael, was born in 1963. They were responsible young adults and set out to fulfill the American Dream in the prescribed manner during the short-lived era of the New Frontier. Duane got a job as a machinist at Jorgenson Steel and Rosalie became a homemaker to rival Donna Reed, Barbara Billingsley, or any of the other TV moms of the '60s.

But Duane remained cool in the high school sense of the word years before his only son ever understood that *cool* was a word with meaning beyond temperature.

Michael Cluck's old man was a drag racer—a real pioneer in the sport. The family photo album showed Duane in his Navy days, down in southern California during the late '50s, when the summer months at the Los Angeles County Fairgrounds were punctuated by the sounds of squealing tires and the acrid smell of hot Valvoline. It was a grand memory that aged into something more mellow and comforting than the reality of sweaty Sunday afternoons in the pits. In retelling it to his son, Duane forgot that spinning wheels kicked up the kind of dust that rims the nostrils and makes molars grind like wet emery boards.

Hotshots like Duane Cluck revved their flathead six engines past the 40,000-rpm mark in an ancient time when there was no such thing as a built-in dashboard tachometer. They used to get high on beer and gasoline fumes. That was all that anybody needed back then.

Then came fatherhood.

"I gave up drag racing in '71, but I still have a one-of-a-kind Corvette out in the garage," Duane said. "I get along with other kids in the neighborhood real good. Everybody comes up to see it."

It was a '75 Corvette Duane had customized himself: a foot wider and three feet longer than the stock model. And his teenage son, who should have been beaming, seemed like he could have cared less. It didn't frost Duane that Mike didn't look up to the old man that much for his customizing accomplishment. It did stick in the craw a bit when the rest of the Kentwood High guys would come by the house and want to see the Corvette and Mike just kind of shrugged the whole thing off.

"We just didn't relate," he said. "Mike looked at me as part of the Establishment and we didn't get along. You know, high school does funny things to you. It's different from when I was in school. Lots of peer pressure. And Michael was a follower, not a leader."

Mike Cluck didn't get in trouble, but he didn't fare well in school either. Against his father's advice, he dropped out in his junior year. He played a little guitar, loafed around the house, spent hours on the phone with giggling young women who hung on his every word. If there had ever been a chance that Duane or Rosalie ever acted so ditzy or so irresponsibly in their teens, they had both forgotten it long before the kids were ever born. Duane threatened to put in a pay phone if Michael didn't knock off the marathon phone calls and do something with his life.

In March of 1981, the year that Mike should have been a high school senior, he went to southern Idaho to join the federal government's Youth Corps—a latter-day resurrection of Franklin D. Roosevelt's highly successful Civilian Conservation Corps of the '30s. He figured it would be a grown-up version of the Boy Scouts.

"He tried it out ten days, maybe a week, and it wasn't what he thought it would be," remembered Duane. "So we had to drive over there and pick him up."

Mike was a big, strapping boy by then, with a strong handshake, a shock of blond hair, and a shy smile that disarmed almost everyone he met. Although he seemed deferential, almost passive to his peers, he was headstrong to the point that his parents often felt like screaming when it came to domestic matters. If they said jump, he'd answer no. If they said don't jump, he'd be in the air before the last syllable rolled off their tongues.

After they brought him home from the Idaho backwoods, Mike got a call from Scott Herr, another Kentwood High dropout who had gone down to Bakersfield in southern California to live with his uncle and work in the oilfields. Herr had big-money stories to tell Mike. Roughnecking on one of the San Joaquin Valley rigs was not only romantic as hell, it paid big: $18 to $20 an hour. Someone with muscle enough who could take orders and didn't mind getting a little dirty could pull down $20,000 to $30,000 a year easy.

Twice Mike told his father he was going and twice Duane Cluck talked him out of it. He sat him down on the living room couch and tried mightily to bust through the wall that seemed to separate them: Duane didn't even make that kind of money. What made Mike believe he was going to waltz into some Standard Oil employment office, requisition a hard hat, and start knocking down $200 a day? It was not possible.

One morning in April, when Duane was working the graveyard shift at Jorgenson, he came home from work and found Mike with his red duffel bag packed with everything he owned—shirts, shoes, a shaving kit his grandmother had given him. He was standing on the front porch. He was going, he said stubbornly.

Duane started in. Rosalie came out on the porch and put in her pitch too. How was he going to get there? Hitchhiking was dangerous, he had no car, and flying or taking the train was too expensive.

Duane wasn't so worried about how he planned to get there. Mike was big enough to take care of himself. He was more worried about what would happen to him when he got to Bakersfield and found out that God and Standard Oil don't just hand out $20-an-hour jobs to every dropout who has a winning smile and a husky pair of shoulders.

He knew something about being male and seventeen and having big dreams though. He also knew that he'd tried twice to talk logic to the boy when it was clearly not a logical issue. When he was a young man himself, bumming around southern California while he was in the navy, he used to put out his thumb and catch a ride between Long Beach, where his ship was home-ported, and San Diego, where he trained before shipping out to Korea.

He quietly reached into his back pocket while his wife went on pleading with her only son and pulled out a handful of currency. Mike took it, gave them both a hug, and told them not to worry.

His body was found the next morning outside the Short Mountain landfill on Peebles Road, just off the I-5 freeway near Goshen, Oregon. He was naked from the waist down and his T-shirt had been pulled up to his armpits to expose his chest. Blood, still warm to the touch, had coagulated in a pool around his skull, which had been pounded with a heavy instrument—maybe a rock or a tire iron or a jack handle—at least thirty times, so that the back of his head was the sticky red consistency of half-dried catsup mixed with bits of bone fragments and brain matter.

Blood was all over his body and his face and his clothes too. His anus was ripped and bleeding, and the killer had raked his fingernails over his thighs and groin.

Michael Cluck's resting place was a ditch about five hundred feet off the I-5 freeway. The spring grass was green and high, maybe as tall as a foot in some places, waving in the morning breeze when the Lane County Sheriff's cars showed up shortly after eight A.M. A crime scene photographer took closeups, long shots and medium photos of the body from every disgusting angle. There was an empty pack of Marlboros near the body, a knife with bloodstains on the blade, and some white pills strewn around nearby. They found more in the pockets of Cluck's jacket. They also found a Washington state driver's instruction permit issued to Michael Duane Cluck.

The autopsy turned up a .09 alcohol level and large doses of antihistamines, codeine, and flurazepam in his bloodstream.

Cluck's murder was shocking to local law enforcement for its sheer savagery. The killer obviously had gone into an animal frenzy, kicking and hitting and wreaking a bloody wrath on the dead youth that went far beyond simply murdering him.

But rural Oregon had witnessed its share of inhuman cruelty. Michael Cluck's death was disturbing, but not unprecedented.

"At the time, we looked at two or three locals as suspects because just after the Cluck case we had another individual we found wrapped in a tarp in his own horse barn," said Sergeant John Peckels, one of the first Lane County Sheriff's deputies at the murder scene. "We arrested two people who did him, but they didn't do Cluck."

Duane and Rosalie were heartbroken for a while and then outraged even longer because the Lane County Sheriff's deputies couldn't get even a lukewarm lead on their son's killer.

The awful truth, said Peckels, was that the murderer was just too careful and too clever. Every year, there are one or two unsolved homicides in or around Eugene. Every year, there's a mother or father or some other relative who feels that law enforcement isn't doing enough.

But some crimes really do seem as though they have been committed by a phantom: some evil wraith who swoops in, does his dirt, and moves off without a trace. The murder of Michael Cluck was one of those crimes.

One of the things that happened after he died was a round of warnings of teenage hitchhikers, published in the local newspaper.

"You can't stop it. Most kids hitchhike when they're in school. That's quite common, you know," said Duane Cluck. "They listen to you but they just hear what they want to hear. Kids have big dreams. They'll get to them any way they can."

Mike's friends and former classmates reacted with predictable shock and disbelief. There were outpourings of sympathy, both among Duane's co-workers at Jorgenson and the neighbors up and down Black Diamond Road.

But it all blew over after a while. Mike was in the ground and life went on without him. His younger sister got married. So did his old girlfriend. Duane and Rosalie alone seemed to keep their anger alive.

Mike's friends grew up and moved on too. A new crop moved into the neighborhood, where they heard about Duane Cluck's bitchin' old classic sports car. He talks with them, maybe even a bit more earnestly than he did while Mike was in school and the boy brought his buddies around to check out his cool, drag-racing father. Duane laughs out loud, remembering how ridiculous it was to be able to relate to every other kid in the neighborhood, but not to his own son.

"Kids still come around to see the Corvette," he said. "We do a lot of bullshitting, like we used to—what we call bench rapping."

He sighed, regretting the missed moments he and Mike could have spent bench rapping.

"I guess I'm what the neighborhood kids consider a nice old man," he said.

While the Lane County Coroner's Office was picking up Michael Cluck's body, a few miles away Randy Kraft was carefully driving his rented car to an outpatient clinic at a nearby hospital, putting as little pressure as possible on the bruised big toe of his right foot.

"The joke around the office was that he was chasing a girl around the bed at the Ramada," Jean Geddis remembered. The office gossip extended to the faint scratches that Randy had on his face. Nothing too serious, but prominent enough on his fair, teutonic complexion to provoke some giggles in Peerless Corporation's ladies' room about the possibility that Mr. Southern California Professional might have gotten a little too passionate the night before.

Randy seemed embarrassed by the whole incident and tried to shrug it off as best he could when Geddis and the other young women employees at Peerless teased him about his accident. The story he told them was that he got hungry in the middle of the night, hopped out of bed and tried finding his way to the light switch only to trip over the furniture and stub his toe.

He told the on-duty physician at the clinic a slightly different story: he got out of bed around three A.M. to switch on the TV so that he could watch the Space Shuttle landing and, being in an unfamiliar motel room, tripped and whacked the toe of his kicking foot.

It wasn't serious, but it had been stubbed a good one. The doctor recommended he stay off of it as much as possible and prescribed a phenobarbital compound as a painkiller and sedative to help him sleep.

The toe business put a crimp in his style. Randy liked to drive a lot when he wasn't working, exploring the wineries and the Columbia River gorge area up toward the Dalles and central Oregon, down around Bend. With his injured foot, Randy's natural restlessness made him even more like a caged lion than normal. When he got ordered back down to California, it wasn't a moment too soon.

His next assignment for Lear Siegler was Sierra Electronics in Menlo Park, near Stanford University, where he again worked his magic on the employees.

"I worked closely with Randy for a while," said Sierra programmer Lonny Schwartz. "There was nobody that he did not get along with. He was liked by everyone. People actually looked forward to his visits."

As at Peerless, having some corporate efficiency expert sniffing around normally put the troops into a bunker mentality. But Randy had charm.

"He was very conscious that he was in a sensitive situation. Company people didn't like to see corporate types come around," Schwartz said. But Randy struck his patented shy-guy pose, planted his hands in his front pockets, and came on more like Jimmy Stewart than Attila the Hun.

In a few days, he figured out what was wrong with the Sierra

MAPICS project team and reported back to Lear Siegler headquarters without alienating any of the people who were bogging down the team.

"He could do things in a couple of minutes that I couldn't get through in two days," Schwartz said.

From Shobe's office on down, Lear Siegler managers, new hires and lifer employees were starting to use words like "genius" and "computer whiz kid" to describe Randy Kraft. Besides being brilliant, he worked well under pressure, stayed with a project until it was done, and never complained about overtime.

He was also a social activist and a self-improvement fanatic. His est group got together at Christmas time to gather gifts to give to invalids at convalescent homes, and he continued to monitor local and national political causes, throwing his support increasingly to Democrats who seemed to be more sympathetic to gay causes. He scored high on entrance exams for USC's M.B.A. program, promising Shobe that he would measure up to Lear Siegler's middle management standards for people with post-graduate degrees.

At $31,460.68 a year, he had gone about as far as he could go on the strict corporate salary chart for someone with his background and training. Shobe was pushing to get him more money, but it didn't look promising beyond a 6 percent boost that managers were allowed to give their top employees.

In many ways, Randy was typical of many young people who had protested their way through the '60s, lapsed into a comfortable and hedonistic identity search in the '70s, and didn't really get started in their professional lives until the '80s. They had the ability and a full head of steam, but were not acquainted with the corporate inertia that tends to reward loyalty and longevity over instant results.

Randy was a classic overachiever, almost childlike in an odd way. He wanted his needs, as well as his wants, satisfied immediately. He didn't mind working hard, but he didn't like waiting to be rewarded.

On August 20, 1981, the body of seventeen-year-old Christopher R. Williams was found clothed, except for shoes, socks, and underwear, lying off a mountain road in the San Bernardino mountains southeast of Los Angeles. His nostrils had been stuffed with paper and the cause of death was signed off on the death certificate as pneumonia due to aspiration. He choked to death on his own mucus.

Williams might have been able to move his limbs and pull the paper out of his nose, but he had been drugged to the point that his arms and legs and hands and feet were useless. His body was loaded with the sedative and hypnotic drugs phenobarbital and benzodiazapine.

There might have been more made of the death, but Williams was the kind of victim that the more cynical cops like to refer to as a "misdemeanor murder." He was a male prostitute who worked the bus stops in Hollywood, offering his body or his mouth or his hand in exchange for a few bucks or a place to stay the night. Police weren't so callous as to simply write him off. The case remained open. But the newspapers didn't care enough even to publish a little squib about the body being found, and the leads were virtually nonexistent. Sure, people had seen him out soliciting tricks. He did it every night. Nobody paid attention to whether he was picked up or by whom.

There wasn't much to go on when a prostitute—male or female—wound up dead. In a way, they were just asking for it.

"A driver pulls up, opens his door, waves a $20 bill at them, and they get in. They become the perfect victim," said one veteran homicide detective. There's no connection between killer and victim to trace. Usually the prostitute's family either doesn't care about the victim or they don't know the prostitution is even going on. And once the killer does his deed, the body is dumped far from the scene of the crime with little or no evidence that can be traced back to the murderer.

So it was with Christopher Williams. No fingerprints. No murder weapon. No leads. No suspects. No media outrage.

No investigation.

iriam Phillips found talking
to Randy as easy and as comforting as sharing secrets with an older
brother.

It had always been that way, from the first time they met around
the swimming pool at the Laguna Hills complex where Jeff Seelig and
Randy first shared an apartment back in the mid-'70s. Miriam and her
financée, Russ, liked them from the beginning and invited Randy and Jeff
to their wedding back in New England in 1978. When they settled down
in southern California, they counted the candymaker and the computer
whiz among their closest friends.

The Phillipses understood that the two men were gay and that
theirs was a life-style very different from their own. But there were just
as many striking similarities. As is the case with many heterosexual
relationships, Jeff was the "gregarious, outgoing, friendly" half of the
couple while Randy was "quiet and agreeable," according to Miriam.
The two couples shared dinners and Saturday afternoons and movies
together.

"Jeff and I usually picked the movie. I don't ever remember Randy
getting his way. Let's put it that way," Miriam remembered. "Throughout the years that I've known Randy he's always been very sensitive,
but he's a very easygoing guy."

The Phillipses were looking for a house to buy at about the same
time as Randy and Jeff. They bought in a new tract in El Toro, in
southern Orange County while Randy and Jeff found their fixer-upper in

an older neighborhood in Long Beach, just a block from a high school.

After their housewarming, Russ and Miriam were among the first people Jeff and Randy had over to dinner. They were all young upwardly mobile professionals long before the acronym became a dictionary word. They shared disco music, the *Star Wars* movies, Andrew Lloyd Webber musicals, and a modestly affluent urban life-style in common. If the early '80s represented the Armageddon of the Age of Aquarius, then they were all survivors, bravely moving toward middle age with one eye on their social consciences and the other on their bank accounts.

Miriam liked her friends' new home well enough. Besides the ramshackle doghouse Randy had built for his mangy white mongrel, Max, one of the first things Miriam noticed in the backyard was the vegetable garden. With his own age now creeping past the thirty-five-year mark, Randy preached a healthy sermon of vitamins, exercise and lots of good, wholesome food, especially fresh vegetables. You are what you eat, Randy believed, which made Miriam a walking, talking Mars bar.

Miriam remembered, "When he saw the amount of junk food I continued to accumulate, he would bring me vegetables from his garden: great tomatoes and things. And I remember specifically, one evening we were . . . it might have been a brunch, I'm not sure. He was cutting tomatoes and vegetables at the sink and I was talking about junk food—about trying to get away from that and go for the vegetables. Randy was always very concerned."

Randy revealed to her that he had hypoglycemia, a fluctuating blood sugar imbalance that brought on all sorts of debilitating side effects, ranging from severe headaches to fatigue, irritability, and mood swings. He'd always had the condition, but it hadn't been diagnosed until recently. Miriam confided in him that she had some of those very symptoms and was probably a borderline hypoglycemic herself.

Randy's case was particularly severe, giving him chest pains and insomnia when he didn't eat right. Twinkie lunches and Kentucky Fried Chicken were an invitation to trouble. Of course, only each individual has control over what he eats, he chided Miriam in his most sagacious voice.

As a result of his est conversion, Randy was also becoming a strong believer in psychological counseling and pontificated on its benefits whenever he was given half a chance.

When Miriam became pregnant with her first child, she went

through a stage where she wasn't certain she wanted to have a child. She tried to explain her dread to several people, but it didn't come out right. Nobody seemed to get it. She felt selfish and angry and guilty and afraid, all at once. That's when she turned to Randy.

"We went out to dinner one night and I was trying to explain to him how I was feeling and he sat very patiently and he showed a lot of support," she said.

He told her to see a professional counselor—a step that Miriam rejected out of hand. Counselors were for crazy people and she was not crazy. Randy persisted.

"What he said specifically was where else in life can you get someone to look at you and make no judgment calls on who you are?" Miriam remembered.

She did finally go to a counselor and work through her anxiety. In 1981, she gave birth to a daughter. From that point on when the Phillips family visited Jeff and Randy and Max, there were three of them too: Russ and Miriam and Jenny.

Randy represented a kind of rock to Miriam—a strong, sincere teacher and friend who was always there when he was needed. He was as gentle and compassionate with the new baby as he had been with Miriam, and he demanded nothing from her in return. A gentle yet self-confident soul. Like most of his co-workers and other friends, not once in all the years she knew him did Miriam recall ever seeing Randy truly angry.

Randy was pissed when he got his Lear Siegler employee performance appraisal. He felt like someone had just handed him a report card filled with C's after he'd busted his ass up and down the Pacific Coast for more than a year and a half doing A+ work. He genuinely believed that Dan Shobe had been his friend as well as his supervisor, so he felt betrayed as well as humiliated. Instead of Dan Shobe, the appraisal should have been signed by Brutus Shobe. And Randy told Dan as much—in writing.

"As you know I am in strong disagreement with the latest appraisal you made of my work," his letter began.

Shobe replied that he hadn't rated Randy as outstanding because that would give him nothing to work for.

Randy interpreted Shobe's reluctance to call him "outstanding" as an attempt to oversee Kraft's personal growth, as though Shobe were the parent and Randy the child.

Randy was outraged. All he wanted was to be judged by his performance on the job and to be rewarded accordingly with appropriate merit pay increases and promotions. He did not need Shobe acting as his father too.

"I am exceptionally good and talented at what I do and it leaves me incredulous to believe that there is no upward mobility for such a person within Lear Siegler Industries," he wrote.

Besides his problems at Lear Siegler, Randy was also having trouble with Jeff. As winter turned to spring 1982 was proving to be rocky. They fought and Jeff moved out for a while. No sooner did he come back than it started all over again.

Their age difference probably had something to do with it. Jeff was ten years younger and so were his hormones. Besides being more demanding sexually, Jeff was not as well educated. Randy liked having Jeff look up to him and depend on him for advice about life and love and the world in general, but he craved conversation with his intellectual peers as well. The Friday Night Poker Club crowd satisfied part of that need, but not all of it.

He also began to resent Jeff getting in the last word. Jeff made the plans for both of them, as Miriam Phillips noted, and Randy exercised little say-so over it. Jeff called the shots about what they ate, where they went, what they did. And Randy, though he might grouse about it a little or try putting his foot down, always seemed to give in.

Jeff was a mixed bag of emotions—a real up-and-down personality type in a way—and sometimes it drove Randy nuts. Jeff liked smoking pot, but Randy felt like he was pretty much beyond that stage in his life. He was more worried about growing older and maintaining his health. His stomach was beginning to give him problems, adding to all his hypoglycemia symptoms. He'd watch his diet, get it under control, and then, just as quickly, let it get out of control.

When the ups and downs, mood swings, battles with Jeff, and the job hassles got to be too much, Randy took his own best advice and sought professional counseling help. Through the Krafts' longtime family physician, Dr. Wilson McArthur, he and Jeff began weekly sessions with Sandra Hare, a registered nurse and counselor with Associated Therapists in Huntington Beach.

Following their first appointment on June 22, 1982, she described Jeff as defensive and anxious and concluded that it was difficult for either man to hear what the other was saying.

Her thumbnail sketches boiled the two men down to their bare relationship essences: Randy, the bright, anxiety-ridden older gay with no feelings of attraction to women, who liked control but didn't like to be controlled, and who didn't have the insatiable sex drive that his roommate did. Grew up in Westminster and still visits his family often, but has difficulty describing what his family is like. Not much affection or communication between his parents and seems to idealize his mother over his father. Never attracted much to girls in high school or college.

Jeff, the youngest child of a close-knit Jewish family. Close relationship with—but also rivalry with—an older sister who married and moved to Beverly Hills. He remained somewhat attracted to women and maintained friendships with several women, despite his long-term commitment to Randy.

In a letter thanking Dr. McArthur for referring the pair to her, Sandra analyzed their relationship this way:

"At the moment, neither Jeff nor Randy feels the other partner sees or tries to meet his needs. Age difference, money, and energy level are also some factors entering into their relationship. On the whole, there appears to be a good chance to make some adjustments and changes for the better with these two men."

A month later, on July 27, she had an even better grasp of the issues. The objections Randy was leveling at her during their sessions began to resemble the hurt and frustration of a spouse who suspects his or her mate of having an affair.

Jeff worked long hours at the candy shop and Randy was getting fed up with it. He wanted him home where they could spend more time together. Jeff also had his own network of friends, exclusive of Randy, and sometimes he simply left Randy at home to stew while he went out and had a good time.

Randy felt increasingly like the responsible partner, planning for the future, while Jeff acted flaky and lived only for the moment. Just as Miriam Phillips had said, Randy was the rock, always there for advice and comfort and calm, commonsense suggestions.

At any rate, that's what he told Sandra Hare the last week of July.

The last week of July was hot and dry in Los Angeles. In the afternoons, a little sea breeze might waft in off the ocean or a Santa Ana might kick up through the Cahuenga Pass, but it did little to bring the temperature down. Sometimes, if the wind came in from the ocean along the concrete spillway of the Los Angeles River, it caught the rank stench from the Vernon slaughterhouses right at sunset and settled like a beefy blanket of death over the central city.

That's what the predominantly Hispanic residents along the 1400 block of Bellevue Avenue in the Echo Park section of Los Angeles thought they were smelling at first. But it got worse every day and, by the time the odor was strong enough to make mothers and toddlers physically ill when they stepped out on the sidewalk, it seemed too close by to blame on Jimmy Dean Sausage or Farmer John. Neighbors began talking to neighbors and started a phone campaign to find out what it was.

The LAPD Ramparts Division kicked the series of phone complaints over to CalTrans and asked them to see if, maybe, a dog had been hit on the Hollywood Freeway and crawled into the weeds to die.

A CalTrans cleanup crew found something dead all right, buried under some leaves and dirt in a landscaped area next to the south Rampart Boulevard offramp of the Hollywood Freeway. It weighed thirty-eight pounds and wore one Nike tennis shoe. It also had on jeans and underwear and green and white socks and a black Derby jacket over a blue T-shirt. In the pockets of the jeans were a green Afro-style comb and a Vicks inhaler.

It had been a thirteen-year-old boy from the northern California town of Pittsburg, visiting relatives in Echo Park several weeks before. Now, as the crew members held their breath in order to get close enough for a look, it had been reduced to a skeleton with some patches of putrefied skin stretched over sun-baked pockets of maggot-infested flesh.

He was Raymond Davis. His mother confirmed it when police brought her his clothes. It appeared he had been strangled with his own shoelaces, judging from the tightly wrapped string knotted and looped five times around the loose leathery skin of his neck. Similar string was wrapped around the wrist bones, behind the vertebrae where he once had a back.

The last anyone had heard from him, he was going out in the neighborhood to try to find his dog.

When detectives arrived, the rush-hour traffic had already started. There was some slowing up on the freeway as a few curious drivers craned out the window to see what all the police activity was about down on the Rampart offramp, but most rolled their windows back up once they caught the odor.

As they spread out and started scouring the landscaped area for clues, one cop hollered out loud for the others to scoot over to a spot about forty feet south of where they had found Raymond Davis.

The second body had also been bound with shoelaces. It had been strangled, but with a length of stereo-speaker wire, not cord. It weighed eighty-one pounds and wore Levi's and a green and white scarf. It was loaded in a van along with the remains of Raymond Davis and transported to the LAPD Forensics Science Lab for tests and an I.D.

It remained John Doe 270 for a few days until a grieving mother showed up at the county morgue. She had been to the police, relatives, a priest, neighbors, even a psychic, trying to find out what had become of her sixteen-year-old son. When the two detectives from LAPD Major Crimes Section laid out the clothes to her, she knew in a few unbelieving moments that it was her boy, Robert Avila.

By August, Randy seemed to be doing better, but Sandra Hare was experienced enough in such matters to know that early progress didn't always translate into a long-term cure. He and Jeff were back together, socializing a bit more, and planning a trip to Europe together in the fall to celebrate Oktoberfest in Germany.

His anxiety level was far better than it had been when he first came in the office. She had him questioning his own impulsive behavior as the source of a lot of the problems he was having with Jeff, his job, his health, and everything else that he told her he valued in his life. She helped him trace his depression and sense of helplessness back to his own behavior patterns, and it seemed to be helping.

She continued to try to see Randy once a week, though his job tended to interfere whenever he had to travel to the Bay Area or up to northern Oregon for one of his troubleshooting visits for Lear Siegler. Sandra felt certain she could pull him out of his psychosomatic troubles, including the sour stomach and insomnia, as well as the deteriorating love-hate cycle with Jeff, if she could just keep him in therapy.

She told Dr. McArthur that Randy had motor tension, with shakiness, jumpiness, fatiguability, and an inability to relax. His autonomic hyperactivity included sweating, heart pounding, stomach discomfort, flushing, anxiety, worry, fear, and rumination. Randy was obsessively preoccupied with his relationships and didn't seem to feel pressure from the normal activities of living, she wrote. His appetite and sleep were affected, and he had feelings of worthlessness and difficulty in concentration. His hypoglycemia had something to do with it, but not totally, she concluded.

* * *

The morning after Governor Jerry Brown lost the California Senate race to San Diego mayor Peter Wilson, Randy's morale dropped into a quiet, pained tailspin.

He and Jeff had been back from Europe only a couple of weeks, refreshed by many steins of Hofbrau house brew and lots of homemade German sausage. They made plans to put in a hot tub in the backyard and invited the poker club crowd over to check out the pictures from their trip. Things were on an even keel and life seemed to be good once more.

Then the election results started rolling in on November 2, 1982, and Randy and Jeff watched the Reagan landslide on their newly installed cable TV with sinking hearts. By the time the morning papers spelled out the new conservative direction the country and the state were headed in, Randy followed the principles he'd learned in psychotherapy and tried turning his despair into something positive.

"There is a difference, apparently a dichotomy, between what we *as a people* see ourselves to be and what we really are," he wrote. "Our answers to problems seem to be containment of the symptoms rather than eliminating or reducing the root causes of the problems." Crime, he wrote, was answered by guns, prisons, and police. Energy was answered by oil. Society didn't seem capable of diagnosing and solving long-term problems. The nation seemed confused, bewildered, and hesitant about which road to take. Where were America's positive and forward-looking leaders? Its Ben Franklins and Tom Edisons? "When will we stop trying to contain the status quo and instead forge an enduring commitment to our future development and survival?" Randy wanted to know.

They were lofty questions Randy was apparently not prepared to answer immediately. Within the week, he was preparing for yet another trip to Oregon.

Brian Whitcher didn't care for homosexuals. "There's a way to take care of these queers," said Whitcher. "They're not so damned smart." He did a lot of boasting in his twenty-six years but most of it fell flat when measured against his eternal need for a drink. Whitcher played out his hand on Burnside Avenue in southwest Portland, where boasts are worth less than a quart can of stout malt liquor or a single night's lodging in one of the dead-end hotels.

Burnside was Portland's beer bar row, and that's where Whitcher spent a lot of his time. Rotten Robert's and Terrible Terry's were the kind of watering holes Whitcher favored. Rotten Robert's was the last place Earl Davis remembered him saying he was going on the night he died. A retired Army cook in his early sixties who had spent his own share of downtime in Portland's mean streets, Davis met Whitcher at a health club where they had both worked briefly a couple years earlier. He considered theirs almost a father/son kind of relationship and he took Whitcher in as an occasional roommate despite his drug use. Earl was a drinking man himself and had no use for drugs.

It was after ten when Davis answered the phone that night.

"How are you, Earl?" Whitcher shouted into the receiver.

Earl heard the steady shudder of hard rock and party conversations in the background. He asked Brian where he was.

"I'm not at a joint. I'm at a house," Brian shouted again. "Come on over."

Earl started sputtering that he wasn't interested, but Brian had already handed the receiver over to someone else who came on the line, spewing out directions. Earl nearly hung up halfway through, but waited long enough to talk to Brian again. When he came back on the line, all Whitcher wanted was $5 that he claimed Davis owed him. Davis hung up. He'd had enough of Whitcher's nonsense for one night.

Davis only half-remembered the phone conversation when Clackamas County Sheriff's investigators came around a month later with the news. It seemed that Whitcher had wound up dead the day before Thanksgiving on Canby Hubbard Highway, near the I-5 freeway south of Portland.

Davis wasn't sure the cops suspected him or not, but he had nothing to hide. Brian was a bum in a lot of ways, but Earl Davis regarded him as a friend. The very week Whitcher disappeared, Earl advanced him $85 to get his teeth fixed and literally gave him the shirt off his back—a warm long-sleeved brown velour to keep him from freezing on his late night bar-hopping.

They told him Brian was found lying in a pool of blood with his sweater pulled up to expose his chest—no jacket, no shoes, no socks, no long-sleeved shirt. They figured he'd been robbed and dumped from a moving vehicle. He had no identification and it took them a while just to figure out who he was. He might have been hustling gays to roll them for beer money, but the cops weren't sure about that.

He had a lethal combination of alcohol and Valium in his system when they opened him on the autopsy table, but the coroner laid his death to asphyxiation.

He wasn't a bad kid, Davis told them. He was from California originally and tried to work at his father's print shop in Portland once. He chased skirts when he wasn't loaded, especially around Rotten Robert's, but he never had a steady girl. Whitcher's folks lived nearby in southeast Portland, but Brian stayed away from them much of the time. Most of his friends were down-on-their-luck guys like Brian: epileptic Tom, who lived off Social Security benefits; Carl, who had bunked with him at the Broadway Hotel before he moved in with Davis; and Frank, who worked at the Star Theater and went out to the bars with Brian at night. Whitcher had a tendency to go out drinking with damn near anybody, said Davis. He was not too particular about the company he kept as long as they paid for the drinks, he told the cops.

There was one guy Davis remembered. A sloppy guy, in his early thirties perhaps, with messy blond hair and blue jeans. He was probably about five foot eight or nine and had a big mouth. Whitcher knew him from the Locker Room bar on Burnside at Broadway.

"The guy kept putting his hand on Brian's shoulder and asking for a cigarette," Davis remembered. Brian told him he didn't have one so the guy looked at Davis and said, "Maybe Gramps has one."

Davis didn't like the looks of that guy from the first moment he saw him. In fact, he told police, he was pretty sure it was the same guy he'd spoken to on the phone the night that Brian was murdered. The fellow who gave Davis directions over the phone to the party Brian said he was going to.

Medium pitch. Unfriendly tone. A high but mature masculine voice that was easily understood. Yes, Davis told them. It sounded like the same guy all right.

"I'd do anything to catch the person who murdered Brian," he told them.

But he had no idea where to tell them to start.

17

Boone's Ferry Road, which runs parallel to Interstate 5 just outside of the Oregon coastal town of Hubbard, isn't half as romantic to look at as its name sounds. Motorists toss their tissues and candy wrappers and soda cans off by the roadside as they pass through, especially out-of-state types who don't care all that much whether Oregon stays scenic or not.

To Boy Scout troops and people with gunny sacks who just want to make a few bucks, the roadside north of Hubbard is a treasure trove of returnable aluminum cans and bottles. In the weeks between Thanksgiving and Christmas, when the daytime temperature drops into the forties and the rains come almost every day to northern Oregon, the can and bottle patrols lighten up. Only the hardiest or most desperate go searching through the mud, the high grass and the bushes for returnable refuse.

Late one morning a week before Christmas in 1982, just such an ecological explorer was picking through the wet underbrush along Boone's Ferry Road when he came upon Anthony Jose Silveira.

Outside of being stark naked, the most curious thing about Silveira's body, which lay facedown in the weeds, was that a red plastic object appeared to have sprouted from between his buttocks. The aluminum can collector didn't bother to inspect any further. He dropped his bag of returnable empties and hyperventilated all the way to the nearest pay phone.

The Marion County Sheriff's Office showed up, squad car lights ablaze, just a little before noon. Sergeant Will Hingston was among the first to take a closer look at the stalk of red plastic poking out of Silveira's rectum. It was a red adult-sized Tek toothbrush, run five inches up an anus that had been used as a repository for something much larger. The rectum of a dead person relaxes, but not so much that it opens up over an inch in diameter. Before Silveira was impaled on a toothbrush, something the size of a table leg was jammed inside his colon.

Silveira had been there long enough to become a meal or two for field mice and a few crows. Something a bit bigger—a dog perhaps—had gnawed the meat off his toes. Despite a dozen years on the force and lots of dead bodies, Hingston couldn't eyeball this one without a wave of nausea welling up the back of his throat. There was no way to guess how long he'd been there, lying in the weeds.

He'd been there a while, though. No doubt about that. With the weather acting as a kind of natural icebox, the twenty-nine-year-old carpenter could have lain peacefully in the brush until spring before anyone smelled him. By then, most of his flesh would probably have been in scavenger bellies and there wouldn't be much of anything to recognize.

Lyla Silveira was able to identify her husband, though. She helped Hingston with times and dates too. He'd guessed right; the body had been there at least a week. It was actually closer to two weeks, if Mrs. Silveira's memory was correct.

On Friday, December 3, the young husband and father had a few beers after work at a construction site some distance from his home where he had gotten a job. He had no car. He told his drinking buddies he planned to hitchhike back home to Eagle Point, the next county over, and then do his regular weekend duty with the National Guard. He never arrived, said Mrs. Silveira.

He was a big drinker and a real pushover when he had a pitcher or two, Hingston learned from his wife and fellow workers. He wasn't a gay-basher like some of the guys he worked with, but Tony Silveira was definitely not homosexual. He and Lyla had two kids, and if she was at all worried about the possibility of his sleeping around, it certainly wasn't with men.

Still, everyone Hingston talked to said when Tony was loaded he could be talked into damn near anything. One of the things that showed up in the lab results was that he was intoxicated in a big way: a .23 blood alcohol level mixed with Valium. He also had semen in his rectum, along with the toothbrush.

Circling his cold, gray neck like a thin maroon belt was a one-inch-wide mark, still visible two weeks after he'd been strangled to death.

Lyla Silveira was worried sick about her husband from the day he disappeared. He had his binges, but he never stayed away long and, drinks or no drinks, he was responsible enough to make his monthly reserve training weekends. It took her a little while to calm down when Hingston and the other investigators came around seeking a description of what she had last seen him wearing.

Nothing special. His old jeans and work shoes and a T-shirt. The only thing she could remember that was at all distinctive was his National Guard coat—an old green fatigue jacket with his last name stenciled across the top of the right-hand breast pocket.

Randy Kraft, the overachieving towheaded kid from Midway City, tooled down the highway behind the wheel of his rented Lincoln, taking in the grand winter scenery of Washington state as he drove from Portland to Seattle.

He was no longer a second-class citizen, consigned to driving a forklift or tending bar. The first week of December 1982, he was laying claim to his rightful place among the Lear Siegler professional elite, traveling around the U.S. first class at company expense. He had been asked to come back to Michigan for a two-day conference on Lear Siegler's future computerization plans. They had even asked Randy to make his own presentation to the brass during the seminar.

Beforehand, however, he flew to Portland and spent a couple days following up on the new computer system he had helped create at the Peerless Division in northern Oregon. He was acting data-processing manager by now, and his quiet, deferential demeanor commanded respect among his subordinates and his peers. It didn't seem to matter what his background was or where he came from or what he did on his own time. Corporations were interested in the bottom line: could he perform or not? The answer in Randy's case was a resounding "Yes!" and that was all that mattered.

When work knocked off Friday afternoon, December 3, Randy took off in his Hertz Town Car, beginning a short journey up the coast to Seattle to visit friends he'd met through Jeff back in 1979.

Gary Newell and Leonard Brouette had met Jeff Seelig during a trade show in Los Angeles and he had brought them home to meet Randy. They had become fast friends, visiting each other a couple of times a year. So when Randy got the word from Shobe that he had been picked to go back to Michigan, he called Gary, told him he was going to be in Portland, and asked if he'd like a house guest Saturday night before the last plane left Seattle for Grand Rapids.

Gary said he and Leonard would be delighted when Randy told them he'd be up after work Friday.

It wasn't more than a four- or five-hour drive from Portland, even when the traffic was bad, but Randy didn't pull into Newell's driveway until late Saturday afternoon. He knocked on the door, greeted Gary and Leonard, and told them he had a little stash out in the car. Gary said he was going to make dinner and wasn't interested, but Leonard wasn't opposed to a little toke before sitting down at the supper table, so he accompanied their house guest back to his car.

Randy handed him the marijuana and then reached across the seat, proudly holding up an olive-green military jacket for Leonard's inspection. There was a Hispanic name stenciled in over the right breast— something that started with an S. Randy seemed taken with it, so Leonard held his tongue, but his gut reaction was that it looked like the kind of cheesy Army surplus item somebody might pick up at a thrift store. Instead of commenting on the coat, he complimented Randy on the Lincoln and suggested they go have a joint before dinner.

Later on, when they all went out for a nightcap, Randy insisted on wearing his new jacket.

"We'd had dinner and went out to have a beer and we ran into a friend," Newell recalled. "The friend looked at the jacket and looked at Randy and said, 'You don't look Hispanic.' And we all just laughed."

Back at the house, they did a little more grass and retired. The next day, the three went out for Sunday brunch and talked a bit about Jeff's burgeoning candy business down in Long Beach, the Oktoberfest trip they'd taken together in the fall, and the progress that Randy and Jeff had made in remodeling their house. A hot tub was the next item on their agenda, he said.

Then, shortly before noon, Randy bid them adieu with handshakes and hugs. He would be staying at the Amway Grand Hotel in Grand Rapids, he told them. He waved out the window as he pulled from the driveway and punched the gas, racing south to the airport to drop off the rental car before catching his flight to Michigan.

Newell and Brouette waved and went back inside to get out of the chill Seattle wind.

He was always something of a paradox, this lover and friend of Jeff Seelig's: perpetually in a hurry, but never hurried. A man with a lot more on his mind than he ever seemed to want to share over a dinner salad, a joint, or a glass of beer. Still, he was a pleasant sort. He didn't let his preoccupation lapse into brooding. Say what you will about Randy Kraft, he was a good listener and a good friend.

One remark he'd made while they were in the car together alone continued to bother Leonard, though. It resonated literally for years after Randy's last visit that December weekend in 1982. He and Randy were in the car driving to a store or someplace, probably while Gary was either making dinner or off on his own somewhere. Leonard remembered, "Just off the wall, he told me, 'The ultimate orgasm is when you're dying.' "

Schoenborn Orchards sits on Conklin Ridge, about twenty minutes northwest of Grand Rapids, up a gravel road that winds into the gently rolling hills overlooking Grand Creek. For nearly 140 years, the 750-acre farm has been in the Schoenborn family. For most of the '70s and early '80s, Robert Schoenborn and his brother worked with Robert's two sons, Chris and Rick, raising apples, cherries, prunes, and field crops like oats and barley.

When his own father was shepherding the land through the Depression and World War II, using hand tools and horse-drawn plows, Robert helped coax his old man into more modern, mechanized farm methods. Chris and Rick were doing the same with Robert: pushing for more efficient use of equipment and an organic approach to horticulture that would maximize their fruit yield without producing apples that tasted like mush.

The Schoenborns operated a big spread—a good ten miles wide. It was something to be proud of. They pretty much lived off the land, though Carol Schoenborn worked at a fertilizer plant for a time after the boys were grown. From the time Rick and Chris were small, Robert and Carol instilled the agrarian mystique in them: the farm would all be theirs one day, and it was their responsibility to learn how to work it and make it work for them.

They were a warm, closely knit family, built around the Protestant work ethic, populist politics, and a deep moral sense of right and wrong. Chris and Rick were always up early, even in the winter months when they were both in school, so that they could get the chores done: slopping the hogs, pulling baled alfalfa down for the livestock in the barn, gathering up eggs from the henhouse for breakfast.

As far as following in his father's footsteps, Chris was especially gung ho. He was active in 4-H from the time he could walk, and while he was in high school, Chris took a course in small engine repair, which helped out plenty when something went haywire on a pump or one of the tractors. His father began to depend on him as the semi-official Schoenborn Orchards mechanic. After graduation, Chris bought a four-wheel-drive Silverado pickup and zipped around the farm in it. The truck was also pretty terrific for making the run into Grand Rapids to impress the girls.

Chris Schoenborn wasn't exactly a bad catch. Not only did his folks own one of the biggest spreads north of Grand Rapids, he was also husky, farm-boy masculine, and kind of cute. Blond hair, six foot two, 190 pounds, friendly but not brash, Chris was just as appreciative of the sloe-eyed heifers looking for weekend action in downtown Grand Rapids. The young single women who bundled up bravely against the winter cold to go window shopping in the warm indoor mall on Monroe Street, near the Amway Grand Hotel in the center of the city, were as good a reason as any to make the drive into Grand Rapids, even in the worst weather.

The first week in December of 1982 a storm had left the city blanketed in snow, but it had cleared up and the sun was actually out over the weekend. The following Tuesday, December 7, Robert Schoenborn and the younger of his two sons headed into town together. The elder Schoenborn had read about a three-day horticulture convention at the Amway Grand and Chris was eager to go, as much for the beer and the women as to learn the latest techniques in tree-grafting.

The Amway Grand Plaza Hotel wasn't more than a dozen years old, and it was already a Grand Rapids institution. On the east bank of the Grand River in the heart of downtown, it billed itself as the city's "most luxurious hotel": two blocks long, 682 rooms, a health club, shops, and an enclosed skywalk to get from the hotel itself to the Grand Center, which houses both a concert and convention hall. In addition, the hotel has a dozen restaurants and nightclubs. In the restaurant at the top of the elevator, patrons could see the Gerald Ford Museum across the river and, on a clear summer day, the white sandy beaches that made Grand Rapids one of the nicest spots in western Michigan to spend a lazy afternoon.

But during the cold winter months, the Amway was the very hub of Grand Rapids nightlife. Out-of-towners, in for a convention or a business meeting, mingled with the locals. Guys picked up girls at places with names like the Rendezvous and Tootsie Van Kelly's. Other parts of town rolled up the sidewalks after nine P.M., but the taps flowed at the Amway Grand until midnight.

The day Chris and his father were there for the horticulture convention, the Lear Siegler people were also holding a seminar. When things began to break up, around seven P.M., it seemed like everybody decided to hit Tootsie Van Kelly's at once.

While his father was upstairs schmoozing in one of the convention hospitality suites, Chris went down to the bar, ordered a beer, and started to loosen up. He tended to get sarcastic and a little mischievous when he had a drink or two and this time, almost immediately, he and a friend fell into a mild argument. The friend got disgusted, found a girl, and went with her to sit at a booth. Chris sneaked outside and appeared at a window, next to where the couple were sitting. He gave them both the finger through the glass, laughed, and, tickled with his minor adolescent triumph, returned to the bar.

The place was packed when Chris came back. He ordered up a brew and discovered after a few casual questions that the new crowd was made up of half the computer nerds who had come to the Amway for a three-day Lear Siegler business conference. Chris went into his aw-shucks country bumpkin routine when he struck up a conversation with a couple of consulting types from California. He earned a lousy $4.50 an hour as a farmer, wore clodhoppers, and drove a Chevy truck, he told them. He couldn't afford to lie around a tanning salon all day long sipping Mai Tais like the computer hotshots from "El Lay."

Besides, Stroh's on tap was a more honest drink.

About nine P.M., when things were just getting rolling, Chris left for a bit to go upstairs and see if his father was still there. They spotted each other and Robert said he was taking the truck and going home, but Chris decided he'd stay awhile longer. He'd find his own way home.

Meanwhile, Chris's second cousin, Dennis Alt, had been hitting the hospitality suites too, partaking of the free food and drinks laid out by the fertilizer and pesticide companies eager for some of the farm business that the convention might draw. Alt's mother drove him to the Amway about seven P.M. from their dairy farm in Comstock Park. As he clambered out of Thelma Alt's car, Dennis told her he'd probably find a way home so she wouldn't have to come pick him up.

A horticulture convention was a terrific excuse for a party, and that's exactly what was going on. Dennis got a buzz on right away and started making the circuit, hitting on women when he could. It was a strange crowd, full of good ol' boys in their dungarees and white collar workers still in their white collars. On the periphery were college students, young farmers like Dennis and Chris, and a few hookers looking for an overnight trick. At one point, a few beers into the evening, Dennis even ran into a black transvestite waltzing through the lobby as if he/she owned the place.

For a Tuesday night, it was a strange if hot and happy crowd. Shortly after eleven P.M., Dennis ran into his cousin Tom Alt in the lobby and asked if he could count on him for a ride home. Tom said sure, after he went to the restroom and got his jacket. They agreed to meet back in the lobby, but when Tom returned, Dennis was gone, so Tom shrugged and figured he'd gotten a ride home from someone else. He left without him.

Through the smoke and the constant buzz of conversations, Dennis had seen Chris across the room at Tootsie's. His distant cousin (Dennis's grandmother and Chris's grandmother were sisters) was chatting animatedly with a thin, short blondish fellow who nursed his beer and nodded politely at Schoenborn's story. He knew Chris had a truck and the stranger seemed to be picking up the bar tab, so Dennis forgot about catching a ride with Tom and moved toward the bar. He'd just have one more free beer and hitch home with Chris.

Randy was showered, shaved, and packed before eight A.M. Wednesday, December 8. He was supposed to meet another LSI computer troubleshooter, Ronnie Titgen, at the checkout desk so that they could share Randy's rental car to corporate headquarters in downtown Grand Rapids. The seminar was over, but they both had to go through their annual performance reviews with their immediate supervisors before they flew back to Los Angeles.

Randy amazed Titgen in a way. He'd been to all the sessions during the three-day conference, put together his own well-received presentation on computer management techniques during the final Tuesday afternoon session, and then proceeded to out-party everyone, closing down the bars long after Titgen, Roger Thomas, Larry DeJarrett, and all the rest of the guys headed for their rooms. The last thing Titgen remembered was Randy standing at the bar in Tootsie Van Kelly's, listening to the prattle of one of the local yokels and buying one more round.

But it was morning now and Titgen figured he'd find Mr. Kraft the Whiz Kid still hung over in his room.

He was wrong. When Ronnie rode the elevator up to Randy's room on the eleventh floor of the Amway Grand, a fresh-as-a-daisy Randy met him at the door. He told him he'd already checked out and instructed Ronnie to meet him out in front of the hotel: the car was parked in the garage across the street.

Titgen was a little nonplussed, but he didn't show it. It took him fifteen minutes to check out, and then he stood in the frigid morning air another fifteen minutes, waiting and wondering what had become of Randy. About 8:30 A.M., just as Titgen was about to go ring him up in his room again, Randy's car pulled up at the curb and Randy hopped out to help Titgen put his luggage in the trunk. Ronnie looked for signs of sluggishness or lack of sleep, but Randy looked like he'd just done a four-minute mile and didn't have to catch his breath. They made it to corporate headquarters in plenty of time, heard their respective performance reviews, and were back on the road to the Grand Rapids airport by ten A.M.

At the terminal, they shook hands and went their separate ways. Titgen was flying directly back to Los Angeles. Randy had unfinished business back in Portland. Before noon, they were both in the air and winging their way west.

Back at the Amway Grand Plaza, floor security guard Ron Ortega was making his morning rounds on the eleventh floor when he noticed a green military-type jacket lying on a couch near the elevators. He picked it up and looked it over. The name SILVEIRA was stenciled over the right front pocket. He admired it for a moment—even thought about trying it on—but then did his duty and took it down to lost and found.

At about the same time, a dozen feet away, maid Kimberley Ann Kinney was just letting herself into Room 1169. Almost the first thing she noticed was that the guest, who had already checked out, had left a set of keys on the nightstand. They appeared to be car or truck keys. Another absentminded guest who would remember where he left them and be back for them later in the day, but her job called for taking them immediately to lost and found.

Lost and Found. They had everything there, from wigs to shoes to whole suitcases. People even left their pets behind. Lost and Found was where everything that got left behind at the Amway Grand ultimately seemed to wind up: chiefly wallets and watches and hand-bags. Unless they contained money, credit cards, or identification, like a driver's license, people often wouldn't bother to come back. That's why the Lost and Found room often resembled a small garage sale, loaded with goodies that nobody cared enough about to want returned. It was an eclectic assortment to say the least. About the only thing security or housekeeping hadn't found abandoned in a corridor or forgotten in a guest room was a dead body.

Detective Lieutenant Jack Christiansen got the unenviable duty of acting as liaison officer between the Kent County Sheriff's Office and the Schoenborn family. He had to make the run out to their farm Thursday morning after the two young men were found.

A power company meter reader found them laid out neatly on the ground, next to the Plainfield Township water tower. The naked one was lying on his back with his legs spread out in a V. The clothed victim was lying on his back too, perpendicular to the naked man.

Police identified the naked corpse as Christopher Schoenborn, age twenty. The shorter one with its clothes still on was Dennis Patrick Alt, age twenty-four. They were both frozen and covered with an inch of freshly fallen snow.

There was something eerie and evil about the scene long before anyone got close enough to see that the two forms lying in the open field were young men. From a distance, Alt looked like he had been carefully and symmetrically aligned at a right angle to Schoenborn in order to purposely form the bottom of a triangle. Schoenborn's legs formed the other two sides of the triangle and one of his bare feet rested on Alt's belly. It was geometric in a grisly, satanic sort of way.

A ballpoint pen from the Amway Grand Hotel had been run up Schoenborn's penis and into the soft tissue of his bladder. The only blood at the scene had seeped out of his urethra. It took a little while for the Kent County Sheriff's deputies to run down just who the boy was because there was nothing else—no tattoos, scars, marks—to identify the body. It was just a lean, muscular corpse, relieved of life in its prime and now radiating a translucent bluish-white tint, like Grecian marble, in the icy morning sunlight. A ligature ring circled the neck like a deadly red ribbon.

Alt wore a sweater that was pulled up, exposing his chest. His pants were completely unzipped and his genitals hung out lewdly. He wore socks but no shoes.

Like the other detectives, Lieutenant Christiansen kept the un-
pleasant details imprinted indelibly in his memory. He didn't rehearse
them again for the victims' parents. He knew they knew. But the angry
vision stayed with him when he tried to be sympathetic yet businesslike
during his visit with Bob and Carol Schoenborn. He kept notes from the
interview that might help in the investigation in a small notebook. From
the moment he stepped through the front door, the entire session was
remarkably sensible and pragmatic, under the circumstances.

"A detailed clothing description was obtained at this time," he
wrote in his report. The middle-aged couple didn't "tell" him anything.
They "advised" him.

They advised him that Chris was last seen wearing a yellow velour
western-style shirt, size sixteen and a half with size thirty-three
sleeves. They also advised him that Chris was wearing a blue T-shirt
with the word ADIDAS printed across the chest. His notebook cataloged
the rest of the clothing Chris Schoenborn had last been seen wearing
the Tuesday night he disappeared: a pair of blue jeans, Levi's brand; a
pair of blue men's bikini-style underwear; a tan and maroon ski-type
jacket, Mighty Mac brand. Bob and Carol Schoenborn advised him that
there was a nametag on the inner left front panel of the jacket with
Chris's name written in ink.

Lieutenant Christiansen's notes also reflected the fact that the
victim was wearing a pair of black work boots with nine-inch tops and a
heavy cleated sole. The boots were fairly new and in good condition.

The parents also advised that Chris was carrying a man's wallet,
brown fold-over in style and color, with photos, identification and papers
in the name of Chris Schoenborn, including a Michigan state driver's
license, a Social Security card, and an identification card. When he left
the house, he probably had about $20 with him, they advised the
detective.

"It is also believed that the keys to his Chevrolet pickup truck
would have been in his possession as they have not at this date been
located," Lieutenant Christiansen jotted down in his notebook.

What he couldn't record in his notebook was Robert Schoenborn's
profound grief or his wife's tears. When she described the Mighty Mac
jacket, it became more than a garment. It was a lovingly selected coat
that Chris wanted because it resembled one his older brother, Rick,
owned. He and his mother had bought it together at a shop in Grand
Rapids that catered exclusively to tall men. Chris was so long-limbed
and lanky that she had to buy most of his things there. The tan and

maroon jacket Chris and his mother found together was just like Rick's only a little bit different; it had a slightly different trim, and that made it Chris's very own, Carol said, clearing her throat to keep from breaking down.

"I took a marker and marked both the boys' coats, just in case they could get lost somewhere," Carol said years later, a small shudder still resonant in her voice. "The last time I saw it was on my son."

The Schoenborns tried to buy quality and passed the clothes down, from father to son to younger son.

It was the same thing with the shoes: Wolverine Worldwide lace-up boots, made and sold in western Michigan. Carol explained softly that she had to yell at Chris to take them off in the "mud" room on the back porch during the winter so that he wouldn't track up her house. She used to tease her boy about his Wolverines because they had a high heel on them, and the last thing Chris needed was to be taller.

And the belt he wore that night wasn't just any belt. It was his Sagebrush leather belt, one and a half inches wide and hand inlaid with feathers. When she bought him jeans, she had to look for the ones with the special large button loops or he couldn't even wear the Sagebrush belt. In 4-H, Chris taught the younger kids in one of their leathercraft classes how to make such belts, Carol said.

It wouldn't help either of his parents to know that Chris might have been strangled to death with his own treasured Sagebrush belt.

When he was finished with the Schoenborns, Lieutenant Christiansen excused himself, maintaining his dour but sympathetic manner. While he was getting the clothing description from the Schoenborns, he didn't mention that their son's blood alcohol level was .16 and his cousin's was .14—or that both of them had taken Valium along with their beer, effectively turning them both into comatose vegetables while the killer had his fun with them.

And the killer definitely had his fun—sadistic, cruel fun to be sure, but great fun, if playing both God and the Devil was your cup of poison. It was like the sick work of some deadly five-year-old who took murderous glee in spitting in the eye of his elders. He not only killed and dumped, he degraded and debauched with energy and imagination. The white Amway Grand pen that turned the poor Schoenborn kid's phallus into an obscene, dead erection was a particularly grotesque signature.

Christiansen's department, led by homicide detective Sgt. Larry French, spent the next week futilely retracing the last hours of the two young men, interviewing everyone who might have come in contact with them at the hotel. Every lead failed. As one week passed into another, the case began to grow as cold as the victims' bodies when they were found that Wednesday morning in December.

It didn't take long to realize that their suspect was probably an expert from somewhere far removed from Grand Rapids. Homicide detectives put out a teletype on the crime to other agencies and other states before the end of the year. Then they kept their fingers crossed.

Jim Reed from the Oregon State Police started putting two and two together around the same time as Will Hingston, a homicide sergeant from Salem, the state capital.

"The killings occurred so sporadically, with a various assortment of victims who were scattered over such a large distance that we figured it must be someone from out of state," said Hingston. "Maybe California, but we were looking at people in other states too. I can remember one guy we were really hot on at one time. A guy from Colorado. Lane County Sheriff's down in Eugene was sending out teletypes and came up with that guy."

If there had been any doubt that there was some sort of pattern to the Oregon killings, it was dispelled by the middle of December. Even the press began to catch on when Silveira's body was discovered. The *Eugene Register-Guard* and the Portland papers printed maps, pinpointing the location of each of the bodies that had been found near freeways during the previous three years and stories speculating on the possibility of a common killer.

By December 9, a full week and two days before a can collector would discover Anthony Silveira's body lying off the side of Boone's Ferry Road in Marion County, the press and the police would have yet another victim to add to the list.

This time, the Clackamas County Sheriff's Department got the call. At about six A.M. a man driving to work saw Lance Trenton Taggs lying in the weeds off Airport Road near Wilsonville. Just two weeks earlier, Brian Whitcher's body had been dumped on the side of a road that ran parallel to Airport Road—a fact that did not escape either the homicide detectives or the media.

Taggs was nineteen years old, barefoot, and wearing a T-shirt and sweatshirt imprinted with the words HAWAII and LOCAL MOTION. He had been drinking and had Valium in his bloodstream, according to the coroner, but died from choking to death on a sock stuffed down his throat. His pants were unzipped and one of his pockets was turned inside out. He had no I.D.

Until September, Taggs had lived with his grandparents on the Koauka Loop in Honolulu. He fancied himself a beach bum and a martial arts buff and was not especially pleased about having to move back to the mainland to live with his mother. He'd been arrested in Hawaii for smoking marijuana, however, and his grandparents found him just too much to handle. He was immature, unambitious, and plagued with learning disabilities that made him an unlikely candidate for college. The arrest was the last straw. His grandparents shipped him home to his mother.

Taggs lived with her in the Portland suburb of Tigard, where sun and surfboards are about as familiar as penguins and polar bears. It didn't take long for the dreary gray skies and constant rain to get to him. He told his mother that he didn't want to live there and he certainly didn't want to work there. Almost as soon as he arrived, Lance was on the phone to a cousin who lived in Los Angeles, looking for a way to get back to his true calling: surfing.

On December 8, 1982, he set out hitchhiking south on I-5, carrying a tote bag with all the essentials a beach bum has to have to get by: baggie shorts, tank tops, sandals, as many shirts as possible emblazoned with insignia bearing the name HAWAII. He also threw a pair of homemade nunchakus in the bag—part of his Bruce Lee legacy.

But he never even made it past Wilsonville, ten miles south of his mother's front doorstep. Sometime on the night of December 9, he caught a ride with a killer—the same killer, Oregon State Police investigator Jim Reed guessed, who had been picking up hitchhikers, drugging them, and then killing them for a couple of years.

It was certainly possible that the murderer was homegrown. Oregon had its share of nut cases. But the pattern seemed far more likely to fit someone who just passed through from time to time, either on business or as a tourist, who did his deed and then disappeared for months at a time. For a while, Reed and the other homicide investigators from Marion, Clackamas, and Lane counties, who had banded together to share information on the murders, thought a mad trucker might be responsible. It made sense that the victims—all young male hitchhikers—could have jumped in the cab of a friendly down-home diesel driver who offered them a beer or two, followed by a couple of pills.

But the teletypes that Reed and the others started getting from out of state began to give them other ideas. The first ones were from Orange County, in southern California, where drugs and booze kept turning up in the systems of ligature strangulation victims who had been molested and dumped by the side of the freeways. When Reed saw the similarities, he called the name on the teletype: a Sergeant James Sidebotham with the Orange County Sheriff's Department.

There were no clear-cut clues or solid suspects down there either, Reed learned, but the killings had been going on a hell of a lot longer. Maybe ten years or more. By the time he hung up, Reed didn't feel any closer to putting his finger on the killer, but he had more ideas than before. Perhaps the guy they were looking for was a southern Californian who occasionally had the opportunity and the inclination to export his murderous hobby to other states.

Reed and Will Hingston devised a plan to check every airline, hotel, and rental car agency in and around Portland and Eugene during the times when the six bodies were dumped. It would be time-consuming. Might take up to a year to do it, Hingston said. And it might just be a big waste of time.

But if the same name turned up enough times on enough rental car slips or motel registration ledgers, and that same name could be traced back to someone from southern California, well . . . they would certainly have somebody worth putting a few questions to.

Randy checked out of the Wilsonville Holiday Inn and got in his Hertz rental car the morning of December 9. The flight from Grand Rapids might have been the coup de grace for a Ronnie Titgen or a Roger Thomas, following an exhausting, intense weekend of travel and preparation for the computer conference, but it only seemed to get Randy's juices flowing. When he met his immediate supervisor at Peerless, Jim Bremkamp, for lunch at Lee's Kitchen, he felt energized, confident—almost pompous, it seemed to Bremkamp.

What Bremkamp had to tell him wasn't particularly uplifting, however. To begin with, his work at Peerless was about finished. He'd done a good job, but the new system was in place and he probably wouldn't be shuttling to and from Portland as often as he had in the previous couple of years. In fact, there might be no need for Randy's talents at all, but Bremkamp kept that part of the news to himself. He hinted that the state of the economy was forcing a lot of layoffs, but didn't go beyond that generalization.

Secondly, he said, Randy had violated corporate policy in renting from Hertz. Employees, whether on loan from Lear Siegler corporate or not, were supposed to use a cheaper rental car agency and were certainly not supposed to run up mileage on as expensive a model as a Lincoln Town Car. Randy also had a tendency to drive all over the state from the looks of the odometer, and then charge it off to the company. Bremkamp had the evidence: a copy of a rental agreement that showed that Randy had managed to chalk up 993 miles on a single weekend back in July of 1980, during one of his very first trips to Portland on behalf of Lear Siegler.

It didn't take a genius to figure out that the distance between the Portland airport and the Peerless plant was a scant twenty-five miles.

Peerless and Lear Siegler both were experiencing the sting of the early '80s recession and Kraft's profligacy—as minor as it might be—was not the action of a team player. Randy took his scolding stoically, but Bremkamp's reprimand was only a mild harbinger of worse things to come.

Within a month, he would be out of a job—a victim of the layoffs that Bremkamp predicted might happen.

But as he flew home, Randy was still confident that things would get better. Bremkamp's warnings aside, he felt impervious and optimistic. At his next regular session with Sandra Hare, he told her so. Things were improving with Jeff and he had done a good job at Peerless, which would surely result in another raise and, perhaps, his long-awaited promotion to management. Things couldn't be better in a lot of ways.

On December 2, after seeing her patient again, Sandra Hare wrote Dr. McArthur once again, thanking him for referring Randy to her the previous summer.

Randy was moving toward changing his life to deal with the stress of work and his relationship with Seelig, but anger and guilt were two emotional issues that kept cropping up. Nevertheless, she wrote, Randy was "very capable of working through these issues to improve his life."

18

Coventry, Connecticut, is as green as an Irish glade in the summertime and as cold and white as death in winter. When Eric Church was growing up here in the '70s, it used to be a good place to raise children.

There are drugs and petty crime there nowadays. Kids who have moved here from the Bronx or South Boston, or even East Hartford a couple dozen miles to the west, brought all of that with them, to hear the old men tell it around Lyon's Barber Shop or Hale's Country Kitchen. These days, the Coventry police seem to bust someone every other month selling crack or marijuana in Patriot's Park.

Nobody hitchhikes in Coventry, Connecticut,anymore.

Patriot's Park took its name from Nathan Hale who was born here nearly 250 years ago in a rambling two-story farmhouse surrounded by green fields and hardwood forest. He was a child of privilege, studied at Yale, and became a schoolteacher. At the outbreak of the Revolutionary War he joined the militia and rose swiftly to the rank of captain. The British strangled him to death with a gallows rope in 1776 after Captain Hale uttered his famous regrets that he had only a single life to give to his country.

He was twenty-five years old.

Eric Church grew up in Coventry too, the fourth of five children raised in a single-story four-room dusty beige bungalow with brown shutters, up a gravel road about a mile from Nathan Hale's birthplace. He never had his own room or went to college like Captain Hale. He didn't even graduate from Coventry High School. Eric didn't care much for school even though he was bright enough. He never seemed to be able to concentrate. Hyperactive, his father would say.

"He made friends everywhere he went," Clayton Church said of his slim, youngest son. "Girlfriends mostly. He got along pretty good with girls. I don't know why. I don't know how he got girlfriends, but he did. He was a good-looking kid but I don't know what he had that attracted them. He always seemed to have a girl on the string."

Eric could have joined the military like his old man, who did time in Korea before he met Eric's mother in the mid-'50s, when they both worked on the Royal Typewriters assembly line in Hartford. But the army wasn't Eric's destiny either. He was restless, always moving, never happy standing in one spot too long. He wouldn't have lasted through boot camp without getting an itch to leave and wind up getting himself in a pack of trouble.

"He liked to go," said Clayton. "Eric took off early. Even when he was little he used to go a little farther up the road than he was supposed to. Every kid's different. All of them have their own way. He liked to travel."

When he hitchhiked, girls picked him up as often as guys. He loved women and the great outdoors, roughly in that order. Clayton still has a snapshot, showing Eric in New Hampshire surrounded with trees still holding on to their bright orange and yellow and red autumn leaves. The Churches keep the picture on a knickknack shelf in the living room, next to a porcelain statue of the Virgin Mary and a big red and white button that says I'M SOMEONE SPECIAL.

Before Eric hit the road on his first big cross-country journey in 1981, everything he did seemed to point toward an itinerant existence. The same year he dropped out of high school he enrolled in a trucking trade school and lasted there for a few months, but that was all. He was good with engines, but he didn't like standing in one place all day long. In hopes of earning enough to buy his own car, he got a job cooking eggs and bacon for the International House of Pancakes in Hartford.

His father invited Eric to make use of his own mechanical skills and learn the trade of typewriter repair, but Eric didn't have the patience. Besides, he wanted something more in life than a tiny mortgage payment on a tiny house brimming with microwave do-dads and souvenir coffee mugs and state-of-the-art video equipment and clocks that announced the hour with a computerized voice. He loved his parents, but he didn't love their life-style—and he didn't want to fall into the same trap they had.

He still couldn't afford the car he wanted, so he learned to use a backpack and his thumb. A grin full of teeth, a slightly cocky stance, and a glib line about where he was coming from or where he was going to always seemed to do the trick. It was actually better than having a car, in a way: no gas, no oil, no responsibility. Just an open road.

In the beginning, Eric flagged down cars at the turnpike onramps out of Coventry just to get back and forth to work in Hartford. When he learned how easy it was, he expanded his horizons and began exploring a wider world. He could hitch to New York City in a couple of hours on a Sunday—the same distance it took Captain Hale a couple of days to cross two hundred years earlier. Woodstock, where fragments remained of the rock 'n' roll culture Eric and his friends still worshipped, could be reached in the comfort of a friendly truck driver's cab in less than three hours.

It was so easy. Besides, there was a chance to meet interesting people who did more in life than sit around a color TV like his parents, watching cable, sitcom reruns, and wrestling matches. Coventry was placid but stifling. A person could die there without having seen much beyond Nathan Hale's tombstone across the road from Patriot's Park.

By the time he was nineteen, Eric was off on a cross-country jaunt, hitching to California. He printed up the obligatory cardboard signs proclaiming CALIFORNIA OR BUST and put the essentials in his orange knapsack—underwear, toothbrush, deodorant, an old Norelco shaver that his father had picked up at a flea market the previous year and rewired for him so that it would work. Then he hit the road.

Along the way he took a job as a short-order cook at a restaurant near the Grand Canyon, passed through Glitter Gulch in Las Vegas, and ogled the California girls who took pity on the poor long-haired boy standing in the sun by the roadside in his open sports shirt and faded blue jeans. When he got to L.A., he dropped his parents a card about the Hollywood sign. It was there, sure enough, bigger than life, up on the hillside above the Capitol Records building, which resembled a fourteen-story stack of pancakes, like the buckwheat cakes Eric used to serve up at the IHOP back in East Hartford.

"He told us they made 'M*A*S*H' in those same hills where the Hollywood sign is," said Clayton Church. "They look pretty much like the hills in Korea. Almost the same on TV as they were when I was there."

After L.A., Eric hitched up to Sacramento, where he fell in love. It didn't happen right away, but he was smitten enough to start writing her postcards along with those he dropped in the mailboxes around the country for his folks.

By 1982, Eric had the hang of it. He felt like he could hitch around the world. His mother was always wringing her hands, warning him to watch out because he never knew who might pick him up. But Eric told her he was careful. He knew a weirdo when he saw one. He watched himself when they pulled over to the side of the road to pick him up, making certain he wasn't catching a ride with some degenerate faggot looking for a handjob in exchange for a lift to the next town. He felt much safer—and he got much better mileage—when a female stopped to pick him up.

It was no longer summer by the time he headed back to the East Coast and Eric had had enough Connecticut snow to last him a lifetime. So he veered south to Florida where he found another fry cook's job at a Sambo's Restaurant in Naples, near the coast.

He blamed his bad luck in New England on the colder climes. He did so much better where it was warm, like California and Florida. His problems always seemed to crop up when he was back home, in the cramped cottage Clayton and Liz Church called home. But that's where he headed when the money ran out. When he lost his job in Florida, he was back in Coventry by spring, driving a school bus and grousing about it the whole time. He never did get his final paycheck from Sambo's and wasted several stamps and letters writing to Naples and to the restaurant chain's corporate headquarters in southern California, trying to get his money.

Autumn came and the chilly winds turned the Connecticut countryside yellow and gray. Eric felt the old restlessness. He stuck his thumb out one day and wound up in New Hampshire, only to find that the girl who offered him a ride was underage, out-of-state, and driving a stolen car. Clayton had to go up to Ossipy, New Hampshire, to smooth things over before the local gendarmes would turn his long-haired prodigal son loose.

When he got back home to Coventry, he hadn't learned a thing from Clayton's point of view. He wanted to go back to California, back to Sacramento where his old girlfriend lived. Liz and Clayton argued against it, but Eric told them that this was his chance to be happy. He had a job as a tree trimmer waiting for him on the Coast and a girl that cared enough about him to carry on a transcontinental love affair via the post office.

"We spotted him $150 so that he wouldn't hitchhike," remembered Liz Church. A one-way bus ticket was $99.

His father gave him a postcard to mail when he got there so that his mother wouldn't worry.

After the first of the year, Eric kissed his mother, waved good-bye, and got on the Greyhound. Snow was still on the ground and ice caked the edges of the Connecticut River flowing through the center of Hartford as the bus pulled out for California. Eric rubbed the steam off the inside of the bus window to watch his home state recede behind him.

He was starting out the new year, 1983, heading for a new life in a new state with a new girl where the sun always shined and people weren't stuck for life in a shabby existence, sentenced to living their lives vicariously through "M*A*S*H," "Mary Tyler Moore," and "Monday Night Football," unless they were fortunate enough to be "born to the manor," like Nathan Hale.

"As I'm writing this my pulse rate is ninety . . . I'm sitting at a desk . . . over the past two weeks the lowest I've monitored my pulse is eighty-four."

When Randy scribbled out a "catalogue of symptoms" he'd been developing during the months prior to the initial counseling sessions he and Jeff had with Sandra Hare, he couldn't help but remember his father's own health problems: high blood pressure, irregular heart beat, fatigue. . . .

But there was something wrong here. Harold Kraft was about to celebrate his seventy-fifth birthday. At that age, symptoms like lightheadedness or a sudden onset of clammy shivers were to be expected. But Randy was only thirty-seven.

He found himself bumping into walls and desks. He experienced faintness, trouble with writing, driving, and his vision, and a weakness in the back of his knees. Chest sensations, headaches, minor numbness, and clammy hands and feet plagued him, along with a pounding pulse in his stomach, neck, and chest.

"Sometimes wake up with this," he wrote. "Hot face. . . . Sudden onset of cold sweat, welling up in throat. Tremors [in] hands. Feeling of impending convulsions. Muscular tightness [chest, neck] . . ."

The second week of January, Randy took a treadmill test. He told

Sandra Hare he didn't have heart disease to the best of his knowledge and both of his parents were still alive and fairly healthy. But the symptoms weren't his imagination either. He was not being a hypochondriac. There were inexplicable attacks of rapid, irregular, or skipped heartbeat.

Granted, the computer business was not conducive to lots of physical activity, and he was smoking two packs of Half & Half cigarettes a day. He endured bouts of angina pectoris and took pills Dr. McArthur had been prescribing for him for years to calm him to the point where he could relax the pain away.

But the pills just treated the symptoms, not the cause. Randy laid it to his ongoing relationship problems with Jeff and the tension at work. His layoff at Lear Siegler was imminent and inevitable. Reaganomics had not yet taken hold in early 1983, and the slump in the economy, especially in defense-dependent Lear Siegler, was finally hitting home.

Randy knew he'd get through it all right because he had salable skills. As he told his old friend Phil Crabtree, he could walk in the door anywhere and get a job programming. But Randy was at a point in his life where he wanted something more than just a job. That's why his appointment as data-processing manager at Peerless up in Tualitin had been such a big deal. He still had the letter from Bart Hoemann, his Peerless supervisor, dated February 18, 1981. He'd made a lot of good friends, straight and "in the life," up there in Oregon and he would miss them now that LSI had effectively clipped his wings for a while.

He was a little bitter. In the short time he'd been with Lear Siegler, he kept hearing praise about how good he was. Knowing the axe might be coming for a lot of junior employees didn't make it feel any better when he got his final check.

Randy wanted to get beyond his health problems, pick up the pieces, further his career, and boost his standard of living: put in a Jacuzzi at the house or take more trips like the Oktoberfest vacation with Jeff.

The river-rafting trip he and Jeff had taken in the Sierras the previous spring stood out as one of the highlights of their relationship, running the rapids during the day and sleeping out under the stars at night. They horsed around in the woods, mooning each other for the camera and drinking beer around the camp fire. People could be friendly, and a lot less judgmental, once they got back to nature and broke bread with each other a long way from the maddening workaday world. Randy's nerves and heart palpitations hadn't seemed to bother him at all on the rafting trip.

It was back in the city that the anxiety attacks began anew and he and Jeff renewed their constant bickering. They separated, got back together, then separated all over again—sometimes for a week, sometimes longer. Theirs was beginning to resemble the love-hate relationship Randy's own parents had developed over the years. Sandra Hare hadn't been able to cure their problems, but Randy had to admit that she seemed to have helped them.

She just couldn't seem to help the underlying stress that Randy insisted he didn't even understand. It just seemed to hit him when he least expected it. Following the Christmas holidays, they fought yet again and Jeff left in a huff.

On January 18, Randy missed his regular weekly counseling appointment with Sandra.

"Jeff had hoped he would show," she jotted in her client notes.

Randy missed his January 24 appointment too. The following day Jeff showed up and told her that he felt things were going better, even though there continued to be poor communication between them and with Jeff's family. The separation had not been all bad. They were learning something about each other individually and about living together.

Despite their differences, Jeff knew from years of experience that his relationship with Randy was worth fighting for. Here was a genuinely concerned, loving, compassionate human being whose deep reverence for life was so exaggerated that he would find a paper towel and carefully lift a ladybug off the sink and put it out of the house rather than harm it.

Witness the worry he devoted to his dog, Maxer. There was no question Randy Kraft cared. It was as simple as that. If he could just get him back into counseling, Jeff felt certain they would discover what was wrecking his health and making Randy impossible to live with.

Southern California had its worst rainstorm in years on January 26, 1983. The Pacific Ocean was so angry it beat down the one-hundred-year-old Seal Beach pier and the wind-whipped waves washed the pilings up on the beach before anyone from the Coast Guard could do much about it.

The following day at about eleven A.M., a workman with the California Department of Transportation saw a mannequin in the ice plant off the shoulder of the 605 Freeway onramp. Upon closer inspection, he saw that it wore a black shirt and pants and that its hair had been plastered down by the rain. He also noticed that its eyes were shut and that the skin was very, very gray—almost white, like the smokestack snow of a New England winter. There were no shoes on its feet and no belt around its waist. When he knelt down beside it, he noticed something else: it wasn't a mannequin.

"When they called me from the funeral home, I brought out his pajamas," Clayton said softly in the cramped front room of the tiny Coventry cottage that Eric strove so hard to escape.

Eric's postcard from Sacramento telling the Churches that everything was just fine arrived just a couple of days before Clayton got the call from the Seal Beach police. The card said that he had a couple of days of free time before he started his tree-trimming job in Sacramento and that the Sambo's Restaurant people still owed him about $200 from his last week's work in Florida the previous summer, so he was going to check out of his motel and hitch down to Sambo's corporate headquarters in Orange County to collect his money.

When he got there, the Churches later learned, he was told that his final check was in the mail—to Coventry. Furious and frustrated, Eric turned around and stuck his thumb out one more time, heading back north to Sacramento.

Clayton flew out to California to formally identify the body and made a scene in the funeral home when they refused to cut his hair. He raised holy hell until they made his boy look respectable.

"They put him in a shipping casket. Just a plywood shipping casket," he said.

He had died at one A.M., January 27, according to the coroner. He'd had a couple drinks mixed with Valium, but it was strangulation and crushing blows to the right side of his forehead that did him in. There were rope burns around his wrists too. The autopsy also revealed that he had been sodomized.

He had no I.D., but he was reclassified from John Doe Seal Beach a week later, to Eric Herbert Church.

"He always wanted to try something different but he wouldn't ever stick with it, like the guitar, or almost anything," Clayton said with sad, helpless exasperation. "He was just too hyper."

His older brother picked up Eric's restless ways after the funeral. He started working in health care and moving all over the country, just like Eric: Florida, Los Angeles, New Mexico, Idaho. He doesn't hitchhike though. Nobody from Coventry does anymore. With drugs and degenerates in the parks and on the roadways, a person would have to be nuts to thumb a ride.

Eric's headstone is modest and his grave plot out of the way, in a cemetery not far from his parents' home. It isn't anywhere near as ostentatious as Nathan Hale's gravesite. A huge stone obelisk rises twenty feet above the ground where the American patriot lies buried in the ground. Perhaps his parents could afford it.

Clayton and Liz Church's son did have a couple of things in common with Captain Hale. Eric died when he was young and he died by strangulation, at the hands of another. No one will ever know if he could have been as eloquent with his own last words.

Eric Church only had an audience of one at his execution.

About an hour's drive from downtown Sacramento, twenty-four-year-old Mikeal Laine got on a southbound Greyhound around the same time of year that Eric Church caught his final bus ride to the West Coast.

He left his hometown of Modesto, California, and told his mother he was traveling the 150 miles or so south to Bakersfield to look for a job. Laine had a drug problem and he knew it. The cops had busted him for possession once and Modesto—the inspiration for George Lucas's classic comedy *American Graffiti*—was still small enough that word got around pretty quickly who was a doper and who was not.

Mikeal Laine couldn't get a job cooking pancakes, driving a bus, or pushing a broom. He needed work and he wasn't going to find it in Modesto. He didn't find it in Bakersfield either. Mikeal kept right on traveling down the road, using his thumb to take him all the way to Orange County.

But his mother didn't know that when she went to the police the following week, trying to get a line on what had become of Mikeal. Like Liz Church, Mrs. Laine kissed her son and waved good-bye through the window as the Greyhound pulled out of the depot. But unlike Clayton and Liz Church, she never heard from him again.

Another year to the day passed before San Diego County Sheriff's deputies found the skeleton of Mikeal Laine on a remote mountain hillside near the town of Ramona. As in the Eric Church case, there were no shoes nor belt. In fact, there was nothing to indicate that the body had been anything but naked when it was tossed out the door of a passing car. The remains were so old it was impossible to tell what he died of.

But, by then, police had a pretty good idea who killed him.

Part of the defense's strategy was to show Kraft as an ordinary person. This photo of Randy, age eight, was one of several the defense made available to jurors. *(Photo from Defense exhibits, Kraft family photo albums)*

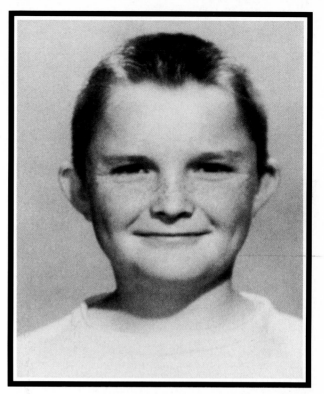

Randy Kraft graduation photo, Westminster High, Class of 1963. *(Photo from Defense exhibits, Kraft family photo albums)*

Airman Randy Kraft in 1969, age twenty-three. *(Photo from Defense exhibits, Kraft family photo albums)*

Randy and his dog, Max.
(Photo from Defense exhibits, Kraft family photo albums)

U.S. Marine Donnie Crisel in full dress uniform.
(Prosecution exhibit no. 89)

Donnie Crisel's body, dumped on the side of the road.
(Police photo)

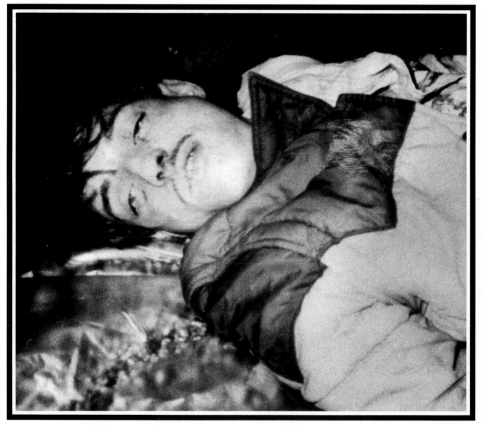

Police photo of Rodger DeVaul, Jr., who was found on a San Bernardino
mountainside in February of 1983.
(Prosecution exhibit)

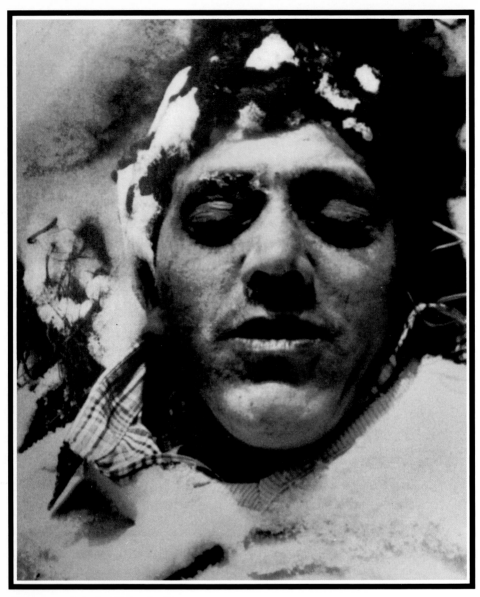

Close-up of victim Dennis Alt.
(Michigan police photo)

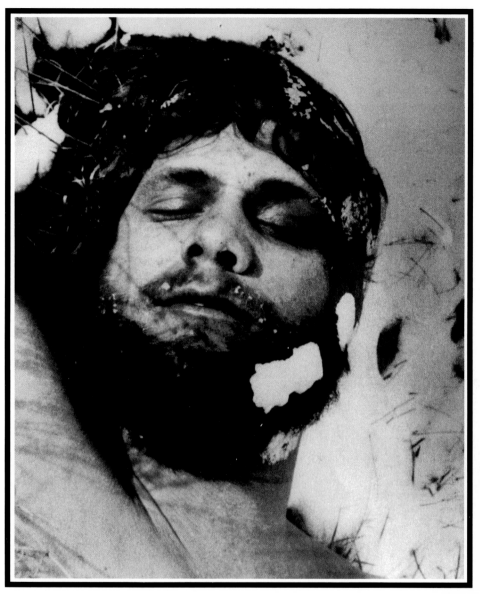

Close-up of victim Chris Schoenborn.
(Michigan police photo)

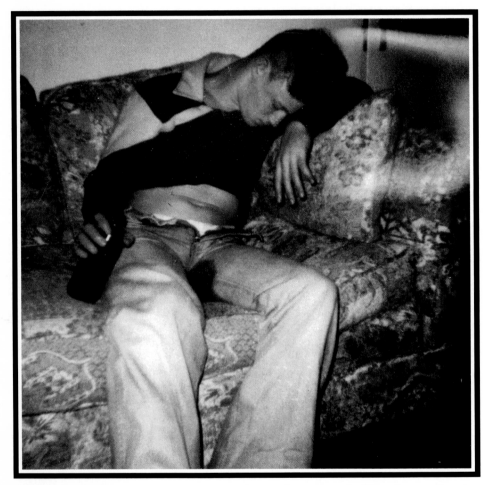

U.S. Marine Robert Wyatt Loggins, Jr., slumped on a couch. The photo, taken in the living room of Kraft's Long Beach home, was among a collection of forty-seven such snapshots of young male victims found by police in Kraft's Celica. *(Prosecution exhibit no. 38B)*

Loggins's body, wrapped in a trash bag, at dump site in a southern Orange County housing development.
(Prosecution exhibit no. 86F)

Eric Church, a twenty-two-year-old Connecticut native, lies in a field of an ice plant just off the San Diego Freeway, following a severe rainstorm.
(Prosecution exhibit no. 82)

The hand-printed, encoded list of entries —later characterized by prosecutor Bryan Brown as the "scorecard" or "death list"— found in the trunk of Kraft's Toyota Celica the day he was arrested.
(Prosecution exhibit no. 38A)

Joseph Fancher, Kraft's earliest known victim, testifying for the prosecution. *(Photo by Leo Hetzel)*

Prosecutor Bryan Brown, Orange County deputy district attorney. *(Photo by Leo Hetzel)*

Chief defense attorney
C. Thomas McDonald.
(Photo by Leo Hetzel)

Orange County Superior Court judge Donald McCartin.
(Photo by Leo Hetzel)

Four faces of Randy Kraft during his trial in Orange County Superior Court in the spring of 1989. *(Photos by Leo Hetzel)*

Rodger DeVaul, Sr., hugs his daughters after hearing Judge McCartin deliver Randy Kraft the death penalty.
(Photo by Leo Hetzel)

19

No one in the household seemed to really understand—or even know—anyone else, least of all Geoff.

For months following his June 1982 graduation from Cypress High, the strains of Journey and other mellow pop/rock groups flowed from Geoff Nelson's bedroom like loud reverb molasses, sticking to his family's eardrums from morning to night. It was a stalemate. They tolerated the music and he tolerated the rest of the family.

It was the year Geoff Nelson had turned eighteen, and he was going to "find himself," he told his mother. Sometimes he was pretty secretive about just how he was going to do that, but Judy Nelson had faith in her son. He'd snap out of it eventually. It was also the year Geoff's parents broke up twenty-one years of marriage and went their separate ways. And it was the year Geoff Nelson went out slumming one Friday night in February with a guy he'd only met a couple weeks before, and never came home.

The guy's name was Rodger DeVaul. He was a couple years older than Geoff. He'd been in the navy up in San Francisco, gotten discharged on medical grounds, and lived out on his own for a while in an apartment with another guy. But he came back home to live with his folks too when he found he couldn't live life the way he wanted—beer money, movie money, video game money—on the salary he earned as a maintenance man at Anaheim Stadium, where the California Angels play baseball. DeVaul was also enrolled in an auto mechanics class at

Cypress Junior College and needed a cheap place to crash while he was going to school.

In a way, it was a little weird that Rodger and Geoff hadn't hooked up before. In many ways, they were opposite sides of the same coin: a righteous young Mutt and Jeff, wise to the soothing properties of marijuana and other controlled substances and hip to what was *really* going on in the world. They both grooved on the ripe sounds of Kansas and Journey while, at the same time, they paid homage to the heavy mystic beat of Aerosmith and Led Zeppelin. Geoff was dark blond and clean-shaven, while Rodger was brown-haired and had a thin mustache, but they were both long in the locks. Together, they looked a little like Darryl Hall and John Oates—a couple of street-smart young rebels with every right to be disgusted but a little hopeful about the world they were inheriting.

Both of their mothers and fathers had their problems, but they cared for them in an exasperated way. There was no way either of them were going to get locked into any long-term commitments that could go awry like their folks' marriages. They each had worlds to conquer and the last thing they needed was a relationship that could go sour.

Geoff and Rodger were the kind who went out prowling when the lights had gone down in the city of Buena Park, where they both lived. They liked the evening air and the anonymous blanket of darkness and the action down on Lincoln Avenue, where dudes could hang out and score a little dope if they were lucky.

Jeff Wojick, once one of Nelson's best friends, remembered that Nelson, and possibly DeVaul too, had been part of a loose-knit crowd that called themselves the Wasteland Fiddlers. They did a little marijuana, a little acid—anything they didn't have to shoot up. Sometimes, they hung out in a couple of abandoned houses in Cypress where they would occasionally spend the night, getting loaded. There was also talk that they were into other tawdry activities as well. Maybe they rolled gays for thrills and money. Maybe they did other things for money and thrills too.

When Geoff wasn't out picking his way through the midnight streets, he stayed at home in his room and picked out a few chords on his red electric guitar, mimicking the rhythms on the radio.

"When the lights go down in the city, and the moon shines on the bay . . ." he'd warble along with Journey's Steve Perry.

A bunch of the guys he hung out with in the west Orange County neighborhood where he grew up had gotten together and tried to form a band once. They'd settled on Night Fall or Night Moves as a name, but had never gotten much beyond that.

Like Rodger, Geoff was a night person, with an ineffable darkness to his otherwise ebullient, surfer-blond personality. At 18, Geoff Nelson was both effusive and elusive. He wouldn't commit to his girlfriend. He wouldn't commit to a job or even to school. He was signed up at Cypress Junior College, but he didn't go.

Geoff worked as a waiter at the restaurant adjacent to Los Alamitos Race Track while he was in high school, but after graduation, he just kicked back. Experimented with life. Checked the scene. Wrote poetry. Scored dope. Slept until noon.

He was so witty and artistic and clever with his hands that his mother was certain he was the reincarnation of Benjamin Franklin. He made an intricate underwater scene in origami when he was thirteen and sold it to his aunt for a dollar. He did what he wanted in high school and almost didn't graduate because he was one credit short and took his slow, sweet time about picking it up.

"He used to say, 'Don't worry, Mom. Don't worry about it.' He always used to say that," recalled Judy Nelson.

But his elusive attitude also drove his friends, his brothers, and his parents nuts: up one day, down the next, and never quite certain what he wanted to do with his life. His father, Dale, was a medical administrator and his business had recently been computerized. He brought a new personal computer home one night and Geoff went crazy over it. He spoke enthusiastically about going into programming and even discussed the possibility with his uncle, who owned a fledgling computer business. But, then, the languishing side took over again and he was back to hanging out with other lost young souls, in search of . . . something.

On the one hand, Geoff would go to great lengths to be outgoing and creative, once even building a replica of the console used on the Starship Enterprise in his bedroom. On the other, he'd closet himself and write brooding songs and poetry, like the one he entitled "The Raven," about a lone killer who stalked the city streets at night, preying upon the naïve and the unsuspecting.

He had recently taken to wearing a diamond stud earring in his left ear—a new fad among his peers. On the back of his denim jacket, he wore a skull and crossbones, and he played "chicken" with his friends to see who could stand the pain from a burning cigarette the longest, often until a red welt rose where the glowing tip of tobacco singed the flesh.

Whenever his elders took him to task for his aimless friends, his lackadaisical attitude, or his sloppy housekeeping, he'd give the standard Geoff Nelson reply, "Don't worry about it."

Rodger regularly served up roughly the same catch phrase to his own folks. They had broken up even more recently than the Nelsons. In fact, it was the morning of the very day that Rodger and Geoff went out bumming around together for the last time: February 11, 1983.

His mother, Shirley, just left home after an angry battle with her husband. Rodger Sr. broke the news to Rodger Jr. and his two sisters over breakfast: their mother had left. She said she wasn't coming back. They were getting a divorce.

Rodger Jr. had seen it happen before and was not nearly so crushed as his old man. He gave him a pat on the shoulder and told him not to worry—she'd be back.

He didn't hang around to talk, though. It wasn't his style and, besides, there was more to life than parental angst. He told his dad he'd be gone for a while—maybe the weekend. He was going to try to get up to the mountains, his father remembered Rodger telling him. He borrowed a ten-speed bike from a friend, Mark Gaukler, and pedaled over to his girlfriend's house to spend the day.

That same morning, Geoff was rolling out of bed at his girlfriend's house where he and another buddy, Bryce Wilson, had spent the night. They weren't broadcasting it to the world, but it was common knowledge among their friends that Geoff and his steady were sleeping together. Someday, maybe in six or seven years, they might even tie the knot.

From where his girl sat, Geoff was cute, even if he didn't have much in the way of goals at the moment, and she was staking a lot in him. She bought him a pair of Sergio Valente jeans to go with his denim jacket and stood back to admire the finished product. There was no question about it: Geoff Nelson was one sexy dude when he wanted to be.

By the time he and Bryce left her house Saturday morning, however, Geoff was good and pissed at her. She had told him over breakfast that she was going to Disneyland that night—without him. She was going with someone else.

And whether she was teasing him to make him jealous or Geoff just had missed something in the conversation, he was convinced that she was going to the amusement park with some other guy, not only betraying him but also leaving him and Wilson to figure out for themselves how they were going to spend Friday night without her.

That's what he told his mother a few hours later when he called from Wilson's house to let her know what he was up to that day. What he was doing, he told her, was hanging out at the Electric Palace video arcade on Lincoln, near Valley View. His mother told him fine, just stay out of trouble.

"Don't worry about it, Mom," he muttered wearily into the receiver.

Later on at the arcade, he and Bryce ran into Rodger and his girlfriend. They b.s.'ed for a little while about women and dope and parents. Rodger understood better than the others just how Geoff Nelson felt. Girlfriends could be so fickle and parents could be so foolish. At times, a joint and an electric guitar seemed as though they were the only things a growing boy could depend on.

Just before sundown, Rodger walked his girl back home, leaving Bryce and Geoff to loiter along Lincoln Avenue. The neighborhood itself isn't remarkable. There are fast-food franchises and grocery stores and neighborhood mini-malls, like the one on the corner where the Electric Palace was located. Traffic isn't particularly heavy, even on a Friday night, the way it is on some of the bigger cruising streets like Beach and Whittier boulevards. There, kids are always thumbing down rides or gawking at the endless, bizarro parade of convertibles, souped-up VWs and customized pickup trucks. By contrast, Friday night traffic on Lincoln is tame.

A few years back, when Geoff had still been in high school, one of his family's acquaintances had been picked up on one of the cruising boulevards and murdered by Bill Bonin, the guy they called the Freeway Killer. There was a wave of hysteria in the community until the cops finally nailed the son of a bitch. Everyone, from homeroom teachers to counselors to clergymen were harping on the age-old cliché that every son hears from about age two forward: don't ride with strangers.

The Nelsons drilled it into Geoff and both of his brothers: never, ever hitchhike. Geoff scoffed. He would never be so stupid as to climb inside a van driven by somebody he didn't know. Did he *look* like a retard, for Christ's sake? There wasn't much danger of that happening on Lincoln anyway. It wasn't exactly the Sunset Strip.

After he dropped his girl off, Rodger was supposed to meet Geoff and Bryce back at Bryce's house around eight P.M. At the arcade,

Rodger learned about Geoff's interest in starting a band, and he was into the guitar himself, so they talked about getting together on some sounds. It looked to Geoff like Rodger might be the missing musical link in Night Moves. In the meantime, he and Bryce got bored hanging out on Lincoln and wandered back to Wilson's house where they sat on a retaining wall and schmoozed until DeVaul showed up and joined the conversation. They had a few beers and philosophized into the night.

It was 11:30 P.M. when Bryce stretched, yawned, and told the other two he had decided to pack it in. He was heading inside to get some sleep. But Geoff and Rodger weren't even tired. They said good night and sauntered off into the night to get something to eat.

Around one A.M., Geoff was back, knocking at Bryce's front door. Wilson was sleeping, but his mother and stepfather had just come home from the Red Rooster bar, which his stepfather owned and where his mother tended bar.

"Geoff had come to see my son, but he was asleep on the couch," recalled Sharon House, Bryce's mother. "I tried to wake him up, but he wouldn't wake up, so Geoff said he would see him the next day and he left."

He might have been drinking, but Mrs. House saw no swaying or speech slurring signs—and she had seen Geoff and Bryce blotto together often enough in the past. If there was someone with Geoff, she didn't see him either. When the Nelson boy stuck his hands in his brand new Sergio Valentes and stepped off the porch, back into the night, he appeared to be all alone.

But apparently he wasn't.

Donald Batchelder, an off-duty officer with the Los Angeles Police Department, was on his way to work four hours later when he spotted the body up ahead in his headlights. According to the records of the Garden Grove Police Department, Detective's Report 83-2552, it was Saturday morning, February 12, 1983, at approximately 5:20 A.M., when it was still dark out.

Batchelder started to get out of the car until he saw what he was certain was a twitch of the bare right foot. He figured it out instantly: some kid got so shit-faced he just passed out on the pavement. Batchelder backed off the offramp, pulled into a service station and called for a patrol unit.

When they showed up three minutes later on the westbound onramp of the Garden Grove Freeway at Euclid Avenue, Garden Grove police found no pulse, even though the body was still warm to the touch. He was stark naked.

When they flipped the boy over, they cringed. It wasn't just a drunken teenager. A gaping red hole still dripped crimson gore from the gash where his genitals had once been. By the time paramedics arrived, he was pronounced dead.

There was no identification. Judging by the skid marks, the body had been pushed onto the roadway from a moving vehicle. A trail of skin, blood, and hair showed in the asphalt where he had bounced and rolled before coming to a dead stop at the side of the road. He had a single diamond stud in his left ear lobe.

There were no missing person reports on a thin, white male, about five foot nine, blond. So he was tagged, given a John Doe number, and autopsied before finding a berth in the county morgue. The most intriguing thing turned up on the coroner's table was the contents of his stomach: diazepam, aspirin, and a drug called propranolol, used in the treatment of heart trouble and hypertension, along with some undigested potato skins and grapes. He had been drinking, of course— probably a six-pack or two.

The most disturbing thing, however, was something the police had seen before, far too many times. A neat red ring, about the width of a pencil, encircled his neck. The drugs and the booze and the mutilation hadn't helped matters, but it was strangulation that had killed him. As recently as two weeks earlier, on an offramp of the 605 Freeway near Long Beach, they'd seen the same thing with a twenty-one-year-old hitchhiker from Connecticut.

That kind of killing had seemed to lapse with the close of the '70s. Since the arrest of William George Bonin and his cronies in 1980, the occasional body of a derelict or a gay prostitute turned up near a roadway, but not so viciously mutilated nor so blatantly on freeway display as this last couple. Recent teletypes from Oregon and as far away as Michigan seemed to imply that, maybe, the predator who had been stalking the southern California roadways for a decade had finally moved on to other pastures, if, in fact, he was still on the loose and was *not* Bill Bonin.

But this latest ghastly discovery seemed to end that speculation for good.

The task at hand, though, was to get an I.D. on John Doe Garden Grove, and the best way to do that, homicide detectives had learned from past experience, was to get some handbills printed up pronto so they could be distributed within the gay community: bars, restaurants, community centers. Time was of the essence in any murder investigation. Trails grew cold quickly, and any leads, witnesses or evidence could simply vanish altogether if you didn't find out who your victim was and start interviewing friends and family as soon as possible.

It was possible that the victim was not gay. The kid from Connecticut hadn't been. But chances were good that he was. For some years, the Freeway Killer task force had been convinced that their suspect or suspects were active in some way within the growing gay community.

One sometime transvestite recognized the picture on the handbill immediately and called the Garden Grove police.

"I was devastated. Shocked," said Humberto Franco, describing his reaction when he saw the flyer. "I couldn't believe it."

Franco knew the victim as Coco, a gay prostitute who picked up men at the DOK Bar in Garden Grove where Franco worked cleaning restrooms. Around Christmas, Franco met the kid outside the bar, obviously looking for money in exchange for a little friendly sex, Franco told the Garden Grove cops.

"He always wore plaid shirts," said Franco. "Like corduroy plaid shirts."

They saw each other four times. Their second "date" was at the Rumor Has It, another gay bar. The last couple of times they met, at a hotel and at Franco's apartment, they had sex. Franco half-expected the worst from Coco, but it didn't happen. He didn't hit him or hurt him. He just sort of faded away, out of his life. There were no names, addresses, or phone numbers. It was just the clandestine, quick encounters with a stranger that characterized a large share of the sexual liaisons in the gay community at the time. Get each other off, no questions asked.

Franco did give Coco one token of his affection before the boy disappeared from his life. It was a single diamond stud earring that Coco wore on his left ear lobe. It was the same earring that Humberto spotted right away in the picture on the flyer.

That still didn't help the police. Coco could be anyone. The only real lead Franco was able to give them was that the boy said he lived somewhere near Knott's Berry Farm, in Buena Park.

Somewhere in the neighborhood of one Geoffrey Alan Nelson, as it turned out. Years later, Franco maintained that Coco and Geoff Nelson were one and the same.

But Sunday afternoon, the thirteenth of February, when the flyers were just getting distributed to places like the DOK and Rumor Has It bars, another big clue to the identity of the dead man with the diamond stud in his earlobe was being hauled up a mountainside forty miles away.

Shortly after three P.M., a ranger from Mount Baldy Village stopped on Glendora Ridge Road to take in the panorama. In a ravine fifteen feet down an embankment off the west side of the highway, he spotted what he thought was a person lying precariously in some dead tree branches at the edge of a cliff. When the ranger called out to him, the figure didn't move. If it had fallen, the body would have tumbled another one thousand feet down the mountainside.

An hour later, Los Angeles County Sheriff's deputies carefully hauled the body up the hillside. He had on an orange and white nylon windbreaker, a long-sleeved T-shirt with a palm tree design on the chest, and black denim jeans with the fly and top button peeled back. His underwear was rolled down past his genitals, so that they hung out of his pants. He had a tattoo on his right arm, a short mustache, and abrasions next to the right ear and under his right eye. His I.D. and wallet were missing and he was lightly coated from head to foot with beach sand.

Whoever had taken him on his last trip to the beach had sodomized him, according to the lab tests. He also had been tied up and strangled with a small cord after taking sizable—though not lethal—doses of diazepam, propranolol, and beer. He also had some undigested potato skins and grapes in his belly.

Cause of death: asphyxia due to compression of the neck.

From the turnout where the ranger had first spotted the body that Sunday afternoon, the sun could be seen dropping into the Pacific fifty miles away while the white top of Baldy towered directly behind. It was an imposing though calming view, even in wintertime.

Twenty years earlier, students from the Claremont Colleges just a few miles below Glendora Ridge Road used to drive the twenty minutes up Mount Baldy Road just to get to that very spot, settle back, take a girl for some sunset smooching, or maybe drink a beer while hitting the books.

"It's breathtaking up there," remembered an alumnus of Claremont Men's College, class of '66. "It's very soothing. They found the body within five hundred feet of where we used to go up and study."

Randy left the poker game a winner on Friday night, February 11, chiefly because he played bridge instead.

"He rarely lost," said Bob Day. "He had a knack of knowing when to get out of the game. Everybody raved about what a great bridge player he was. He remembered cards. He remembered as they went through the deck.

"He was *such* a good bridge player. Everyone wanted to be his partner. He never lost. A few chips here and there maybe. But he never really lost. He dropped out of a game instead of bluffing. If they wanted the pot, he just let them have it."

He took his winnings and ducked out of Joey Carrissimo's Huntington Beach condo a little early that night—maybe around 11:30 P.M. or so.

Jeff wasn't with him. They were still at odds with each other and sorting things out with Sandra Hare, though Randy found he just didn't have the time to make her regular weekly counseling sessions. Since his layoff from Lear Siegler, there were also problems with getting his medical insurance to cover the sessions, leaving open the question of whether he and Jeff could afford to continue with them at all.

But for this particular weekend, Randy had a full schedule ahead of him and little time to worry much over headshrinker bills. He had to be up early and drive over to the Palos Verdes Peninsula by nine A.M. the next morning, Saturday, February 12. When Bob Day and Harry Eylar and the rest of the Friday Night Poker Club regulars waved good-bye, they assumed Randy was headed back to Roswell for a few hours' sleep.

He might not have the cushy position with Lear Siegler anymore, but he was still in demand. He had a standing job each Saturday morning at St. Ives Laboratories in Palos Verdes, and it called for a full day at the computers. He also had his old consulting chores at Jay El Products in Gardena to fall back upon—a part-time working relationship that dated back to 1977.

And there were other calls coming into the house from small businesses that needed programming help. Randy was back in the freelance consulting business, but losing Lear Siegler had not turned out to be the traumatic end of the world he had thought it would be.

He showed up right on time for work Saturday morning at St. Ives. Saturday afternoon after work, about six P.M., Randy called his niece, Mindi Lane, who worked at Grandma's Sugar Plums, the thriving specialty candy shop Jeff had co-founded in Belmont Shore. For several days, they had been planning a surprise seventy-fifth birthday party for Grandpa Harold Kraft. As the Saturday six o'clock TV news blared the headline item about another dead young man being found on a freeway offramp that very morning, Randy and Mindi wound up plans to meet early the next day to pick up the cake for Harold's party.

And, on Sunday, February 13, at about the same time that a second body was being hauled up a steep slope near Randy Kraft's alma mater some forty miles to the east, the thirty-eight-year-old computer consultant was sitting down to dinner at his sister's home in Westminster, warmly toasting the family patriarch and wishing him another year of happiness and good health, in spite of his chronic bouts with heart trouble and hypertension.

He was out of regular work thanks to Lear Siegler, Randy explained to his family, but not out of luck or skill or the strong work ethic he had learned from his hard-working, salt-of-the-earth parents. Sunday was a good day for the Kraft clan. Harold smiled for the camera and Randy smiled with him as he blew out the birthday candles. Both their faces froze in the snapshot at the sound of "Say cheese!" like happy death masks.

Monday was Valentine's Day.

Geoff's girlfriend showed up at the Nelson's front door with an explanation and a present for Geoff. She had gone to Disneyland with her mother and she was sorry they had had a fight.

But Geoff hadn't been at either his father's house, his aunt's, or his mother's place all weekend, she was told. The Nelsons thought he had been at her house.

They checked with Bryce Wilson and several other of Geoff's friends. No one had seen him since Friday night. His girlfriend went to the police.

Two days later, Rodger DeVaul, Sr., did the same thing. He told Buena Park police that his twenty-year-old son had supposedly gone to the mountains and was to have returned by Tuesday, but that he had never showed up.

By Thursday, both young men had been found, tagged, and sealed at the Orange County morgue. Judy Nelson's daughter broke the news to her mother. Rodger DeVaul, Sr., told his wife.

Geoff Nelson's body was cold, gray, and naked. The Sergio Valentes that his girlfriend had bought for her boyfriend were never found, but the windbreaker he had been wearing the night he disappeared was. Rodger DeVaul was wearing it, along with the T-shirt that he got for his twentieth birthday just two weeks earlier.

Rodger DeVaul, Jr., and Geoffrey Nelson were buried a week after they disappeared together. Both had big turnouts at their funerals. Both had mothers who grieved for years after the last spade of dirt was patted into place.

Shirley DeVaul swore that she didn't recognize some of the names signed in the guest register and later speculated that her boy's killer might have been so perverse that he attended and signed the memory book for Rodger's funeral.

Judy Nelson spent hours going over old family albums, gathering together poems and pictures and creating a small shrine to the memory of the boy with the laughing "Venetian eyes." She and her husband created a small endowment at Cypress High in Geoff's name so that, each year, a promising art student would be awarded a scholarship and remember Geoff Nelson, who also showed promise, but never had the opportunity to fulfill it.

20

D

ear Mr. Kraft," wrote eight-year-old student John L. Lewis. "Thank you for coming in, talking to the class and I thought your presentation was interesting. I learned things I didn't know about computers. You told me things I found really interesting about data processing. Yours truly, John L. Lewis."

John's was only one of more than two dozen notes that were delivered in a big envelope to Randy's Roswell Avenue home in early March. Some of the letters had pictures of computers drawn on them and some were signed with "love." Randy kept them all.

The week following their father's seventy-fifth birthday party, Randy's sister Kay asked her younger brother to speak to her third grade class at Eastwood School about computer careers. Randy accepted without hesitation and turned out to be the hit of the semester. As far back as she could remember, Randy was great with children: patient, light-hearted, and considerate.

Like most of the kids in her class, Kay wrote Randy a special thank-you note too, congratulating him on the impression he'd made on the children. She signed the note, "Your big sis, Kay."

To the outside world, the Krafts appeared to be a well-adjusted, close-knit family who relied on each other in times of celebration, tradition, and trouble, and to a large extent, that was true.

"Randy did not ever miss Christmas or any other family get-together," said Kay.

"The custom was to exchange names on Thanksgiving and, then, give gifts on Christmas eve. We'd have supper at six or six-thirty, and sing carols and sometimes go to church services. It probably would not go past nine-thirty. Our whole family was there."

By 1983, when Randy devoted almost all of his time to his profession, his house, and Jeff Seelig, he continued to be closest to his oldest sister. But even she scorned his choice of a mate.

"I often wondered what Randy saw in him," she said.

Both Kay and her sister, Doris Lane, saw Jeff as a negative influence on their little brother.

But according to Jeff Seelig, the Krafts were "loony tunes"— always bickering and closed off to the outside world. Once he and Randy began living together, he encouraged Kraft to break away and spend more weekends and vacation time with Seelig's own family, whom Jeff characterized as "normal."

If the Kraft clan had problems, one almost had to be a member of the family to see them. The Krafts' prevailing credo seemed to be the same one that governs many American families: don't advertise family concerns to outsiders. Individual family members may have had a bout with alcohol, a need for tranquilizer prescriptions from the family doctor, or a domestic crisis such as divorce, but it was not information for public consumption. That information was kept all in the family.

Randy's relationship with Jeff continued to be rocky, though, and the progress that they appeared to have been making in psychotherapy looked like it was in trouble by the end of March.

Sandra Hare logged in five missed, or rescheduled and missed, appointments for Randy before she called him on March 28.

"Phoned Randy at home," she wrote. "Voice strange, disconnected. Discussed bill. Angry."

His anger, he told her, stemmed from the failure of his insurance company to pick up the cost of his counseling sessions. He owed $100, but the company was obligated to make the payment—not him. Randy told her he was considering suing them. He rescheduled his next session with her for April 4, but he never showed up.

She tried rescheduling again April 6 and on into May. But despite the fact her notes reflected his need for some sessions, she couldn't seem to get Randy back into therapy, no matter how persistent or patient she was.

On Friday, the thirteenth of May, Randy met with John Robert Moutier, a marketing executive for the Anchorlok division of Lear Siegler Industries in Compton.

He was no longer on the regular payroll, but Randy was still consulting for Lear Siegler and, in a way, enjoying the work a lot more. As an independent contractor, he came and went as he pleased without having to put up with the corporate politicking or the whims of some local executive. They either liked his work or they didn't. He succeeded or failed based on the merit of his work, not his personality or his life-style, and that was exactly how he liked it.

Randy showed up right on time at nine A.M. in a shirt and tie. Moutier had worked with him at least fifty times during his long association with LSI, and Kraft was always businesslike, easygoing, and punctual.

He had started the latest programming project for Moutier on Thursday and had to wrap it up before early afternoon so that he could head over to St. Ives Laboratories in Palos Verdes and finish up a system problem that had developed there.

But now that he was back on his own again, he quickly relearned the self-discipline a small businessman has to have to survive. No more long lunches or pleasure drives between jobs. Randy had to deliver the goods and manage his time to earn his keep. He had both the Anchorlok and St. Ives jobs wrapped up in time to get back home by four P.M. so that he could supervise the construction contractors he'd hired to install his dream: a backyard hot tub. He also arrived in time to help Jeff get ready for a weekend marketing convention in Los Angeles.

By 1983, Seelig was no longer an apprentice cook consigned to sweeping up the backroom at Grandma's Sugar Plums. The business was thriving, with Jeff as a partner and frontline chocolatier. There were two locations: the original candy store in Belmont Shore and a second operation in the west Orange County city of Cypress. Jeff worked both stores and, like Randy, had to juggle his time just to be able to see his mate.

On May 13, Jeff had called on Carl Herringer, a Grandma's employee as well as a longtime friend, to come help him get ready for the convention—the first of its kind in Los Angeles. For one weekend in May, the Los Angeles Convention Center was turned into a chocolate lover's fantasy, with candy shops, bakeries, and dessert specialists from throughout southern California dispatching representatives to man booths and dispense confections.

Randy pitched in, helping Jeff and Carl load chairs and tables and tablecloths into the car so that they could get down to the Convention

Center and set up their booth. Jeff had already laid in a generous supply of his hand-dipped chocolates for the show.

After helping Jeff and also seeing the building contractors off for the evening, Randy took a moment to show off his $3,000 hot tub extravaganza to Carl. There were still two-by-fours and sawdust all over the driveway and scattered throughout the tiny backyard, but the finished product was already taking form: a round, heated Jacuzzi set into a deck discreetly set off to one side of the yard, where residents of the three-story apartment building next door would not have a clear view.

Carl, a sometime bridge player who visited the Friday Night Poker Club on occasion, was impressed. He was invited to come try it out once it was finished. Randy had already issued informal invitations to the rest of the poker group to break out the champagne glasses and help christen the Kraft-Seelig tub at a party in a week or two, when the decking was finished.

By nightfall, Carl and Jeff were packed and ready to go. Jeff gave Randy a good-bye squeeze and Randy wished him well.

The next time Jeff spoke with him, Randy told him a monstrous mistake had been made and that he needed Jeff to find him a good lawyer as soon as possible.

Shortly after one A.M. on Saturday, May 14, 1983, two California Highway Patrol officers pulled over a brown 1979 Toyota Celica in the southern Orange County community of Mission Viejo. The remote stretch of the San Diego Freeway, also known as Interstate 5, where Officer Michael Sterling and Sergeant Michael Howard made the routine traffic stop, runs parallel to the Atcheson, Topeka, and Santa Fe rail line, about fifty miles south of Los Angeles.

It looked to Sterling as though they were about to bag their second drunk driver of the evening. That was about par for the Saturday morning graveyard shift. Cops call it the "deuce" shift—a shortened slang reference to Section 502, the old California penal code for driving under the influence. From seven P.M. Friday to four A.M. Saturday, as any law enforcement officer will tell you, drunks are most likely to roam the freeways.

Sterling and his supervisor, Sergeant Howard, had been following the Toyota in the far right-hand lane for several minutes, watching it weave northward, on and off the freeway shoulder. When the driver made an illegal lane change, they switched on their red light. The

Toyota slowed down from forty-five to, perhaps, thirty miles per hour and the driver steadied his steering, but he didn't pull over. Sterling flashed his "wig-wag" high beams and shone a spotlight into the car.

The driver reached into the back seat and grabbed a dark jacket that he tossed onto the passenger seat. When Sterling went on the public address system, ordering the car over, the driver finally pulled off and parked next to a guard rail on the right freeway shoulder.

Randy Steven Kraft, a thin, wiry middleweight with a prominent chin, mustache, sandy blond hair, and dark piercing brown eyes, got out of his Celica. He walked briskly back toward the CHP black-and-white. Drivers don't normally do that unless they've got something to hide, according to Sterling, a veteran of close to five thousand drunk-driving arrests in the three years he had been working the highways of Orange County.

"It usually means they've got an open container, usually an open beer can," Sterling said nearly seven years after that warm spring night in 1983.

Randy did have beer in his car, as it turned out. A whole cooler, in fact, packed with ice and Moosehead lager. As he got out of the car, he dumped a half-empty bottle on the pavement before walking back to the patrol car. But the broken beer bottle was the least of the damning evidence Sterling, Howard, and other officers would eventually turn up.

"I did a field sobriety test on him. You know: finger to nose, walking a straight line," Sterling recalled.

Sterling noticed, too, that the fly on Kraft's Levi's was open except for the top button.

The thirty-eight-year-old Long Beach computer analyst admitted having three or four drinks, but told Sterling he was sober. At that point, Sterling saw Randy Kraft as just another guy who thought he could toss off a few at the local bar and still drive home safely.

"He wasn't drunk by any means, but he was under the influence," Sterling said.

While Sterling went through the routine of cuffing Kraft and telling him he was under arrest, Sergeant Howard walked up to the passenger side of the Toyota and saw that Randy hadn't been traveling alone. Howard tapped on the glass to get the man's attention.

No response.

"So I banged on the window a little harder and shouted at the guy. Still no response," Howard recalled. "Obviously I wasn't going to get one, but I didn't know that at the time."

Terry Lee Gambrel, a twenty-five-year-old Indiana farmboy who had joined the marines and was stationed at nearby El Toro Marine Air Base, was slumped in the seat, a black jacket draped over his lap. He appeared to be sleeping.

While he continued drumming on the window, Howard hollered to Sterling that Kraft had a passenger.

Where did his friend live? Sterling asked Kraft.

Kraft didn't know. He was just a hitchhiker he'd picked up several miles back.

Normally, highway patrolman give sober passengers an opportunity to drive the car home so the arrested driver doesn't have impound fees to pay over and above bail and fines.

But it seemed likely to Howard that the Marine corporal was as drunk as Kraft. When he tried to open the door on the passenger's side, he found it locked. So he went around to the driver's side.

There he saw the first signs that he was probably right about Gambrel's drunken stupor. A couple of pill vials and some empty Moosehead bottles lay on the floorboards. And resting on Randy's seat was a folded, five-inch buck knife.

Howard allowed himself a weary little sigh of disgust. Gambrel was so intoxicated that he had actually passed out. But the veteran patrolman recoiled when he reached over and touched the clammy flesh of the young marine's forearm. It was obvious the young marine wasn't just dead drunk. He was dead, period.

Howard set the pill vials and knife up on the roof, reached across the still marine to unlock the door on the passenger side, and walked around to check Gambrel's pulse and pupils for signs of life.

"I didn't notice any real loss of color in the face," he recalled, "but his arms were a kind of waxy yellow color."

Then he lifted the jacket.

Gambrel's fly was open, the V of his jeans pulled up tight around his scrotum so that his penis and testicles waved obscenely in an upright position. His lap was wet—damp testimony of a bladder draining as the pelvic muscles relaxed into death.

His hands had been bound with the laces from his shoes. Fresh pink ligature marks were still branded deep into his wrists, "like a rubber band or something had been around each wrist," Howard remembers. The shoes had been removed from his feet and carefully tucked beneath the front seat.

There were marks on his neck, made by the tightening and loosening of Gambrel's own belt.

He wasn't breathing.

Howard walked back to the patrol unit where Sterling had just buckled the benign, handcuffed suspect into the back seat. The sergeant nervously asked Sterling to go up and check Randy's passenger for a pulse while Howard waited in the patrol unit with Kraft.

"He had been dead for some time," recalled Sterling. "Not a long time but, you know, a while."

Even describing the moment years later, Sterling's voice takes on a chilled urgency. At the time, Sterling was the same age and build as the strapping six-foot corpse sitting in the passenger seat of Randy Kraft's car.

"My regular partner was off on a personal holiday and they won't let you drive on patrol alone at night," he said. "That's how Sergeant Howard and I wound up together. If Gil [his regular partner] had been with me, I don't know if we would have been on that particular stretch of road at that particular time. I just don't know. It was pure chance."

Like Howard, Sterling knew within seconds of touching Gambrel's limp, clammy wrist what they had stumbled upon.

"I had just been transferred down there to south [Orange] county about four or five months before and I remember a sergeant at the briefing we get before heading out on patrol each night who had talked about dead bodies turning up on the freeways and that there was some killer out there."

Indeed, bodies had been showing up on offramps and near hilltops and in the underbrush for more than a decade. Bodies of young men—hitchhikers, for the most part.

"At first I didn't give it much thought except to think, 'Wow, that's weird.' And later, after the paramedics came and we were talking about it, I said, 'Could this be the guy?'

"And then everything snowballed."

They radioed for paramedics at 1:17 A.M. and then waited in the patrol car with Kraft. It took four minutes for the team of firemen and paramedics to get there. The two officers remained grim and silent, realizing they might have something far more menacing than a drunk driver in the back seat of their patrol car. Kraft was equally silent.

"He did ask us, 'How's my friend?'" Howard remembered. "Well, 'How's my friend?' is completely different from 'He's a hitchhiker I picked up,' you know?"

By the time paramedics arrived at 1:21 A.M. and hooked Gambrel up to an electrocardiogram monitor, the line reflecting his heart activity was flat.

Paramedic Dan Deslauriers stuck his head in the back of the patrol car to ask Kraft what Gambrel might have taken to go into full cardiac arrest. Kraft volunteered that he had given the marine some of his Ativan.

In the meantime, Deslauriers's partner, Steve Werth, was furiously working to pump life back into Gambrel's body. Jerry Flores, a paramedic intern at the time, later said that the two CHP officers tried to prevent them from treating Gambrel at first. He was dead, they said, and they did not want to disturb evidence.

"We put the monitor on him and we had some electrical activity in his heart and I said, 'We've got to work this guy,'" Flores recalled.

He wasn't breathing and he had no pulse, but his body temperature, color, and moistness were still within the normal range. The paramedics insisted on pulling the marine out of the Toyota. They put an EOA (esophagal orbitrator airway) tube down his throat.

"It's got a little balloon on the tip of it and we blew that up so that he wouldn't start vomiting and get it into his lungs," Flores said.

After cardiopulmonary resuscitation and intravenous drug treatment, Gambrel's heart showed faint electrical activity. "I've been a paramedic over six years now and the thing that stands out in my mind to this day is how many drugs we pushed on that guy," Flores said. "We used everything. That's the most drugs I've ever used on any one call."

With a doctor instructing them via radio what to use and in what dosages to use it, the paramedics gave Gambrel every life-preserving treatment they had: sodium bicarbonate to neutralize acid in his bloodstream; dextrose to boost his blood sugar; Narcan, a general antidote to most narcotic overdosages; calcium fluoride to balance the electrolytes in his system; dopamine and epinephrine to increase his blood pressure; and atropine to stimulate his heart.

They used a pair of electric shock paddles in a vain attempt to stimulate his heart back into a regular beat, artificially lifting Gambrel's body off the pavement each time a rush of electricity ran through it.

But the pupils of the young marine's eyes remained fixed in a death stare.

By 1:35 A.M., he was loaded into an ambulance and rushed to Saddleback Community Hospital, the paramedics pumping his chest throughout the entire ten-minute ride. Sterling and Howard followed close behind, Randy sitting quietly in the back seat. When they arrived, Sterling stayed in the car with Kraft.

"I had to be around him for a while by myself," Sterling said. "There was nobody else around. He was handcuffed in the back seat and, you know, I've got my service revolver. But still there was that eerie feeling being around him, knowing that he could be the guy."

At 2:19 A.M., the on-duty emergency room physician examined Terry Gambrel for vital signs. In less than five minutes, he declared him dead.

Jim Sidebotham's phone rang at 3:45 A.M.

The long, tall homicide investigator with the cheekbones of a Cherokee and the deep-set eyes of a hound dog had received that kind of middle-of-the-night call before. More often than not it meant murder.

In twenty-five years with the Orange County Sheriff's Department, the forty-eight-year-old Sidebotham had been called out of bed on dozens of killings. Though most were of the domestic violence or convenience-store robbery variety, he had investigated his share of grisly murder mysteries.

There was the time two years before when a Mission Viejo man, Cody Schreiber, reported that his home had been burglarized and his lover killed. For two hours, Schreiber told the first two investigators who interrogated him the details of how the home was ransacked and his roommate murdered. Sidebotham listened from another room.

When it was over, Sidebotham sidled up to Schreiber in the hallway, leaned up against a water cooler, and commiserated with him. How tough it must be, Sidebotham said, not to get something as traumatic as murder off his chest. He asked Schreiber if he was ready to talk.

The man stammered, reluctant at first. Then he nodded. Talking with the sallow-faced Sidebotham has been likened by some who marvel at his interrogation techniques to the rocking-chair patience of a grandfather. In the hallway and, later, on videotape, Sidebotham sympathetically coaxed the truth from Schreiber.

Schreiber had decapitated and buried his roommate.

But now the phone was jangling and his wife was beginning to stir. Sidebotham answered in his low, cautious drawl before his wife awakened, and then he listened. The CHP had a man in custody—five feet ten inches, about 160 pounds, mustache, probably gay. He was pulled over on the I-5. He had a dead marine with his pants pulled down around his thighs sitting in the passenger seat of his car.

Sidebotham's thin, bony fingers dropped the phone back in its cradle. He got dressed quickly.

He had said all along that a chance CHP stop would be how the killer would finally be brought down. All the detective work and evidence gathering and witness questioning in the world couldn't beat blind luck in a case like this.

Sidebotham was looking forward to finally meeting this suspect. He didn't know how many of the mysterious bodies found along the freeway during the past decade had been this Kraft fellow's responsibility, but he was certain that the marine was probably not the first to die at his hands.

By the time he reached Saddleback Community Hospital, the body had already been transferred to the county morgue in Santa Ana and the CHP officers had turned Kraft over to Sheriff's deputies. Sidebotham drove the dozen miles to Santa Ana north on the I-5, in the opposite direction Kraft had been driving just three hours before.

By five A.M., he and Deputy Coroner Joe Luckey were gazing down on the body of Terry Gambrel. Pinpoint ruptures in the capillaries behind his eyelids were mute testimony that he had died of asphyxiation. The tiny blood vessels burst in the cheeks and eyelids of victims who choke for lack of oxygen. Most often those are drowning victims.

But the two-hundred-pound Marine corporal who stared up at them had not drowned. He had the alcohol equivalent of two beers in his blood and enough of the tranquilizer Ativan in his system to synergize the beer into a bona fide Mickey Finn. But not enough to kill him.

The autopsy that medical examiner Dr. Walter Fischer conducted later that morning would confirm that Gambrel had been strangled to death.

At daybreak, Sidebotham walked from the coroner's office to the Orange County Jail where Kraft was being held. He was not the sinewy bruiser that might have been expected to cruise the highways in search of marines to murder. The man Sidebotham and Sergeant Doug Storm met in a jail interrogation room was very nearly as thin as Sidebotham, though shorter and younger. Without his neatly trimmed mustache, Kraft could have passed for twenty-eight instead of thirty-eight years old, though his hairline was beginning to recede. He seemed amiable, calm, and sober, but when Sidebotham asked him about Gambrel, Kraft refused to waive his rights. He would give them no statement without a lawyer present, he said.

The sun was coming up as Storm and Sidebotham left the jail. They were more certain than ever that the freeway murder case might be cracked. Finally.

Sidebotham linked up with Deputy District Attorney Bryan Brown, the homicide specialist in the Orange County Prosecutor's Office, and the first thing they did was roust Superior Court judge Richard Beacom out of bed. Once they had Beacom on a conference call and informed everyone that the call was being recorded for legal purposes, they began the formal Q&A necessary to secure a search warrant:

Sidebotham: I've been a deputy sheriff for twenty-four years. I've been assigned to robbery-homicide with more emphasis on homicide for the past seven and a half years.

Brown: Did you receive a call sometime this morning with respect to an incident that occurred on the San Diego Freeway in the south portion of Orange County?

Sidebotham: Yes, I did.

Brown: What time did you receive the call?

Sidebotham: I received a call at 0345 hours this morning, or at three-forty-five. A.M.

Brown: And what was the substance of the call you received?

Sidebotham: I received a call that a person was deceased at Mission Community Hospital. He had ligature marks on his wrists. He was a passenger in a vehicle and that the driver had been arrested.

Brown: Did you then go to the hospital?

Sidebotham: Yes, I did.

Brown: What did you do when you got to the hospital?

Sidebotham: The body had already been transported to the Forensic Science Center, also known as the morgue, in Santa Ana. I proceeded to the Forensic Science Center in Santa Ana to view the body.

Brown: Okay. Now, what do you seek to search that car for?

Sidebotham: I want to search . . .

Sidebotham paused long enough to catch his breath and begin a recitation from a prepared list of wants.

Sidebotham: Since there hasn't been an autopsy performed on the body, I would like to search the vehicle for a gun, a knife, a blunt instrument, sharp instrument and scabbards, sheaths, and containers for weapons, blood, fingerprints, footprints, and shoe prints, tissue, body fluids, shell casings, bullets, fragments, and ammunition, packages, hair samples, fiber samples, photographs, measurements, metal fragments, secretions such as saliva, perspiration, and semen liquid; powder or other drugs or narcotics that may tend to cause death; articles containing apparent blood tissue, gunpowder, body fluids, victims' clothing; identification of the body, papers, and identification from the body; any written material pertaining to the homicide, papers and identification from area of death scene tending to show identity and relationship of victim to potential suspect or suspects; papers and identification showing owner, occupier, or person who has dominion and control of the vehicle such as, but not limited to, letters, envelopes, vehicle registration card, Valium, propranolol, homosexual drawings, photographs, and literature; homosexual killing, beating, or abusive literature.

Brown: Okay. Based upon your experience in the robbery-homicide division, have you had occasion to investigate cases that involve homosexual-type homicides?

Sidebotham: Yes, I have.

Brown: About how many occasions have you had that opportunity?

Sidebotham: I would have to estimate that it's been in excess of twenty-five.

Brown: Okay, and from the information that you have at this time, do you believe that this particular homicide is a homosexually-related homicide?

Sidebotham: Based on the information . . . the condition of victim's body, the way he was clothed, the condition of Mr. Kraft's pants being unbuttoned, the ligature marks on the victim's wrists, and the ligature mark on the neck, yes.

At the same time that Sidebotham started the procedures for obtaining the search warrant for the car, he dispatched an investigator to stand by at Kraft's home, located about thirty minutes north of Santa Ana in Long Beach.

But he and Bryan Brown had to go through the same authorization procedure—conference call, formal Q&A and warrant request—from Judge Beacom in order to go through Kraft's white stucco bungalow at 824 Roswell Avenue. That would take another prepared list and more time to make certain they had an airtight search warrant before going in.

Sidebotham decided early on that they would take every precaution to make certain they did this case correctly, from the reading of the rights down to the dotting of the *i*'s and the crossing of the fingers. If Kraft was the guy and they had caught him red-handed, Sidebotham had no intention of going down in history as the man who blew the case.

While he waited for the second search-warrant session with Judge Beacom, he turned his attention to Kraft's Toyota, now parked in the county garage.

Sheriff's Department forensics expert James White and several other department personnel joined Sidebotham on Saturday afternoon and began digging through the car, coming up with routine bric-a-brac: keys, gum, toothbrush, an open roll of Rolaids, a can opener, computer manuals, a package of Zig Zag cigarette papers, a disposable cigarette lighter, hand lotion, old newspapers, a Montecito Las Palmas brand Dunhill cigar.

In the glove compartment were matchbooks from the Charthouse restaurant and a San Diego bar called the Hole, as well as a couple of minor collector's items: a Lyndon Johnson/Hubert Humphrey matchbook from the 1964 presidential campaign and a matchbook advertising the movie and song "Take This Job and Shove It." There were also several pin-on buttons, ranging from I'M AN EXPERT WITH EXPERT VERSYTEC, A XEROX COMPANY to one that proclaimed IT'S YOUR TURN IN THE BARREL.

Investigators also found a half-used bottle of Styx, a "spell spinning spray" guaranteed to act as an aphrodisiac on a prospective gay lover. "The magic of its vapors twine and tangle with his mind," read the ad line. "With Styx and a smile, he'll understand."

Behind the driver's seat, they found Gambrel's brown leather belt. It matched the width of the clear, neat ring that had been left around Gambrel's neck by the instrument used to garotte him to death.

Two unopened bottles of Moosehead lager were still in the cooler in the back seat of the Celica. Beyond the empty beer bottles and the two Ativan vials that Sergeant Howard had found in the car the night before, the search team discovered several more vials. In all, they found nine different prescription drugs, including Ativan, Valium (diazepam), the depressant propranolol, and Inderal, a painkiller used in the treatment of angina and migraine headaches. Most of the vials still contained pills.

They also found a thick, well-thumbed paperback, *The Essential Guide to Prescription Drugs: What You Need to Know for Safe Drug Use.* The "new and revised edition" contained "profiles" of 212 generic and over-the-counter drugs and 1,466 brand-name drugs, detailing when not to take each drug, side and adverse effects, and interactions with other drugs, with nineteen ready reference tables and "much, much more," according to the advertising blurb on the front cover.

White lifted the floor mat on the driver's side of the car and came up with an envelope. Inside were forty-seven photographs, all of young men. Some were nude. Some were clothed. Some, observed Sidebotham, were dead—or, at least, they looked that way.

One depicted a naked young man draped on a couch made of fabric with a distinctive floral pattern. He appeared either stoned or dead. His eyes gazed at the camera but did not see, and his mouth hung in a loose, lolling gape.

Others looked like they might be sleeping. They were generally the same height and weight as Kraft, many with distinctive military haircuts.

But there were further shocks to be found, even as Sidebotham and White leafed through the photos.

The seat that Gambrel had been sitting on was soaked with blood. It couldn't have been Gambrel's, Sidebotham noted. The dead marine had no open wounds.

By the time the investigators got to the trunk, there was both expectation and dread in the air. They were prepared for the worst and they weren't disappointed.

They found a briefcase that contained a wood-grained binder, and there they discovered a tablet bearing sixty-one neatly printed notations. At first glance, they made no sense. The list began with "STABLE," "ANGEL," "EDM," "HARI KARI," and ended with "EN-GLAND," "OIL," "DART 405," and "WHAT YOU GOT."

But Sidebotham had a pretty good idea what the list meant. Each entry appeared to be a meticulously encoded memory trigger for a murder. Sometimes, more than one, as in "2 IN 1 HITCH," "2 IN 1 BEACH," and "GR2." The investigating team concluded that what they now had in hand was a two-column list of murder victims dating back for years. Including the four "2 in 1" notations, the list added up to sixty-five victims. If Sidebotham's hunch was correct, it would make Randy Steven Kraft the most prolific serial killer in modern times.

It would also open up "an investigator's nightmare," as he became fond of telling newspaper reporters. Matching photos to bodies and bodies to the death list would become Sidebotham's full-time occupation for years to come, and several of the cryptic entries would never have a body to match them.

Sidebotham left the fingerprint dusting and microscopic work that would take place over the next weeks in the hands of the experts while he returned to his office and got back on the phone with Bryan Brown and Judge Beacom.

He was not one to show excitement, but Sidebotham had a tough time keeping his emotions under control during the formal Q&A that followed. There had always been a low-key but very real kind of competition among homicide detectives in southern California to find and convict the true freeway killer. Bryan Brown, who was in the process of trying William Bonin on four counts of murder in Orange County at the time of Kraft's arrest, was as aware as Sidebotham that Bonin had been awarded the title of the Freeway Killer under false pretenses.

The real one had always been out there, operating right under law enforcement's nose—tweaking it from time to time with a naked, emasculated body right in the middle of a freeway offramp.

And now it appeared as though the cat and mouse game was over. Sidebotham described the forty-seven-snapshot collection he found in Randy's car to Judge Beacom, including a picture he was sure depicted Eric Church, and another flash photo that had to be Rodger DeVaul, Jr., wearing a nylon windbreaker, orange in color with brown shoulders and white bodice. It was the same windbreaker that Judy Nelson had described as the gift Geoffrey Nelson's grandmother had given to him a short time before he wound up naked and dead on the Euclid onramp of the Garden Grove Freeway.

In the photo, DeVaul's hands were jammed in the pockets of the jacket and the bottom button was buttoned while the rest of the coat gaped opened—just like DeVaul's loose, stunned mouth.

"The person appears to be dead," Sidebotham said.

"The photo depicting Mr. DeVaul?" asked Brown.

"Right," answered Sidebotham.

"Appears to be taken of him after he was . . ." Brown began. Sidebotham finished his sentence for him.

". . . of a person being dead, yes," said the homicide detective.

"Judge, do you have any questions with respect to the three victims, Church, DeVaul, and Nelson at this point?" Brown asked.

"No," answered Beacom. He signed off on the search warrant request for Randy Kraft's house with no further comment.

Following the second phone session with Judge Beacom, Sidebotham was on his way to Long Beach. At 5:30 P.M., he rolled up to 824
Roswell Avenue, search warrant in hand. He announced himself and
knocked at the door, but there was nobody home except Kraft's dog,
Max. The police barricades went up around the house and Sidebotham
let himself in, followed by a small army of police: two Orange County
Sheriff's forensics experts, four other Sheriff's detectives, and several
investigators from the Los Angeles County Sheriff's Office as well as the
Seal Beach, Long Beach, and Garden Grove Police departments.

Jeff Seelig returned from the chocolate convention, demanding to
know what was going on, but he was kept outside the barricades.

Inside, the investigators were literally tearing the house apart, as
Seelig would later complain. Part of the den wall would be removed and
a pair of couches, with a distinctive floral pattern would be hauled out
the front door to a waiting Sheriff's van later in the week. The wall, as
it turned out, was stained with blood, and the couches matched the one
in the photo taken from Kraft's car, depicting a dead, naked young man.

In the bathroom, they found a brown shaving kit with the name
MIKE CLUCK inscribed on it.

In the garage, they found a tan and maroon jacket that had once
belonged to Chris Schoenborn, the twenty-year-old farmer from Grand
Rapids, Michigan. Loose threads in the lining marked the spot where a
label had once been sewn to identify the jacket as Schoenborn's.

And the horrifying bits of evidence continued to pile up: A camera
that had once belonged to Michael Sean O'Fallon, a dead Colorado
youth. A Norelco shaver with two floating heads, still in its dark gray
carrying case with red felt lining, that Clayton Church gave to his
twenty-one-year-old son, Eric, before he took a bus across the United
States. A tote bag emblazoned with the word HAWAII and a pair of
Japanese nunchakus, once the property of Lance Taggs of Oregon. A
signed sketch pad that belonged to Greg Jolley, whose dismembered
body had shown up in a trash bag in the San Bernardino mountains.

By the time Sidebotham and his troops left the modest, single-
story home at 824 Roswell at 2:05 the next morning, they had enough
rugs and clothing and furniture to fill a moving van and enough
apprehension about what they had stumbled upon to fill the most
terrifying of nightmares.

But it was only the beginning.

21

The list itself is not particularly startling.

It takes up the top half of a single sheet torn from a yellow legal pad, and the carefully block-printed entries are innocuous enough. There are thirty names or phrases on the far left side of the page and thirty-one on the far right. A smear of something dark and inky that spilled on the paper decorates the center of the page, like an out-of-place Rorschach blot. At first or even second glance, the sheet of paper could represent an old checklist for a scavenger hunt or an encoded "things to do" list.

Kraft explained it away as a list of nicknames he had given to his friends in the gay community. Phil Crabtree was "Airplane Hill," another Kraft acquaintance was "Jail Out," and so on. But Sergeant Sidebotham and, later, prosecutor Bryan Brown called the inventory in the trunk of Randy's car a catalog far more sinister than any grouping of friends.

Early on in court proceedings, Brown began referring to the sheet as the "scorecard." Each entry, he said, represented a victim—and, sometimes, two victims at once—of the most prolific serial killer in modern U.S. history. Beginning with the cryptic "STABLE" and ending with the equally mysterious "WHAT YOU GOT," the list was slapped under seal by the prosecution nearly as quickly as it was discovered, for fear that it would lead to charges of foul from Kraft's defense lawyer. Indeed, linking the entries to anything as horrific as serial murder appears to be pure speculation upon initial examination.

But investigators looked closer.

To begin with, there were the seven entries that began with the word "PORTLAND":

> PORTLAND
> PORTLAND DENVER
> PORTLAND BLOOD
> PORTLAND HAWAII
> PORTLAND RESERVE
> PORTLAND HEAD
> PORTLAND ECK

It didn't take long for Oregon state homicide investigators to match those entries with six unsolved murders of young hitchhikers along the Interstate 5 freeway, south of Portland, beginning with Michael O'Fallon—"PORTLAND DENVER"—in the summer of 1980. The one-word entry "PORTLAND" would continue to be a mystery. No murder would be linked to it.

Following the Portland entries is "GR2," one of four notations on the list containing the numeral "2." Dennis Alt and Chris Schoenborn, two young men from Grand Rapids, Michigan, died the same night in December of 1982, shortly after sharing a drink with Kraft at the bar of the Amway Grand Hotel.

From there, the mix-and-match game became as baffling at times as the *New York Sunday Times* acrostic puzzle, if a shade more macabre. The game for investigators became one of locating a body or a missing person who fit the description of a Kraft victim and looking for a characteristic, setting, or key word that fit the death list.

Lynn Wierman, the woman who hired Randy as a dispatcher at Aztec Aircraft in 1973 and first introduced him to computers, theorized that the entries represented the names of data files in an IBM business computer system. Kraft never owned a personal computer of his own, so Wierman suggested that he might have either hidden the files in one of the computer systems at businesses where he worked or kept the information separate, on a floppy disk, that he could remove and carry with him from location to location.

"Randy was familiar with the RPG2 system," Wierman said, "and those kinds of entries [on the so-called death list] would be just the sort of title that you would use with that system."

It was a theory that intrigued law enforcement as well, though nothing was ever made public if, indeed, computer files about murder victims were ever located at Lear Siegler or any of the other businesses where Randy worked.

Six years after Kraft's arrest, detectives had pieced together only about two-thirds of the puzzle. Of the sixty-one entries, detectives managed to tie forty-one to the deaths of forty-three young men, killed between 1971 and 1983. Two of the entries—GR2 and 2 IN 1 BEACH—represent episodes where Kraft murdered two victims at the same time, according to the prosecution.

But twenty entries on the list remain a mystery. They were still showing up on the screen of the Compaq computer in the district attorney's *Randy Kraft* Inventory Room on the ground floor of the Orange County Courthouse, seven years after his arrest. Each entry is followed by the phrase "Name unconnected to any unsolved murder."

Two of those entries carry the disturbing numeral "2": 2 IN 1 MKV TO PL and 2 IN 1 HITCH.

And two of Kraft's final victims—Eric Church, the young hitchhiker from Connecticut, and Marine corporal Terry Lee Gambrel, found dying in the seat next to Randy on the night he was arrested—were not entered on the death list, according to Bryan Brown's investigative team. He apparently had not found the time to jot them into his catalog by the time CHP officers Howard and Sterling pulled him over on the San Diego Freeway.

But the alarming box score of identified and still unmatched names on the list added up to a frightening total if investigators were correct: by the time he was caught, Randy Steven Kraft was responsible for sixty-seven murders over a twelve-and-half-year period.

Texas drifter Henry Lee Lucas claimed responsibility for more than two-hundred serial killings following his arrest just four months after Kraft, but that figure was pared down to less than sixty—and perhaps as few as two—by law enforcement officials who discounted his confession as exaggerated to a large degree. Other notorious serial killers—from Jack the Ripper to John Wayne Gacy—have been connected to far fewer killings. London's turn-of-the-century lust murderer's reputation rests on the murder of five prostitutes, while Gacy's reputation as Chicago's premier serial killer relies on the discovery of thirty-three bodies of young men buried beneath his suburban home.

Randy Kraft, however, outdistanced all of them. If his scoreboard is accurate, not since the execution of French aristocrat Giles de Rais in the fifteenth century, when the Catholic church found him guilty of murdering several hundred young boys for pure sexual pleasure, has a single serial killer been identified as responsible for more thrill killings.

On Sunday, May 15, the day after Randy's arrest, police contacted Ronald Phillips, a corporal in Terry Lee Gambrel's unit at El Toro Marine Corps Air Station. In Gambrel's pants pocket, Sidebotham's investigators had come up with a folded piece of paper that contained directions to Phillips's off-base apartment at 4902 Oakfield in Santa Ana.

That didn't surprise Phillips. He and Terry had been roommates in the barracks and they had lunch together around noon on the Thursday before he died. Phillips had invited him to a party at his new place on Friday night, but Gambrel had never arrived. Ron personally wrote out the directions to his apartment for Terry, a simple Indiana farm boy with a big heart and a taste for beer—lots of beer. Gambrel also smoked a little pot from time to time, Phillips told investigators, but then so did a lot of guys on the base. He didn't use anything harder than that, though the story around the barracks was that he did keep a regular stash in a shoe box he locked away in his personal locker.

The investigators also got through to Gambrel's girlfriend on Sunday, back in Austin, Indiana. Diana Richie told them she had been going with Terry since December and that they planned to get married. He did like his beer, she said, but she knew nothing of any drugs. Names like lorazapam or nordiazepam were gibberish to her.

She and Terry were from different towns, but they had been acquainted for several years, southern Indiana not being the kind of place where people can remain anonymous for long. In any of the tiny farm hamlets that dot the map south of Indianapolis and north of the Ohio River, natives spot strangers in a minute.

Terry and his twin brother, Jerry, were no strangers. Jerry used to kid his brother that he was the baby of the family because he had been born a few moments after Jerry had. They grew up on an acre of land between Brownstown and Crothersville that once belonged to their grandmother, who raised them after their mother and father separated. In addition to the twins, the Gambrels' grandmother also raised their older sister.

They all graduated from Brownstown Central High in a close-knit rural community where very little changed and everyone knew every-one else. When Jerry got the news that Terry was dead that Sunday afternoon in May, he was living in the small wood-frame house on Rural

Route 1, Crothersville, Scott County, Indiana, where he and his twin brother had grown up.

Their grandmother didn't have a car, so Jerry and Terry learned to entertain themselves out in the country. They played football and softball, and Terry, the quiet one, became proficient at chess. In high school, he became a power hitter on the intramural baseball team, but just an average fielder. He was a southpaw at first base for the Brownstown Huskies.

He joined the marines in 1976, right out of high school, in order to get out of his stifling small-town existence. Jerry wasn't quite so adventurous: he took a job in a nearby shoe factory.

For the next three years, Gambrel was stationed at Camp Pendleton in southern California. He liked it well enough, adopted the nickname "Luke," and joined a basketball team on base. But he grew homesick. When his enlistment was up in 1979, he moved back home and went to work in the same shoe factory where his brother and older sister worked.

In the meantime, Jerry Gambrel quit the shoe business and took a job in a neighboring town with a larger company—a subsidiary of Lear Siegler Industries. There, he linked up with friends who got him to join the softball team at a church in Austin, and he started going with the minister's daughter. He also brought his southpaw twin into the fold to play first base Saturday afternoons, even if he was a reluctant convert on Sunday mornings.

But Terry still didn't have the wanderlust out of his soul. He and another restless ex-marine, Tim Kenton, backpacked across Europe in the summer of 1981. When they returned, Terry reenlisted in the marines rather than go back to work in the shoe factory.

He went back to California, this time to the Marine Corps Air Station in El Toro, but things had changed. It wasn't the corps he remembered, in part because he had changed. The group he had been through boot camp with had moved on, replaced by a younger contingent with slightly different tastes in music, pop heroes, TV shows, and other cultural icons. At twenty-three, Terry was suddenly no longer "Luke" Gambrel, one of the guys. He was "the old man" in the El Toro personnel office—out of touch with the young hot-doggers just out of boots or technical school.

The "quiet" half of the Gambrel twins had developed a taste for the party life as an adult, but his new unchosen role as a base elder statesman precluded him from many off-base invitations. Again, Terry began getting homesick and took every leave he could get to go back home to Indiana.

Jerry Gambrel was a permanent fixture at the Austin church by 1982. During one of his brother's leaves, he introduced Terry to his sweetheart, the minister's daughter. She, in turn, introduced Terry to her girlfriend, Diane Richie. They'd run into each other before, but never socially. Diane did in a few weeks what no one else—including Terry's own twin brother—had been able to do since high school: get Terry to talk about settling down. She even convinced him that the church was more than just a sponsor for softball games. Terry got religion at the same time that he got roots.

From that point forward, Terry Gambrel ached to get his enlistment with the corps over with so he and Diane could get married. He had a little over a year to go.

She was first astonished, then distraught when she was told about Terry Gambrel's last ride. People hitchhiked in Indiana, but they didn't lose their lives when they did. After she collected herself, she told police that Terry owned a Mercury Bobcat station wagon and, normally, he wouldn't have been dependent on anyone for transportation. He had left it in California during his most recent visit to Indiana in early May because he was having trouble with the exhaust system.

The station wagon had apparently conked out in the parking lot of an Irvine shopping center, and by the time Gambrel returned to California on May 8, the local police had ticketed it and towed it away. Sidebotham's investigators found it in a Costa Mesa impound yard.

Early Friday evening, the thirteenth of May, Terry played softball on base with his intramural team, then showered in the barracks and read a letter he'd just received from Diane. Then, shortly after dark, he pulled his overnight bag out of his locker and headed out to the highway with directions to Ron Phillips's new apartment in his pocket.

"He didn't say when he'd be back," said his roommate, Lance Corporal Kristofer Lake.

Five days later, on May 18, 1983, Terry Gambrel was buried with full military rites in the Russell Chapel Cemetery, Crothersville, Indiana. Diane Richie was there. So was Gambrel's mother, Nellie Lewis, and friends like Tim Kenton who had listened with kind patience to Terry's talk about his recent rebirth as a Christian.

At the funeral, Jerry asked the minister to say a few words about seeking salvation before it's too late, and the clergyman obliged. Death, he told the assembled friends and family, can come when one least expects it, and it is best to be prepared by asking God's forgiveness before your soul passes over. Terry was prepared.

Or, at least, his soul was.

While one member of the team of investigators that Jim Sidebotham and Bryan Brown had assembled was on the phone to Terry Gambrel's family and fiancée, a pair of Los Angeles County Sheriff's deputies took on the job of interviewing a second suspect in the case: a chubby chocolate-candy maker who shared the home at 824 Roswell Avenue with Randy Kraft.

Since the house search the previous evening, when a half dozen camera-toting, fingerprint-dusting detectives had found two foot-long dildos, a container of Crisco, and a jar of petroleum jelly in the nightstand next to the bed that Kraft and Seelig shared, Doug Storm, Sidebotham, and all the rest of the investigative team were curious as to how someone Kraft knew so intimately could not have known about his roommate's extracurricular activities.

Jeffery Alan Seelig started out by telling police that he and Randy were both gay and had lived together since Seelig graduated from high school in 1975. Jeff said that he was into S&M—sadomasochism—but Randy wasn't.

"Mr. Seelig related that he and the defendant sometimes picked up hitchhikers on the freeway and brought them home to have sex with them," wrote one of the investigating deputies. "However, whenever he and the defendant would have an argument, the defendant would drive the freeways by himself, sometimes going as far south as San Diego and sometimes bringing back hitchhikers to the house."

For two and a half months prior to the arrest, Randy hadn't been able to have sex with him, Seelig said. It was partially for that reason that the two of them were seeing a couples counselor. It was Jeff, too, who confirmed in his interview with the deputies that Randy had traveled frequently to places like Portland, Grand Rapids, and Washington state while he was employed by Lear Siegler. He also confirmed that Randy often carried a supply of tranquilizers in his car, including Equanol, meprobamate, and drugs used to treat anxiety disorders and high blood pressure.

Following his meeting with the deputies, Jeff got to a phone and called Sandra Hare, who recorded her notes from that 4:30 P.M. conversation.

Jeff Seelig, she wrote, was hysterical and fearful. Randy had been stopped on a 502 and had a half-dead body in the car. "I love that man. I can't hardly stand up," Jeff told her. "I can't stand not having him close. He is a good person. Why did this happen to me?"

Jeff asked her to call Dr. McArthur and to pray for Randy.

For the first several weeks following Kraft's arrest, Seelig was an active suspect in the case. At one point during the first week, Orange County sheriff Brad Gates publicly confirmed at a press conference his department's contention that Seelig might be as guilty of the crimes they believed his roommate committed as Kraft himself.

But, as more and more friends and acquaintances of the pair were interviewed, that belief began to change, and an even more astonishing possibility arose: that Seelig might have lived with someone for more than eight years, at three different addresses, and never known about his lover's secret life.

"I am his only living victim," Seelig said many years later, after he had broken off all communication with Kraft.

Immediately following his arrest, however, Jeff was his single greatest defender. By week's end, he called his own press conference at his attorney's office in Laguna Hills, disarming the fact-hungry journalists by serving up two trays of hand-dipped chocolates from his candy shop before answering any of their questions. He barred cameras and TV crews from the conference.

"He and I worked very, very hard," he told reporters. "We built a home together as a partnership. We recently did some very extensive remodeling on our home. We never went out really anywhere because we spent so much time at the house, and one of the reasons for doing all the remodeling . . . was because we spent so much time at home. We just wanted to kind of make it real nice and comfortable so we can have friends come over.

"I'll tell you, Randy and I in our spare time sat around and drank a lot of beer and relaxed and went to the movies and we always were entertaining friends. I'm basically a gourmet chef by hobby and Randy and I always would have dinners and have special people with us."

Randy had already eaten into the equity of their Roswell home by taking out a second trust deed loan in order to put in the hot tub, but Seelig took out a third trust deed loan to supply a retainer for Randy's defense attorney. For more than a week after the arrest, while police were going through his house, Seelig stayed with friends.

He refused to tell reporters about his own personal relationship with Randy or his speculation on his guilt, but he did have blistering words for Sheriff Gates and Sidebotham's heavy-handed sleuths.

"They turned the place inside out," he said. "Rooms were torn up, walls were chopped, antiques were damaged, sofas were removed. . . . Three-fourths of the things they confiscated were mutual things of Randy's and mine."

In all, Jim Sidebotham's investigators made three trips to 824 Roswell. By the following Thursday, homicide detectives from Michigan, Washington, and Oregon had flown in to help in the search. They had been able to identify positively several of the items found in the house and the garage as belonging to murder victims in their jurisdictions.

In the cluttered single-car garage, a sign on one wall read FINDERS KEEPERS—UNUSUAL OLD STUFF. There, among the power tools and lumber and half-used cans of house paint and redwood stain, they found a box containing an unusual collection of chains, shoelaces, and belts. There were also some shirts and jackets that Randy or Jeff might simply have outgrown or decided for whatever reason to store in the garage. One of them, however, turned out to belong to Chris Schoenborn, and speculation turned to the rest of them as being souvenirs of some long-forgotten night of horror.

They also found an old yellow rug that intrigued forensics expert Dan White. He took a sample of the nylon fibers and tried matching them up back in the police lab with similar fibers that homicide detectives found on the body of Marine Scott Michael Hughes five years before. He wasn't absolutely certain Hughes had been lying on that rug before he was dumped on an onramp to the Riverside Freeway, but the fibers appeared to have come from the same source when scrutinized under a microscope.

Back in the house, police found *Blues Harp* by Tony "Little Sun" Glover—an instruction book for the blues harmonica, just like one Eddie Moore once used to teach himself how to play the blues.

Next door neighbor Penny DeWees went on and on about how meticulous the two men were about their gardening. She also praised them for taking the time to walk their dog regularly. They were quiet, unassuming, and friendly—just the kind of neighbors anyone would want. Sure, they were gay. That was common knowledge in the neighborhood. But it was the 1980s, after all, and people who couldn't live and let live were likely to be hypocrites and probably weren't worth bothering with anyway.

As long as they weren't in the bedroom, it was difficult for the dozens of police, lab, and forensics personnel wandering in and out of the bungalow on Roswell to tell that two gay men lived in the house at all. Seelig, who had recently completed a gourmet cooking class, had all the most up-to-date cookery tools in the kitchen, including a food processor and an espresso machine. A framed Oktoberfest poster hung over the toaster, a memento of their autumn vacation in Europe.

Ferns and ficus plants decorated every corner of the front of the house and a pair of *Vogue* posters hung in the dining room, where the two entertained family and friends like the Phillipses or members of the Friday Night Poker Club. In the den, they found a bookshelf, topped with a picture of Max, and a gold, yellow, and white brocade couch and chair facing each other across a hardwood floor.

In several of the forty-seven photographs that had been found under the floor mat of Randy's car, a nude and dazed—or dead—young man was posed on a couch bearing the exact same coloring, shape, and pattern as the one that belonged to Randy and Jeff.

The young man in the photos was identified by his mother, Barbara, as Marine corporal Wyatt Loggins, whose body, stuffed in a gray plastic trash bag, had been discovered by children in an El Toro housing development on a hot August day in 1980.

Early in the investigation, Bryan Brown strung a half dozen of the most graphic and most brutal of Randy's color Polaroid shots over his desk as a constant reminder of the perverse and vicious nature of the defendant. Then he assembled a team of investigators and paralegals and went to work.

One month after Randy's arrest, a handwritten letter arrived on Bryan Brown's desk. It had no return address, but was postmarked from the City of Industry on the east side of Los Angeles County:

I am Les. I have been here in California since last October and I am the new Zodiac, who has come to liquidate the evil boys and men of this area. My method will or has been the rope.

I will get to them mainly seeking from them a so-called sexual relationship, but I will act on a plan of liquidation for I must. For these evil licentious people in the Army of Satan must be stopped, so I must kill them. I can tell you Randy Kraft didn't kill a few of your found bodies.

I am giving you those nude bodies of these evil men and boys by pushing them out of my van or parking my van near a freeway. I have done this in New Jersey, Long Island, Pennsylvania, as well as in other states so far across our land.

Tell the police of California, I will have to dispatch others, as I have dispatched a few so far in Orange County.

Les

For the men and women of Orange County homicide, as well as detectives from Los Angeles, San Diego, and as far away as Eugene,

Portland, and Grand Rapids, it was one more small but disturbing bit of information potentially clouding the Kraft investigation.

One of the major concerns from the beginning was the possibility that Kraft might be one more accomplice in Bill Bonin's loose network of lust murderers. That was quickly discounted after a series of fiber, blood, and chemical tests showed no matches between evidence taken from Randy's home and automobile and similar evidence gathered by Los Angeles County authorities in the misnamed Freeway Killer case.

But even with Bonin ruled out, the idea that one small, bookish homosexual could have acted alone in the worst killing spree in modern times defied logic.

Just days after Randy's arrest, anonymous calls began filtering into local police departments in Long Beach, Signal Hill, Seal Beach, and other places where Randy lived or worked, offering clues as to who might have helped the mustachioed thirty-eight-year-old computer consultant capture and kill so many victims over such a long period of time.

One anonymous caller blurted out the name of a Long Beach transvestite, thought to be involved in child pornography. Another suggested that Kraft was only one of several murderers with the same murder method and that the others were still on the loose. Still other tipsters pointed the finger at a secret coven of satanic worshipers, performing human sacrifices in the hills and mountains that ring the Los Angeles basin. Kraft, they said, was only a sometimes member of the group.

But Randy Steven Kraft, who was charged with the murder of Terry Gambrel and held at first on $250,000 bail in the Orange County Jail, maintained his absolute innocence of any killings from the very beginning. And family, friends, co-workers—in fact, almost everyone who had ever had a conversation with him—gave him their unconditional support. Like Jeff Seelig, they simply stated for the record that it was utterly absurd even to consider Randy Kraft a suspect in any crime of violence, let alone murder.

Municipal Judge Gary Ryan did not agree and boosted the bail to $750,000 after hearing Kraft's innocent plea the Monday following his arrest. At Kraft's request, he postponed his formal arraignment for a week until his parents and sisters could hire an attorney to defend him.

Ten days after his arrest, Randy appeared before Municipal Judge Robert Thomas in a different courtroom, defense counsel Doug Otto and Bruce Bridgman at his side. While they sought a bail reduction by trying to show Judge Thomas that their client was "passive, non-violent and hard-working," as Bridgman put it, prosecutor Bryan Brown had something else to offer the court: four new counts of murder, based on the photos and other physical evidence that Sidebotham's crew had found in Randy's Toyota. In addition to Gambrel, Kraft now faced charges of violating California Penal Code 187—homicide—in connection with the deaths of nineteen-year-old Wyatt Loggins, twenty-one-year-old Eric Church, twenty-year-old Rodger DeVaul, and eighteen-year-old Geoffrey Nelson.

He pled not guilty to those counts too.

Judge Thomas revoked bail, Randy returned to his cell, and Sergeant Sidebotham continued his investigation. So far, there were no other solid suspects in sight, despite the sudden gush of leads that had come in the mail and over the telephones.

The news of several out-of-state murders began filtering into the press too. Reporters quoted unnamed police sources in Oregon and Michigan who said that more indictments were expected to be delivered against Kraft in those states within a short time, based on evidence found in his house and garage. Like the Orange County authorities, they said that they had not been able to develop any proof that Kraft killed with anyone else who might have come along for the ride.

Seelig seemed less and less likely a candidate as an accomplice with each passing day. He was genuinely stunned, then hurt, and then as blindly supportive of his jailed lover as Randy's sisters and parents. One month after his arrest and just a few hours after speaking with Seelig through the Plexiglas in the jail visiting area, Randy wrote him from his jail cell. In his letter, Randy repeated to Jeff what he'd told him in person: that his arrest was all a big mistake and that the authorities would have to correct their error very soon. It was a love letter and Jeff believed every word.

Randy told Jeff how it hurt to look at him so closely and not be able to touch and hug and kiss him. "Ever so I need to be with you and talk and hear your voice and know that you are there for support and encouragement," Randy said. It was all a big mistake. It would end and everything would return to normal, he told Seelig.

The following week, Kraft was formally charged with a sixth murder: the brutal 1976 rape, torture, mutilation, and murder of twenty-year-old Mark Howard Hall.

The summer of 1983, homicide detectives representing a half dozen different police departments from throughout southern California traveled across the country, interviewing prospective witnesses in the case against Randy Kraft.

A Seal Beach detective flew back to Hartford, Connecticut, and drove the twenty miles outside of the city to the small New England town of Coventry. He had a Norelco double-head electric shaver with him when he knocked at Clayton and Liz Church's front door. Clayton had to catch himself on the door jamb to keep from falling when he saw it. The last time he had seen his son Eric alive, he was packing the same shaver into his knapsack and walking out the screen door to catch a one-way bus for Sacramento.

In one of the first searches for information about Kraft's early brushes with the law in Long Beach, a still-open but long-forgotten case involving a floating head in the Long Beach Marina was located at the back of a filing cabinet in the homicide division. The reason for Keith Crotwell's death, as well as the whereabouts of the rest of his body, were still a mystery to Long Beach police. But the old file did yield the name of one Kent May, a fifteen-year-old high school sophomore who had gone riding with Crotwell in Randy Kraft's Mustang that fatal night in 1975.

Robert Bell, one of the Long Beach detectives who had worked the case, tracked May down to the small northern California town of Yountville. There, Bell and Detective Bill Collette met the now twenty-three-year-old salesman in a city park. They showed him a group of mug shots and, without tipping their hand as to specifically why they wanted to know, asked May if he could identify the man who had taken him and Crotwell for a ride that night.

May sorted through the pictures and pointed to Randy's picture without hesitating.

In the town of Sebastopol just a few miles away in nearby Sonoma County, Orange County Sheriff's detectives Stan Kinkade and Dan Martini sat down with a thirty-four-year-old grocery store manager named Jeff Graves and questioned him about that same night back in 1975, when Keith Crotwell took his last ride.

Graves, Randy's first long-term lover, remembered the parking lot where Crotwell and May were picked up as a meeting place for homosexuals.

"It was a hangout for gays," he told the two detectives. "I don't know what the situation is now, but Ripples was across the street and you almost had to park there unless you parked on Ocean Boulevard. So you just walked across the street [to the parking lot]."

He and Randy had been on the outs by then, and the night Kraft took them for a ride, Jeff "was out with someone, probably at Ripples, and I didn't even see Randy that night. So I came home the next day—I mean I came home that night—and the phone rang and it was Randy and he ran out of gas or [had] car problems or something. He said, 'Come and help me.'"

Graves had done just that, he told Martini and Kinkade. When he showed up at daybreak in his Volkswagen, however, there was no sign of a companion, living or dead, in or near Randy's Mustang. Later, Graves took a polygraph test to confirm what he told the two detectives.

During the interview, he added one oddly out-of-place comment that defense and prosecution attorneys turned to again and again years later.

"I'm really not going to pay for it, you know," he said.

A thousand miles away, in Aurora, Colorado, Kinkade and Martini found another piece of the puzzle several weeks later, living in a small apartment with another down-on-his-luck friend. Joseph Fancher, now twenty-six years old, was a drug user on probation from a three-year Colorado prison term for burglary and auto theft.

When he met Randy Kraft for the first and last time, he told the detectives, he was still just a troubled teenager who couldn't get along with his strict, punitive stepfather. He had chosen to rebel by running away from home one day in the spring of 1970.

"Thirteen years ago? And did you know him at the time by the name of Randy Kraft or was there some other name that he used?" asked Kinkade as the three men sat in the front room of Fancher's cramped apartment.

"No, he just went by Randy," answered Fancher, a large, burly man with a gruff, monosyllabic manner.

"By Randy. Did you know his last name at the time?" Kinkade persisted.

"No," barked the heavyset ex-con.

What had brought them to his door was a yellowing police report from that incident, in which Kraft was investigated by Long Beach police for allegedly supplying drugs to a minor, though he was never prosecuted. The Fancher incident, like the Crotwell case, just seemed to have disappeared into the back of a filing cabinet.

Fancher's memory of the incident was still vivid and far more detailed than the police report. To begin with, there was much more involved than smoking marijuana and overdosing on Seconal, as he had told his parents and police at the time.

"They were the red devils, the big ones," Fancher told Kinkade and Martini in a halting voice. "Ah, I had took . . . eight of them . . . and, in the process of taking them, I was—I ate a couple sandwiches, and then . . ."

Fancher stopped to wipe his nose and clear his throat. Kinkade gently urged him to continue.

"I realize it's not easy what you're telling us, okay, but it—it may be super important in this investigation, whatever the details were," Kinkade said in a soothing voice.

Fancher sniffed again, clouding up like a vanquished teenager rather than a hardened felon. "I mean, okay, from detail to detail, the dude asked me if I ever, you know, made love with a dude before. And I said no," Fancher said, stumbling from one difficult phrase to the next. "The dude forced me . . . onto the bed. . . ."

He lapsed into a long silence before continuing.

"All right, he made me commit sexual acts towards him," he said finally. "In other words, oral copulating or how would you say it in police, ah, just . . ."

"Okay, you orally copulated—sucked him off," said Kinkade.

"Ah, I sucked him off," Fancher mumbled, unable to look either detective directly in the eye. "He slapped me around a couple times, then he molested me. In other words, ah . . ."

Fancher's voice trailed off again.

"Sodomized?" asked Martini.

"Sodomized," Fancher nodded.

Until he met Randy Kraft, Fancher told the pair of cops who had come all the way from California to visit him in his tiny, run-down apartment, the total extent of his sexual exploits was a kiss he had stolen from a girl he had a crush on in seventh grade. Randy Kraft—who seemed so kind and so understanding when he first picked Fancher up on his motorcycle down at the beach—changed all of that forever. When Fancher was drugged and helpless, the kind samaritan who took him home went through an astonishing and terrifying transformation.

"He looked like a fucking monster to me," Fancher recounted for Kinkade and Martini. "Face, attitude, everything. I mean if I could put everything that he looked like together, he looked like a fucking monster."

"Totally opposite from when you first met," said Martini.

"From when I first met him," Fancher agreed.

Fancher had no idea what homosexuality was until, in his intoxicated and defenseless state, he saw a series of pictures Randy displayed in front of his glazed-over eyes. In the photos, Randy was, himself, sodomizing and orally copulating another male.

When he asked Fancher to do the same to him, the boy dully refused and Randy hit him. Relating the incident thirteen years later to Kinkade and Martini while the two detectives taped the conversation, Fancher stopped fidgeting and started fuming. His descriptions of the slight, 160-pound Kraft as a huge, towering Frankenstein seemed absurd considering Fancher's massive 250-pound bulk, his lengthy arrest record for violent crimes, and his menacing appearance. But Kinkade and Martini weren't laughing.

Fancher: Now I'm starting to get mad, I mean . . .

Martini: Okay, I can understand that.

Fancher: You know, I just . . . it's nothing against you people.

Kinkade: I understand. All right.

Fancher: And ah, this really pissed me off, I mean I . . . the only people that ever know about this shit is you two.

Kinkade: Okay. You . . .

Fancher: And I ain't never told them. I never told my parents and I guess that's why I'm the way I am now. I mean, now if I had never went through this whole deal, I don't think I'd ever went to prison or anything. I mean it just screwed my life up.

Martini: That was the question that, that I was gonna ask you. Do you feel you've suffered? Because of this incident?

Fancher: I've done nothing but suffer.

Martini: Emotionally?

Fancher: Emotionally, yeah.

Martini: Okay, and you feel that maybe your life would have been entirely different had this not occurred?

Fancher: That's right. But I was having problems when I was a kid. Every kid does.

Martini: Sure.

Fancher: But after I went through that ordeal, I didn't want to be around my dad, not my brothers, nobody. And that's why I kept wanting to run away. I finally went to Juvenile Hall. I always stayed in my cell by myself too. I mean you can call Orange County Juvenile Hall and they'll tell you the same thing.

Martini: You were afraid of being assaulted?

Fancher: I was afraid, you know, just . . . I put a block in my head. I tried to block it out but every time somebody would get around me, you know—male, female, didn't make any difference—I'd just clamp up. And I'm still that way today.

Martini: Have you suffered any medical problems?

Fancher: Emotional-wise, I've suffered a lot. I've suffered for the last thirteen fucking years if, you know, if . . . Now, I don't know if I should say this on tape or not . . .

Kinkade: You say whatever you feel.

Fancher: . . . eh, you know, if I was in the same cell with this dude right now, I'd kill him. I mean that's the way I feel. I mean he ain't done nothing but put me through a goddamn bunch of shit!

Martini: You suffered that much.

Fancher: You know, thirteen years ago this happened and, you know, finally somebody is, you know, picking up what the fuck is going on, you know. I don't think the dude should live. I think . . . I, on the serious side, I think they ought to just cut his fucking nuts off, shove 'em in his mouth, and kill him. . . .

All through my life, I can't even . . . the dude I live with I can't even get close to. I mean he's a good brother of mine, you know. I've tried everything. I've tried shooting dope. I've tried smoking my brains out. I've tried taking heroin. I've done everything. I've tried to commit suicide plenty of times. And nothing is releasing what I got inside . . .

By July, Randy was as chipper as he could be under the circumstances. Some of the deputies harassed him by withholding his mail or suspending privileges, but he told Jeff and his family that he was holding up well. He ate well, learned self-hypnosis, and ran every other day. There was a walled-in exercise area up on the roof of the jail and Randy got to the point where he was doing a mile or two each time he was allowed to do laps. He hadn't fully adjusted to jail life, but was finding ways to cope.

He wrote his sister Kay that he had gotten into meditation, which he described as "a complete and prolonged yielding of one's soul to whatever creative essence, universal order or God that you value." He quoted philosopher Alan Watts to her: "When you allow thinking to stop, you find you are an internal here and now."

Randy spoke to Jeff and his other friends by mail and in person as though he would be out soon and nothing had really changed. His letters read like notes sent home from summer camp.

"How's my man?" he wrote Jeff, complimenting him on a recent weight loss and chiding him for going to bars where his new, svelte body was on display.

He wasn't above scolding Seelig, and did so regularly. When his former roommate started dating other men, Randy told him he understood his physical needs, but warned him that the two of them still had a commitment.

But Randy was particularly incensed when he heard from his parents that Seelig was planning to sell the Roswell house after Randy's defense expenses began to mount. In a crisis, Seelig was the first one to push the panic button, said Randy. Jeff was a grown man who ought to make good decisions in times of crisis and not just spout off, hurting people's feelings. Instead of saying that everything was sinking and saying he was going to act hastily, Seelig should ask other people for advice, Randy said. The worst possible thing Jeff could do, he said, was sell the house in a panic.

He also worried with Jeff about his privacy. Court proceedings were likely to display their private lives all over everybody's living room via television and newspapers, but Randy saw no way around it.

He also worried about his dog. If Max should ever get killed, he wanted Jeff to bury the dog in the back yard. He didn't want the pound to grind Max up. Max, he instructed Seelig, should have something of Randy's by his nose and Jeff should read a poem or some other good words over the dog's body. Max was, after all, family.

Randy also worried about an entirely new menace that was just beginning to get attention in the media. When a mutual friend died of AIDS, Randy told Jeff to give his condolences to the friend's surviving mate. The dead friend and Randy had once been sexually intimate, but it had been twelve years earlier, Randy told Jeff. He had been very promiscuous and "liked to use his number 2 a lot," according to Randy, adding his warning to Jeff to be careful. "Keep choir practice to a minimum for awhile," he advised.

In a letter to Phil Crabtree, Randy went through the usual, chatting about the summer weather, asking about mutual friends, and even joking a little before launching into a pitch that Crabtree himself recognized much later on as classic Kraft manipulation. He invited Crabtree to visit him in jail and to bring a whole gaggle of others to stand outside and weep. More seriously, he wrote, he needed Crabtree to help create positive press in order to counteract all the negative. "The evidence isn't going to convict 'cause it isn't there," he wrote. Some circumstantial evidence existed, but it wasn't particularly damning. Negative press could hurt him though if left uncontested. People would believe Kraft no different from Kenneth Bianchi, Bonin, and all the others. They would assume he was a loner or a weirdo, with no responsibilities. The real story had to come out, he said, and the only place it could come from was folks like Crabtree who knew him.

Most of the time, Randy read or meditated alone in his cell, but sometimes, during exercise hours up on the roof of the three-story jail, he stopped and did a 360-degree survey of the area where he used to drive late at night. It left him breathless and more than a little impatient, but not the least bit defeated. Being locked up and restricted was harsh, he wrote. Most people wouldn't be able to handle it. Since he had to, he let his mind dwell on being at home with Jeff.

Randy chose to look at jail time as being away at some school taking some class that he'd never signed up for before, but learning some lesson—although he didn't know what it might be that God had willed him to learn. Jail was like the military "but much more restrictive, demeaning, and punishing," he told Jeff.

On September 8, 1983, Orange County sheriff Brad Gates called his second press conference in the matter of Randy Steven Kraft. This time, he told the TV cameras, his deputies had "been able to establish Randy Kraft's propensity, without a doubt, for sexually deviant behavior that goes back to the 1970 period."

After interviews with over seven hundred witnesses and the gathering of over 250 exhibits, he announced that Deputy District Attorney Bryan Brown was ready to go to court on ten new murder counts as well as the six that had already been leveled against Kraft. The new counts included a John Doe found in Huntington Beach in 1973, four marines—Donnie Crisel, Richard Keith, Edward Daniel Moore, and Scott Hughes—and five other young men who were unlucky enough to have hitched a ride from Randy Kraft. He named the remaining five victims as Michael Inderbieten, Keith Klingbeil, Roland Young, Ronnie Wiebe, and Keith Crotwell.

Kraft's attorney, Doug Otto, condemned Gates's tactic as "headline grabbing" and pointed out that Freeway Killer Bill Bonin had been initially suspected by police of having committed those same unsolved crimes.

But inside the Orange County Jail, Randy was crushed. In a letter to Jeff the day after Gates's press conference, he called the ten additional charges devastating. Brad Gates and the Sheriff's department were shoddy and despicable. Their hogwash would not only make it impossible for a fair trial but would also make it very difficult for Kraft to live in southern California once he was freed. Gates was a nincompoop trying to bury him with sheer numbers. They were trying to make Randy and Jeff buckle under. But it was all lies, he assured Seelig. Stay with the truth, he told him. Jeff Graves had told the police nothing was happening and Randy was sure his other friends would also help clear his name. "If they tell the truth, there can be no other outcome," he told Seelig.

In August, just before the preliminary hearing was to begin, Randy's classmates from Westminster High held their twenty-year reunion. Most of them expressed utter shock, though one or two professed to have known all along that Randy was a little odd and probably gay. One of Randy's classmates, Penelope Spheeris, had gone on to become a successful filmmaker and, ironically, would produce a critically acclaimed feature, *The Boys Next Door*, about two disaffected teenage killers who randomly murder for thrills.

"There was a lot of chat about Randy all right," said class of '63 student body president Clancy Haynes, who had become a criminal defense attorney in the years following his and Randy's graduation. "They gave away door prizes, and one of the door prizes was a two-hour consultation with Randy's lawyer. I wasn't sure if that was a joke or not."

After five postponements and an attempt by Kraft's attorneys to close the proceeding to the public, the preliminary hearing—to determine whether the district attorney's evidence was strong enough to try Randy Kraft for murder—began at nine A.M., September 27, 1983, in a small courtroom on the third floor of the ten story Orange County Courthouse.

Judge John Ryan forbade cameras in the courtroom, so artists hired by local TV stations sketched Randy in his jail dungarees for the evening newscasts. Most of the front row of spectator seats were taken up by reporters from the *Long Beach Press-Telegram*, the *Los Angeles Times*, the *Orange County Register*, Associated Press, United Press International, and City News Service.

Randy had trimmed his hair and mustache and sat relaxed but alert through most of the testimony of the prosecution's first five witnesses. He smiled calmly without showing a hint of his contempt for the media. Privately, he continued to rail against the trial that he felt was being conducted on television, over radio, and in the daily newspapers. One of the first things he asked his attorneys to look into was a change of venue if they were unable to have the preposterous charges against him dismissed.

Doug Otto, himself a former Orange County prosecutor, was joined in defending Kraft by attorney Fred McBride, who had stepped in to replace Bruce Bridgman. Sensing a marathon trial that might take years to prepare, Bridgman bowed out of the case shortly after Randy's arrest.

A former high school football star, Otto was a meticulous researcher and legal strategist who knew full well the risk of allowing the prosecution to lump several murders together in one trial, before one jury in as conservative a stronghold as Orange County. The Kraft family retained him and, later, McBride, with their own funds, but Otto knew that couldn't last. Sooner or later, the county would have to take over the cost of defending his client.

Otto also knew the evidence and that much of it was circumstantial. Strongly circumstantial, to be sure, but circumstantial nonetheless. The legal battle would be long and expensive, regardless of the outcome.

Bryan Brown was also aware of the stakes and the strategy, and having reviewed over one thousand pages of documents, witness transcripts, and police reports on the case, he was totally convinced that Randy Kraft was the man that law enforcement thought they had nailed when they first brought down Bill Bonin: the single worst mass murderer Orange County had ever seen, possibly the worst killer in state history, and one of the worst in U.S. history.

Ironically, all three men—Brown, Otto, and Randy Steven Kraft—were born and raised during their earliest years within a few miles of each other in Long Beach, the city where Kraft returned to live when he came of age, out of the closet, and began his computer career.

The first day, Michael Howard and Michael Sterling, the two CHP officers who first arrested Kraft, took the stand, as did Orange County Sheriff's deputy Michael Mitchell, one of the first local police officers to arrive at the scene of Terry Gambrel's death. Kristofer Leake, the Marine corporal who bunked with Terry Gambrel at El Toro Marine Base and bid him good-bye for the last time on May 13, 1983, also testified about his roommate's final hours of life.

But it was veteran pathologist Walter Fischer whose bland, monotonic description of Terry Gambrel's demise captured both the nightmarish horror of the night Gambrel was found near death in Randy Kraft's car as well as the collective imagination of the assembled members of the press.

Fischer, a fifty-four-year-old Illinois physician who had become one of the leading autopsy specialists in Orange County, had cut open hundreds of corpses in his years with the coroner's office, attempting to unravel the mystery of their deaths. Terry Lee Gambrel, he told Bryan Brown in a polite, clipped, matter-of-fact manner, died of anoxia, due to ligature strangulation. The ligature that killed him, Fischer testified, could have been a belt, about seven-eighths of an inch wide—a belt not unlike the one Gambrel had been wearing when he left the base, but which lay on the back seat of Kraft's Celica when Officers Howard and Sterling pulled the car over.

McBride tried shaking Fischer's testimony, but only got his affirmation that pinpoint-sized hemorrhages in the eyes, eyelids, neck, and cheeks only show up as a result of lack of oxygen delivered to the tissues, and that Terry Gambrel's face and neck were dotted with such tiny ruptures.

Two weeks later in the hearing, after Bryan Brown had walked more than two dozen witnesses through the deathly details of the murders of Rodger DeVaul, Geoffrey Nelson, Eric Church, Wyatt Loggins, and Donnie Crisel, Dr. Fischer made another appearance on the stand. This time, he testified about another autopsy he had performed five years earlier on a twenty-one-year-old truck driver from Long Beach named Mike Inderbieten.

At the time he came under Fischer's scalpel, however, Inderbieten was still just another John Doe, found early one morning on the Seventh Street offramp of the San Diego Freeway.

Police delivered the corpse to Fischer around noon on November 18, 1978, Fischer told defense attorney Fred McBride during cross-examination. It was probably one of the worst cases he had ever worked, but Fischer showed no emotion in describing for McBride what he witnessed, lying on his clean, stainless-steel table inside the windowless operating room at the back of the county morgue.

McBride: Now you testified as to the fact that the man had been emasculated. Is that correct?
Fischer: Yes sir.
McBride: Both testicles missing?
Fischer: Yes sir.
McBride: Scrotum missing?
Fischer: Yes sir.
McBride: Penis was present however.
Fischer: Yes sir.
McBride: Was there injury to the penis?
Fischer: Yes sir.
McBride: Would you describe that injury?

Fischer: A portion of the skin of the posterior shaft of the penis was also missing.

McBride continued, wanting to know whether Inderbieten's scrotum had been removed and his penis skinned before or after he died. Fischer calmly testified that the massive bleeding was enough to tell him that the young man was emasculated while he was still alive.

With equal scientific detachment, Dr. Fischer politely described under cross-examination the bloody, torn state of Michael Inderbieten's rectum and how it probably got that way because the young man had been impaled on a large, coarse object.

"There was some dilatory . . . either some dilation of the anus either prior to death or in some prior time. In other words, if constantly dilated, [it] can lead to a dilated anus in a relaxed state," the pathologist testified. "With the constant dilation of the anus, it can be dilated to some degree with something having been inserted into it."

Dr. Fischer was exactly the kind of placid, methodical professional Bryan Brown liked to put on the witness stand. His unruffled delivery, even under the toughest, most pointed cross-examination, showed an expert's unclouded vision under the most trying of circumstances.

The wizened veteran continued to display a crisp, objective persona on the witness stand during the Inderbieten phase of the hearing, until his testimony came to a description of the circular burn marks engraved into the young truck driver's nipples. Even then, he maintained a businesslike detachment about the evil nature of deliberately inflicted torture until McBride steered the questioning onto something he seemed reluctant to talk about.

"Your selection of a cigarette lighter as the possible instrumentality of these wounds, is that just based on our common understanding of what a cigarette lighter looks like or is it based upon some other similar burns that you have seen and have an expert experience with?" McBride asked.

Fischer told him he knew what a cigarette lighter looked like and what a burn from one might look like.

"My question is, do you have some special experience?" McBride persisted. "I mean all of us perhaps without being an expert could have an opinion as to whether something *looks* like a cigarette lighter burn or not. But I'm inquiring whether you have any special expertise or experience that would cause you to identify that as a cigarette lighter burn. Have you seen similar burns in the past?"

He had. It was on a murder victim.

"On the nipple?" McBride wanted to know.

"I don't remember where the area was, but I believe—" Fischer began.

"Sounds like you were talking about one other incident," McBride interrupted.

"Yes," Fischer said quietly.

"So in your career you have seen only one other time when you saw wounds which you thought were cigarette lighter wounds," McBride said.

"Yes sir," Fischer said.

"How long ago was that?" asked McBride.

"A number of years ago," Fischer answered in a clipped voice.

"Was that on an infant?" McBride asked.

"It was on a child," the pathologist answered.

Two years after Randy's hearing, Dr. Fischer put a gun to his head one Monday afternoon in a parking lot off 700 City Drive South in the city of Orange and pulled the trigger.

"Doing what he had to do for a living would have depressed anybody," said one veteran criminal attorney.

Randy had taken to quoting Edna St. Vincent Millay, Ogden Nash, and the Beatles in his letters from jail. By late October, when his preliminary hearing was nearly a month old, he had also begun composing his own poetry, like that he sent Jeff after receiving a letter from Phil Crabtree and his lover, Jay Boulton. The former Friday Night Poker regulars openly questioned Randy about the nonstop damning evidence that kept cropping up in court and getting reported in every new edition of the morning newspaper. He answered with a seventeen-line poem he sent Seelig about being too quick to judge others.

In court, Randy continued to project an inscrutable appearance, dressed in casual street clothes. First-time visitors to Judge Ryan's courtroom often had trouble determining who was the infamous defendant they had read about in the newspapers.

Randy's family had quickly come to his defense, putting up the necessary money to pay the lawyers. His sisters were still convinced that the entire matter was a horrible misunderstanding and that all that was necessary was to show a reasonable jurist how ridiculous the charges were and their brother would be released. As the legal costs mounted and the evidence continued to pile up at the hearing, it became clear that the expenses were going to be insurmountable. By year's end, Randy had to declare himself indigent in order to get the court to appoint Otto and McBride to continue as his lawyers.

For his own safety, the Orange County Jail deputies had him housed in the medical isolation wing during the preliminary hearing, but he had a steady stream of visitors during regular visiting hours allowed each week.

Randy by this time had taken a keen interest in his own defense and was actually getting used to the isolation. In addition to his meditation and poetry, he was beginning to read the law and become something of a jailhouse lawyer. Weeks before the preliminary hearing was over, he was haranguing Otto to let him join the defense team as co-counsel. Otto answered with the old adage that a person who acts as his own attorney has a fool for a client.

Jail deputies were also going through his mail and turning over copies to the district attorney, prompting Otto to file a protest with Judge Ryan.

"Kraft's ability to personally correspond with persons outside the Orange County Jail is critical to the preparation of his defense," he argued. Reading it not only violated his privacy; it also had a chilling effect on many of his friends who were gay and did not want the fact publicized for fear of losing their jobs, family or friends.

Judge Ryan rejected the protest on grounds that law enforcement had a right to prevent Kraft from using the mail to threaten witnesses, smuggle in drugs or weapons, or plan an escape.

Kraft answered what he saw as his continuous persecution with a poem about freedom and how good men, like himself, too often take their liberty for granted.

At approximately eleven P.M. on January 3, 1976, Robert Richards had performed the autopsy on what was left of Mark Howard Hall. He died of acute alcoholism and suffocation, Richards told Bryan Brown as he leaned forward in the witness chair in Judge Ryan's courtroom and spoke into the microphone.

It was now the third week of testimony and the horror had become so commonplace that there were not even occasional gasps in the courtroom anymore. Just fascinated, dazed silence.

Brown held out pictures and autopsy reports for the witness and persisted through the inevitable line of questioning. He wanted to know, specifically, how Hall came to suffocate.

"The trachea was packed with dirt," Richards answered.

He also had had his penis cut off and stuffed up his rectum, Richards testified.

"Was there anything placed in the penis?" Brown wanted to know.

"I don't understand," Richards said, shaking his head with a puzzled look on his face.

"Did you find any foreign objects within the penis?" Brown asked.

Richards—who would eventually take the stand more times than any other witness—described a plastic object that had been jammed with such force through the urethra of Mark Hall's sex organ that one end of it lodged deep into the bladder itself.

"I found a yellow swizzle stick," Richards said. "You know, that you get from a drink in a casino with Las Vegas, Nevada, on it?"

He also described the scrapes and "meanderings" of the point of a sharp instrument—probably a knife—over the legs of the dead man.

"Is there one cut on one of the legs that is more prominent than the superficial scraping?" asked Brown.

Yes, answered Richards. A long wound, deep into the muscle. When it came to burns, the damage to Hall's body made Michael Inderbieten's torture seem merciful.

"The one eye here is, you know, just charred," Richards said, pointing to a black and white photograph of Hall's face. "The anterior part of the eye is almost gone. In other words, whereas the opposite eye, just the eyelashes are burned a little bit, and the skin is seared a little bit, the orbit itself doesn't appear to be too significantly involved."

He went on.

"One side of the nose is burned. Then there are burns of the chest. These are all the same type of burns, you know. Cigarette lighter burns . . .

"Here is a picture. There is a burn on the head of the penis. There is a burn on the shaft of the penis. It seems to me I remember one on the scrotum as well."

"Were there also cigarette lighter burns on the nipples or the nipple of Mr. Hall?" Brown asked.

"Left one," answered Richards.

Orange County Sheriff's fingerprint expert Edward Carson, who testified directly before Richards, also spoke about Mark Hall's death, but not about his body. A shattered liquor bottle lay next to it, the neck of the bottle caked with blood as though it might have been forced inside Hall's body before it was broken on the rocks.

A latent thumbprint was carefully removed from one of the shards of glass and preserved in the Sheriff's property room for nearly eight years until they were able to find a match. The print from the bottle and Randy Kraft's right thumb were identical, Carson testified.

Jim Sidebotham looked like a deadpan undertaker on the witness stand. All he needed was a chaw of tobacco in one cheek and a spittoon next to the clerk's desk to complete the portrait of a cynical lawman who used a dusty dry sense of humor to mask a basic disgust for men and women who violate human dignity.

He had testified in court before and would be there again, and he knew exactly how to play the game.

This day, the testimony was about pictures—forty-seven of them, found in a drugstore photo-developing envelope beneath the floormat in Randy Kraft's Toyota.

Twenty-two of the snapshots were pictures of Rodger DeVaul and Wyatt Loggins, Sidebotham told Brown. DeVaul appeared dead. Loggins appeared nude and dead. There were twenty-five other photos in the envelope too, depicting young men in various stages of dress and undress. Some looked asleep or dead and some didn't, but Sidebotham said that he and his deputies had not yet been able to identify who they were.

On November 18, eight weeks after it had begun, the marathon preliminary hearing for Randy Kraft ended with Doug Otto's impassioned reaffirmation that the district attorney had not proven that his client had killed anyone, that the evidence presented was all circumstantial and inconclusive, and that Randy should be set free.

Bryan Brown answered by introducing his last, and most damaging, bit of evidence: some of the entries from the list he and his investigators had kept under wraps since the day Sidebotham had found it in the trunk of Kraft's car.

"What we have here is a true scorecard killer," said Brown.

Otto and McBride called the list meaningless and accused Brown of guessing, but Ryan took the list seriously enough to order it sealed until trial.

After some wrangling at the sidebar and several objections from Otto and McBride, Judge Ryan agreed that eleven of the entries on the list could be tied to twelve of the murders: "EDM" for Edward Daniel Moore; "2 IN 1 HITCH" for Geoff Nelson and Rodger DeVaul; "JAIL OUT" for Roland Young; "EUCLID" for Scott Hughes; "MCHB TATTOO" for Wyatt Loggins; "AIRPLANE HILL" for John Doe Huntington

Beach; "SEVENTH STREET" for Ronnie Wiebe; "MARINE DRUNK OVERNIGHT SHORTS" for Donnie Crisel; "MARINE CARSON" for Richard Keith; "PARKING LOT" for Keith Crotwell; and "NEW YEAR'S EVE" for Mark Hall.

He ordered Kraft bound over for trial in Orange County Superior Court for the murders of sixteen young men over an eleven-year period.

The following week, Randy granted his first and only interview to a news organization, inviting *Los Angeles Times* reporter Jerry Hicks to visit him in jail, over the objections of Kraft's defense attorneys.

Throughout the entire preliminary hearing, Kraft sat mute, day after day, but in the interview Hicks published the day following his interview, Kraft added little new information to answer the cornucopia of questions raised during the lengthy court proceedings. After watching Kraft's back throughout most of the hearing, Hicks now faced the accused killer, separated from him in a jail visiting room by a plate of glass.

"I don't belong here," Randy told the reporter over a telephone receiver.

He had come in contact with one or two of the victims, he said, but did not kill them. The so-called scorecard that Judge Ryan put under seal was "only a code list of some friends of my mate's and mine," he told Hicks.

What hurt him the most, he said, was how the press portrayed him as a Dr. Jekyll and Mr. Hyde.

When the *Times* interview was published the day after Thanksgiving, Randy felt betrayed by the media once again.

"You likely noticed I tried my hand with the press, *L.A. Times* no less," he told Michael Wiles. "I chose them because I thought I'd get a better shake than with the [Orange County] *Register.*"

Most of his message—that the authorities had no real hard evidence—got through in the article, he said. Even so, he was irritated that things he felt should have been included, weren't. He pooh-poohed the death list as prosecutorial showboating that could only be chalked up to a lack of evidence and limited mental ability.

By year's end, Randy had abandoned hope of a quick reversal of his case. The District Attorney's Office announced in December that, if Kraft were convicted of the sixteen murder charges, the prosecution intended to add another twenty during the penalty phase of the trial, when it would be determined whether Kraft went to the gas chamber or spent life in prison without parole.

Randy reregistered to vote, giving the Orange County Jail as his legal residence. Outside of a miracle, he wasn't going to be home for Christmas, so he wrote a general letter of good cheer and got it off on Christmas Eve to his friends and family, praising their support.

An otherwise bleak holiday season brightened for Randy when he remembered sharing the joys of the season with family. He advised all of his loved ones to appreciate the moments they had had together for the wonderful and irreplaceable times that they were. He would shut his eyes and sense all of their transcendental hugs over the airwaves, he said. Then he quoted a line from *Star Wars*: "I think, Master Luke, there is a joyous swelling in the Force."

God bless everyone, he wrote in his closing. Love, hugs, and kisses—including all dogs, cats, and other "allegedly dumb creatures" who also deserved extra Christmas hug rations for companionship above and beyond the call of duty, Randy said.

The new year was right around the corner: 1984 had to be better than 1983.

24

Drawing was sort of fun, Randy wrote to his niece in Arizona. It took up time and that was a godsend. It was rewarding, too. The first thing he drew with his new sketch pad and eraser was a picture of Reggie Jackson from the newspaper. It turned out good, surprising even Randy. He'd drawn before but never had so much time to devote to it.

By the time he wrote about discovering his hidden talent as an artist in March of 1984, Kraft had been in the D wing of the Orange County Jail for nearly ten months. His was one of twenty-eight cells on the protective custody floor where prisoners least likely to survive unharmed in the general jail population—often gay prisoners—are housed.

His isolation rankled him enough that he complained frequently about it. He even filed habeas corpus petitions in state and federal court, where he bitterly called his quarantine a blatant violation of his Eighth Amendment right against cruel and unusual punishment.

But when Deputy County Counsel Edward Duran agreed to put Kraft into the general jail population, there was resounding silence from the D wing.

"If Randy wants to sign a waiver, we'll move him out into the general population today and save the expense of a trial," said Duran.

One plot to kill Kraft had already been uncovered, when a snitch turned in two inmates after overhearing them talk about wasting Kraft. A search by jailers turned up the weapon they were going to use.

Kraft's cell furniture consisted of an uncovered toilet, a sink, a small table, a stool, and a steel plate bunk with a one-and-a-half-inch-thick mattress pad. Except for a couple of hours a day in the dayroom for TV or his thrice-weekly forty-minute exercise periods up on the roof of the jail, Kraft saw no one, spoke with no one. His meals were served to him in his cell for fear that one of the inmates might make good on their rumored threats to kill Kraft if he showed up in the mess hall. Randy's sisters, Kay and Doris, complained that the guards oversalted his food on purpose to make it unfit to eat. And, always, Randy felt that his privacy was invaded.

Jailhouse informants chronically plagued him. There seemed to be a never-ending stream of people who spoke about getting Kraft so that they could lessen the time they had to do. They talked to the D.A., claiming that Randy admitted one thing or another, but he never did. He continued to keep to himself and not discuss his family, friends, or case with anyone.

Everything he owned was confiscated when he was booked into the jail, Kraft complained. His watch was taken away, so he didn't even know what time it was from day to day. Jail rules forbade putting posters, clocks, or calendars on the wall. He wanted to put up a few male pin-ups, but his request was turned down. His jailers also prohibited playing pop music on a small tape recorder that his lawyers had brought him to play legal advisory tapes on.

An indignant Kraft cataloged his wants: Kleenex, Rolaids, cotton balls, dandruff shampoo, ear plugs, dental floss, nail clippers, soap dish, Band-Aids. He got none of his requests filled. He was forced to dress "like a hobo" with a freshly laundered denim jail uniform or an orange jumpsuit brought in every three days. He got a haircut once a month and a shower every other day.

Kraft kept a diary and did have a tiny three-inch pencil to use for his artwork. He used the heel of his tennis shoe as an eraser. Besides self-portraits and pictures of his hands, knees, and shoes, he turned his artistic gifts toward a more practical application when he drafted a picture of his seventy-inch-wide cell as an addendum to one of his many habeas corpus petitions.

He wrote often to friends and relatives, but his visitors dwindled following his preliminary hearing. Jeff continued to write and visit regularly, but even he stopped making the thirty-minute trek from Long Beach to Santa Ana after a few years.

"How's my birthday boy?" Randy wrote Jeff on his birthday, nearly three years after his arrest. He praised him for his fortitude and promised that they would someday be together again. The cruel joke would end and the sun would shine on them again, Randy vowed. He didn't know when, but he shared faith and love with Seelig. Trial and oppression would pass but love—deep love—would not.

The following year, Seelig sold the Roswell house and moved in with another roommate. Though he continued to maintain that he loved, supported, and believed in Randy, he told friends that he realized after months of therapy and an emotional hell, which included bouts with alcohol and bulimia, that his own life had to go on.

Randy's mail often arrived three months late, according to his sister Kay Plunkett. When it did arrive, his guards opened every letter and sent copies to the District Attorney's Office. Randy was obedient, even tolerant of his jailers, and did his best to get along, but just below the surface was a haughty contempt for the men invested with the duty of depriving him of his freedom.

Once a sergeant called him out without warning and chewed him out because he didn't like the mail Randy was receiving. The guard said it was "bullshit" and he was tired of having to "put up with it," Randy recalled. The two examples that the guard had waved in his face were a pocket guide to the Hollywood Bowl summer season and an advertisement for Bach Orbond men's toiletries. There was no jail rule concerning such things, said Randy. Why they even bothered to concern themselves was "mystifying," he said.

Outside the jail, the strategy and members of Kraft's defense team were shifting. Fred McBride quit after Kraft publicly berated his defense style during the preliminary hearing, and Doug Otto left in August of 1984, after Kraft insisted upon acting as co-counsel in preparing for his trial.

They were replaced by a trio of Orange County public defenders who quit their county jobs to devote their full time to Randy Kraft. Ultimately, their earnings from the Kraft case allowed the three of them—C. Thomas McDonald, James Merwin, and William Kopeny—to create a new law firm and establish an office a city block from the Orange County Courthouse.

The expense of trying the state's most prolific serial killer quickly became a *cause célèbre* in conservative, cost-conscious Orange County. The *Orange County Register* went to court in a failed effort to force the presiding Superior Court judge in the case to reveal how much the three defense lawyers and their team of investigators and expert witnesses had cost the taxpayers. Judge Luis Cardenas turned them down with the explanation that revealing defense expenses might unduly prejudice the public and potential jurors against Kraft.

The most expensive case in California history until Randy Kraft was arrested was another serial killer's: Juan Corona, convicted of killing twenty-five migrant farmworkers in the early 1970s in the northern California town of Yuba City. Corona was tried and convicted, but then an appellate panel overturned the first trial because he was not accorded an adequate defense. The trial and retrial (he was convicted of all twenty-five murders both times) cost taxpayers $4,776,012.

By April of 1986, after Kraft had been in jail for three years, the taxpayers' expense for his defense alone was already estimated by the Orange County District Attorney's Office to have exceeded $2 million. District Attorney Cecil Hicks asked the county Board of Supervisors for eight new clerical and investigator positions just to help in preparing Bryan Brown's case against Kraft and to keep pace with the defense's discovery requests. An entire section of the first-floor office space of the Orange County Courthouse was turned over to Brown, where several computers, a half dozen investigators, and several paralegals and clerks worked for over five years transcribing, cataloging, phoning, taping, and preparing information for the trial.

Similarly, the new firm of McDonald, Merwin, and Kopeny was a beehive of activity. In addition to their new offices, they also rented space in two office buildings for storage and work space to prepare for the case. They, too, hired a battery of investigators and set up their own lab with their own forensics experts inside the Orange County Sheriff's Department to test evidence gathered by the prosecution.

Each time Bryan Brown showed up for trial, McDonald appeared with a request for more preparation time. Over the next five years, Kraft's lawyers were granted a dozen delays. But, as McDonald successfully pointed out each time he sought a few more months to prepare, the number of charged and uncharged murders against his client was unprecedented. By the end of 1985, Randy was charged with sixteen murders in Orange County, two in Michigan, and six in Oregon. He was also the leading suspect in at least another thirteen cases in Orange as well as Los Angeles, San Bernardino, Imperial, and San Diego counties. If his staff devoted two months to developing a defense for each killing, trial preparation would take more than six years.

And that only accounted for a little over half the names on his "death list."

The *Register*'s legal attempt to force open the defense expenses for Randy Kraft went all the way to the California Supreme Court before Judge Cardenas's decision was ultimately upheld. The costs remained under seal throughout his trial. But legal experts estimated that the cost of bringing Randy Kraft to trial easily exceeded $5 million.

Clayton Church flew in from Coventry to testify at the preliminary hearing. Liz Church, who had gone on disability following news of her son's death, stayed home. Darwin and Lois Hall made and postponed plans several times to come down from Idaho for the trial, canceling out when word came back that it had been delayed again and again. Barbara Loggins likened the long wait for justice to an open sore that would not heal.

Shirley and Rodger DeVaul, Sr., reunited, following Rodger Jr.'s funeral. Together with Judy Nelson, they became the most visible standard bearers of the more than two hundred fathers, mothers, sisters, brothers, wives, and other close kin directly affected by the murders with which Randy Kraft was charged. They stayed in loose contact with each other through a court-supported Victim/Witness Assistance Program.

Shirley became an outspoken member of the Crime Victims' California Justice Committee, leading candlelight vigils for crime victims and their families and helping draft a thirteen-point Crime Victims Justice Reform Act that would speed up trials and make public the defense expenses of murder defendants like Randy Kraft. At one point in the years between Kraft's arrest and trial, she tried organizing the families of the sixteen victims whose deaths were formally charged to Randy, so that they could publish a memorial book containing biographies and pictures of each of their dead sons.

"My son would do very special things for me for my birthday," said a tearful Mrs. DeVaul outside the courtroom the day after her birthday. "The only special thing I can do for him now is be here, regardless of how much it hurts. I'm going to see it through, whatever it takes."

Judy Nelson maintained that Geoffrey's grandmother died within a year of his murder as a direct result of the news.

"I tell people that she was also Randy Kraft's victim," she said.

But Judy could see an equally shattered set of victims in the close-knit family that supported Randy, too. Once, early in the years of court proceedings, she confronted Opal Kraft in one of the hallways inside the Orange County Courthouse, accompanied by her daughter Kay Plunkett. Mrs. Kraft, then well into her seventies, offered her deepest condolences to Judy about the loss of Geoffrey, but quickly added that her son, Randy, could not have done it. Before the otherwise friendly encounter deteriorated into an argument, Kay hustled her mother away, Judy recalled.

"None of his family can believe it. They just can't believe their son would do such a thing and I guess, if I were in their shoes, I wouldn't be able to either," said Mrs. Nelson. "I genuinely feel sorry for his family. They seemed like good, decent people."

Not long after that meeting, Opal Kraft suffered a stroke and entered a rest home.

"She is living in the past right now," said Doris Lane, the second of Randy's three older sisters. "She thinks she is home and she talks to her teddy bear all day long. Every time I see her, I ask her, 'Where is Randy?'" Mrs. Kraft's response, said Doris, is that her son is either playing in the yard or off at work.

Harold Kraft, too, had difficulty remembering the past, Doris said, though he was not so disabled that he had to be institutionalized. He continued to live in the family home on Beach Boulevard, attended most of the time by Doris and occasionally by Kay.

Confined to a wheelchair, Harold attended some of the court proceedings, but made no comment to newspaper reporters beyond gruffly putting his faith in the justice system. A fan of the TV program "The People's Court" and a veteran of several juries himself, Harold said only that a jury could ultimately decide what the truth was.

Jury selection did not get underway until the summer of 1988, more than five years after Randy's arrest.

To pick twenty jurors, the Orange County jury commissioner mailed out fifteen thousand summonses—more than any ever sent out for a single case in county history. Because the trial was expected to last as long as two years, eight alternates were to be selected to prevent a mistrial should people die, be disqualified, or otherwise become incapable of seeing the case through over such a long period of time.

Construction contractors were called in after courthouse officials picked the largest courtroom in the building, located on the eighth floor, as the site for the trial. The workmen were asked to enlarge the jury box to accommodate twenty jurors.

Several months before jury selection began, Randy's lawyers tried unsuccessfully to have the case dismissed on grounds that Jim Sidebotham's exhaustive search and seizure of material in Randy's car, house, and workplaces far overstepped the legal boundaries for gathering evidence. Superior Court Judge James Turner, who had inherited the case from Judge Cardenas, listened to five months of testimony—chiefly from Sidebotham himself—before he ruled that the searches were legally correct.

Several attempts to get the trial moved out of the county because of prejudicial pretrial publicity failed.

McDonald, Merwin, and Kopeny also tried to sever the murder counts so that Kraft would have to be tried sixteen different times, once for each case. They lost that battle as well—this time, at the hands of Judge Donald A. McCartin, who inherited the case from Judge Turner after Turner had to quit the bench because of heart trouble.

In one significant victory, the defense team was able to prevent the prosecution from formally introducing even more murders against their client. Due process demanded that new felony counts be heard in preliminary hearings before they could be added on to the growing list of charges, they argued.

And Bryan Brown finally had to agree. Adding on more and more murder victims to the list of charges against Kraft only added more and more delays. Though the prosecution's investigators had tied Randy to more than forty murders committed over thirteen years, Brown agreed to go to trial only on the original sixteen just to save time and money.

By the time Brown and Defense Attorney Tom McDonald finally got around to interviewing prospective jurors for the trial, Kraft had already spent more time in the Orange County Jail than any other prisoner in history. The two adversaries spent the long, hot month of August 1988 challenging prospective jurors. After most of the original 5,000 potential jurors who had answered their summonses were weeded out for various reasons, Judge McCartin winnowed a list of 1,653 possible jurors down even further to a pool of 215 people who might be able to last economically and physically through a two-year trial. The process of elimination then went to a fifteen-page written questionnaire, handed out to each man and woman. Potential jurors who flatly told the judge and attorneys that they did not want to serve on the jury likened the entire process to applying for a job. The prosecution wanted jurors who were not opposed to California's recently reinstated death penalty. The defense looked for just one juror who would vote against death under any circumstances in order to get a hung jury in the event they were unable to get an acquittal.

While the idea of up to two years of gory photographs and explicit descriptions of torture disgusted most jurors, others wanted to serve on the Kraft jury.

"I have this theory about jurors, that they're all liars," said Clancy Haynes, who was defending five murder cases of his own in Orange County when Randy was on trial. "What strikes me is how some of them will go to such great lengths to cover up their feelings about the death penalty because they want to be on one of those juries. They want to be on a death penalty jury. They want to send somebody to the gas chamber. They want that chance."

Among the Sheriff's deputies who worked in the jail, the tacky running joke went:

Q: What kills more gays than AIDS?
A: Randy Kraft.

AIDS was no joke to Randy nor to any of his friends, however. Phil Crabtree had the disease. Many other former friends had also tested positive for the HIV virus.

Randy held the public health crisis to be the one bright spot in his incarceration. He'd heard a little about it in jail and read newspaper accounts, but usually only discovered that a friend had AIDS after they had died. In at least one way, he said, being in jail was lucky: He couldn't catch it even if he wanted to.

On July 27, 1987, Jeffrey P. Graves died at Sonoma Community Hospital in Santa Rosa, California. According to Michael Whitwhere, his doctor, Randy Kraft's former lover during the early 1970s died of complications brought on by AIDS. He was buried at Sebastopol Memorial Lawn in Sebastopol, California. He was thirty-eight years old.

Exactly fourteen months later, after spending five years and four months in the Orange County Jail, Randy Kraft went on trial for murder.

At 9:25 A.M. on September 26, 1988, Randy emerged from the side door lockup area of Judge Donald McCartin's courtroom, sandwiched between Tom McDonald, his ruddy-faced attorney, and a slender but muscular bailiff whose neatly trimmed mustache and regulation haircut could pass for that of a marine.

In a blue dress shirt, dark tie, beltless Levi's and white sneakers, Randy radiated the kind of poise he'd learned to project during his est period in the early '80s. He also wore a confident smile that he flashed at the three TV news camera crews jockeying for position on the west side of the courtroom. When he sat at the defense table facing the bench with McDonald and his second lawyer, James Merwin, Kraft pulled a long yellow legal pad from McDonald's briefcase and began writing. He whispered to McDonald from time to time, but never stopped taking notes during the entire proceeding.

As the twelve jurors and eight alternates filed in, the television camera lenses whipped around to catch them crowding into the two-tiered jury box on the opposite side of the room: three men and seventeen women—one black and two Hispanics. Everyone else was white and ranged in age from early twenties to midsixties.

McCartin waited at his chamber door until everyone had a seat before making his own entrance. His gaunt, gray figure wrapped in black robes made him look a little like an absentminded grim reaper who'd misplaced his scythe.

Donald McCartin, Orange County Superior Court judge, speaks in a slow, graveled drawl that matches his cranky grandfatherly appearance. His sunken cheeks, wavy steel-gray hair, thin nose and stiff, deliberate stride make him look more like an aging gunfighter than a jurist.

"He looks like Howard Hesseman's father," whispered one courtroom regular.

Beneath his robes, he wears rumpled shirts and casual slacks and thin, dark ties, if he wears them at all. Occasionally he shows up for court in blue jeans and bolo tie. McCartin radiates a tired competence: the day-in, day-out moodiness of a man who has assumed the tedious responsibility of meting out punishment to too many men and women who probably deserve to be punished but routinely deny that they ever broke the law.

Of the fifty-four Superior Court judges in Orange County, McCartin had sent more convicted murderers to the gas chamber than any other: six condemned men.

As the TV cameras whirred, he climbed the platform behind the bench and sat in the larger of two chairs there, beneath a large, round, plastic copy of the Great Seal of California. The symbol hung askew, so that the eyes of the relief Amazon woman in the center of the seal looked over the heads of the jurors toward a blank corner of the courtroom.

Defense and prosecution tables butted up against each other, facing the bench. Adjacent to the clerk's desk stood a six-foot easel with a pad of four-foot-by-four-foot blank white paper resting against it.

There was a chorus of rusty squeaks as friends, reporters, families of victims, and the just plain curious all leaned forward in the 143 folding seats in the eighth-floor courtroom.

The clumsy medieval ritual of trial for murder began. McCartin ordered the reading of the charges.

Court clerk Gail Carpenter began reciting all sixteen murder counts leveled against Randy Kraft, beginning with the murder of U.S. Marine Edward Daniel Moore on the day after Christmas 1972.

". . . on December 26, 1972, the defendant did kill Edward Daniel Moore . . ."

Fourteen minutes later, Carpenter finished with another marine: Terry Lee Gambrel, who died on the San Diego Freeway in the early morning hours of May 14, 1983, nearly eleven years later. In all, she read off sixteen counts of murder, two counts of sodomy, and one count of mayhem—the act of purposely mutilating another human being.

Bryan Brown stood slowly. In his dark blue suit and crisp white shirt, the Orange County DA's homicide expert seemed boyish despite his brush-cut graying hair and terse, clipped delivery. Five years earlier, Brown had shepherded a jury through the Orange County trial of William Bonin, in which the Freeway Killer was convicted of four lust murders in addition to the ten he was found guilty of having committed in Los Angeles County in 1982. Better than any other prosecutor in the Orange County Courthouse, he understood the master manipulation and utter lack of conscience of the serial killer.

Brown was not above a little manipulation of his own, however, kicking off his opening statement by moseying up to the rail that separated the jury box from the rest of the courtroom and addressing the twenty jurors as "folks."

"You will hear evidence during the trial about various victims," he began, suggesting that they take notes on the sex, race, age, height, and weight of the victims and the manner in which each one had been killed.

Pay close attention, he suggested, to how each man died:

- Whether ligature strangulation was the cause;
- How and where each body was discarded;
- Whether drugs were found in the victim's blood;
- Whether "aberrational activity" had taken place with the body;
- Whether the victim had shoes on and whether those shoes had laces in them or not;
- Whether the victim was naked;
- What day of the week the victim was killed.

It was a complicated case, he told the jury. Very complicated. Brown stepped to the easel he'd set up in front of the defense table so everyone—jury, judge, and defense—could see. Then he picked up a black crayon and, in reverse chronological order, Brown walked the jury through all nineteen felony counts facing the pale, fragile-looking man who sat calm but attentive between his two defense attorneys.

For two hours, Brown spelled out his theory of just how each young man had met his death. The homicide expert gave thumbnail sketches that included only the sparest details of the obscenities and horrifying tortures inflicted on each of them. At the defense table, Randy never stopped feverishly taking notes.

From Kraft's back-seat beer cooler, a gullible Terry Gambrel accepted a Moosehead lager laced with prescription drugs, Brown began. Only when he was fading into a semicomatose state and found himself helpless to fight against the seemingly friendly fellow who had stopped to pick him up did Gambrel sense that something was terribly wrong. By the time the Mickey Finn he'd swallowed took its full effect, Gambrel had been garroted with the shoelaces from his own boots.

Roger DeVaul and Geoffrey Nelson shared a last supper of grapes and potato skins, Brown told the jury with a bitter deadpan expression drawn across his face.

Randy liked to take pictures of his victims, he continued. He flashed off a head shot of a dead, dazed Roger DeVaul, half sitting and half lying in the back seat of Kraft's Toyota before his body was dumped. The jury would get to see those snapshots, Brown told them.

Scrawling the name "CHURCH" under "Count 14" on his easel, Brown told the jurors that Eric Church may have already been dead when Randy finally got around to taking his picture. Likewise with Wyatt Loggins, another of Kraft's models. With the victim either drugged into stupefaction or already dead, Randy had shot a regular portfolio of the marine on Randy's living room sofa, holding his penis, baring his anus, and lying about in several lewd poses.

And the list of victims went on.

Donnie Crisel. Michael Joseph Inderbieten. And Keith Klingbeil and Richard Keith and Roland Young and Scott Hughes.

And Mark Hall, probably the worst case in the whole catalog of Kraft atrocities, according to Bryan Brown. Penis burned, swizzle stick run through the entire length like a barbecue spit, and the entire bloody mess rammed up the young man's rectum while his killer packed dirt and leaves down his windpipe.

Two of the male jurors and several spectators in the packed courtroom winced and uncomfortably crossed and recrossed their legs during Brown's description. Brown drawled on, describing the lonely coastal mountaintop where Kraft dumped Hall's body.

"There Mr. Kraft probably makes his biggest mistake," Brown told the jury, leaving them hanging for a few dramatic seconds before revealing that two pieces of glass found next to Hall's naked corpse had Kraft's fingerprints on them and that he had left an empty package of Half & Half, his favorite brand of cigarettes, within a few feet of the body.

Brown continued to take the jury on a macabre tour of Randy's bloodlettings until he'd finished up with Marine Eddie Moore.

"What I've tried to do is give you a road map, folks," Brown said softly as he took a seat adjacent to the defense table and turned the floor over to Tom McDonald.

McDonald, a stocky man in a gray suit and gold wire-rim glasses, stood beside his client. His florid complexion, coupled with the fuzzy strawberry-blond fringe that tonsured his deeply receding hairline, gave Tom McDonald a somewhat comic bearing. He appeared to be all bluster, especially when he pulled his coat back and planted his fingers into his pants pockets, rocking on his heels like a latter-day W. C. Fields.

But his message to the jury was neither humorous nor very long. Whereas Brown spoke softly, stoically describing each horror with calm, detailed detachment, as if he were delivering a well-rehearsed toastmaster's speech, McDonald began and ended his abrupt opening statement with barely contained fury.

Brown's list of names, from Moore to DeVaul to Church, were victims of somebody, to be sure, but not Randy Kraft.

"This is a tactical maneuver made by the prosecutor to color your thinking," said McDonald, barely pausing to catch his breath. "The basis of the building blocks of the people's case which you will hear from that witness stand are suspicion, innuendo, and prosecutorial rhetoric. There will be no concrete evidence that my client killed anybody."

Randy Kraft, he told them, was a "homeowner, taxpayer, and hard worker, just like many other citizens of our country."

He was gay, but had exhibited the maturity and stability it takes to involve himself in an eight-year relationship with the same partner.

"What you have heard is prosecutorial rhetoric, designed to inflame you and color your thinking," he warned. "Mr. Kraft killed no one."

Randy said nothing, but gave McDonald a thin smile and an all but imperceptible nod of approval.

By the end of the first day of testimony, Judge McCartin had allowed the prosecution to unseal Randy's so-called scorecard or "death list" and introduce at least part of the list to the jury as Exhibit 165. After years of mix and match, law enforcement had been able to link forty-one of the entries on the list to forty-three murder victims, but twenty entries remained a mystery.

"Kraft collected murder victims like one would collect matchbooks," Brown wrote in his legal brief accompanying the list.

In the days that followed, Brown walked the jury through mounds of evidence extracted from the trunk and glove compartment of Kraft's car, his house, and several of his victims. Jim Sidebotham took the stand briefly to describe a box of shoelaces and belts he'd found in the garage, holding the long, thin pieces of leather up for the jury to study like live rattlesnakes.

Brown described the seat cushion of the passenger's seat of Randy's Toyota as a sponge, soaked with human blood. Investigators didn't know whose blood, however. It didn't match Terry Gambrel or Eric Church or any of the more recent victims they had been able to link to Kraft, though the blood was fresh enough to have seeped through onto Church's pants when he had been riding in Randy's car.

"This vehicle," Brown told the jury with the nearest thing he had to offer in the way of a dramatic inflection, "is used basically as a platform of death. With a buck knife, prescription drugs in the glove box, and alcohol in the cooler, he's ready to roll."

He even carried his death list and a 110 camera in the trunk to record it all, Brown continued.

When Brown moved on to other evidence that had been lost or misplaced during the sixteen years between Randy's first murder and the day he was finally brought to trial, defense co-counsel William Kopeny began the first of several calls for dismissal of various murders charged against his client.

The trash bag in which Wyatt Loggins had been found smelled so bad that a criminal cataloging clerk took it out of the property room in the Sheriff's building and put it up on the roof to air out. When he returned, it had blown away in a rainstorm.

Similarly, evidence collected from the 1972 killing of Edward Daniel Moore and the 1979 garroting of Keith Klingbeil—matchbooks, hair samples, blood samples—was also missing. Brown said he presumed that police who believed it was old, taking up storage space, and no longer serving a purpose had gotten rid of it.

McCartin denied Kopeny's request to dismiss the Loggins or Klingbeil or Moore counts, or any of the other murder charges, as he would repeatedly throughout much of the year-long trial.

By October, the first of more than 150 witnesses began taking the stand. Among them was Clayton Church, back from Connecticut one final time to formally identify Eric's Norelco shaver, found in Randy's house, and to testify against the man who killed his son. This time, he brought Liz Church with him and they sat together quietly through a morning of testimony until McCartin ordered the room darkened so that

Bryan Brown could show slides to the jury. Eric's dead, rain-soaked face, lying in the ice plant off to the side of the onramp to the 605 Freeway, appeared in color on a screen visible both to the jury and the courtroom spectators, including Eric's mother.

Upon seeing her son's face up on the screen, Liz rose, her hand to her mouth, and raced from the courtroom. Clayton was at her heels. Shirley DeVaul and several other victims' kin followed, consoling and hugging in the hallway outside the courtroom. She waited outside, sobbing, until the slide presentation was over.

At the end of the first full month of trial, the jury had heard from more than ninety witnesses and Brown had logged in over eight hundred exhibits. McDonald and Merwin, who had told McCartin at the outset that they believed the trial would last eighteen months, complained that it was moving too fast and asked for a mistrial. McCartin denied the motion and moved on.

By Thanksgiving, the trial of Randy Kraft appeared as though it would be lengthy by criminal trial standards, but far from the marathon that jurors, prosecution, defense, and the public had thought it would be. For one thing, Bryan Brown had dismissed the idea of introducing any more murders, even though Chief Investigator Dan DiSanto and his team of three full-time assistants had come up with evidence linking Kraft to two-dozen cases beyond the sixteen the computer consultant was originally charged with committing.

"This case is so spread out—one day you're in San Diego, the next day you're in Oregon," said the impeccably dressed investigator, decked out each day in a different Dior shirt, silk tie, and tailored suit. "Witnesses die. They retire. They move. They get married. We got over thirteen hundred witnesses contacted over a three-year period. You lose track of them when you're talking like ten years between when the crime was committed and the trial happens. With some of them, it's closer to twenty years. You have to track the witnesses down all over again. We finally found one of our key witnesses on a cruise ship operating out of Hawaii."

DiSanto had less sympathy for Kraft each time he investigated a fresh lead on yet another murder that might be linked to the death list.

"There's four things I want to do before I die," DiSanto said outside the courtroom. "Kill me a boar, shoot a wild turkey, catch a marlin, and throw the switch on Randy."

On November 30, Bryan Brown called his last witness: toxicologist Raymond Kelly. Twelve of the sixteen victims were near-comatose when they died, Kelly said. They had been doped up on pain killers, heart medicine, or sedatives, mixed with alcohol, and could not have put up much of a fight, if any.

When the prosecution rested, 157 witnesses had testified and 1,052 pieces of evidence—photos, belts, blood samples, coats, hair, etc.—had been tagged, logged, and locked away in the exhibit room in the basement of the courthouse.

McCartin ordered the jury back after New Year's and sent them home for the holidays. Randy returned to his cell to spend a sixth Christmas alone.

Randy's defense was a double A strategy: alibis and alternate suspects. The battery of defense investigators were ordered to dig up people who were likely to have committed one or more of the sixteen charged and twenty-nine uncharged murders that Bryan Brown's small army of investigators had traced to Randy Kraft by the time the jury reconvened in January of 1989.

"The prosecution itself has developed the following list of alternate suspects," Jim Merwin wrote in a declaration he gave to the court asking Brown to turn over more discovery information. The list contained thirty-three names, including that of a woman. Patrick Kearney was also on the list.

William Bonin, whom prosecutors had ruled out early on in connection with the kinds of victims Kraft was accused of killing, was not on the alternate suspect list, even though McDonald and Merwin were certain many of the deaths attributed to Randy were attributable to either Bonin or one of his minions. Merwin speculated that a carved symbol on one of Mark Hall's limbs was a satanic sign and probably put there by Vernon Butts, until Brown pointed out that Butts and Bonin didn't even know each other in 1975, when Hall died.

The mysterious "Les," who had written the note to Brown calling himself the new Zodiac killer, just a few weeks after Randy was caught, also wasn't on the alternate suspect list.

And neither was Jon Michael McMellen, who would have been four days younger than Randy Kraft, had he been alive. McMellen came to be a key part of the "alternate suspect" defense strategy when Merwin and Tom McDonald began parading their own witnesses before the jury. All that they had to do was establish a "reasonable doubt" in the mind of one of the jurors, and Kraft would not be convicted. At least for two of the murder counts—Donnie Crisel and possibly Richard Keith—

Randy's lawyers thought they had a perfect alternate in Jon McMellen.

Police from the city of Irvine, as well as military intelligence, had been watching Jon McMellen off and on for years, but never made a connection between him and Randy Kraft. In his own way, McMellen was an even more unlikely candidate for a murder suspect than Kraft.

A six-foot-three, two-hundred-pound, bespectacled family man with a wife, a two-story tract home, and two small daughters, McMellen first surfaced in connection with the murder of Marine corporal Donnie Crisel.

McMellen held a job, drove a camper, and enjoyed watching football on TV, armed with a Miller High Life in one hand and a remote control in the other.

But like Kraft, McMellen led a double life. He cruised gay bars in Santa Ana, had an arrest record, and occasionally picked up hitchhikers at military bases, sharing marijuana with them as a prelude to sex.

Irvine police developed an interest in McMellen in the fall of 1979, when a marine named Andy Wilhelm told Irvine Police sergeant Jim Potts about a man in a brown pickup truck with two toddlers in the front seat and a white camper shell on the back who stopped one October morning in front of the Lighter Than Air bar in Tustin to offer him a ride.

"Where are you going?" the guy hollered out his window. Wilhelm told him he was heading back to the El Toro Marine Base.

"I can take you as far as Culver," said McMellen.

As soon as he was in the car, McMellen asked him if he'd like to stop by the house and "smoke a couple of doobies." Wilhelm agreed, so they drove to his house and Wilhelm parked in front of the TV set while McMellen put his two small daughters to bed. Then he brought out some Thai stick and the two of them proceeded to get high. McMellen rambled on about how he liked driving up Silverado Canyon, where he'd park and smoke and watch the jets land at the Marine base. He worked as a superintendent at Leisure World, a retirement settlement in nearby Laguna Hills, and babysat for the children on his off time, while his wife worked. Somewhere in the marijuana haze, Wilhelm recalled McMellen's conversation turning to sex.

Mrs. McMellen, he told Wilhelm, had just had a hysterectomy, and McMellen spent most of his waking hours in a sustained state of lust. He had a girlfriend on the side named Cathy, he said, but as good a lay as she was, she didn't always satisfy him. He asked Wilhelm if he'd like to go trolling for women in Anaheim. Getting a nod from the anesthetized marine, McMellen told him to go wait in the camper until his wife got home from work. He didn't want to leave his daughters at home alone, but as soon as his wife had returned, the two of them could go off together and get laid.

A few minutes later, McMellen came out to the driveway and told Wilhelm to come back in the house. His wife had called from Alpha Beta with car trouble, he said, and wouldn't be home for a while.

Back inside, Wilhelm got worried for the first time.

"He kept sizing me up," Wilhelm told Sergeant Potts. McMellen also did not appear to be as loaded as Wilhelm, leading the marine to reassess, too late, just how much Thai stick he'd smoked compared to McMellen. It was at that point that McMellen went into a shocking personality switch.

"What's the best way you get off?" he wanted to know. "Head? Fucking? Are your nuts tight? Do you shoot big wads?"

McMellen bounded upstairs to his bedroom. While Wilhelm weaved in amazement at the foot of the stairs, McMellen called down to Wilhelm, asking him to come upstairs and sodomize him. Wilhelm's jaw dropped open like a boxer's who's been caught in the solar plexus. Unfazed, McMellen asked Wilhelm if he liked to use Vaseline.

Wilhelm was barely able to utter a "no" before he hurried out the front door. He tripped over the hose in the front yard as McMellen followed him out the door, apologizing for frightening him and asking him to stay awhile longer. Wilhelm snapped out of his cannabis trance in a hurry. He ran down the street and out of the housing tract.

Just four months before the Wilhelm incident, Sergeant Potts testified, Donnie Crisel was found strangled to death just off the San Diego Freeway in Irvine.

Naval Intelligence officials invested with the responsibility of finding out who was killing off southern California's marines, as well as the local police, considered McMellen a prime suspect. But in a classic case of law enforcement officials jealously refusing to share witnesses or information, the federal investigators didn't cooperate with Irvine police and vice versa.

In the course of their own investigation, Irvine detectives Mark Hoffman and Ron Veach, who suspected that federal authorities were not telling all, began secretly following Sergeant Brooks Mason, one of the naval investigators. What they discovered was that Sergeant Mason had a gay informant who knew about McMellen's double life. The informant led Veach and Hoffman to McMellen's suburban home, where they found that McMellen did, in fact, cruise Taylor's Restaurant just outside the main gate of the Tustin Marine Base where Crisel was last seen alive and that he did, indeed, know about Crisel's murder.

"He had details that he shouldn't have had about Crisel's death," Veach testified under McDonald's questioning.

Jim Espinoza, one of Crisel's Marine buddies, related from the witness stand an incident that had happened just three weeks before Crisel died, in which a couple of men in a van parked outside the Lighter Than Air bar were offering beer and weed to anyone who would hop in and take a ride. One of the two men matched the description of McMellen, he said.

Furthermore, another defense witness testified, a brown and white camper with heavy-duty tires like those likely to have been on McMellen's truck had been seen idling near the side of the road where Marine Richard Keith's body was found early one Monday morning in June of 1978, one year before Crisel died.

Keith was found naked. Crisel wore boxer shorts with tire marks on the back. McDonald suggested to the jury that the tire marks might have come from McMellen's camper, but Brown brought in his own expert witness to dispute that.

For several months following the Wilhelm incident, McMellen remained a suspect, but ultimately investigators seemed prepared to concede that he was just one of the hedonistic casualties of the '60s sexual revolution whose addiction to kinky sex was pathetic but usually consensual and not necessarily illegal.

Exactly one week after Kraft's arrest in 1983, McMellen committed suicide.

Despite question marks like Jon McMellen that McDonald and Merwin were able to toss into the prosecution's case, Bryan Brown had a ready answer for most of the reasonable doubts the two defense attorneys tried implanting into the jurors' minds.

McDonald tried showing that Randy was working the night Rodger DeVaul and Geoff Nelson were picked up, and had worked as well the following day at St. Ives laboratories in Palos Verdes, for example.

But Brown pointed out that a roll of film containing several frames of Rodger was found in Kraft's possession. In some of the photos, DeVaul's hands could be seen lashed together with shoestrings, and a ligature mark was visible on his neck. At the end of that same roll of film, several frames of a parking lot near St. Ives labs had been shot, as though Randy were trying to finish it up so that he could get it developed.

The conclusion Brown wanted the jury to reach was that Kraft took pictures of his dead victim, dumped the body, and immediately drove to his regular Saturday morning job at St. Ives, shooting up the rest of the film on the way so that he could rush it to a drugstore for developing.

Over and over, as McDonald would try to establish a credible alibi, Brown countered with an equally credible—and, in some instances, damning—piece of evidence or set of circumstances that pointed the finger back at Kraft.

One thing Brown could not do was defend the victims.

"Let's face it," said his chief investigator, Dan DiSanto, "none of these guys was going to grow up to be president."

Out in the hallway, friends and family of the victims complained bitterly throughout the four-month-long defense portion of the trial that their dead sons, not Randy Kraft, seemed to be on trial in Judge McCartin's courtroom. Judy Nelson was mortified when transvestite Humberto Franco took the stand and identified Geoff as the male prostitute Coco. Shirley DeVaul winced and wept when DeVaul's former roommate Stanley Goheen conceded, under McDonald's questioning, that Rodger was a frequent recreational drug user. McDonald succeeded in getting Judge McCartin to order the ever-present Mrs. DeVaul to sit at least two rows back from the front of the courtroom so that her angry eyes did not intimidate his client's witnesses.

The ultimate slap in the face for the victims' families, however, was the day Jim Merwin called Barbara Loggins as a defense witness.

"Did Wyatt own a gold necklace with a roach clip?" Merwin asked.

"I never saw it," answered the nervous, stout mother of the victim identified on Randy's death list as "MCHB TATTOO."

"Did Wyatt have a drinking problem?" Merwin continued, amiably but persistent.

"Wyatt drank more than I thought he should," said Barbara Loggins, measuring her words as she wrung her hands tightly in her lap. "He had been treated in the military for it. I know that he took some . . . I know that he smoked marijuana. He told me that he never did anything else."

Merwin wanted to know if he ever left his wallet at home or loaned his car to friends or if he took antihistamines, and Barbara, looking more and more as though she might explode from anxiety, stumbled through another half hour of painful answers before she was finally allowed to step down.

She maintained her composure until she went into the ladies' room outside the courtroom. There, surrounded by other outraged members of other victims' families, she broke into deep, uncontrollable sobs.

"What's the point?" she cried hysterically over and over and over while four different women tried comforting her. "What's the point?"

Judge McCartin knew the players in his little courtroom drama well enough. From his perch a few feet above everyone else, he looked down upon an intelligent and attentive jury of mostly women who had taken to playing fashion games with him. One day, they would all show up in red. The next, they were all in pink or green or some other uniform color. It might have been coincidence, but from where McCartin sat, it didn't seem like it.

"All those not wearing red will change during the noon hour," he said in a deadpan voice before excusing the jury for lunch.

He was stern, and had the face for it, but McCartin had a wry sense of humor too. As the trial of Randy Kraft dragged on, month after month, a sense of propriety and rigid courtroom etiquette often disappeared. There were times when even Kraft joined in the laughter.

When the defense case finally started winding down and talk turned to the question of sequestering the jury, McCartin suggested they spend their deliberation time in the Bates Motel. The offhand reference to the out-of-the-way inn where Anthony Perkins murdered guests in Alfred Hitchcock's *Psycho* did not go unnoticed by the *Orange County Register*. A political cartoon on the newspaper's editorial page the following day depicted the jurors trudging up a grim knoll, topped by the Bates Hotel.

But McCartin was not always so fun-loving, especially when the defense case seemed to poke on interminably. At one point, he threatened to charge McDonald with contempt for failing to have his witnesses ready to go and asking for repeated trial delays. Furiously, McDonald yelled back at him that he would answer such intimidation by asking for a mistrial.

"I don't think we've gone at an average of two hours a day in the last month," McCartin said. "If we go any slower, we'll stop."

"Frankly, I'm going as fast as I can!" McDonald shouted indignantly at the judge.

Bryan Brown agreed that the defense seemed to be slowing things down on purpose, but he, too, complained about the terse, acerbic treatment that he received at McCartin's hands. If McCartin was a dog, he said, then he was a fire hydrant.

"Do you want to ask for a mistrial too?" McCartin teased.

McCartin ordered McDonald and Merwin to move the case along, if not for the jury's sake, then for McCartin's.

"My wife may kill me if I go home early again," he said. "I may be . . . emasculated. Is that the word?"

Denver Sayre, father of one of Kraft's alleged victims, agreed with Judge McCartin. "It's very slow and very unproductive," he said in mid-March as the trial ground sluggishly toward its climax. As to the man on trial who sat face forward, as inscrutable as a Buddhist monk, day in and day out, he left the smallish, soft-spoken Mr. Sayre dumbfounded.

"It's hard to believe," he added, more wonder in his voice than anger or hurt.

But there was that too, for himself and his wife, Arvetta. On November 24, 1979, his fifteen-year-old son, Jeffery Bryan Sayre, had disappeared following a date with his girlfriend in Westminster. He left her house at approximately 10:30 P.M., intending to ride the bus home to Santa Ana. But the bus stopped running in Westminster at 7:30 P.M., and Bryan never came home. After months of desperate searching, believing but praying that he had not been one of the Bonin gang's victims, the Sayres settled into an eternal holding pattern of hope. One day, they told themselves, Bryan would walk through the front door.

One day, after Randy Kraft was arrested, a homicide investigator showed up at the front door instead. He told Denver and Arvetta Sayre that there was still no sign of the remains of their son, but that police had found something that they believed might end the Sayres' vigil.

On a list Randy Kraft kept in the trunk of his car was an entry reading "WESTMINSTER DATE."

News of the death list had spread across the country, with requests coming in from parents whose sons had set out on the road years before and never come home. But the prosecution could only make a couple of calculated guesses when they didn't even have the benefit of a corpse. Sayre's was one of those. Paul Fuchs, who left his mother's paprika chicken on the Sunday dinner table in 1976 and never returned, was another. Kraft killed both of them, according to police, even though they never learned what he did with their bodies.

But McDonald pounded home alternative suspects as his theme, day after day in the courtroom. The Nelsons and the Churches and the Crotwells, and certainly the Sayres and the Fuchses, needed to look somewhere other than at Randy if they wanted to know who had killed their sons. Brown preferred a different term than alternate: "phantom" suspects is what he called them for the jury's benefit.

McDonald, perturbed and inflamed by Brown's low-key, Cheshire-cat approach to arguing the case, railed on with the righteous fury of a Southern politician in midfilibuster. Whenever he finished with a witness, instead of humbly thanking them for testifying as Brown regularly did, McDonald simply said, "That's it," and called for the next witness, his indignation always glowing as brightly as his neck.

Roland Young didn't die at the hands of Randy Kraft; he was killed by drug dealers, he said. So was Rodger DeVaul. Mark Hall was murdered by satanists, and both Donnie Crisel and Richard Keith were picked up in Jon McMellen's camper.

They all had an explanation just as plausible as those offered up by the prosecution, McDonald argued.

The toughest one to explain, however, was Gambrel. That, McDonald said, Kraft would explain himself once he got on the witness stand.

Throughout the long judicial ordeal, Randy's demeanor never altered. He was as placid the first day as he was the last. The *Orange County Register*'s daily columnist, Bob Emmers, sat in McCartin's courtroom and closely studied Randy, sitting in the middle chair at the defense table, for just fourteen minutes during one day of the trial. He wrote:

"During these 14 minutes, Kraft conferred with his attorneys, Tom McDonald and James Merwin; smiled briefly; once tapped his chest rapidly as if to signify that his heart was beating rapidly; turned and searched the faces of the jurors; wrote rapidly on his tablet with a gold pen; conferred again with McDonald; turned toward the spectators and scanned the faces, his gaze pausing here and there. His face was relaxed although a little puffy around the eyes, but the eyes themselves were bright. He looked like an accountant awaiting the start of a business meeting."

Indeed, when Judy Nelson or Denver Sayre or Darwin Hall, or any of the other parents first laid eyes on Kraft, every one of them walked away shaking their heads in bewilderment.

"One thing that puzzles me is your choice of clothes, Mr. Kraft," blurted out Judge McCartin in one of his rare comments aimed directly at Randy. "A tie one day and jeans the next."

Randy altered his inscrutability ever so slightly and responded with a quiet chuckle, but no words. Then he returned to his incessant note taking.

The jury got Easter off before McDonald and Brown wound up their respective cases. McDonald explained to McCartin that he had canceled his plan to put Randy on the stand because Brown refused to exempt him from cross-examination.

All that left for the defense team was a theatrical beer-and-drug demonstration, put on by pharmacologist Lawrence Plon. For the benefit of the jury, Plon mixed Valium with Moosehead lager to demonstrate that the bottles overflowed in a chemical reaction if laced with the drug.

"I don't know if Moosehead would want that in a commercial or not," deadpanned McCartin.

"Your honor, I was going to say something like 'This Bud's for you,' but I'm going to resist that feeble attempt at humor," quipped McDonald.

Brown asked Plon, who reportedly charged several hundred dollars for the thirty-minute demonstration, to take his remaining drugs with him when he left or he might take them to "help me tolerate the judge."

Brown did his closing argument with the aid of a black Magic Marker and an easel of white paper. McDonald used a four-by-six-foot computer console, operated by a gray-haired keyboard operator whose anonymous presence off to one side of Judge McCartin's bench seemed like that of the Wizard of Oz as he manipulated control panels just out of the jury's line of sight.

Both of them used charts and graphs to walk the jurors through the charges one last time. McDonald's just happened to be far more sophisticated and expensive than Brown's.

"There's been a gloss put on these charges by a clever prosecutor painting with a real broad brush," said McDonald. "Nothing could be further from the truth."

The lights dimmed and he signaled the little man at the console to show the first of ten computerized color charts, showing how different each murder was from the others. Different physical characteristics.

Different methods for dumping bodies. Different blood alcohol levels. Different causes of death.

The one graph that showed disparity and, therefore, Randy's innocence, more than any other, said McDonald, was a pie chart depicting thirteen different categories of drugs found in the bodies of the sixteen victims. Far from being similar, he suggested, the charts showed that each death was very different and probably done by different killers.

Brown was more direct.

"Burning the nipples on a victim is so gross there aren't other people around that are going to do that," he said.

Brown's checkerboard chart focused on similarities among the killings, including the use of an automobile cigarette lighter as a branding iron. When he had finished darkening in the square to show which victim met each of his criteria, his chart depicted similarities ranging from their age and alcohol use to their military status and the drugs found in their body.

Randy had sought out the same kind of victim—male, white, single hitchhikers, eighteen to twenty-five years of age. He drugged them, tied them up with their own shoelaces, tortured and sodomized them, and dumped their bodies on the freeway. He didn't follow the scenario exactly in every case, conceded Brown, but more often than not, he did.

Jim Merwin spoke last. "When evidence falls short, Mr. Brown ad libs," he told the jury. "He does it in such a matter-of-fact way that you just sort of take it as fact."

Unlike his flamboyant partner, Merwin was steady and calm. Convicting Kraft based on similarities as minor as the type of shoelaces the victims wore or did not wear was unjust and unfair.

"If you put up enough different charges, you could probably come up with enough evidence to convict the Pope," Merwin said.

At the end of the third day of closing arguments, the defense rested. Judge McCartin held up the cartoon from the *Register* that depicted the Bates Motel and ordered the jury off to an Irvine hotel to begin deliberations the following day.

Outside the courtroom, victims' relatives, led by Shirley and Rodger Devaul, groused before the TV cameras about Kraft's cowardice in failing to take the stand and answer directly for his crimes. Before she caught the elevator down to the courtroom lobby, Kay Plunkett told reporters that a long-lost relative from San Antonio, Texas, had been reading about her brother's trial and had told her to send Randy down for a visit when he was acquitted.

It took eleven days for the ten-woman, two-man jury to return their verdict. On May 12, 1989, they found Randy innocent of sodomizing Rodger DeVaul, Jr.

On the remaining eighteen counts, including the emasculation of Geoffrey Nelson and the sodomizing of Michael Inderbieten and the murders of sixteen young men between 1972 and 1983, Randy Kraft was declared guilty in the first degree.

"I didn't know what to expect, but I was hoping for the best," said Kay Plunkett. "Randy's the only one who knows the truth. It's been six years and I believe Randy is trying not to burden the family."

On the morning he was arrested, she remembered, Kay was one of the first people Randy called.

"He said, 'Kay, I've been arrested.' I said 'For what?' in complete shock," said the fifty-eight-year-old schoolteacher. "He said, 'Murder.' Then he said, and these were his exact words, 'Don't tell Mom and Dad—it would break their hearts.'"

"Anyone who has genuine feelings would hope that their loved one would never do anything as serious as murder," she said.

Doris Lane, her younger sister, was more tight-lipped in her assessment of the jury's verdict. "One word: wrong. They didn't believe the family," she said.

The *Times* and the *Register* were both reporting that the trial of Randy Kraft would have a final pricetag of $10 million and, still, the ordeal was not over.

Under California law, the jurors who had convicted Kraft of multiple murder still had to decide whether to send him to his death or put him in prison for life with no chance for parole. A "penalty phase," in which Brown and McDonald drastically changed their respective tactics, got underway on June 5, 1989.

Bolstered by the near-total victory given him by the jury, a less folksy and far more aggressive Bryan Brown waived his opening statement and immediately put witnesses on the stand who would paint a picture for the jury of a rabid wolverine, suitable only for the gas chamber. Instead of introducing all twenty-nine additional victims that Brown's investigators had been able to link to Kraft and his "death list," the more self-confident prosecutor decided to limit the additional evidence to just eight: the six hitchhikers killed in Oregon and the two Michigan farm boys whose bodies had been left in a snow-covered field in Grand Rapids. That was all Bryan Brown felt he needed to get the jury to vote execution for Randy Kraft.

Once his client had been convicted, Tom McDonald showed a warmer, less apoplectic side in the courtroom. Jim Merwin remained his unruffled, professional self, keeping his cross-examination terse and logical while performing for the jury as a kind of intellectual Sancho Panza to McDonald's blustery Don Quixote.

And their tactics outside the courtroom changed too. Their defense support team was no longer searching for alternate suspects as much as it was searching for ways to reach the hearts of the ten women and two men who would decide their client's fate.

One investigator, Johanna Ramsey, spent weeks piecing together a pair of family albums containing photos, memorabilia, and letters that would show the jury just how human, warm, and good-hearted a person Randy Kraft really was. The albums, containing photos dating back as far as Randy's infancy, became part of the court record.

John Blackburn, another investigator, had been hired because he was openly gay and, the attorneys believed, would be able to penetrate the gay community. They wanted him to come up with valuable character witnesses who could give the jury a sense of the general normalcy that usually exists in the gay world, despite its obvious differences with the heterosexual majority. Blackburn was also invested with the task of getting reluctant gay witnesses to come out of the closet and into the courtroom.

Other investigators scoured the Orange County Jail deputy roster for guards and former guards who had come in contact with Randy during his six years behind bars. They found nearly a dozen willing to take the stand and testify to Randy's behavior as a model prisoner.

"You might have shut down the jail with all the deputies you've got testifying," quipped McCartin.

One guard who was studying computer programming had even asked Randy to tutor him.

But not everyone in the Orange County Jail got on so well with Kraft. One prisoner who guards kept far away from Randy's wing was a heavyset thirty-two-year-old felon from Colorado who was doing a six-month stretch for violating parole. He had been caught driving drunk one night on an Orange County street, and a computer record check had turned up the fact that he was still on parole from an auto theft conviction near Denver.

His name was Joseph Alwyn Fancher, and he was the first witness Brown called to the stand during the penalty phase of Randy's trial.

The boy Kraft had raped nineteen years earlier had tattoos on his large Popeye-sized arms and fine, blond—nearly white—hair, beard, and mustache. He wore handcuffs and entered McCartin's courtroom escorted by Sheriff's deputies. His gruff, monosyllabic voice, his hulking profile, and his high, flat forehead with bony protrusions where his eyebrows knit together made Joe Fancher look like a wounded bear in a yellow jail-issue jumpsuit.

When his gaze fell on Kraft, his eyes narrowed to slits and Randy looked elsewhere. Ironically, the man on trial for his life sat unshackled a few feet away from the prisoner in the witness stand. Randy was dressed in gray cotton slacks, white Oxford shirt, dark striped tie, dress shoes, and black leather belt.

Brown ordered the cuffs removed and offered Fancher a Styrofoam cup of water before he testified. He and Fancher had been through this ritual six years earlier during Kraft's preliminary hearing, but the jury had never witnessed it.

For the next hour, in hoarse single-sentence replies that Brown had to extract from the hulking figure on the witness stand one ponderous question at a time, Fancher related how the skinny young naïf he once had been was repeatedly raped by Randy Kraft. While Fancher spoke, Kraft rested his head on his left hand and furiously took notes.

"What happened when you got up to his apartment?" Brown asked.

Fancher growled slowly, inserting long pauses to swallow away his dry throat.

"He asked me . . . if I liked music," he managed to utter. "I guess, from the way I looked . . . he asked me if I was nervous."

He rubbed the back of his neck.

"Look," he said suddenly, a dangerous edge to his voice. "This ain't easy, so what do you want to know? This is starting to agitate me."

For the first time, Brown looked slightly nervous. He stepped up the line of questioning, gingerly steering Fancher through the crucial information about being drugged, shown pornography, and forced to perform oral copulation.

"What happened then?" Brown asked gently.

The witness's huge hands interlocked in his lap and he looked down at them for several seconds, searching for the answer.

"What happened?" Brown coaxed.

"He . . . ah . . ." Fancher began, reaching his left hand to the back of his neck again. "He so—sod—sodomized me."

When Jim Merwin took over cross-examination, he confronted his most hostile witness since the trial began. Fancher was just as gruff, but no longer hesitant. When Merwin asked Fancher if he belonged to a motorcycle gang, the bruiser on the stand looked defiant and began to answer until Brown hopped to his feet with an objection. McCartin ruled Merwin's question irrelevant.

"Do you have a two-page rap sheet?" Merwin asked.

"Yep," said Fancher.

"What crimes were you convicted of?" Merwin continued.

"Ain't none of your business as far as I'm concerned," Fancher shot back.

Merwin reeled slightly from Fancher's impudence. He looked to McCartin for help and, finding none, rephrased his question. But it did little good.

"It ain't got nothing to do with this case," Fancher said.

Kraft grinned slightly in Fancher's direction, and Merwin stepped to the bench with Brown close behind. After a hasty conference, McCartin ordered Fancher to tell the jury the crimes that he could recall having committed.

"I still ain't gonna answer," he said.

Brown asked for a ten-minute recess and took his witness back to one of the holding cells off behind the courtroom for a cigarette break. Fancher was soothed enough when he returned to answer Merwin's questions: fifteen convictions, including assault with great bodily harm, three stints in Colorado state prison, a history of explosive violence. When Merwin asked if the district attorney had offered to pay Fancher for his testimony, Fancher chuckled. He told the now profusely sweating defense attorney that he had asked Brown to buy him a truck for $650 when he got out of jail and that the prosecutor had refused.

After Merwin sat back down next to Kraft, Brown asked, "Did anybody from the DA's office give you any benefits?"

"No," barked Joe Fancher.

As he was recuffed and escorted back to a holding cell to await transport back to the Orange County Jail, Fancher came within inches of Kraft, still sitting head down, carefully taking notes at the defense table. Two of the women in the jury box held their breath and one of the male jurors appeared to brace himself to duck down behind the barrier that sets the jury box off from the rest of the courtroom.

But Joe Fancher did not even look at Randy Kraft as he passed.

The remainder of Bryan Brown's case was more of the same grotesque evidence and heart-tugging testimony that he'd offered since the trial began nearly a year earlier. All that was different was that the killings had occurred in different states, different terrain.

Michael O'Fallon's mother and brother told about the seventeen-year-old high school graduate from Colorado who was bright and daring and independent enough to hitch across the Pacific Northwest all by himself. The jury also saw his autopsy photos.

Rosalie Cluck spoke of a headstrong boy who was determined to make a million dollars in the oil business and might finally have developed the gumption to do it if he hadn't caught the wrong ride south. The jury also viewed blow-ups of Michael Cluck's skull, hammered thirty-one times, the coroner estimated. Characterized on the death list as "PORTLAND BLOOD," the seventeen-year-old from Kent, Washington, was the bloodiest of all of Kraft's victims.

Lyla Silveira identified for the jury her dead husband's jacket with the name SILVEIRA stenciled across the pocket. After he had died, she had gone back to school, gotten a job, and remarried, providing their two children with a stepfather.

She did not remain in the courtroom to see the color photographs of Anthony Silveira's strangled, decomposing body lying in the weeds off of Boone's Ferry Road with a red Tek toothbrush rammed into the rectum.

Even the most jaded of the jurors gasped at the autopsy photos of Chris Schoenborn. They'd repeatedly seen the Y incision medical examiners routinely cut into victims' torsos, with human organs exposed to view like so many sweetbreads. They'd grown shell-shocked to the many different views of scalped cadavers with their brain pans opened for inspection. But the sight of the young Michigan farmer's genitals sliced open to expose a ball-point pen run all the way through to the bladder nearly sent a young woman juror out of the courtroom with her hand covering her mouth. One uncomfortable male juror crossed and recrossed his legs.

After only five days of testimony, Bryan Brown wrapped up his case against Randy Kraft. He put into evidence the forty-five entries from the death list that he and his investigators had linked to known victims, giving the jury a better idea of just how extensive Randy's killing spree may have been. Because of defense objections, none of the jurors had ever seen the full list, and the defense had no intention of allowing it to happen now.

"This is rank speculation!" protested Bill Kopeny, the defense team's procedural specialist. Kopeny rarely made court appearances, but McCartin gave him grudging respect for his skill whenever he did.

"It's highly speculative," he continued, railing on for several minutes about his objections to Brown's attempt to put the death list into evidence while the court reporter sat up taller in her chair and furiously tapped out notes to keep up with Kopeny's staccato.

"I feel it meets the relevancy test," a grumpy McCartin finally said, cutting Kopeny off. "If Mr. Kopeny wants to add more, the court reporter will have to change paper. He's so long-winded."

A more serene, at times almost jolly, Tom McDonald had a surprise for everyone in the courtroom on the second day of the final phase of the trial.

In a departure from his abrupt interrogation technique before the jury brought in its guilty verdicts, he was asking the procession of character witnesses who knew Randy over the years to "share your views on Randy as far as who he is, as a human being."

He also introduced each witness with a short but weighty explanation of why they were asked to appear: to help the jury decide whether or not to "kill" Randy Kraft.

"They would lose a very brilliant mind," said Carol Barnett, who had once worked with Randy at Jay-El Products. "I've often wondered why the prison doesn't use his capabilities."

He was always patient, competent, a vegetarian, said Barnett. He came over to her house twice for dinner, and she went river rafting once with Randy and Jeff. She never would have survived in her job if it hadn't been for Randy's help, she said, her voice quavering and her eyes verging on tears.

Then McDonald delivered his surprise. "Randy would like to ask you a few questions," he said.

In a brown tweed jacket, blue jeans, and knit tie, Randy looked more like a New Age defense attorney himself than a defendant in the nation's worst murder spree. From his seat at the defense table, his voice was a calm, articulate tenor.

"Hi, Carol," he began softly. "Before I began working at Jay-El you had already been working there?"

"Yes."

"When IBM sold computers [to the company] did they try to give help to the employees?"

"No."

Randy's questions followed the same nonsensical pattern throughout the remainder of his trial. Once the jury and spectators got over the initial shock of actually hearing him speak, the line of questioning quickly

became predictably innocuous. He seemed more determined to demonstrate his humanity for the jury than to elicit crucial information from
the witnesses. What he managed to show was how pleasantly mundane
and manipulative he could be when his life depended on it, according to
Brown.

When his old friend Fred Barrow took the stand, he did manage to
raise a chuckle in the courtroom. He asked the male nurse whom Kraft
had met when he was still tending bar at the Buoy's Shed twenty years
earlier, whether or not he, Kraft, had ever shown any interest in young
boys.

"Have you ever heard the expression 'chicken queen'?" Kraft
asked.

"Someone interested in younger people?" said Barrow, shrugging
his shoulders as if to ask a question as much as to answer one.

"You've never seen me in the company of teenagers?" Kraft asked.

Barrow answered that he hadn't, nor had he seen him with any
marines. Under Brown's cross-examination, Barrow said he'd never
heard the expression "chicken queen" before.

Neither had Carl Herringer, Jeff Seelig's candy store employee,
who had seen a perfectly calm, normal Randy at the Roswell Avenue
house early Friday evening on the night that Randy was arrested.
Herringer said he might not use the term "chicken queen" or "chicken
hawk" as Randy had, but he never knew Kraft to hit on teenagers or
marines. More than a dozen witnesses who followed Herringer, some
nearly in tears like Carol Barnett, echoed the aging candymaker's final
assessment of the Randy Kraft they had known—in some cases, for
more than twenty years.

"I'm not aware of any enemies that he had," said Herringer. "I
never knew anyone who didn't like Randy."

The Reverend Joe Morris Doss, an Episcopal priest, had known
Kraft for only a few hours before McDonald called him to the stand, but
he praised him as though they had known each other for years. He was
the first of several clergy with anti–capital punishment views who
testified against the death penalty as much as they did for Randy Kraft.

"He's warm and gracious . . . a person of real humility," said
Reverend Doss. "This is a human being. He breathes. He has
sensations. He cares and is cared for."

Before Bryan Brown caught on, Doss switched his testimony from
Randy to execution in general. He lectured the jury on the inherent evil
in the institutional killing of another human being and, by the time

Brown had gotten to his feet to object, Reverend Doss had told the jury that killing Kraft would be participating in a ritual of death that would only hurt one more family: Randy's.

"These questions are completely out of line," McCartin scolded. "The evidence should focus on the offenders and the offense."

McDonald's kindly demeanor of the previous few weeks suddenly vanished. His face grew scarlet as he raised his fists and began shouting at McCartin that he had every right to question Doss about the death penalty.

"It's silly," McCartin shouted back. "It's so far afield it's stupid. I've heard all I want to hear."

"Your Honor, may I add just one thing?" asked Reverend Doss.

"No sir, you may not!" McCartin hollered, staring the priest into secular silence.

While McDonald continued to loudly protest, McCartin ordered the jury to disregard Reverend Doss's philosophizing. Then he warned McDonald to stick to defending his client instead of attacking public policy. Shaking a slender forefinger at the defiant attorney, McCartin told McDonald to watch himself.

"That's like asking the wolf to watch the chicken coop," muttered Bryan Brown.

Brown took his revenge two days later when another minister, this time a Methodist, took the stand. After McDonald finished eliciting the anti-execution testimony from Reverend Ignatio Castuera, Brown leaned into the clergyman with a sympathetic question. "Help us out here, sir. Did Mr. Kraft show any remorse whatsoever for these kids?" Brown asked.

The Reverend Castuera shrugged, answering that the short time he visited with Kraft in jail, they spoke only in general terms about philosophy and religion and not murder.

"So I would guess the answer would be he didn't show any remorse," said Brown.

McDonald objected. Brown smiled.

Dr. Monte Buchsbaum was a balding, owlish academic who taught psychiatry at the University of California campus in Irvine. What hair he had on his egg-shaped scalp was thin and graying and tended to look unkempt no matter what he did with it. He wore tortoiseshell glasses that rode low on his nose and spoke in a pensive, but not impenetrable, professor-ese.

He looked like TV newsman Charles Kuralt in a laboratory coat. In a way, Dr. Buchsbaum was McDonald's secret weapon.

Kraft and his attorneys had consistently dodged the psychological testing that tends to be routine in most multiple murder cases. The backbone of Randy's case, even following his conviction, was that he was innocent. He maintained to lawyers and family alike that there was nothing wrong with him. The logic seemed to be: if the defendant is innocent, why submit to psychological testing?

But now that the jurors had voted that they did not believe Randy's innocence, McDonald said he was going to show them that his client was not "evil" and simply could not help himself if, in fact, he did commit the crimes they believed that he had committed.

"It's something that he had no control of," McDonald said.

By calling Dr. Buchsbaum to the stand as an expert witness, McDonald was able to get around Randy's innocent plea without submitting his client to a battery of potentially damaging or inconclusive psychological tests.

Back in 1984, Merwin had retained Buchsbaum to conduct an electroencephalogram on Kraft. It came out normal, but that tried and true brain defect test only records electrical impulses from the surface of the skull. An electroencephalogram can uncover castastrophic brain malfunctions, such as tumors or Alzheimer's or epilepsy, but not emotional disorders.

Since the first time he tested Randy, however, Buchsbaum had become one of a handful of teaching psychiatrists in the U.S. who began putting their faith into a new technology called Positron Emission Tomography or PET scanning. The new test procedure called for patients to be injected with radioactive sugar tracer and then X-rayed at different levels, or "slices," of the brain. What the X-ray scans reveal, according to Buchsbaum, are the "hot" and "cool" spots inside the brain, where electrical activity is either rapid or sluggish.

When it came to measuring the organic potential for emotional abnormalities, Buchsbaum believed in PET scan technology. In May, just two weeks after Randy's conviction on sixteen counts of murder, McDonald and Merwin invited Buchsbaum to try PET scanning Kraft's brain.

When Buchsbaum studied a set of colorized sections of the convicted killer's brain, he discovered lethargic electrical activity in parts of the frontal lobes, where an individual's judgment is controlled.

But in the portions of the temporal lobes that govern emotion, impulse, and sex drive, electrical activity was abnormally high.

"The two systems are out of balance," Buchsbaum concluded, relating his findings on the witness stand. "The planning systems are decreased and the emotional systems are increased."

Buchsbaum used twenty-four volunteers at UCI to create a control group. The same scan that Buchsbaum performed on Randy was also performed on each of the volunteers. When the X rays were in, Buchsbaum concluded that fewer than 5 percent of the general population would have as aberrant a PET scan as Randy's.

Furthermore, he said, people who did have the kind of skewed brain activity that Randy's PET scan showed would probably have suffered from a childhood head injury and would become obsessive-compulsives as adults: people who are sane and even viewed as normal by their peers, but who act out obsessive, irrational impulses.

An obsessive-compulsive behavior can be as simple and inconsequential as uncontrollable hand washing, Buchsbaum offered, but whatever it is, it's usually ritualistic and recurring.

When Randy fell and was knocked unconscious at the age of one, Buchsbaum said, the accident could have caused irreparable but undetected brain damage that allowed him to act normally much of the time, but made him susceptible to emotional outbursts over which he may have had no control.

When Brown asked Buchsbaum if he'd done any psychiatric evaluations of Randy beyond the PET scan, the psychiatrist said Kraft didn't want any done. But showing a little nonacademic eagerness, Buchsbaum leaned forward to say that he would have been interested in doing some.

Shooting to his feet, McDonald said, "Didn't we say that you were only responsible for the PET scan and that others would do the rest?"

"Yes," Buchsbaum answered meekly.

Buchsbaum was followed by Dr. Craig Haney, a professional witness who charged $95 an hour to testify in capital cases up and down California. Haney said he had interviewed Kraft three times over five years for a total of six hours and concluded that he would adjust to prison life with little problem.

"Would you call him abnormally normal?" Brown asked him, demanding to know what experience Haney had in interviewing serial killers.

McDonald objected on grounds that the term "serial killer" might inflame the jury. Brown waived further questioning and, mildly amused at McDonald's attempt to shield the jury from inflammation, sat down to wait for the next witness.

On August 2, Jim Merwin brought up four new killings in one desperate last-minute attempt to buy some more time for the defense.

He read from an alert dated May 4, 1989, which had been sent by an official of a gay community center in Long Beach to gay bars throughout the old beach haunts and coastal neighborhoods where Randy used to cruise so many years before:

"We regret to inform you that there is a good possibility that a serial killer is preying upon the gay men of Long Beach," wrote Bill Geiger of the Center. "During the past month, at least two murders— actually, severe mutilations—may be attributed to the same man or men, possibly gay. Both victims were gay men. It's possible that the contact was made at local gay bars, later deciding to go home and have sex."

In all, Merwin told Judge McCartin, there had been four—not two—unsolved murders, with gay serial killer overtones, committed within a ten-month period. Implying that the maniac who had actually committed Randy's crimes was still on the loose, Merwin asked for more time and a discovery order to force the Long Beach police to give him their investigation reports on the four cases.

But Long Beach homicide detective George Fox not only discounted the relation of any of the four killings to Kraft's case, he flatly stated that none of the murders were related in any way. Three of the victims were stabbed to death and one was strangled, but in each incident the circumstances varied significantly from the string of killings attributed to Randy. To begin with, all three stabbing victims had been murdered in their homes or places of business.

Only the one strangulation victim—a thirty-six-year-old gay waiter who worked at the Long Beach Holiday Inn—had been dumped after he was murdered.

Roy Allen Griffin's body was found floating in a lagoon about a mile from Randy's old house on the morning of April 26. It was the same day that closing arguments ended and the jury began deliberating Randy's fate, but Long Beach homicide investigators saw no significance in the coincidence. Detective William MacLyman said robbery—not sex— appeared to be the motive.

In one case that did bear the signature of a Kraft murder—

castration—police had arrested a twenty-eight-year-old Montana drifter, who had refused to talk to them. The victim didn't fit the Kraft profile either. He was a sixty-one-year-old carpet cleaner who had a history of picking up young men at bars and taking them home with him.

Brown scoffed at the last-minute maneuver, but Merwin was insistent. A killer might still be out on the streets, and the defense needed more time to track down leads, turn up witnesses, find corroborating evidence . . .

"I'll review the reports," McCartin said.

It was 10:10 A.M. by the clock at the back of the courtroom when Bryan Brown began addressing the jury for the final time.

"It gives me the shivers to talk about it," he whispered to them confidentially, invoking the ghost of Mark Howard Hall one last time. "It is the most dehumanizing thing to do to another human being."

The chart he used in his closing statement for the penalty phase was a scale, not a grid like the one he used in the guilt phase of the trial. On one side, he told them, he was writing down the reasons that Randy, should live—the mitigating factors. On the other, he was writing down the reasons he should die—the aggravating factors.

And Mark Howard Hall, he said, addressing the jurors as "you guys," figured large on the aggravating side.

"Mr. Kraft puts these people in a position where he can dominate them. Where they're at his mercy," he said. "The one that cries out to me is Mark Hall. The one up there on Bedford Peak with everything cut off.

"Mr. Kraft wears a mask out in society, at work, and at home. But when it's in his interest to have sexual euphoria, he takes the mask off."

One by one, he walked the murder-weary men and women of the jury through each killing one final time. As the clock at the back of the courtroom ticked off hour after hour, on into the afternoon, the wretched details of each thrill-killing Brown enunciated became as indistinguishable from each other as the casting call of names: Keith, Crisel, Inderbieten, Hughes, Young, Crotwell, Cluck, O'Fallon, Alt, Schoenborn, DeVaul, Church, Nelson, Loggins, Gambrel. . . .

"Gambrel represented the end of an era of Mr. Kraft, flying the freeways," Brown finally muttered with savored sarcasm, after exhausting the catalog of killings.

As for the PET scan evidence that Kraft just could not help himself, Brown saved his harshest words.

"There's nothing wrong with Mr. Kraft's mind other than that he likes killing for sexual satisfaction," he said. The tears from family members on the witness stand, the testimonials from friends and co-workers "just show what a good salesman he is," Brown said bitterly.

Looking at the balance chart he had set up for the jurors, the side marked M for mitigating factors was blank. The A side, for aggravating factors, was covered with names and facts that Brown said could lead the jury toward only one conclusion: "Mr. Kraft is just plain evil. It has taken me four hours to go through the evil. If this case is not appropriate for the death penalty, there isn't any case that is."

The clock at the back of the room read 3:05 P.M. as Brown sat down and shut his notebook. The jury shuffled out of the room and Randy scribbled a few last notes. He whispered in McDonald's ear and they both chuckled before the bailiff came to escort Kraft back to jail.

On the last day of the trial, Jim Merwin brought out every detail that cast a doubt: the impossible task of carting around bodies, or getting to work on time, clean-shaven and alert, after a night of murderous debauchery, or attending a family gathering both before and after a killing.

How could little Randy lure big, strapping marines to their death? Why couldn't he have picked up the so-called souvenirs Sidebotham found in his car and house at a swap meet? Were a used Norelco shaver, a Mighty Mac jacket, and a set of nunchakus strong enough evidence to send a man to the gas chamber?

"I don't see how it's possible not to have some doubt," he concluded in a soft voice. He shook his head dramatically before yielding the courtroom floor to his partner.

Tom McDonald's final argument was not so much a defense of Randy Kraft as it was a condemnation of the death penalty.

"Most of the industrialized world has abandoned the death penalty," he said. He lumped the United States together with Iran, South Africa, China, Nigeria, Saudi Arabia, Pakistan, Malaysia, and the Soviet Union as nations that still execute.

A righteous, almost pious McDonald ordered everyone on the jury to ask themselves one important question. But when he slowly recited it out loud, he focused in on one timorous young female at the center of the jury box who might cast the one vote that could hang the jury. "Ask yourself: 'Am I so damn sure that my position on the death penalty is correct?'"

Bryan Brown's "cavalier casual treatment" of the clergymen that McDonald brought before the jury was reprehensible, he lectured.

"These gentlemen are in the moral guidance business," he said, finding his old familiar choler rising with his voice. He showed the jury grainy photographs of Charles Manson sitting in his jail cell. Randy, he told them, would never get out of prison if they sentenced him to life without parole.

Something was wrong with Randy's brain, McDonald said. The PET scan confirmed that. Opal Kraft could not have known that the unconscious baby she rushed to the emergency room had brain damage.

"Is Randy protecting someone?" he asked in a voice hoarse with emotion. "I don't know. Is there a split personality? I don't know. I wish I had the answers, but if we kill Randy, we're never going to have them."

He quoted Thomas Jefferson and Barbara Graham on the death penalty. The nation's third president pledged his opposition to the gallows "until the infallibility of man's judgment is proven to me. . . ." Graham, the last woman to die in California's gas chamber, told her executioners, "Good people are always so sure they're right."

"This decision will say much more about you than about Randy," McDonald said, an ominous note rising in his voice.

Break the cycle of violence, McDonald pleaded. Capital punishment is only institutionalized revenge. "If you condemn Randy, all that would happen would be that another family would lose a loved one and another mother would bury another son," he said.

McDonald paused to let the thought sink in. Then he sniffled and his eyes welled up with tears behind his gold wire-rimmed glasses. Before preparing his final argument, he had spoken with his seventy-four-year-old mother, he told the jury.

"'Tommy,' she said, 'there has to be a better way,'" McDonald said.

"You're going to be asked to make a Godlike decision," he continued, pounding the flat of his hand on the railing around the jury box. "I pray that you exercise Godlike wisdom. Please don't take his life. Not so much for Randy—I care a great deal about Randy. But I care more about us, about our society. Violence has to stop. We have to learn.

"It's a surrender to our worst instincts. The use of the power to kill . . . All it's done is to perpetuate more hate and violence. What we need is information and answers. The choice is yours. Do we go forward or do we kill needlessly? I beg you to make the right decision. You have to live with it. We all have to live with it."

Randy wrote furiously on his legal pad and barely looked up to see when his lawyer finished. He smiled blandly and pulled the chair out for him when he returned to the defense table.

One day later, the jury recommended that McCartin sentence Kraft to death.

Someone had finally straightened up the Great Seal of California hanging over Judge McCartin's chair. Instead of staring up at an angle at the ceiling on the west side of the courtroom, the Amazon in the seal was looking straight ahead when Randy Kraft entered from a side door shortly after nine A.M.

The convicted killer with the winsome smile and clean-cut features was flanked by all three of his attorneys. They all wore suits, but their client was dressed as though he were meeting friends for Saturday morning brunch. Kraft wore a starched long-sleeved blue-checked dress shirt, buttoned at the sleeves, no tie, and faded blue jeans. He apparently saw no irony in wearing an inch-wide black leather belt around his waist. As always, he appeared relaxed but attentive. His cheeks crinkled with laugh lines around his eyes as he grinned at something lead counsel Tom McDonald whispered in his ear.

But for the next two hours, the laugh lines around his eyes disappeared. If he looked up at all from the legal pad he scribbled on, it was not to twist around in his chair to smile at those who had come to see him sentenced. Kraft confined his blank stares to the tired, dour man in black robes who sat beneath the straightened Great Seal.

Donald McCartin shuffled papers, scratched, and ran his long, thin fingers through his scalp before getting down to business. He glanced at Kraft, but not in a stern way. His own eyes seemed a touch gloomy and even a little more fatigued than normal, but not angry. There was nothing of the stiff formality of a year before in his courthouse, when the trial had begun. His clerk, Gail Carpenter, shook her shoes off and waddled around the bench in stocking feet. She fussed with the potted plant hanging from the top of her desk, pinching off a dead leaf. Even the usually stiff and by-the-book bailiff was trading smiles and small talk with newspaper reporters, bragging about his new baby who had been conceived and born in the time it took to try Randy Kraft for murder.

Instead of jurors, TV camera crews and a small army of still photographers occupied the jury box. Several of Kraft's jurors, including foreman Jim Lytle, had returned to Department 30 like high school alumni to a homecoming game. But, this time, they sat in the gallery with newsmen and the regular retinue of court watchers and victims' relatives.

"I spent a year of my life here," Lytle explained. "I've got to see what happens."

Shirley and Rodger DeVaul, Sr., sat in the front row for the first time, Rodger's arm draped around his wife's shoulders. Judy Nelson sat nearby, arms and legs crossed. She hunkered down, almost as if she were hiding.

Three rows back sat Darwin and Lois Hall, who had flown in from Pocatello to watch the sentencing of the man who had killed their only son thirteen years before.

In a row of seats at the back of the room sat Jim Sidebotham, uncomfortably decked out in suit and tie, looking more sunken-cheeked and cadaverous than ever.

On the opposite end of the ancient walnut-stained table from where Randy and his lawyers sat, Bryan Brown and Dan DiSanto took their seats. And Judge McCartin called Randy Kraft's death-sentencing hearing to order.

Bill Kopeny moved that the jury verdict and the entire trial be set aside, pointing out again that he didn't believe Kraft had had an even chance facing sixteen separate counts of murder in a single trial.

"It's an oppressive number of charges," he said, at the same time seeming to contradict himself by chiding the district attorney for not adding on the twenty-nine additional murder counts of which Sidebotham and his investigators eventually came to believe Kraft was guilty.

Kopeny denounced Brown's easels, artwork, and photos, blown up beyond life-size throughout the trial for the jury. McDonald, who had remained silent with his arm draped protectively around the back of Kraft's chair, stood and joined Kopeny in condemning the hundreds of pictures entered into evidence, calling it "an array of death" that Brown used to "avalanche" the jury.

McDonald objected to the testimony Joseph Fancher had given about being raped by Kraft when he was thirteen years old. The evidence surrounding the eight out-of-state murders in Michigan and Oregon was also unwarranted in that Kraft had never been formally arraigned in any of those crimes, he said.

And both lawyers blasted McCartin for allowing Brown to show the jury Randy's "death list."

But when it was his turn, Brown had his own blasts for the defense. He stood slowly and, in an indignant drawl, rebuked McDonald and Kopeny for criticizing McCartin, the prosecution, and even the jury for finding Randy guilty on all sixteen murder counts following the evidence "avalanche."

"The jury in this case was a very dedicated group," Brown told McCartin. "They gave up over a year of their lives to ensure that Mr. Kraft got a fair trial."

The Fancher testimony and evidence from the two Michigan and six Oregon murders were all permitted under California law because the evidence was given to the jury after Kraft had already been found guilty, Brown said, slowly working himself into a quiet fury.

The one criminal count where Brown conceded that the prosecution "had a little proof problem" was in the sodomy of Rodger DeVaul, Jr.—the single crime that the jury did not find Kraft guilty of committing.

"The court, I think, has bent over backwards for this defendant," he continued. "What do we have here? The defendant complaining that there were too many charges. He was charged with sixteen murders. And the court allowed a list in. Really only a part of a list.

"The defendant authored a list that has sixty-one entries relating to sixty-five young men whom he has murdered. Yet the court handcuffs the People in this case and allowed the jury only to see a small portion of that list."

If anything, Brown fumed, McCartin acted like a pussycat for the defense.

"I don't like that pussycat remark," McCartin deadpanned, sending the courtroom into one of its few bursts of laughter.

But the sixteen counts, the numbing horror of a daily replay of morgue and murder photos, Joseph Fancher's sad story of homosexual rape, the recounting of Kraft's killings during out-of-town business trips, and the "death list" itself were all legitimate parts of the prosecution case, McCartin declared.

He ruled against granting Kraft a new trial.

The chief bit of business McCartin had to dispense with before getting to sentencing was addressing Section 190.3 of the California Penal Code—the so-called "aggravating vs. mitigating circumstances" legal rule that California judges must always invoke in a death penalty case.

As written, Section 190.3 is designed to be a final, thorough set of eleven specific guidelines that a judge must weigh before passing sentence. Each guideline demands that a judge spell out the good and the bad in a criminal's behavior in a last-ditch effort to absolutely justify the gas chamber over a sentence of life without parole.

At the top of the Section 190.3 list are the aggravating vs. mitigating circumstances surrounding the crimes themselves.

"The court has the obligation and duty to review the evidence and state on the record why it has so ruled," McCartin began. "It seems ludicrous for the court to go through these sixteen counts, Fancher, and the eight counts in the penalty phase. I'm going to just address myself to basically one of the counts and I'm not even going to identify the victim by name. But it's practically too hard for me to comprehend."

For the first time, McCartin's voice reflected the exhaustion evident in his slack features and slumped posture. The occasional squeaking of the folding seats out in the gallery ceased as everyone in the courtroom craned to hear what the tough old bird sitting on the bench had to say.

"Normally, this court has dealt with people who have shot, killed, or raped in passion," McCartin began. "But here we're dealing with a man who put these victims through a long, torturous death for what some of the evidence indicates may have been possibly over as long a period of time as a weekend. They were made helpless, manipulated . . . this was sophisticated killing."

McCartin cleared his throat and absently tugged at the neckline of his robe.

"In the beginning, where there was strangulation, there were obvious ligature marks," he said. "In the end, the individual hardly had a mark on the neck. Mr. Kraft got so sophisticated that it almost became impossible to tell how these victims died: was it ligature or otherwise? What he did with these victims, I can go chapter and verse. It doesn't help. . . ."

If the death penalty had to be justified, McCartin said, just the details of how one of the sixteen victims died was enough. He read with dull clarity from a list of the horrors inflicted on Mark Howard Hall on that New Year's Eve nearly fourteen years before.

Darwin Hall wrapped a beefy arm around his wife and ground his jaws down hard as McCartin read in a questioning chant from a list of unspeakable tortures that had been inflicted upon their only son.

McCartin set the list aside and focused on Kraft. "I don't know of any type of person who could do that to another human being. And I could go on. That's the tip of the iceberg. I could sit here and dwell on the circumstances of the crimes that everybody probably don't want to hear."

Kraft showed no reaction. He simply returned McCartin's stare. The judge went through the remaining aggravating vs. mitigating factors quickly, amazed contempt now edging into his voice.

"Getting back to the presence or absence of criminal activity by the defendant," he said. "This activity had been going on over a decade. I'm not going to say any more about that."

Kraft had no prior felony convictions, but that was only because police didn't catch him killing for over a decade, the judge observed.

"I don't know what kind of a plus that is," McCartin muttered. "Don't know whether it's a mitigating circumstance that he didn't get caught for ten years. . . ."

Dr. Buchsbaum's PET scan of Kraft's brain showed an abnormality "possibly caused by a head injury or activity in the part of the brain controlling the sexual controls," McCartin acknowledged. But that evidence, too, didn't mitigate Kraft's crimes.

"As far as the defense's desire to have the jury believe that Mr. Kraft was mentally handicapped and so forth, I'm a long way from reaching that conclusion," McCartin said in an increasingly grim voice.

He whipped through the remaining mitigating factors quickly:

- Whether or not the death of the victim was consistent with homicidal conduct;
- Whether or not the defendant acted under extreme duress or substantial domination from another person;
- Whether or not the defendant appreciated the criminality of his conduct as a result of mental disease or defects with respect to intoxication;

• Whether or not the defendant's behavior was good when he wasn't committing his crimes.

"The defense spent two or three weeks, putting on evidence of everything that they could possibly come up with," McCartin muttered. "Day after day, volumes of Kraft baby pictures, evidence from the school where he taught, about what a good teacher he was. They had chapter and verse from every religious denomination known to man that came in and testified for him. It was all there."

Character witnesses and testimony about Kraft's good works did not persuade the jury, however, and they did not persuade the judge. The list of aggravating vs. mitigating circumstances exhausted, McCartin picked the sheet of paper off the bench with his thumb and forefinger and held it aloft for a moment like a dead fish.

"The mitigating circumstances equated against the enormity of the crime here doesn't meet the test by a long shot," he said, no longer trying to keep the disgust from lacing his speech. "In summary, unsuspecting victims were killed and mutilated in excess of ten years," he continued. "He demonstrated an unbelievable aggressive violent tendency toward humanity. It was done clearly to satisfy his own sexual desires. I can't imagine anyone who could do that in a scientific experiment. On a dead person, not a live person. It's unbelievable.

"I sat here for a year and I looked at Mr. Kraft and heard him ask a lot of questions. What I got was I didn't see any remorse, any feelings of regret. It was like he was in another world while his trial was going on. He showed no emotion or breakdown, nothing.

"It was like a breach of contract case, where someone is suing someone for I don't know what.

"To have something like this take place in our society, I . . . I think I've sent eight or nine individuals to their death in my courtroom before. I can take all those aggravating circumstances in those other cases and they don't match Mr. Kraft's record. I just can't comment. If anyone ever deserved the death penalty, he's got it coming."

McCartin dropped his eyes and, for the next ten minutes, read a dull litany of California Penal Code sections, laced with the dates of Kraft's court appearances. His singsong delivery gave a soporific lilt to the formalizing of the counts of murder and mayhem and sodomy lodged against Randy Kraft for the official court record.

McCartin finished the long list of charges and the chronology that led to this moment with the pronouncement that "the defendant, Randy

Steven Kraft, be put to death by the administration of lethal gas within the walls of the State Prison at San Quentin according to California Penal Code Section 190."

In an ironic but necessary anticlimax, McCartin ordered consecutive life sentences for the sodomy and mayhem charges. Then he ordered Orange County Sheriff Brad Gates to deliver Kraft to the warden of San Quentin for execution.

"The case automatically goes to the Court of Appeal," McCartin said for the record. He looked squarely at Kraft.

"Do you understand your rights?" he asked.

"It's an automatic appeal?" Kraft said, in an even, unruffled voice.

"Yes sir," McCartin said.

Kraft nodded calmly that he did, indeed, understand his rights.

"You have any other questions regarding appellate rights?" McCartin asked.

"No," Kraft said simply.

"The court will order a transcript to be prepared and filed forthwith," McCartin said brusquely.

But he couldn't let the moment pass. He cocked his head slightly to the right and tried one more time to break through.

"Mr. Kraft, this is probably your last chance in this courtroom to say anything," McCartin pleaded.

"I have a few things to say," Kraft said, his tenor trembling slightly. "I wanted to say a lot more, but Mr. McDonald's advised me not to. I take his advice. But just briefly I would like to say I have not murdered anyone, and I believe that a full review of the record will show that. That's all."

McCartin had stopped being stunned months before, when Randy Kraft's Jekyll-and-Hyde behavior kept coming up Jekyll each time the evidence of Hyde's atrocities was paraded before the jury. If there was any head shaking to do, it had been done the first few weeks that he watched the daily "array of death" that Bryan Brown displayed, all attributable to the hands of Randy Kraft.

Now, there was no incredulity left.

"I have no further comments," McCartin said. "Mr. Kraft, I . . ."

The judge stopped momentarily to summon up the right words to link his own and Kraft's common humanity. With a deep breath, he began:

"Between you and me—and this has nothing to do with my sentencing. And it may not be proper. But now that the case is all over,

I'm talking now not as a judge but just as a person. I want to make it clear that there's nothing here that can influence my thinking on the record as far as your comments about not being guilty. That's your prerogative.

"One thing that occurred to me after the conclusion of this case, though, was I received two letters: one from Corona Del Mar and one from the state of Iowa. And I turned them over to the District Attorney's Office. They were from parents of children who were missing and who wanted to know if they were on the list. The famous list we've all referred to as containing sixty-one or sixty-five victims. There were many unknown entries on there that have never been tied down.

"Somewhere down the line with response to your legal grounds for appeals, maybe you might give some thought in your waning moments to helping these people out."

McDonald was on his feet, demanding that the letters be made a part of the court record. Kopeny joined him, demanding to know whether or not McCartin's sentencing might have been unduly influenced by the unsolicited letters from the mothers and fathers of missing sons in Iowa and Corona Del Mar.

And Randy Kraft remained seated, scribbling on his legal pad, apparently oblivious to McCartin's entreaty.

"One was from Corona Del Mar and the other was postmarked from somewhere in Iowa and I didn't respond," McCartin sighed. "I didn't think it would be proper and I didn't know actually if there was anything I could say to those boys' parents."

McDonald and Kopeny persisted, demanding that the letters be copied and turned over to Kraft's defense team immediately.

Donald McCartin suddenly seemed to age, expelling a cheerless sigh that ricocheted off his courtroom walls like a melancholy echo. He agreed to the lawyers' demands in a small voice, with nods and listless gestures. The language he spoke and the language Kraft and his attorneys spoke may have been English, but all communication between them ended there. McCartin declared the proceedings over, and the courtroom gallery came to life with squealing chairs, clearing throats, and moving feet. He sat stock-still as a pair of deputies stepped to the witness table to escort Randy Kraft out through the same side door, stage right, where he had entered two hours before.

In the midst of the bustle and buzz of hugging relatives and scrambling journalists, ravenous for a few quotes from the victims' families about their elation over the sentencing, Darwin Hall was on his feet, shouting at the top of his lungs.

"Burn in hell, Kraft!"

The aging fireplug of a man raised a clenched fist in the air and hollered again at the figure of Randy Kraft who stood with his back to the audience and packed up his papers.

"Turn around so we can see you!"

Randy Kraft didn't look back. He disappeared through the courtroom door with his head held high, like some sulking, arrogant angel who had fallen in all other eyes but his own.

EPILOGUE

Randy Kraft's trial became the longest (thirteen months) and most expensive (estimated to be in excess of $10 million) in Orange County history. When he was transported to San Quentin State Prison two days after his sentencing, he became the twenty-first Orange County resident to take up residence on death row.

The Orange County probation office asked the families of his victims how they felt about the death penalty and their answers were, predictably, unanimous:

"A lot of families have suffered because of him," said Patricia Moore, sister of the first marine Randy killed. "Execute him," she said.

"I don't fully believe in the death penalty," Lyla Hampton, Anthony Silveira's widow, told the probation office.

Despite her own beliefs, though, execution seemed appropriate for someone whose guilt was certain "beyond a shadow of a doubt." In Kraft's case, she said, spending tax dollars to keep him alive was wrong. Not only had he killed scores of human beings, Kraft had actually put an end to family lines by killing off the only male offspring, such as Rodger DeVaul, Jr., and Mark Howard Hall.

Darwin and Lois Hall said Kraft deserved "to be put to death and as soon as possible. Something is terribly wrong with a judicial system that allows Mr. Kraft and his attorneys to delay this for six years."

Charlene Hughes said that her son Scott might have had a shot at playing outfield for the Cincinnati Reds if he had lived. She was "all for the death penalty, given the twenty-five-hundred pieces of evidence" to substantiate Kraft's guilt.

Clayton Church recalled watching Randy in court "without a care in the world" and displaying a "so what?" attitude. That made it even worse. He should be put to death, he said.

Remembering what her son Michael looked like when his body was returned home to Kent, Washington, for burial, Rosalie Cluck angrily told the probation office that Kraft "doesn't deserve to live and shouldn't be allowed to even breathe."

Likewise, Mary Jo Halfin said there is "no justice" that could compensate for any one of Randy Kraft's crimes.

"They are too awful to talk about and who knows how many men he actually murdered?" she said.

Shirley and Rodger DeVaul were the most vocal. For six years, their lives had revolved around the arrest and trial of Randy Kraft. When investigators first found pictures of their only son's dead body in Randy's house and brought them to Rodger to identify, the victim's father began having nightmares that lasted for nearly a year before he was able to sleep through the night.

Those same pictures were blown up to life size and set upon an easel next to the witness stand during the trial when Rodger was called to testify. They triggered nightmares all over again.

The DeVauls blamed each other for their son's death and divorced as a result, though they reconciled and remarried after years of counseling. Rodger lost a series of jobs during the years between Randy's arrest and conviction, blaming his employment problems on the trauma of reliving his son's death. Both of the DeVauls' daughters similarly had their own "defensive" psychological and relationship problems.

From where they sat in the courtroom, Shirley and Rodger saw a laid-back defendant who "smirked and smiled" when pictures of his victims were shown. To them, Randy appeared to be "sexually excited," as if the pictures recalled "joyous times."

"He doesn't deserve to live," said Rodger DeVaul once Judge McCartin had delivered the sentence of death to Randy Kraft. Give him his appeal, he said, but once the conviction has been upheld, "that should be it." The death penalty should be "swift."

Both he and his wife would be happy to attend the execution, Rodger added.

"I'd like to be the one to pull the lever," he said.

Rodger DeVaul was not the only one with insomnia.

Pat Mercantel, a thirty-eight-year-old welfare office worker, and Tracie Melzner, a twenty-six-year-old airline flight attendant, both suffered from recurrent nightmares of Randy Kraft breaking free and roaming the night once again, a razor-sharp buck knife at his side and a cooler of imported beer in the back seat of his Toyota. Mercantel and Metzner were only two of the jurors whose lives were dramatically altered by the Randy Kraft trial.

Jury foreman Jim Lytle quit the electric contracting business to become a full-time recreation director for a youth organization. Juror Carol Neal, a thirty-five-year-old inventory analyst, quit her job to go back to school to become a social worker. Both of them said following the trial that they switched professions in order to keep young people off drugs and to warn them that there are other potential Randy Krafts out looking for prey.

Tom McDonald and Bill Kopeny went on to other cases and clients, as did Jim Sidebotham and Bryan Brown and his team of prosecution investigators. Of the attorneys who prosecuted or defended Randy Kraft during the long trial and all of the hearings leading up to it, Jim Merwin alone seemed to have become obsessed with it.

He could not shake the idea that others were involved somehow, and kept on sleuthing, long after Randy had been sentenced to die. In briefs yet to come, he hoped to show that the prosecution's case was riddled with flimsy circumstantial evidence on most of the charges, and he continued to suggest that the victims were killed by more than one man. The defense investigators, including John Blackburn, also remained convinced that Kraft did not act alone.

"I've only just realized that it's still okay to love the man," said Jeff Seelig six months after his former roommate and lover was sentenced to die. The candymaker, who had remained out of the public eye through most of the trial, had gone on to two other relationships since abandoning hope of living with Randy again.

"Whether he's in San Quentin or not, he can still affect a lot of us out here," said Seelig, referring to Randy in reverential tones as "the Man."

"The Man has ungodlike power, believe it or not. How do you think he did these things? He's his own God. The Man, you know, has his own stuff going on. I mean, anybody in their right mind would have gone bananas already. To be incarcerated for as long as he was in Orange County here and . . . I mean, his power is uncanny. Just uncanny."

Like Kraft's own family, who still refuse to believe Randy committed any of the murders, Seelig has gone through too much over too long a time to be able to open up completely about his life with Kraft. An ebullient optimist armed with a fragile confidence he has worked hard to earn for himself since his days as Randy Kraft's roommate, Seelig talks a mile a minute but slows to a mumble when it comes to talking about the details of his life with a man who many law enforcement professionals believe to be the nation's most prolific serial killer. No one who was genuinely close to Randy Kraft has yet come out of shock sufficiently to talk about it, Seelig said.

"You'll get a version, but you won't get the truth, you know. You won't get the truth. But, of course, what's truth?

"I'm the only living victim. I mean, I really went out the window with this. It took my heart. I've gone through the therapy, the major weight loss, the weight gain, the drugs, the alcohol. I mean there isn't any more ways that I could literally kill myself than to do what I have been doing. And at this point I'm really getting a grasp on all those things, but I'm still at the . . ."

His voice trails away as he carefully ponders what he really wants to say about the enigma that is Randy Kraft. No one will know what made Randy a killer unless it is Randy himself and, in Randy's mind, he is simply not guilty.

"I would not have been a good witness for the defense or the prosecution," said Seelig. "I wouldn't have been good to anybody. There was nothing I could say or didn't say. There were too many things that showed, you know, stuff that . . . yes, something did go on—so that the defense wouldn't want to call me because they hold up this pair of shoes and I would say 'Well, I still don't know whose those were and he told me they were such and such' and they turned out to be Joe Schmoe's."

Since the guilty verdict, Seelig quit seeing Kraft.

"I had special privileges to go see him," he recalled. "I mean, it was like I could go see and talk to him right in front of me and he could hug me and all like that. But it got to be so intense for me because of the personal interaction, and he was just crying out for touch and feel and just to be with me that it was just too hard for me. I couldn't do that anymore. So I did not see him and I haven't spoken to him for quite some time except through investigators and attorneys."

322 • DENNIS McDOUGAL

Though officially Merwin and the other attorneys still represented Kraft during his appeals, Randy began taking his defense into his own hands after his sentencing. With some of the most creative petitions ever to have been filed in California judicial history, he argued persuasively for his release.

On March 27, 1990, Randy had his sister Kay Plunkett carry an emergency application for stay of execution and habeas corpus petition to the California State Supreme Court. In it, Kraft reasoned that he ought to be freed on the following grounds:

1) Execution by lethal gas violates federal and state guarantees of freedom of religion.
2) Execution by lethal gas is cruel and unusual punishment prohibited by both state and federal constitutions.
3) Execution by lethal gas violates Article 1, Section 1 of the California State Constitution.
4) The manufacture of lethal gas, a toxic substance, at San Quentin State Prison and its subsequent dispersal into the atmosphere is dangerous to the public, to wildlife and requires an environmental impact study.
5) The manufacture of lethal gas at San Quentin State Prison as a means to kill non-military citizens violates international treaties to which the United States is a signatory.

In support of each argument, Randy offered the following facts:

Execution by lethal gas is unique among the various forms of execution in that it alone uses the condemned person himself as the delivery vehicle for the means of death. . . . [I]t forces the condemned person to actively participate in his own killing . . . [T]he condemned person can hasten it or slow it by a willful and conscious act—holding the breath or taking a deep breath. . . .[I]t is a form of forced suicide. Without any doubt the State provides the deadly environment, but also without any doubt it is the condemned person who willfully inhales a substance he knows to be deadly.

Execution by lethal gas is unique among the various forms of execution in that by requiring the condemned person to take his own life it drives a wedge between the condemned person and his God at the most critical moment of his life—the moment of his death. Basic Judeo-Christian religious teachings define suicide as a sin. Basic

Judeo-Christian religious teachings define the willful ingestion or inhalation of substances known to be poisonous as a sin.

Forcing a person to sin in addition to ending his life is cruel and unusual. Forcing a person into a moral dilemma at the moment of death is cruel and unusual. Degrading a person by forcing him to kill himself is more than execution. It is cruel and unusual. Forcing a person to take his own life is a dishonorable and cowardly act.

The use of lethal gas to kill human beings on the fields of war is roundly condemned by all civilized nations on earth as being inhumane and cruel. Execution by lethal gas does more than just kill the condemned person. It robs him of his dignity as a human being.

A residential area lies within a few hundred yards of the dispersal vent for San Quentin's lethal gas. The lethal gas is dispersed over the prison itself with its population of prisoners and staff. The dispersal vent for the lethal gas is within 200 feet of San Francisco Bay with its marine flora and fauna.

Every spring, when the rains clear for a few days so that the warm Oregon sunshine can turn the Willamette River Valley green again, a half-dozen homicide investigators gather at a local restaurant and drink tequila until after midnight, swapping stories about Randy Kraft.

Without much fanfare, they reminisce about how they were on their way toward catching the nation's most prolific serial killer before the computer programmer was picked up with a dead marine in the car in May of 1983. Ironically, the Oregon cops were using a computer to track him.

Oregon State Police detective Jim Reed came up with the plan. After Lance Taggs and Tony Silveira turned up dead, Reed figured that the killer must be someone from out of state who visited infrequently and probably rented a car to drive up and down Interstate 5, looking for likely murder prospects. Using that theory, he got a Justice Department grant to obtain records of receipts for gasoline pumped into rented or out-of-state cars that had pulled into service stations along I-5 during the time periods when the six Oregon State victims were found. The information was fed into a computer and collated to see if there were any likely suspects who matched Reed's theory.

Randy Kraft's name came up on the computer eighteen times.

But by then, two California Highway Patrol officers had already pulled Kraft over on the San Diego Freeway a thousand miles to the south and asked him to step out of his car for a field sobriety test.

A week later, Reed and the rest of the Oregon state homicide investigators would be invited by Jim Sidebotham to fly to Orange County and begin identifying clothing and knickknacks linking Kraft to the killings in their state. After a day of sifting through the pornography and victim artifacts at Randy Kraft's Roswell Avenue home, the Oregon investigators held the first of their annual dinners at a nearby El Torito Mexican restaurant. They toasted the end of Randy Kraft's career over and over. By closing time, they still hadn't matched the number of tequila shooters they'd toasted in Randy's dishonor with even half of Kraft's total number of victims.

The worst serial killer in Oregon's history was also the worst in southern California's history. Most people outside of law enforcement would be hard-pressed to remember that small point, though, said an exasperated Jim Reed.

Like the national news media, Oregon's newspapers and TV stations gave the story of Randy Kraft footnote attention before moving on to more compelling stories about presidential politics, international terrorism, and the ups and downs of the logging business. By May 18, 1990, when the Seventh Annual Randy Kraft Memorial Dinner was held, serial murder had become such a commonplace in the U.S. that a monster like Randy could torture and kill the equivalent of six football teams without raising so much as an eyebrow. Jim Sidebotham cited an FBI report that estimated several hundred serial murderers might be at work in the U.S. Kraft might be the worst, but he was only one of them.

"Ask somebody who Randy Kraft was, they couldn't even tell you," said Will Hingston, the Marion County Sheriff's sergeant who originally organized the annual dinners.

In earlier times, before the Eisenhower administration's National Highways Act began interlocking every corner of America with concrete and asphalt ribbons, serial murder was a phenomenon. Jack the Ripper from turn-of-the-century London and the Boston Strangler of the early 1960s were the best known, but there were a few dozen others in between, notably Albert Fish, the Cannibal Killer who stalked New York in the late 1930s, and Jake Bird, the Tacoma Axe Killer of the 1940s.

Gathered around the table at Henry Thiele's Prime Rib restaurant on the banks of the Willamette River in Salem, Oregon, Hingston and the other veterans of the Randy Kraft investigation remembered their own pre-Kraft serial killer in Oregon: a married foot fetishist named

Jerry Brudos who strangled, raped, photographed, and mutilated four victims before he was caught and sent to prison for life.

Brudos had gotten more attention from the media than Randy Kraft.

One of the first topics of discussion after the first round of tequila shooters was the lack of attention that the otherwise bloodthirsty news media seemed to lavish on the Kraft case.

Hingston blamed Randy's homosexuality for the lack of news coverage. That men could do such things to other men was so far removed from the consciousness of mainstream America that the news media and, by extension, most middle-class Americans chose to ignore it altogether rather than address the root causes for that kind of murderer.

Jim Reed pointed out the double standard at work in the public's perception of young female victims, as opposed to young men. Young women were supposed to be vulnerable and protected—a throwback in thinking to the Age of Chivalry. Young, virile men on the other hand, particularly U.S. Marines or National Guardsmen, were somehow exempt from that patent. If they got in trouble, or even got themselves killed at the hands of a sociopath, that was their tough luck.

Or so went the twisted logic of most Americans.

Lynda Estes, the only woman among the Kraft investigation alumni, affirmed Reed's theory from her own personal experience as a wife and mother. When she was working murder cases for the Clackamas County Sheriff's Office in her role as a homicide detective, she knew just how naïve and reckless most young male victims were. But in her role as suburban parent, she saw the double standard at work all the time.

Boys could get away with hitchhiking. Girls couldn't. Boys drank. Girls—at least, good girls—didn't. Boys were taught early on how to fend for themselves. Girls learned by default if they learned at all.

Estes ordered her own round of shooters and, gritting her teeth, swallowed her tequila in one gulp, just like the men. Then she took up the topic of the evening. She guessed that Mr. and Mrs. America simply believed that a gay killer who picked up hitchhikers would never pick up one of their own sons. Most sons, after all, weren't gay, knew better than to hitchhike, and wouldn't drink or take drugs offered to them by a stranger.

So most parents believed.

Duane and Rosalie Cluck learned in the most painful way that their own parental preconceptions about gay murder were wrong. So did Liz and Clayton Church, Rodger and Shirley DeVaul, and Mary Jo Halfin, Michael O'Fallon's mother. Their boys were heterosexuals who experimented with drugs and alcohol and probably even sex. They didn't frequent gay bars or have anything to do with homosexuals, according to their parents. Uniformly, their fatal mistake appeared to have been placing their trust in a normal-looking, generous samaritan who picked them up hitchhiking by the side of the road.

It wasn't just sons either. Lyla Hampton and Ronnie Wiebe's wife, Glenda, were both living testimony that Randy Kraft did not limit his blood lust to unmarried men.

One of the celebrants at the Seventh Annual Randy Kraft Memorial Dinner observed that the eruption of Mount Saint Helens just a few dozen miles from Henry Thiele's Prime Rib had killed only fifty-seven people. Kraft had beaten the volcano by at least eight and possibly more.

The number of parents and brothers and sisters and friends of victims that this single, bland body-snatcher devastated with his killing ways had to run well into the hundreds and, perhaps, thousands, observed Randy Banks, a criminal investigator for the Oregon State Department of Justice. Over a thirteen-year period, Kraft had single-handedly eliminated enough young men to create a small Oregon farming town.

In the beginning, it was a puzzle as to how he did it, but it became clear enough after his arrest that he had the game down to a science. Pick them up, offer them a beer, maybe a joint, always a capsule, and then wait. Randy's favorite drug, diazepam or Valium, had the added benefit of relaxing the sphincter muscle, making the act of sodomy even easier to perform on the victim.

Terry Shaffer, a detective who worked with Lynda Estes in the Clackamas County Sheriff's Department, believed Randy used chloroform on some of his victims. The powerful anesthetic works instantly and dissipates from the body with twenty-four hours, so that an autopsy or toxicology analysis will show no trace.

But speculation on whether or not he acted alone was always a tough call. In Oregon, where Kraft would rent a car and literally drive all night long, sometimes logging as much as 900 miles in a single weekend, it seemed pretty clear that he did in his victims by himself. The two farm boys from Grand Rapids, too, appeared to have been murdered and dumped by Randy, and only Randy.

Some of the other victims, particularly in Orange County, still raised questions.

Samples of semen found on Eric Church's body were not consistent with Randy's blood type, for example. And two sets of footprints indicated that more than one person might have dragged John Leras's body down to the surf at Sunset Beach after impaling him on a wooden surveyor's stake. And there were the twenty entries on the death list that investigators still had been unable to match to any known victim.

One of them, pointed out Lynda Estes, was the entry simply given as "PORTLAND." Whoever that victim might have been, he was given the final tequila toast of the evening by the Kraft veterans that night, just before the moon rose over Salem and the half-dozen homicide investigators headed home down the I-5 freeway.

They would meet again the following year and raise their glasses to the riddle of Randy Kraft. There were enough incongruities, unidentified victims, and unanswered questions to obsess those for and against Randy Kraft's execution for years to come and, at least until the spring of 1990, the one man who knew the answers wasn't talking.

On Randy Kraft's forty-fifth birthday, on Jeff Seelig's advice, I wrote the convicted killer of sixteen young men a letter.

"He is a human being," Seelig told me. "You've got to go to the horse, but how you approach the horse and how you get what it is you want is to calculate. Like the Man himself would say, you really need to calculate. You say a negative, you're going to get a negative back. You say a positive, you're going to get a positive back. That's exactly how he thinks."

Regardless of what has been said about him, in and out of the courtroom, Randy believes in the truth, Seelig said.

"He's a very literate person, believe it or not," Seelig told me. "But that's the part people aren't seeing anymore."

On grounds that we both grew up in southern California, in similar neighborhoods with a similar economic, educational, and family backgrounds, I asked Randy if I might speak with him.

I grew up in Lynwood, a blue-collar suburb of Los Angeles not twenty minutes from Midway City by freeway. We were different people whose lives had taken different turns, I told Randy, but we had common ground. I had spoken with many of his friends and associates and was convinced that, at some level, we had a shared upbringing. We grew up in "Leave It to Beaver" Los Angeles when the world was very different and the tumult of the 1960s had not yet resulted in large-scale drug experimentation, openly gay life-styles, and sociological aberrations like serial murder.

We had common ground, I argued. We could have a dialogue, I said. I wanted to know—needed to know—what went wrong.

On May 2, 1990, Randy wrote back:

I have not killed anyone.

Stop for a moment and reflect on the persons you claim to have spoken with about me. Have they told you things from which you can reasonably infer that I am a murderer? I know they haven't. If you go from the facts as you know them, the only reasonable inference is that something wrong happened in that courtroom in Orange County. Something very wrong. That's where the story is.

Doesn't it bother you at all that there isn't any proof that I killed these people? . . . Doesn't it bother you that the court went to such great lengths to let a jury find me guilty on insufficient evidence? Don't you think Judge McCartin is an experienced jurist who knew exactly what he was doing? And that it was illegal? Have you lost the capacity for independent thought? Have you had a lobotomy? Recently??

But of course, if I'm not guilty then the purpose of your book disappears, doesn't it? So you have something of a vested interest here. You can't pander to the fears of the public, you can't make them feel uneasy about their normal appearing next-door neighbor if the truth is that I was a normal and helpful next-door neighbor and I didn't kill anyone.

When I sit back, right now, and think about what you are poised to do to me, it blows me away. It's appalling. I suppose it is not at all that unusual when one considers the times we live in—the Mike Milkens, Ivan Boeskys, Oliver Norths, the Nixons, the *Star* and the *Enquirer*. But my parents taught me about right and wrong . . . and making a buck, and the difference between the three. With that in mind it seems as though Lynwood was light years from Midway City.

If, as you claim, there is common ground between us, consider yourself on notice that my half is up for sale. I give you the right of first refusal.

Sincerely,
Randy Kraft

At a Long Beach seminar of the California Association of Criminalists, conducted in the autumn of 1990, Jim Sidebotham touched upon
several of the lingering mysteries surrounding the Kraft case. Two and
possibly three of the victims depicted in the forty-seven Polaroid photos
found in Kraft's car the day after he was arrested remain unidentified.
A total of forty-five bodies have been matched to his "scorecard,"
including twenty-five in Orange County. The remaining twenty-two
names on the list are as anonymous as the night into which Randy's
victims disappeared.

The Orange County Sheriff's Department checked everywhere
Kraft traveled—Europe, San Francisco, Florida, New York—in an
effort to link the list with additional victims, but its attempts thus far
have been in vain.

Sidebotham told some two-hundred forensic specialists who had
come from as far away as Africa to hear how the Kraft case was
unraveled that Kraft's motive was sexual, pure and simple. "He liked
the young, tender stuff," Sidebotham said. "There's an unlimited supply
of young people out there."

The wiry, hollow-cheeked detective with the hatchet face and the
dry, hangman's sense of humor, thanked the pathologists, criminalists,
prosecutors, and his own fellow street cops who invested years of hard
work in finally bringing Kraft to justice. But Sidebotham had little good
to say about the task force system or high-level law enforcement
officials who seemed more concerned with taking the credit for breaking
a case than solving it. Those unnamed "politicians," as he put it, were
more of a hindrance than a help in ending Randy's deadly game. If
everyone above the rank of detective disappeared, law enforcement
would operate far more efficiently, he told his audience.

Five hundred miles to the north, in an exercise yard inside the
medieval fortress of San Quentin State Prison, Randy Kraft meets with
three new acquaintances most mornings for a friendly game of bridge. In
addition to Kraft, the card quartet includes a five-time rapist/murderer
named Lawrence Bittaker, convicted "Sunset Strip Killer" Doug Clark,
and Freeway Killer William Bonin. Taken as a group, the four men are
believed to be responsible for more than one-hundred thrill killings
during the past twenty years.

Kraft, whose death list appears to account for more murders than
all three of his bridge opponents combined, is by far the best player. His

is a calculated yet conservative game, whereas the other three tend toward varying degrees of brash or careless play.

Clark, who shot six Sunset Boulevard prostitutes during the summer of 1980, is Kraft's closest competition. Bittaker, who picked up high school girls and recorded their screams on a pocket tape recorder while he ripped their nipples and genitals with a pair of pliers, is next in skill.

Bonin loses more than any of the others. Nobody wants to be his partner because he doesn't seem to know when to quit. He bids foolishly and grouses about it through the rest of the game.

Watching the four of them playing cards at a metal table in the center of the yard, an unenlightened observer might be hard-pressed to pick them out as four of the most vicious sociopaths of modern times. Within a hundred yards of their card table is the tiny green room where each of the four men has an appointment with death. They are among the more than 290 men who live on California's Death Row.

But the California gas chamber hasn't been used for over twenty years. Besides, each of the quartet has several appeals yet to exhaust in both the state and federal courts before their executions are to be carried out. In Kraft's case alone, law enforcement officials estimate that it will be at least four to five years before the last of his legal challenges are reviewed.

Randy remains optimistic. The evidence of his guilt simply is not there, he maintains. His confidence that one or more of his appeals will be upheld and that he will eventually walk out of San Quentin a free man is absolutely unshaken.

In the meantime, there is the satisfaction of cards. From nine A.M. to one P.M. each day, he reigns supreme among his brethren at the Yard 4 bridge table. He doesn't win every hand, but he comes closer than most.

INDEX